Feminist Inquiry

Feminist Inquiry

From Political Conviction to Methodological Innovation

MARY HAWKESWORTH

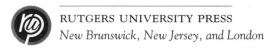

RUTGERS UNIVERSITY PRESS
New Brunswick, New Jersey, and London

Library of Congress Cataloging-in-Publication Data

Hawkesworth, M. E., 1952–
    Feminist inquiry : from political conviction to methodological innovation / Mary
Hawkesworth.
        p.   cm.
    Includes bibliographical references and index.
    ISBN-13: 978-0-8135-3704-7 (hardcover : alk. paper)
    ISBN-13: 978-0-8135-3705-4 (pbk. : alk. paper)
    1. Feminist theory.   I. Title.
HQ1190.H392 2006
305.42'01—dc22   2005011357

A British Cataloging-in-Publication record for this book is available from the
British Library.

Manufactured in the United States of America

For Philip Alperson

Contents

Acknowledgments

In the American colonies during the eighteenth century, restrictions were imposed on women's educational and economic opportunities because of a conviction that "the contamination of the female mind is the necessary and inseparable consequence of illicit intercourse with men" (Abramovitz 1996, 55). Successive generations of feminists in the nineteenth and twentieth centuries decried a very different kind of "mental contamination" that stemmed from women's indoctrination to educational, religious, literary, philosophical, and scientific systems that equated truth with the views of a small group of European and American men. Feminist inquiry emerged in contestation with those androcentric views.

I have been fortunate to have come of age at a time when pathbreaking feminist scholars were launching women's studies in the academy. It has been my privilege to work for the past twenty-five years with pioneering feminist researchers across a range of disciplines who sought to institutionalize an academic field that had not existed when I was an undergraduate student. Through intensive conversations, reading groups, workshops, and curriculum development efforts, we have struggled to develop an interdisciplinary understanding of feminist studies and to devise analytical tools suitable to such an expansive and unprecedented intellectual project.

Profoundly influenced by these collective feminist efforts, this book reflects my attempt to explicate the tacit presuppositions shaping feminist knowledge production and to identify distinctive feminist analytical strategies. My thoughts on these subjects have benefited greatly from discussions with feminist colleagues at the University of Louisville and Rutgers University. I am particularly grateful to Ann Allen, Julia Dietrich, Lucy Freibert, Susan Griffin, and Nancy Theriot whose friendship and intellectual stimulation helped shape my approaches to feminist theory and to feminist pedagogy during nineteen years at the University of Louisville. I owe a special debt of thanks to Barbara Balliet, Joanna Regulska, Mary Hartman, and Barry Qualls, who have devoted their prodigious feminist talents to building a creative and supportive intellectual environment in Women's and Gender Studies at Rutgers. Their thoughtful and probing questions about my work, their generosity in sharing their own innovative research, and their unfailing wit have made it a pleasure to go to work. I have also learned a great deal from conversations with and lucid research briefings presented by colleagues on the graduate faculty in Women's and Gender Studies at Rutgers: Ethel Brooks, Ed Cohen, Harriet Davidson, Belinda Davis, Leela Fernandes, Judy Gerson, Mary Gossy, Angelique Haugerud, Jennifer Jones, Leslie McCall, Jennifer Morgan, Jasbir Puar, Phillip Rothwell, and Sarolta Takacs.

Ruth Mandel and Debbie Walsh gave me the wonderful opportunity to immerse myself in the work of the Center for American Women and Politics and to learn first hand about the struggles of elected women officials to represent the diverse interests of women in the United States. Their vision and their skills in grant writing and fundraising made it possible for me to study the experiences of women in Congress. I would also like to thank Gilda Morales and Kathleen Casey who provided invaluable support and expertise while I was trying to grasp the raced and gendered practices operating within the U.S. Congress.

Many of the ideas incorporated into this book were first aired and debated at conferences. The insights of feminist colleagues across the country have helped me to improve and refine my arguments. I would particularly like to thank Jane Bayes, Eloise Buker, Carolyn DiPalma, Rachel Blau DuPlessis, Kathy Fergusan, Hugh Grady, Judith Grant, Tim Kaufman-Osborn, John Nelson, Anna Sampaio, Manfred Steger, Joan Tronto, and Dvora Yanow for their supportive and constructive criticisms.

Earlier versions of some of the arguments presented here appeared in print. Sections of chapter 2 were included in "Knowers, Knowing, Known: Feminist Theory and Claims of Truth," *Signs* 14 (3): 533–557, 1989. A shorter version of chapter 3 was published as "From Objectivity to Objectification: Feminist Objections," *Annals of Scholarship* 8 (3/4): 451–477, 1991. Selections from chapter 5 were included in "Global Containment: The Production of Feminist Invisibility and the Vanishing Horizon of Social Justice," in Manfred Steger, ed., *Rethinking Globalism*, Boulder, Colo.: Rowman and Littlefield, 2003. Arguments in chapter 6 were published as "Confounding Gender," *Signs* 22 (3): 649–685, 1997. An earlier version of chapter 7 was published as "Analyzing Backlash: Feminist Standpoint Theory as Analytical Tool," *Women's Studies International Forum* 22 (2): 135–155, 1999. The case study in chapter 8 appeared as "Congressional Enactments of Race-Gender: Toward a Theory of Raced-Gendered *Institutions*,"*American Political Science Review* 97 (4): 529–550, 2003.

This book was completed with sabbatical support from Rutgers University for which I am deeply grateful.

The ideas for this book were in gestation for almost two decades. Throughout that time Philip Alperson shared his philosophical insights, constructive criticism, superb cooking, home maintenance skills, and computer expertise. For entering my life and sustaining me across the decades, no words of thanks will ever suffice.

Feminist Inquiry

Introduction

Feminist scholars have been the scrappy interlopers in academia for more than three decades. Working within the traditional disciplines of the humanities, social sciences, and life sciences, feminists have challenged long-established beliefs, contested dominant paradigms, identified new areas of research, and introduced new strategies of analysis. How are we to understand these feminist interventions? Can they be dismissed as misguided, ideological mistakes, as their critics suggest? Are they simply another power-knowledge constellation embodying the "will to power" of feminist scholars? Or do they represent important insights into the nature of knowledge? Do they capture a truth about the nature of raced-gendered existence that mainstream scholarship has missed? Is feminist scholarship an intellectual misnomer, or are feminists excavating aspects of human existence too long neglected by traditional disciplines? What is distinctive about feminist research? How do feminist uses of traditional research methods differ from their deployment by nonfeminist scholars? When feminist knowledge claims differ significantly from those of traditional scholars, how can these debates be adjudicated?

Feminist Inquiry is designed to provide interdisciplinary feminist scholars and students with the tools to answer these questions. It introduces key "problems of knowledge" debated by Western philosophers, assesses competing strategies to resolve these problems, surveys feminist attempts to adapt these strategies to the demands of feminist knowledge production, and identifies a number of methodological innovations that have become central to feminist scholarship across humanities, social science, and natural science disciplines.

Why should feminist scholars be concerned with seemingly abstract questions about the nature of knowledge and defensible strategies of knowledge production? To understand how such abstract questions can have palpable effects on the lives of contemporary women and men, consider the following example.

The *New York Times* Science Section recently featured "New Clues to Women Veiled in Black," an article covering the latest "scientific breakthrough" in the understanding of depression (Gilbert 2004). Twenty-five years after feminist scholars testified before the U.S. Congress about the gendered nature of depression, medical science has acknowledged that depression affects twice as many women as men, and a number of scientists are now trying to explain this disparity. Within feminist scholarship many factors have been identified that contribute to the higher incidence of depression among women: low wages, higher levels of poverty, childhood sexual abuse, rape and domestic violence, stresses related to single-parenthood, the challenge of meeting the competing demands of work and family responsibilities, inadequate leisure time, sexism, racism, and homophobia. These factors are given short shrift in the new "scientific" explanations of the prevalence of depression among women. Instead, the scientists advanced two alternative accounts: The first contends that "about half the risk of depression is thought to be genetic," the second, the newest "scientific theory," links the development of depression to "negative thinking" or "overthinking," "a tendency to dwell on petty slights, to mentally replay testy encounters and to wallow in sad feelings." According to the *New York Times* article, "studies show that this type of negative thinking is far more common in women than in men" (Gilbert 2004, F1). On this view, women are prone to wallow in their misery, nurse their wounds, dwell too long on the recollection of harms that have befallen them, while men have the capacity to let things go. Hence, more women are depressed than men. The article recommends a book, *Women Who Think Too Much*, by Dr. Susan Nolen-Hoeksema for "a variety of strategies to help teenage and adult women cut down on overthinking" (F1).

In this instance, as in many others, feminist analysis of women's lives provides a radically different account from that advanced by nonfeminists. Which view is correct? Resolving this question is not a matter of idle speculation. The quality of millions of women's lives is at stake. The remedies that follow from these divergent explanations of depression also vary significantly. Psychologists and medical practitioners often prescribe mood-altering drugs for depressed women. Feminist scholars, including feminist psychologists and medical practitioners, suggest that, although such therapeutic interventions for particular individuals who can afford them might alleviate immediate symptoms, they are radically incomplete, for they do not address the social causes of depression. Moreover, remedies that "privatize" the problem of depression, treating it solely as an individual problem, may intentionally or unintentionally "blame the victim." As is so clearly demonstrated in the "overthinking theory," women are held responsible for excessive rumination about harms that befall them, while little attention is paid to the underlying social practices that cause the harms. Rather than self-help "advice" books, feminist prescriptions for depression require social transformation in addition to efforts to address the symptoms of particular women.

Are there ways to assess the comparative merits of these competing diagnoses? Are there strategies of inquiry, modes of analysis, standards of evidence, or forms of argument that can resolve a dispute that pits gender inequities and harms that disproportionately affect women against vague references to "genes" and "overthinking"? The goal of this book is to demonstrate that there are ways to assess the comparative merits of such competing accounts, which vindicate feminist knowledge.

During the past thirty years, feminist scholars have developed a rich repertoire of analytic tools and research techniques that support considered judgments about the validity of particular truth claims, while illuminating inadequate and inaccurate representations, faulty arguments, personal biases, social prejudices, distortions, and disinformation. Feminist researchers have also developed a range of concepts to capture dimensions of social relations that had previously eluded investigation. Pushing against that which is most taken for granted, feminist inquiry probes absences, silences, omissions, and distortions in order to challenge common sense understandings that often rely upon evidence taken from a narrow sample of the human population. This book provides an overview of the rich analytic resources that feminist scholarship has introduced to improve understandings of the world.

The Scope of Feminist Inquiry

Marilyn Frye (1993, 104) once suggested that the project of feminist inquiry "is to write a new encyclopedia. Its title: *The World, According to Women*." By situating feminist scholarship in the tradition of the radical eighteenth-century French *encyclopédistes*, whose objective was to systematize all human knowledge, Frye illuminates the enormity of the task of feminist inquiry: to develop an account of the world that places women's lives, experiences, and perspectives at the center of analysis and in so doing, corrects the distorted, biased, and erroneous accounts advanced by men. By suggesting that scholarship from men's perspectives has gotten things wrong and that scholarship that starts from women's lives will get them right, Frye acknowledges that the quest for truth lies at the heart of the feminist project. She also invokes a conception of truth tied to the philosophical enterprise first developed in ancient Greece. Truth is understood as *alethia*, that which remains when all error is purged. Thus Frye construes feminist scholarship as a maieutic art, a form of inquiry that begins with claims that are widely accepted, subjects them to critical scrutiny, demonstrates defects in their assertions, and develops an alternative, corrective account.

Feminist scholarship has grown exponentially over the past three decades, a transformation of knowledge in the humanities, social sciences, and natural sciences. Cutting across the divisions of knowledge that structure contemporary universities, feminist inquiry has been characterized as "oppositional research" because it challenges the right of the powerful across these diverse disciplines to define realities (Devault 1999, 1). To interrogate the dominant paradigms in their disciplines, feminist scholars have to develop expertise in the modes of analysis, investigation, and interpretation accredited within their fields. This book, providing an account of feminist inquiry that is attuned to commonalities and diversities across a wide array of research practices, explicates these points of commonality that feminist scholars share as well as the points of divergence and disagreement across complex modes of intellectual life.

FEMINIST METHODOLOGY

Interrogating accepted beliefs, challenging shared assumptions, and reframing research questions are characteristic of feminist inquiry regardless of specialization. Feminist scholars have taken issue with dominant disciplinary approaches to knowledge production. They have contested androcentric "ways to truth" that universalize the experiences of a fraction of the human population. They have challenged the power dynamics structuring exclusionary academic practices that have enabled unwarranted generalizations to remain unchallenged for centuries or indeed millennia. They have sought to identify and develop alternative research practices that further feminist goals of social transformation.

To examine common dynamics of such diverse feminist research practices, scholars interested in the philosophy and sociology of inquiry have initiated debates about "feminist methodology." In contrast to discussions of feminist "methods," which focus on particular tools to collect and analyze specific kinds of data, debates about feminist methodology encompass questions about theories of knowledge, strategies of inquiry, and standards of evidence appropriate to the production of feminist knowledge. Noting the enormous range of feminist research, many scholars who have written on the question of feminist methodology have taken an inclusive approach in which they describe the variety of methods feminists have deployed, analyze the epistemological assumptions that inform them, and clarify connections between specific methods and the kinds of research questions they are particularly suited to answer (Devault 1999; Fonow and Cook 1991; Hesse-Biber, Gilmartin, and Lydenberg 1999; Hesse-Biber and Leavy 2004; Lather 1991; Letherby 2003; Naples 2003; Oakley 2000; Ramazanoglu and Holland 2002; Reinharz 1992; Winddance Twine and Warren 2000; Wolf 1996). The range of questions and the scope of feminist research surveyed in these discussions are extensive. The epistemological assumptions that inform them vary widely—archaeological, autobiographical, biographical, biological, behavioral, case-study, causal, comparative, cultural, dialectical, deconstructive, demographic, discursive, econometric, ethnographic, experimental, genealogical, geographical, gynocritical, hermeneutic, historical, institutional, intertextual, legal, materialist, narrative, phenomenological, philosophical, primatological, psychoanalytic, psychological, semiotic, statistical, structural, survey, teleological, theoretical, and textual analysis; these have all been deployed successfully by feminist scholars across a range of disciplines to answer particular research questions. Although such an enumeration highlights the breadth of feminist inquiry, it does not resolve the question of how feminist appropriations of these diverse methods are distinctive.

Thinking about methodology in a slightly different way, then, might help to illuminate common dimensions of feminist inquiry amidst this diversity. Etymologically, the term "methodology" arises from the conjunction of three Greek concepts: *meta, hodos,* and *logos.* When used as a prefix in archaic Greek, *meta* typically implied "sharing," "action in common," or "pursuit or quest." *Hodos* was usually translated as "way," but when combined with *logos,* which was variously translated as "account," "explanation," or "truth," *hodos* suggested a very particular path to truth about reality (Wolin 1981). Bringing the three Greek terms together opens possibilities for various interpretations of methodology: "a shared quest for the path to truth," "a shared account of truth," or "the way a group legitimates knowledge claims."

The Greek roots of the term are particularly helpful in laying the groundwork for exploring the distinctive aspects of feminist methodology; the etymology makes clear that methodologies involve philosophical questions about the nature of knowledge, as well as practical questions concerning strategies of inquiry. Moreover, methodologies are group-specific and, as such, political. The appropriate methodology for any particular inquiry is a matter of contestation because scholars often disagree about the "way to truth." Strategies that are accredited as legitimate means to acquire truth gain their force from decisions of particular humans; thus, there is a power element in the accreditation of knowledge. Power is never the only factor involved, but neither is it a negligible factor. One objective of this book is to demonstrate how feminist recognition of the role of power in scholarly investigations and methodological judgments is compatible with an objectivist account of knowledge. This argument turns on a thorough rejection of positivism.

Like all methodologies, feminist research is informed by a politics. But unlike methodologies developed in accordance with positivist assumptions about knowledge production, which explicitly deny any political dimension to "scientific" inquiry, feminist research acknowledges that particular political convictions inspire its existence. As a political movement, feminism seeks to eliminate male domination in all of its various manifestations. As a mode of intellectual inquiry: "What constitutes feminist work is a framework that challenges existing androcentric or partial constructions of women's lives" (Geiger 1990, 169). Knowledge production is a rich terrain for feminist engagement because the authoritative accounts of the world accredited by academic disciplines—whether in the humanities, social sciences, or natural sciences—have profound effects on women's lives and often are riddled with errors and distortions.

FROM POLITICAL CONVICTION TO KNOWLEDGE PRODUCTION

In an effort to explicate how feminist principles could contribute to academic research, Adrienne Rich (2003, 454) noted suggestively that "a politicized life ought to sharpen both the senses and the memory." The "sharpening" that Rich alludes to involves a way of attending to dimensions of existence often overlooked in traditional accounts. Feminist convictions attune scholars to power dynamics that structure women's lives. By making power dynamics visible— probing silences, absences, and distortions in dominant paradigms—feminist inquiry challenges established explanatory accounts and identifies new questions for research. "It is the political commitment that feminists bring to diverse fields that motivates them to focus attention on lines of evidence others have not sought out or thought important; to discern patterns others have ignored; to question androcentric or sexist framework assumptions that have gone unnoticed or unchallenged; and sometimes to significantly reframe the research agenda of their discipline in light of different questions or an expanded repertoire of explanatory hypotheses" (Wylie 2000a, 16).

In recognizing that the researcher's values play a role in scholarly research, feminist inquiry has a great deal in common with post-positivist philosophy of science. These parallels are explored in chapters 1 and 2. There is another dimension of feminist scholarship, however, that far exceeds claims concerning the value-laden origins of research. Feminist scholarship suggests that a particular politics embedded in the research process improves the quality of analysis, heightens objectivity, and enhances the sophistication of research findings. Far from being a source of bias and distortion, feminist convictions and principles are deemed an asset to research. In the words of Linda Nochlin (1971, 1988), "Natural assumptions must be questioned and the mythic basis of so much so-called fact brought to light. And it is here that the very position of women as an acknowledged outsider, the maverick 'she' instead of the presumably neutral 'one'—in reality the white-male position accepted as natural, or the hidden 'he' as the subject of all scholarly predicates—is a decided advantage, rather than merely a hindrance or a subjective distortion."

In marked contrast to positivist conceptions of science, Kantian conceptions of moral reasoning, and the tenets of new criticism within literary theory, feminist scholarship suggests that a tripartite commitment—to struggle against coercive hierarchies linked to gender, race, and sexuality, to promote women's freedom and empowerment, and to revolt against institutions, practices, values, and knowledge systems that subordinate and denigrate women—enhances the truth content and deepens the insights of feminist accounts of the world. Despite widely divergent disciplinary and interdisciplinary backgrounds, feminist scholarship involves "disidentification" from some guiding precepts of positivism, such as value-neutrality, norms of distanced, dispassionate research, and the quest for universal explanations characteristic of many disciplines. The grounds for this break with popular conceptions of objectivity and the implications of the feminist reconceptualization of objectivity and objective knowledge are explored in chapters 2 and 3.

Because it recognizes that values play a formative role in research and that these formative values must be made explicit and subjected to critical scrutiny, feminist scholarship can be situated in the tradition of "value critical research." There is much debate among feminist scholars, however, about the implications of value-laden research. These debates have generated rich discussions of "feminist epistemology," which explore questions concerning the nature of truth and the possibilities of attaining it. Chapters 2, 3, 4, and 5 examine a range of questions central to feminist knowledge production. What is the relation between subjective values and objective knowledge? Does sexed and raced embodiedness influence one's understanding of the world or the validity of the claims one advances about the world? Is there an incontestable ground for feminist truth claims? If so, what is it? If not, what is the status of feminist claims about the world? Are they subjective opinions, willful fictions, wishful thinking, or justified belief? What is the relation between the ambiguities, complexity, contradictions, and diversity of social relations that characterize women's experiences and traditional notions of universal explanation? What kinds of explanation foster feminism's emancipatory objectives? What explanatory frames impair feminist inquiry? What counts as evidence in feminist scholarship? How can we make sense of contradictory evidence concerning the same phenomenon? In the face of compelling evidence, how can we make sense of "evidence blindness?"

Answers to such complex questions concerning feminist knowledge production require some familiarity with basic concepts and key theories developed in the history of Western epistemology. The first part of this book is designed to provide interdisciplinary feminist scholars with the background needed to grapple with these questions. Chapter 1 introduces and defines core concepts, explicates competing theories of knowledge, and traces rich philosophical discussions concerning the possibilities for human knowledge and the factors that impair knowledge acquisition. "Sources of Error, Strategies of Redress" introduces debates about the routes to knowledge (rationalism, empiricism, testimonials), methods of intellection (deduction, induction, intuition, trust), and objects of knowledge (relations of ideas, matters of fact, persons, values, social relations, the past and the future) that have preoccupied Western philosophy. Particular attention is given to discussions of the manifold sources of error that impede knowledge acquisition: appearances, dreams, hallucinations, language, memory, operations of the mind (conscious and unconscious), optical illusions, solipsism, and subjectivism. Chapter 1 also explores the strengths and weaknesses of multiple analytic and research techniques designed to redress the various sources of error. Familiarity with these philosophical discussions can help feminist scholars avoid certain kinds of error in their own research, gain sophistication and critical acuity in their own knowledge production, and draw upon a well-stocked intellectual arsenal in advancing their critiques of problematic claims in traditional disciplinary accounts of the world.

In addition to introducing a basic philosophical vocabulary and elucidating key concepts in epistemology, chapter 1 traces the emergence of "antifoundationalism," a philosophical stance embraced by most feminist scholars, which rejects the possibility of an absolute ground for knowledge. Presenting a sustained critique of classical versions of rationalism and empiricism, as well as positivist and critical rationalist epistemic claims developed in the twentieth century, the chapter draws on post-positivist philosophy of science to explicate the "theoretical constitution of facticity." This view, which suggests that theoretical presuppositions structure every step of the research process from the most elementary perceptions through the accreditation of particular forms of evidence and explanation, plays a key role in feminist inquiry by offering a new way to understand intractable debates and identifying new strategies of critique and new mechanisms for engaging controversies over contentious evidence and explanations, while vindicating feminist arguments concerning the politics of knowledge.

Chapter 2, "Grappling with Claims of Truth," examines three decades of debate in feminist epistemology. Beginning with feminist critiques of masculinist and paternalist epistemic claims that have been wielded as weapons against women in the academy, the chapter traces the development of three ideal types of feminist epistemology in the work of Sandra Harding (1986): feminist empiricism, feminist standpoint theories, and feminist postmodernism. Identifying certain problematic assumptions about knowers and knowing that haunted early arguments in feminist epistemology, the chapter traces the emergence of a feminist consensus on anti-foundationalism. It explicates a conception of cognition as a human practice, which provides an objectivist conception of knowledge consistent with both feminist anti-foundationalism and a recognition of human fallibility in a world of contingency. Although this conception of cognitive practices is anti-foundationalist, it identifies minimalist standards of rationality, evidence, and argumentation embedded in feminist scholarship that lend feminist accounts their justificatory force. The chapter concludes with a discussion of lingering disagreements among postmodern feminists, feminist empiricists, and feminist standpoint theorists over the best methods for scholarly inquiry and the possibility of attaining truth. The chapter shows how these epistemological debates structure continuing arguments over the uses of deconstruction, genealogy, ethnography, structural analysis, randomized controlled trials, and ideology critique in feminist research.

Traditional conceptions of objectivity have relied upon adherence to research methods designed to control for individual idiosyncrasy as the key to attaining objective knowledge—knowledge free from distortion, bias, error, self-interest, and caprice. Feminist scholars have demonstrated, however, that observations, beliefs, theories, methods of inquiry, and institutional practices routinely labeled "objective" fall far short of the norm. Chapter 3, "Reconceptualizing Objectivity," provides an overview of feminist critiques of dominant philosophical and scientific conceptions of objectivity. To assess competing claims that feminists should repudiate objectivity and that feminists should reclaim objectivity, the chapter investigates feminist concerns about an inherent link between objectivity and objectification, the morally objectionable practice of treating a person as a means rather than as an end, as inert matter rather than as autonomous subject. I identify and analyze three efforts to link objectivity to objectification: a contamination model, a commodification model, and a reductionist model. Arguing that none of these models succeeds in establishing an inherent link between objectivity and objectification, I suggest that each provides important insights about the nature and limits of dominant conceptions of objectivity. Drawing upon these insights, I sketch a revised feminist conception of objectivity that avoids the pitfalls of traditional philosophical and scientific conceptions.

Central to the feminist conception of objectivity is an account of social knowledge (Longino 1990) that fosters heightened awareness of multiple sources of error overlooked by Western philosophers. Challenging the conviction that the central problem of objectivity lies with the emotional and perceptual quirks of the subjective self that distort, confuse, and interfere with objective apprehension of reality, feminists scholars have pointed out a remarkable uniformity in the kinds of distortion that impede the acquisition of truth. Shared cultural values, such as racism, sexism, and heteronormativity, pose powerful obstacles to achieving objectivity. Incorporated within the consciousness of individuals within a particular society, these values easily escape detection precisely because they are shared. When objectivity is defined as "intersubjective corroboration," as it is in the dominant approaches to philosophy of science, the distortions introduced by shared social values escape detection. Tracing feminist scholarship's identification of "social knowledge" (Longino 1990) as a hindrance to the attainment of objectivity, the chapter concludes with an exploration of feminist strategies to overcome the kinds of error introduced by social knowledge, linking the systematic interrogation of dominant assumptions to feminist arguments for inclusive research practices that require enhancing diversity within the academy.

Feminist efforts to grapple with complex claims of truth and to reconceptualize objectivity converge in recognizing the role that theories play in constituting facts. Chapter 4, "Evidence," examines how markedly different theoretical frameworks construct and accredit evidence within particular research practices. Within the sphere of textual analysis, it explores competing conceptions of "the text" developed within hermeneutics, history, literary criticism, philosophy, psychoanalysis, and deconstruction. It draws attention to how differently evidence is construed by intentionalists, historicists, formalists, psychoanalysts, semioticians, deconstructionists, gynocritics, proponents of gynesis, and hybridity theorists. In addition to the complex constructions of evidence within competing strands of textual analysis, the chapter also considers how evidence is variously construed within legal studies, phenomenological analysis, systemic analysis, structural analysis, and behavioral analysis.

In seeking to familiarize feminist researchers with the competing constructions of evidence generated by a variety of theoretical frameworks, chapter 4 opens new possibilities for understanding and resolving contestations over evidentiary claims. Chapter 4 also shows how feminist scholars across a range of disciplines have contested the parameters of debate set by dominant paradigms—interrogating the categories of analysis established by prevailing theories, examining how those theories draw boundaries to demarcate their objects of inquiry, how terms are operationalized within those boundaries, and how gendered metaphors and analogies can limit understanding. In surveying these complex contestations over evidence and explanation, the chapter illuminates some shared norms that feminist researchers have developed to assess the merits of competing accounts.

Feminists often encounter "evidence blindness" within the academy and in their daily lives. Despite compelling evidence to support feminist arguments, some people seem unable to accept evidence that impugns their beliefs. How are we to make sense of evidence blindness? Chapter 5 compares several frameworks developed in mainstream scholarship that provide different accounts of evidence blindness. The chapter explicates and compares "level-of-analysis" explanations with claims grounded in the sociology of knowledge, political arguments concerning strategic manipulation, and Nietzschean notions of incompatible wills to power. Demonstrating deficiencies in each of these accounts, the chapter turns to the conception of knowledge as a theoretically constituted human practice for a richer account of evidence blindness.

To show why a sophisticated understanding of evidence blindness is important for feminist inquiry, chapter 5 examines a number of debates that implicate feminist analysis in evidence blindness, debates about the politics of representation and debates over feminist priorities between feminists in the North and feminists in the global South. In addition to tracing the role of contentious theoretical frameworks and methodological approaches in contributing to evidence blindness, the chapter considers how evidence blindness can involve more than misperception or deception. The chapter introduces problems of "sanctioned ignorance," blind spots that can render certain power relations invisible, and "social amnesia," strategies that foster unknowing and forgetting, which are actively produced and legitimated by dominant discourses. Drawing examples from recent discussions of globalization to illuminate sanctioned ignorance and social amnesia, the chapter concludes by discussing strategies devised by feminist scholars to thwart various forms of evidence blindness.

INNOVATIVE FEMINIST ANALYTICAL TOOLS

Dispelling the myth of the given, probing the tacit presuppositions of dominant discourses, challenging the naturalization of oppressive relations, investigating processes that produce invisibility, demonstrating the deficiencies of reductive arguments, and engaging difference and plurality have been hallmarks of feminist scholarship. In undertaking these tasks, feminist researchers have developed several analytic techniques that are quite distinctive. The second section of the book focuses on three methodological innovations that feminist scholars have developed and deployed across a wide range of disciplines: gender as an analytical category, standpoint theory as an analytical tool, and the concept of intersectionality as a guiding research principle.

Innovative inquiry involves more than the creativity of individual scholars; it requires the invention of scholarly apparatus—theories, concepts, language, instruments—that enables new ways of thinking, new ways of seeing, new ways of articulating (Hacking 1999, 76). To describe gender, standpoint, and intersectionality as distinctive feminist analytics is to suggest that feminist scholars have struggled to create these innovative tools to do justice to their subject matter: these conceptual instruments enable feminist knowledge production; these methodological innovations distinguish feminist scholarship across the disciplines from the work of nonfeminist scholars who may be using the same discipline-based methods to study the same subject matter; they are the technical means that feminists have devised to track dimensions of power that remain invisible in traditional scholarship. Chapters 6, 7, and 8 explore the emergence and deployment of these methodological innovations in feminist scholarship and provide concrete examples of the new possibilities for research they create.

With growth and maturation of feminist scholarship, gender has become a central, if not *the* central, analytical concept in Women's Studies. Although originally a linguistic category denoting a system of subdivision within a grammatical class, feminist scholars adopted the concept of gender to distinguish culturally specific characteristics associated with masculinity and femininity from sex-specific biological features, such as chromosomes, hormones, and reproductive organs. Throughout the past three decades as the sex/gender distinction has been questioned and the meanings of gender have proliferated in feminist scholarship, eminent scholars such as Sandra Harding (1986) and Joan Scott (1986) conceptualized gender as an analytic category, as a heuristic device that links psyche to social organization, social roles to cultural symbols, normative beliefs to sexed embodiedness, and social divisions of labor to systems of power that privilege men. Chapter 6, "Gender as an Analytic Category," explores the many meanings of gender in feminist research and considers critiques of the concept raised by both scholars of color and postmodern feminists. Mapping the conceptual terrain of gender as an analytical category, the chapter also identifies a number of danger points in the deployment of gender, dangers that arise in a subtle shift from using gender as an analytical tool to deploying gender as a universal explanation. Examining sophisticated deployments of gender within and across major methodological approaches, including phenomenology, deconstruction, dialectical materialism, and ethnomethodology, the chapter demonstrates how the shift from gender as analytic category to gender as universal explanation implicates gender in the ideology of procreation. It also identifies strategies for avoiding this problematic shift.

Rather than conceiving feminist standpoint theory as an epistemic doctrine, in chapter 7, "Standpoint Theory as Analytical Tool," I suggest that multiple and competing standpoints are better understood as analytical tools, that is, as research heuristics that illuminate questions for analysis, strategies of investigation, and hypotheses to guide feminist research. As analytical tools, feminist standpoints suggest ways of gathering data for analysis that presuppose multiplicity and complexity. Accepting plurality and partiality as inherent characteristics of human cognition, feminist standpoint theory cautions against naïve conceptions of value-neutral inquiry and mistaken notions concerning the immediate apprehension of reality. Instead, standpoint theory acknowledges that claims about the world are theoretically mediated, constructing "experience" in relation to a range of tacit theoretical presuppositions. As an analytical tool then feminist standpoint theory requires researchers to engage competing claims and competing theoretical frameworks. By interrogating tacit assumptions that structure alternative accounts, feminist scholars can develop sophisticated critiques of problematic assumptions that impair an objective account of complex issues.

To demonstrate the potential of this analytical tool, the chapter examines competing theoretical accounts of affirmative action and welfare "reform." Collecting and comparing alternative explanations of these social policies advanced by conservative women, liberal feminists, socialist feminists, black feminists, and postmodern feminists, chapter 7 helps to make "backlash politics" more intelligible and to identify the forces that fuel it, while also suggesting strategies that empower women to resist oppression. By comparing the merits of competing theoretical standpoints and the explanatory accounts they generate, the chapter shows how standpoint theory as an analytical tool enables feminist scholarship to grapple with plurality and complexity without falling into relativism and to differentiate epistemological problems from political issues, thereby avoiding the antidemocratic tendencies of technocratic decision making.

Taking issue with white feminists' generalizations about "women" and "men," feminist scholars of color have pointed out that gender is always mediated by race, class, ethnicity, sexual orientation, nationality, and a host of social vectors of power. Cautioning against overgeneralization, feminists of color have coined the term "intersectionality" (Crenshaw 1989, 1997) to capture the intricate interplay of social forces that produce particular women and men as members of specific races, classes, ethnicities, and nationalities. Chapter 8, "Intersectionality," explores the important contributions that the concept of intersectionality makes to feminist scholarship. Deployed as an analytical tool, intersectionality enables feminists to avoid various forms of reductionist explanation (for example, biological determinism, essentialism, naturalization) that surface far too often in mainstream treatments of race and gender. Instead the concept of intersectionality calls attention to social processes of racialization and gendering through which relations of power and forms of inequality are constructed and maintained. Such an understanding of the political production of difference attunes feminist scholars to operations of power that remain invisible to mainstream social scientists by enabling them to identify new questions for investigation and to develop explanations of institutional processes and interpersonal dynamics overlooked by traditional scholarship. To illuminate the explanatory possibilities created by the concept of intersectionality, this chapter investigates racialization and gendering in the U.S. Congress; I show how feminist research that starts from the reports of congresswomen of color can offer insights into the operations of Congress that are rendered invisible by dominant approaches to congressional research.

Feminist scholars in the humanities, social sciences, and natural sciences have deployed gender, standpoint, and intersectionality in remarkably creative ways. The specific applications considered in these final chapters are meant to illustrate the ways that these analytical tools raise new questions for research, illuminate power relations masked by traditional methods of inquiry, and demonstrate deficiencies in dominant accounts. To reflect my own areas of specialization I focus on issues in feminist theory, public policy debates concerning affirmative action and welfare "reform," and women and politics research. Other feminist scholars could provide compelling examples from their own rich research. As innovations of interdisciplinary feminist scholarship, the analytic possibilities of gender, standpoint, and intersectionality are not limited to any particular discipline, although their particular uses vary markedly from one intellectual context to another. Characterizing them as distinctive feminist analytics should be construed as an open invitation to feminist scholars to consider how these innovative conceptual tools have been used and the potential for their further use to achieve the transformative goals of feminist scholarship.

Part I   Knowledge and
Feminist Knowledge
Production

Chapter 1

Sources of Error, Strategies of Redress

How do feminists know? What is involved in contestation over long-established beliefs? How do feminists produce knowledge to displace misogynist or androcentric claims? How do feminists prove knowledge claims? These epistemological questions lie at the heart of feminist inquiry. Yet outside the field of philosophy, few feminist scholars receive formal training about "problems" of knowledge or how to begin to address them. This chapter introduces debates about the nature of knowledge, discussions of multiple sources of error that can confound efforts to investigate the world, and strategies to overcome error and distortion. Drawing upon philosophical arguments developed in the Western tradition over the past two millennia, the chapter introduces and defines basic epistemological concepts, such as skepticism, rationalism, empiricism, foundationalism, antifoundationalism, positivism, and post-positivism. Because these concepts have been, and continue to be, subjects of contestation, the chapter traces the emergence of multiple versions of these concepts in both antiquity and modernity and tries to illuminate the epistemological issues that have fueled their articulation, repudiation, reconceptualization, and refinement over centuries.

Trying to synthesize more than two thousand years of philosophical argument in one chapter is not an easy feat. Nor is it a simple matter to translate technical philosophical terminology into accessible prose for an interdisciplinary feminist audience. Despite the hazards of such an undertaking, there are strong reasons to make the attempt. Feminist knowledge production is frequently challenged by antifeminist scholars, conservative pundits, and confused citizens whose understandings of the world are under constant siege from misogynist talk-radio hosts, fundamentalist religious leaders, and social Darwinists masquerading as policy scientists. A nuanced and sophisticated understanding of epistemological issues affords feminist scholars a vital resource with which to counter scurrilous attacks. Awareness of important continuities between feminist understandings of knowledge and post-positivist theories of knowledge advanced by contemporary epistemologists and philosophers of science can assist feminists in developing a strong justification of their transformative intellectual project. Moreover, the arguments supporting antifoundationalism offer interdisciplinary feminist scholars an account of knowledge that vindicates feminist knowledge production in all its richness and complexity. This chapter, then, provides the philosophical background necessary for a feminist theory of knowledge sufficiently capacious to accommodate feminist intellectual interventions in the humanities, social sciences, and natural sciences. Subsequent chapters address feminist engagements with the epistemological issues traced here.

From Trust to Skepticism

As children, we engorge a world. From the moment of birth, people speak to us, tell us things, teach us a language, and thereby moor us in a culture and a tradition. Knowledge is conveyed to us on the basis of testimony from others (Alcoff 2000, 236). "The weight of a civilization" (Fanon 1967, 18) is bestowed on us through the tales of others. Absorbing vast amounts tacitly as well as explicitly, we seldom question the validity of what we learn. Our intuitions, our horizons of understanding, and our most basic perceptions are shaped long before we are capable of raising any questions concerning the credibility of our sources or the reliability of their claims. Our earliest accounts of the world are taken on trust.

Philosophical investigations of the world are often rooted in skepticism. The unrelenting distrust of our mental faculties, senses, language, and beliefs can make philosophy seem quite alien. But the constant probing of our assumptions and intuitions has a point. Critical examination of what is most taken for granted can free us from "the myth of the given" (Sellars 1963, 164) and empower us to change oppressive practices. Given the tendency of feminists to challenge existing social relations and traditional conceptions of the world, it could be argued that feminists have an affinity for philosophical investigation. The theories of knowledge developed within the Western philosophical tradition provide rich resources for feminists who seek to interrogate the conditions of our existence. For they identify problems for knowledge production caused by the senses, processes of reasoning, language, beliefs, social relations, and dynamics linked to particular objects of study.

Epistemology is the branch of philosophy that investigates the nature of knowledge. As developed over the past two thousand five hundred years in the Western tradition, epistemology has been concerned with complex questions: What is knowledge? What is the source of knowledge? Do the senses supply, or does reason provide reliable knowledge of the world? What is the relation between knowledge and belief? How much of what we ordinarily think we know is really knowledge? The answers philosophers have provided to such questions have varied markedly, but familiarity with some of the central issues and arguments in these debates can help feminists gain sophistication and critical acuity in our own knowledge production.

Feminist epistemologist Lorraine Code (1991, 224) has defined knowledge as an "intersubjective product constructed within communal practices of acknowledgment, correction, and critique." This definition has the virtue of emphasizing that knowledge is a human product, generated by fallible inquirers through processes of interrogation and contestation that involve many people over long periods of time. Her reference to "practices of acknowledgment" suggests plurality: the multiple forms of knowledge (for example, perception, memory, intuition, introspection, recollection, recognition, conceptualization, contemplation) cannot be reduced to a singular kind. As human conventions, practices have histories; they change over time. Practices also have standards internal to them that provide criteria for assessing quality. Thus Code's definition makes it possible to understand that the criteria for judging recognition (of a person, a place, an object, a pattern) might be different from the criteria for assessing introspection (an examination of one's innermost thoughts, beliefs, motives). Assessing the validity of knowledge claims, then, requires attention to specific ways of knowing that are situated within particular social, cultural, and historical practices, which afford determinate standards of evaluation.

Skepticism: Challenge and Response in the Ancient World

One of the most intensive debates within Western epistemology focuses on questions concerning the sources of knowledge and the standards for assessing the validity of knowledge claims linked to a particular source. This debate was initiated by the Sophists, a group of Greek philosophers in fifth century B.C.E.; these skeptics challenged the possibility of objective knowledge of the natural world. The Sophists asked fundamental questions: How much of what we think we know about nature is really objective, and how much is contributed by the human mind? Do we have any knowledge of nature as it really is, or are appearances all that we can know? The Sophists were the first to suggest that all humans can know are their perceptions of reality. Because individual perceptions vary, the very notion of an objective reality is called into question. Protagoras, for example, asserted the doctrine of *homo mensura*, which insisted that the individual is "the measure of all things." This doctrine quickly devolves into a form of relativism known as "subjectivism." For if each individual's perception is "the measure" of what exists, and individuals differ in their perceptions, then there is

no objective measure. Assertions about the world are merely the subjective perceptions of particular individuals and there is no way to adjudicate competing
perceptual claims. Following this argument to its logical conclusion, Gorgias
insisted that there is no such thing as reality; if there were, then we could not
know it, and even if we could know it, then we could not communicate our
knowledge to another person. Many versions of subjectivism have surfaced since
the time of the Sophists, and potent versions continue to circulate in the
twenty-first century. Recognition of human fallibility combined with individualist assumptions and the overwhelming evidence of diversity in and disagreement
about perceptions lead many of our contemporaries to conclude that subjectivism is an accurate account of the limited possibilities for human knowing.
The earliest epistemological debates, however, challenged the Sophists' claim
that individual perceptions exhaust human's access to knowledge about the
world.

A RATIONALIST RESPONSE

Plato, the first philosopher to develop a systematic response to the Sophists, argued that they went astray because they confused "appearance" with "reality";
they mistook what "seems to be" for "what is." The Sophists made this error,
according to Plato, because they were "empiricists" who relied on the senses as
the source of knowledge. They failed to understand that a carefully trained
mind exercising the powers of reason could correct the faulty observations of
the senses. As the founder of the "rationalist" tradition, which holds that the
faculties of reason provide more reliable knowledge than the senses, Plato suggested that there are multiple dimensions of existence to be known. He distinguished between the realm of appearances, which could be apprehended by the
senses, and the realm of being, which could be grasped only by the a well-honed
intellect, trained to pierce the illusions and distortions of the realm of appearances.

For Plato, the world of appearances was a complex domain, encompassing
the physical or natural world, the "made" world of human artifacts and conventions, as well as the "shadow" world of human beliefs, opinions, myths, and
representations of nature and convention through visual art and literature. Beliefs about reality based on perception of appearances could be mistaken for a variety of reasons, according to Plato. Some of these sources of error are rooted in
the character of the realm of appearances, and some are due to the limitations of
the human senses. The physical world and the world of human convention are
unstable, subject to change, continually in flux. Physical objects such as rocks,
plants, trees, stars, come into and pass out of existence. Similarly, human beings
are born, grow, transform themselves in innumerable ways, then die. The artifacts created by humans are also subject to decay, dissolution, and destruction.

To capture on-going processes of emergence and disappearance that characterize the world of appearances, Plato called this domain, a realm of "becoming." The constant fluidity of the realm of becoming provided one source of error for human observers. A claim made about an object could be true one day and false the next because the object had changed. A claim could also be wrong because it imposed fixity on an on-going process, whose stages varied diametrically. Indeed, Plato suggested that within the realm of becoming, it is not uncommon for opposites to embrace. A massive mountain that seems solid and unalterable may be volcanic; erupting lava flows in liquid form transform every aspect of the stone façade. A beautiful face may convulse in anger or hatred, manifesting profound ugliness.

In addition to errors in perception that arise from changes in the world of appearances, Plato suggested that human senses themselves can also contribute to misperception. Eyes, ears, and noses, for example, are not perfect conduits of information. They play tricks on us. Anticipation may structure perception so that we "see" what we want to see. Settled convictions may influence our perception so that we only see or hear views that confirm our beliefs. Although Plato developed these arguments millennia ago, a good deal of work in social psychology and opinion research supports Plato's claims about "selective perception" and "selective attention." Our senses may also be deceived. Consider optical illusions. Plato used the example of a stick, perfectly straight when observed in the air, which appears bent when submerged in water. Figure-ground relations can produce similar illusions as the famous examples of the duck-rabbit and the chalice-face make clear.

Beyond sources of error in observation linked to the nature of things that exist in the realm of appearances and to the nature of perception, Plato identified several other causes of mistakes in claims about the world derived from the senses. Changing standards of comparison can cause variance in perception. A person who is six feet in height may seem very tall when measured against someone who is four feet, yet seem very short when compared with a person who is seven feet six inches tall. Thus different standards of comparison may generate very different characterizations of the same phenomenon. Perception is further complicated when one observes representations of objects. Whether the representation is a visual artist's rendering, a writer's graphic depiction, or another person's verbal characterization, some features of the object will be emphasized, others downplayed, and some omitted entirely. Plato noted that any inferences drawn from representations were peculiarly vulnerable because of their distance from the original.

Inconstancy, change, fluidity, selective perception, optical illusion, multiple standards of comparison, and mediated representations are all included in Plato's account of the ways that the senses can be led astray. The sources of human error are multiple and various. Plato did not think, however, that humans had to resign themselves to wallow in perceptual distortion. He argued that with sufficient education and recourse to rigorous analytic techniques, individuals could transcend the realm of appearances and gain knowledge of the "realm of being." They could succeed in grasping "things as they are," free from the distortions introduced by the senses and by appearances. Much of Plato's confidence about the power of human reason was derived from his ontology, an account of reality at great remove from contemporary beliefs. Plato argued that the ultimate reality transcended the realm of appearances and all its defects. In contrast to the inconstancy and imperfection of the realm of becoming, the realm of being is a domain of perfect and eternal "Forms" or "Ideas" that provide a template, which the various appearances in the realm of becoming merely approximate. The "Forms" then constituted the essence of existence, which could be grasped by human beings because prior to assuming bodily form, humans existed as immaterial beings in the realm of the Forms. Although the trauma of birth caused people to forget the truth of being and to mistake appearance in the material world for reality, systematic education in mathematics, music, and philosophy could enable them to "recollect" the truth.

There are many good reasons to challenge Plato's ontology as we will see below, but even if one rejects Plato's theory of the Forms, there is much to learn from his account of how to avoid being misled by the many sources of error in the realm of appearances, the domain in which most feminist contestations take place. Plato suggests that inquiry must begin with careful consideration of the nature of the object under investigation, for the kinds of knowledge possible vary, depending upon the objects of study. Images and representations generate inferences that never go beyond conjecture. Appearances of living things, natural phenomena, and human artifacts require close attention to processes of production, growth, change, and decay. Even the most scrupulous observations of such processes are fallible, however; and justified beliefs, or opinions backed by evidence, are the best one can attain about objects in this domain. Abstract ideas, such as those developed in geometry, establish tautological truths amenable to proof by logical deduction and also support applications in the realm of appearances via hypothetical (if-then) reasoning.

The mode of inquiry that Plato endorsed drew upon a form of crossexamination of competing accounts developed by his teacher, Socrates, who routinely began his investigations by gathering together what others said about a topic. Socrates sought to collect as diverse a range of opinions as possible so he could compare them against one another, by drawing insights from the comparison and developing arguments that enabled him to refute faulty views. In this process of reasoning, he paid particular attention to inconsistencies and contradictions that might illuminate errors in perception or reasoning. After purging as many mistakes as possible through this comparative analysis of varying opinions, Socrates probed the competing views for any underlying commonalities to provide clues to a central idea shared by all the conflicting opinions. The common factor or "essential property" underlying all the variations, according to Socrates, provided a definition for the concept under investigation. Although it often differed from the particular claims examined, the concept was "universal" in that it captured the feature that all the differing accounts shared. Once identified, the concept could also provide a standard against which the particular claims could be measured, assessing them according to how closely they approximated the "ideal" or "essential" concept. Plato, appending his ontology to Socratic concepts, suggested that the "essence" underlying all appearances of a particular object was precisely the ideal Form that existed in the realm of being.

AN EMPIRICIST RESPONSE

Aristotle, who had been Plato's student for fourteen years, amended Plato's theory of knowledge, preserving certain insights while jettisoning the ontological assumptions in order to develop an empiricist epistemology—that is, a theory of knowledge that privileges the senses as the source of reliable evidence about the world. Aristotle rejected Plato's theory of the Forms and the notion that a transcendent realm of ideas is the true reality. Like Socrates, he argued that "universals" or "essences" are inherent in the "particulars"—that is, the universal is that which all particulars share in common. But he suggested that there were more mechanisms for gaining information about particulars than Socrates had acknowledged. Inquiry need not be restricted to comparative analysis of conflicting opinions because the senses allowed access to the physical world. Systematic observation aided by reason could generate reliable knowledge about the world, including sophisticated understanding of processes of change and development that characterized the realm of becoming.

The Aristotelian account of inquiry begins with induction, repeated observation of particular cases in order to arrive at a generalization, but Aristotle noted from the outset that individuals must be trained to observe the world so as not to be misled by transitory appearances. By asking the right questions and making careful distinctions, empirical observation could generate accurate knowledge of the physical world. Aristotle agreed with Plato that the physical world is constantly changing, but he suggested that the processes of becoming are themselves characterized by a particular order. Transformations observable in nature, including human nature, are linked to the realization of potentialities inherent in living organisms. Aristotle was a teleologist; he insisted that all processes of development are goal (*telos*) directed. The telos of all life forms is the full realization of potential. The "essence" of any life form is nothing other than the actualization of all potentiality. Appearances depict the amount of potential developed at any particular stage of development, and appearances change as increasing amounts of potential are actualized. A tadpole assumes many different appearances as it progresses toward its development into a frog. An acorn is totally transformed as it grows into an oak tree: its size, shape, complexity, functioning, and uses change dramatically over its developmental process. According to Aristotle, these transformations are governed by an inherent striving to achieve full realization. Given the appropriate soil and moisture and absent intervention by catastrophic forces (natural or humanly created), the acorn will become an oak. At the moment when full actualization occurs, when all potentiality has been realized, actuality and essence coincide. Thus, systematic observation of the developmental process enables a viewer to see the oak's essence, for, at the moment of full flourishing, the oak's essence is manifest in its appearance.

Aristotle noted that a trained observer can provide very different kinds of explanation of developmental processes. A genetic explanation is oriented toward the past, tracing the origin of a phenomenon, identifying its "genesis." A teleological explanation is future-oriented, for it seeks to explain the telos or goal toward which someone is striving or something is developing. A material explanation provides an account of the "matter" or "substances" of which something is made. A material analysis of a human being, for example, would be cast in terms of DNA, RNA, genes, and cells differentiating into specific organs of the body. A formal explanation provides an account of the various stages of actualization over the course of the developmental process by attending to particular forms assumed by the developing organism. An "efficient" explanation provides an account of the mechanisms that cause the transformations from one stage to the next, locating the "engine" of change. According to Aristotle, empirical investigation can generate accurate accounts of all these dimensions of existence. Because each of these forms of explanation focuses on a different level of analysis, the accounts they generate are markedly different. The differences in these accounts do not imply, however, subjectivity in perception. On the contrary, each form of explanation generates objective information about a different aspect of the living organism. A comprehensive account encompassing all these modes of explanation is required to fully understand a particular organism.

Over the course of his life, Aristotle attempted to develop such comprehensive accounts of complex dimensions of existence. His investigations led him to conclude that different kinds of phenomena admit of different kinds of knowledge. Theoretical knowledge, which involves the contemplation of things as they are without attempt to change them, is possible in the domains of physics, mathematics, and metaphysics. In contrast to theoretical knowledge's recognition and acceptance of things as they are, practical knowledge involves the use of reason to guide choices in order to live well. Practical knowledge used to enable individuals to attain happiness is, according to Aristotle, the science of ethics. Practical knowledge of what is necessary to foster the good of communities is the science of politics. Aristotle also identified a third kind of knowledge, productive knowledge, a kind of "know how" essential to making things. The spheres of making and the kinds of "things" that could be made in Aristotle's view are far more expansive than are typically associated with technical knowledge in contemporary understandings of production and construction. *Techne*, the term that refers to "making" in classical Greek, is the etymological root for contemporary conceptions of technology, but in the ancient context techne referred to the knowledge that artisans used to produce goods essential to survival, that poets and playwrights used to produce pathos, bathos, and catharsis in their audiences, and that rhetoricians used to persuade listeners to accept their arguments. Thus, Aristotle's conception of productive knowledge is not only relevant to forms of knowledge that support industrial production and information technology, but it also informs feminist accounts of the manifold practices through which categories of difference are produced and maintained, such as Teresa de Lauretis's discussion of "technologies of gender" and the creative and symbolic production of cultural meanings that structure raced, sexed, and gendered identities, imaginings, and sentiments. On Aristotle's view, the criteria for truth in the realm of practical and productive knowledge is efficacy. The proof of the truth of practical reason's ethical arguments is that they do indeed produce individual happiness. Similarly political knowledge succeeds in promoting the well-being of communities and states. The proof of techne's "know how" is that it succeeds in producing precisely the products, emotions, and convictions that it sets out to produce in particular instances. Practical and productive knowledge succeed because they get the world right; inaccurate or mistaken views fail because they do not.

Skepticism in the Modern World

The version of skepticism that arose in Europe in the late sixteenth and early seventeenth centuries sought to dethrone medieval scholasticism, a system of thought in which Christian theology and Aristotelian philosophy were deeply entwined. Accredited by religious authorities, academics, and rulers of states, Scholasticism governed political life and scientific inquiry, as well as religious convictions. In a world in which "science" had not yet been demarcated from "natural philosophy," scholars like Francis Bacon (1561–1626), Galileo Galilei (1564–1642), René Descartes (1596–1650), and Thomas Hobbes (1588–1659) sought to carve out a space for scientific inquiry free from the heavy hand of church-ruled states and principalities. Skepticism provided a critical tool in these efforts to emancipate knowledge from religious dogmatism. Deploying skepticism to attack religious authorities as guardians of state-sanctioned knowledge, these skeptics also laid the groundwork for drastically curtailing the types of knowledge believed possible.

A MODERN VERSION OF EMPIRICISM

Bacon, often depicted as the "father of modern science," declared all knowledge his province as he set out to accredit certain modes of inductive inquiry. In *The Proficience and Advancement of Learning* (1605) and in *Nine Books of the Dignity and Advancement of Learning* (1623), he championed a utilitarian conception of practical knowledge "for the use and benefit of men" and "relief of the human condition." Where Aristotle had carefully distinguished theoretical knowledge, practical knowledge, and productive knowledge by identifying the kinds of objects in the external world appropriate to each, Bacon reclassified knowledge into three primary categories corresponding to three fundamental faculties of the human mind: history, the form of knowledge associated with memory; poesy, the mode of knowledge corresponding to the imagination; and philosophy, the domain of knowledge tied to reason. Identifying inductive reason as the key to progress in knowledge production, Bacon's reclassification defined philosophy as the domain of "realistic possibility," of everything that can theoretically or actually occur. As the domain of "fact," everything that has happened, history is craftily reconfigured as a subfield of philosophy, for what has happened falls within the larger category of realistic possibility. Poesy is construed by Bacon as "feigned history," the domain of everything that is imaginable. Typically manifested in literature and the arts, empirically oriented Bacon marginalized poesy as far less central to the progress of knowledge, affording merely a means to illustrate scientific discoveries.

Bacon envisioned empirical inquiry as a way to overcome the undue reverence for the past. Yet he acknowledged that for individuals to be able to "open their eyes and minds to the world around them," significant obstacles would have to be overcome. He identified these obstacles in need of clearing as "diseases or distempers of learning." Chief among these distempers, he included "vain imaginations" or pseudosciences such as alchemy, astrology, and magic; "vain altercations," the endless debates and metaphysical quibbling of medieval Scholasticism; and "vain affectations" or "literary vices," preoccupations with words more than matter, and style over substance, which he associated with the revival of Ciceronian rhetoric and classical prose.

In *New Organon or True Directions Concerning the Interpretation of Nature* (1620) Bacon enumerated multiple sources of error that impeded the acquisition and progress of empirical knowledge. The Greek term, *organon*, means "instrument" or "tool," and Bacon constructed this tool as a means to identify, eliminate, or control sources of potential deception and misunderstanding. With lovely literary flair, Bacon called these various sources of error, "idols" from the Greek, *eidolon*—"images" or "phantoms" that cloud the mind and impair an objective apprehension of external reality. He identified four distinct idols, which must be purged to prepare the way for empirical inquiry.

"Idols of the Tribe" refer to basic operations of the human mind, which Bacon understood as fundamental "weaknesses of human nature." As such, they cannot be eliminated, but they can be controlled by adherence to "scientific method." A chief human weakness, according to Bacon, is that the human senses themselves are dull and easily deceived. They can be corrected, however, by use of scientific instruments. Consider how glasses, telescopes, and microscopes assist the naked eye and how hearing aids, microphones, and amplifiers can assist hearing. In addition to sensory dullness, Bacon suggested that we tend to rely too heavily on immediate perceptions, rushing to conclusions and making premature judgments that are more likely to be wrong that right. Human observers also tend to impose more order on observed phenomena that actually exists. We think we "see" similitude when there is singularity or "perceive" regularity when there is randomness. Humans also have a profound tendency to "wishful thinking" in Bacon's view. We tend to accept, believe, and seek conclusive "proof" for what we prefer to be true. These troubling tendencies can be counteracted by rigorous adherence to "the scientific method," inductive techniques, which require careful and painstaking accumulation of evidence by multiple observers who subject one another's claims to strict scrutiny.

"Idols of the Cave" involve peculiar distortions, prejudices, and erroneous beliefs that arise from an individual's upbringing within a particular family within a specific tradition and culture. Whereas the idols of the tribe pertain to all human beings, idols of the cave are social in nature yet vary from one person to another. Tied to an individual's position within a society, education, and personal history, idols of the cave could include biases linked to particular disciplinary training or theoretical orientation, a tendency to rely upon a few select "authorities" to justify one's stance, or to interpret phenomena in terms of one's own narrow specialization. To "dislodge" the idols of the cave, Bacon recommended the use of skepticism as a resource for the individual inquirer. Whatever one's mind "seizes and dwells upon with peculiar satisfaction is to be held in suspicion" (lviii) and interrogated at length. Distortions of this sort can also be corrected by the practice of science as a public enterprise, involving many people, who test one another's claims and subject them to rigorous empirical tests.

Bacon's third and "most troublesome" type of obstruction to the clear apprehension of the world is related to language. Bacon refers to misunderstandings and confusions that creep into the mind through "alliances of words and names" as the "idols of the market place" because the market is a social space in which people associate with one another, engaging in "commerce and consort." Bacon suggests that language has the power to distort perception because it is not the neutral tool that many believe it to be. On the contrary language can shape understanding in a variety of ways. Everyday meanings of words may exact a powerful hold on people that interferes with new scientific understandings. Consider, for example, how the vernacular meaning of "race" as a biological phenomenon precludes popular acceptance of demonstrative scientific evidence that there is no biological basis for "race." Words also lend substance to imagined phenomena so that many people believe that "fairies," "leprechauns," "Fortune," or "the Prime Mover" (Aristotle's term for the originator of the cosmos) exist because there are words that name such "phantoms." Some terms can also be markedly misleading because they have so many different referents that their meaning in a particular instance is always ambiguous. Consider, for example, the multiple referents for "sex" (chromosomal configurations, forms of embodiment, erotic practices, sexual identifications, gendered configurations) and how they can complicate understanding of any particular usage of the term. Bacon also pointed out that when technical meanings of terms proliferate, scholars can devote all their time and attention to fights over the meanings of words and lose all sight of larger questions about processes in the world.

The final source of error identified by Bacon suggested that philosophical systems themselves can distort individual's perceptions of the world. In a caustic critique of their pretense to knowledge, Bacon referred to these distorting theoretical frames as "idols of the theater." He identified three distinctive kinds of mistake that generate these flawed worldviews. Casual observation and anecdotal evidence, made the ground for abstract argument and speculation, generated a particular form of philosophical corruption: fashioning the world out of theoretical concepts and categories absent any kind of experimental testing. Bacon suggested that Scholasticism was one example of the errors introduced by such arm-chair philosophizing. In the contemporary world, one might argue that neo-liberalism is another prime example. Bacon's second example refers to philosophical systems based on a single key insight, which itself rests upon very limited empirical research, but which is generalized to explain phenomena of all kinds, thereby producing a pattern of distortion. Sociobiology is an apt example of this kind of distortion. The potent mixture of philosophy and theology, characteristic of many contemporary fundamentalisms, is the third "parent stock of errors" that impedes objective perception of the external world, according to Bacon.

In delineating these idols of the tribe, cave, marketplace, and theater, Bacon anticipated twentieth-century discussions of the theoretical constitution of facticity, the argument that theoretical presuppositions structure every step of the research process, from the most elementary perceptions through the accreditation of particular forms of evidence and explanation. In contrast to these more recent debates, however, Bacon argued that these idols could be purged. Induction, the systematic observation of particulars as a means to arrive at defensible generalizations, coupled with experimental methods designed to test the validity of inductive generalizations, could generate accurate knowledge of the world. Refutations of mistaken generalizations or axioms could also serve as a "ladder to the intellect," for they indicated wrong directions that should not be pursued any further. Moreover, the use of scientific knowledge to develop instruments to help humans solve problems and improve their condition also generated an important means to demarcate truth from falsity. Bacon anticipated the "pragmatic theory of truth," which links the assessment of knowledge claims to outcomes. On this view, both theories and technological innovations are true if "they work," if they enable people to achieve the objectives that they set for themselves.

Bacon argued that skepticism could be deployed to hone observational powers and liberate people from superstition and error. Convinced that progress was possible through scientific investigation and innovation, Bacon laid the foundation for modern science as a mode of empirical inquiry that relied on induction and experimentation. During the same time period, Descartes also sought to deploy skepticism as a means to achieve truth, but where Bacon vindicated empiricist strategies of knowledge production, Descartes developed a defense of rationalism.

A MODERN VERSION OF RATIONALISM

Like Bacon, Descartes sought to create a new foundation for knowledge to supplant medieval Scholasticism but he did not believe the path to reliable knowledge was through the senses. Tracing a range of errors that typically befall our senses, such as optical illusions, dream images, and misperceptions that stem from physical illnesses or bodily malfunctions, Descartes argued that only reason can save us from falling prey to such distortions. Best known to nonphilosophers for his famous quip, "*Cogito ergo sum*" (I think, therefore I am), Descartes argued that our powers of reasoning provide both the foundation for truth and the requisite guidance to attain it.

In his *Discourse on Method* (1637) and his *Meditations on First Philosophy* (1640) Descartes developed a method of investigation that relied on radical doubt as a primary tool. Conceiving "exaggerated" or "hyperbolic" doubt as a form of philosophical experiment, Descartes suggested that we should push doubt to its absolute limits; we should doubt everything until we arrive at that which cannot be doubted. Such a deployment of doubt is a rational process that enables us to question all existents. During the process of doubting all that exists, we cannot doubt our own existence, however, for the doubting process presupposes the existence of the doubter. We cannot call into question our rational capacity to question. Thus this reasoning process itself becomes the ground for certainty; doubt leads us to the indubitable.

Descartes developed basic guidelines for the production of reliable knowledge that capitalized on the powers of reason. Doubt figures in these as a starting point and as a tool that helps us challenge preconceptions and avoid precipitate conclusions. Descartes suggests that we should apportion belief to evidence. We should never accept anything as true unless we have "evident knowledge" of its truth. Evident knowledge appears in the mind as "clear" and "distinct" ideas, that which remains after the doubting process has eliminated problematic elements. Using a visual analogy of viewing an object up close and in brilliant light, Descartes suggests that "clarity" allows us to understand all the properties and qualities of the object. "Distinctness" enables us to grasp how an idea relates to an object, the dimensions of the object itself, and the scope of its relationships to other phenomena. To apprehend clear and distinct ideas, Descartes recommends a form of philosophical analysis through which we break ideas down to their simplest component parts and scrutinize all the constitutive elements. From the examination of the most simple components, we then proceed in an orderly manner to build more complex ideas and arguments by testing each step of the process so that we understand clearly how the ideas go together. In thereby building knowledge from the ground up, we should seek comprehensiveness, providing an account so complete that nothing escapes scrutiny. The knowledge that is produced by this method, then, will be certain and indubitable.

FOUNDATIONALISM

Versions of rationalism developed by Plato and Descartes and versions of empiricism developed by Aristotle and Bacon are examples of "foundationalism," an epistemological doctrine asserting that a firm foundation for knowledge enables humans to transcend the limitations set by our own fallibility and achieve certain knowledge. As we have seen, these rationalists and empiricists disagree about the foundation for knowledge (reason versus the senses) and human access to it (rational philosophical analysis versus empirical scientific inquiry), but they agree that a sturdy foundation for knowledge exists. Antifoundationalists are not so sanguine. Although antifoundationalists, like foundationalists, wrestle with skepticism, in an important sense certain aspects of antifoundationalists' skepticism remains unabated.

Antifoundationalist Approaches to Problems of Knowledge

Challenges to the epistemological optimism of classical and modern versions of rationalism and empiricism come from various sources, but a common motif in these challenges is our inability to escape or counteract one or more of the sources of error already identified. Convinced that humans can never achieve "indubitable" or "absolutely certain" knowledge, antifoundationalists frame knowledge production within a different set of parameters. Although they do not reject all forms of knowledge, they reconceptualize knowledge as inherently fallible.

Thomas Hobbes, a contemporary of Bacon and Descartes, was profoundly influenced by each of them; Hobbes ultimately broke with their convictions that it is possible to have "absolutely certain" scientific knowledge of the natural world. In Hobbes's view, we can have certain scientific knowledge only of those subjects of which we are the cause, whose construction is in our power or depends upon our arbitrary will. Invoking a conception of productive knowledge as the only ground of certainty, Hobbes insisted that we can know only what we make. Because we do not make "nature"—whether understood as the earth, stars, the planets, oceans, deserts, forests, or as the "cosmos" at large—these natural phenomena remain less than fully intelligible to us. We invent theories to make sense of these phenomena, but according to Hobbes, our theories are and always will remain hypothetical, grounded on nothing more than supposition. Hobbes defines theories as instruments or tools that we create to help us make sense of and "master" nature. Our theoretical tools, then, have a pragmatic purpose, the conquest of nature. The only criteria we need to judge them is also pragmatic: "good" theories enable us to succeed in achieving our ends; "bad" theories do not. All ontological discussions of "truth" can be dispensed with as irrelevant. The natural world remains enigmatic. Instead, humans can proceed with our various projects guided only by an "instrumental" conception of knowledge judged by the criterion of success. Within this frame, the theory of aerodynamics counts as instrumental knowledge because it enables us to fly aircraft. We need nothing more than hypothetical constructs to bend the natural world to our purposes; but in Hobbes's view, we should not confuse our hypothetical theoretical constructs with absolute knowledge of the universe. Although profoundly influenced by Bacon's pragmatic criteria for judging the merits of particular theories, Hobbes contested Bacon's optimistic notion that "successful" theories provide accurate information about the world. Where Bacon argued that the "idols of the theater" could be dispelled by careful adherence to empirical inquiry and experimental method, Hobbes insisted that all theories, including "good theories," are a species of Baconian idol.

Hobbes shared Bacon's recognition that language raised pronounced problems for knowledge, but Hobbes did not believe that these problems could be resolved by scientific methods. On the contrary, he proposed a political solution for the complex issues raised by language. In his most famous work, *Leviathan* (1651), Hobbes defined speech as "the most noble and profitable" human invention, for it enables individuals to create names to register their thoughts, recall them from memory, and declare them to others. Words that "name things and their connections and relationships" enhance our reasoning abilities and make communication possible. But words also raise enormous difficulties in part because they can be "abused." We can misuse words to deceive ourselves and others, we can use words to make "evil appear good and good appear evil," and we can use words to inflict pain upon others. Beyond the "abuses of speech" that Hobbes identifies, words are problematic for another reason. Hobbes is a nominalist, who insists that words are quite arbitrary conventions: any name could be given to any object for there is no inherent or "essential" relation between words and things. Any person could use any idiosyncratic word to refer to an object, and there are no ontological grounds for preferring any particular usage to any other. If each person uses words idiosyncratically, however, no communication would be possible; misunderstanding, confusion, and chaos would ensue. For words to fulfill their communicative function, then, the definitions of terms must be agreed upon, and these conventional meanings of words must be enforced.

Hobbes is well known for his insistence that conventions gain their force only when a coercive power exists to compel compliance with them. Less frequently acknowledged is Hobbes's application of this maxim not only to the "social contract" that creates political sovereignty but also to the convention of speech. In the *Leviathan*, Hobbes defined "truth" as the "right ordering of names in our affirmations" (105). Noting that definitions are the key to truth speaking, Hobbes indicated that the creation and enforcement of a dictionary was a fundamental task of the Sovereign. Arguing that reasoning based on "metaphors and senseless and ambiguous words" ends in "contention and sedition," (116–117), Hobbes insisted that the Sovereign must appoint a judge to resolve all controversies that arise about the meanings of words. Hobbes noted that backed by the coercive power of the Sovereign, the judge's interpretation of words would be final. This did not imply that the interpretation the judge accredited was ontologically exact, an impossibility within Hobbes's nominalist framework, it simply meant that the judge's word was final, bringing the dispute to an end. Any speaker who then refused to use the word as the judge mandated would be liable for the punishment appropriate to "sedition." Hobbes's linkage of politics and language may seem somewhat less draconian when placed in the context of the civil war in England fueled by profound disagreements among certain Catholic and Protestant sects over the "meanings of words," that is, religious doctrines. But it is also instructive to consider the role that political authoritarianism can play with respect to the resolution of contentious claims concerning truth, when the ground for resolution is shifted from an evidentiary basis to politics.

In the eighteenth century, David Hume (1711–1776) launched a strenuous campaign to debunk the foundationalist pretenses of rationalism and empiricism. By a careful "mapping of the operations of the human mind," Hume sought to prove that metaphysical and ontological speculations of moral philosophy and natural philosophy were "fruitless efforts of human vanity . . . [to] penetrate into subjects utterly inaccessible to understanding" (Hume [1748] 1955, 20). In his

Enquiry Concerning Human Understanding (1748), Hume provided compelling demonstrations that neither deductive logic, the tool endorsed by rationalists for the preservation of truth, nor inductive logic, the instrument accredited by empiricists for the discovery of truth, could perform up to the expectations of their respective proponents. Following the demarcation of domains of knowledge developed by rationalists and empiricists, Hume accepted that there are two possible kinds of knowledge: "relations of ideas" and "matters of fact." Hume was willing to grant that deduction operates admirably in some contexts, such as the system of Euclidean geometry where the "relations of ideas" are governed by logical necessity. For example, a triangle is a three-sided figure the sum of whose angles is 180 degrees. It would be logically impossible then for any four-sided figure to be a triangle. We can have "absolute certainty" then about what a triangle is and what it is not. In cases of such "relations of ideas," tautological definitions establish the "truth" of the major premise and demarcate the properties of the geometric figure that may be deduced through syllogistic demonstrations. If rationalists restricted their claims about knowledge to the sphere of geometry or to a limited set of tautological "relations of ideas," their case for deduction would be defensible. The problem arises, according to Hume, when rationalists claim that deduction can provide absolute knowledge about the material world, a domain governed by contingency rather than logical necessity.

As a description of the material world, contingency captures the possibility that things could be other than they currently are. The sun "rises" each day, but not because it is logically required to do so. The physical forces governing the sun and the earth's movement around it could change. As a star, the sun could cease to exist. As a planet, the earth could also cease to exist. What we think we know about the sun and the earth are not matters of tautological definition. Thus the truth-preserving power of deductive logic, which depends on the truth of the major and minor premises in a syllogism, does not hold in cases where contingent propositions supplant tautologies in syllogistic reasoning. In the absence of tautologies, which are the key to "absolute certainty" in deductive arguments, rationalists cannot guarantee the truth of any claim they advance about the world we live in.

Hume pointed out that claims about the natural and social world rest on inductive generalizations, which are themselves prone to error in the face of contingency. In a famous discussion of the "problem of induction," Hume demonstrated that it is not possible to have sufficient empirical evidence to conclusively prove any inductive generalization. The quest for absolute certainty grounded on observation of particular cases is foiled in various ways. To achieve the status of a universal truth, an inductive generalization would have to hold for all past, present, and future cases. Consider, for example, the claim that women are nurturers. To prove this claim "absolutely" true, we would need to have observational evidence of the nurturing behavior of every woman who ever lived in the past, every woman who is currently alive, and every woman who will ever live. While it might be conceivable, given a large enough research team and computer compilation of data, to gather systematic evidence of all living women, it is not possible to gather comparable data about women who either lived in the past or have not yet been born. Hume, therefore, noted that empirical observation cannot provide an "absolute ground" for knowledge: no matter how much inductive evidence we have to support a generalization, it will never be enough to cover all past and future instances. Moreover, in a world of contingency, things can and do change. Thus, even if there were a moment in time when all living women were nurturing, there is no reason to believe that the future will be the same as the present or past. Any number of factors (for example, war, terrorism, domestic violence, rape, anger, animosity, ambition) could cause women to change their behaviors. If even one woman rejects nurturing and refuses to manifest that behavior, then a universal generalization—such as "all women are nurturers"—would be proven false. Contrary to the optimism of classical and modern empiricism, Hume suggested that the impossibility of gathering universal evidence as well as contingency undermine induction as an absolute ground for truth claims.

Hume did not rest content with a demonstration of the limitations of deductive and inductive logic. He also developed an argument that the human mind operated according to principles at great remove from what is commonly considered "reason." Hume agreed with empiricists that thoughts or ideas enter the mind through primary sensory impressions. He suggested, however, that the mind actively organizes these perceptions according to three principles: resemblance, contiguity, and causation. Breaking with a long line of thinkers who characterized the mind as a passive medium that simply receives impressions from the external world, Hume argued that the mind actively imposes order on our perceptions, thereby structuring our understanding of the world. If Hume's claim is interpreted only in the context of memory, then the association of ideas on the basis of resemblance, contiguity, and causation seems relatively unproblematic. According to the principle of resemblance, a picture "leads our thoughts back to the original," a photo reminds us of the person it portrays. Contiguity introduces a train of thoughts that leads our minds from one memory to another that was temporally or spatially adjacent to it. For example, if we see a coffee shop that we once frequented, it may trigger a series of memories of people we used to meet there, of buildings that used to surround it, of streets that led from the coffee shop to home. Similarly with respect to causation, if we think of a wound, our minds may quickly move to the incident that caused it or to the pain caused by it.

Hume does not claim, however, that resemblance, contiguity, and causation—the mechanisms for associating ideas—operate only at the level of memory. On the contrary, he suggests that these principles support inferences that enable our minds to move beyond immediate experience and memory. Indeed, Hume notes that causal inferences, in particular, expand our knowledge of matters of fact beyond our sensory impressions and our memories of them. If we find a watch in the desert, for example, we infer that another person has been there. If we see a pregnant woman, we infer that she has had sexual intercourse with a man. As both these examples make clear, however, causal inferences may be mistaken. A watch may have fallen from a plane and landed in a part of a desert in which no person had ever been. A woman may be pregnant though artificial insemination without ever having experienced sexual intercourse with a man. Hume points out the fallibility of causal inferences as part of a larger critique of empiricist claims about causal knowledge.

Breaking the idea of cause and effect into its component parts as "analytic method" recommends, Hume suggests that a causal relationship typically implies priority in time (the cause precedes the effect), contiguity (the cause triggers the effect by temporal and spatial touching, as when pool balls move when physically hit by a pool cue), and necessary connection (the effect necessarily follows from the cause; its appearance is neither arbitrary nor coincidental). Following empiricist claims that knowledge of matters of fact derive from sensory observation, Hume tries to locate the primary sensory impressions from which the constitutive ideas of cause and effect arise. He points out that priority in time and contiguity are empirically observable, but necessary connection is not. "Constant conjunction" or "correlation" in the language of statistics—two things occurring together—is all that is empirically observable in a putative causal observation. Correlations, however, are notoriously fallible. Consider, for example, claims of nineteenth-century anthropologists that women are intellectually inferior to men because women have smaller brains. The putative causal claim was based on "observations" of a constant conjunction between the weight of women's brains and the absence of women from intellectually demanding positions. The "correlation," however, is spurious. As Stephen J. Gould (1981) and Carol Tavris (1992) have so eloquently demonstrated, brain size is related to body weight, not intellectual capacity; women's absence from intellectually demanding positions is related to discriminatory practices, such as laws and traditions that have barred them from educational and occupational opportunities, not to brain size.

According to Hume, a "habit of the mind" or a "mental custom" imposes "necessity" upon constant conjunction to "render our experience useful to us." Rather than allow us to be paralyzed by skepticism or by a lack of adequate evidence, our minds lead us to believe there is a causal connection when we observe constant conjunction. This mental habit helps us to survive. For example, when we are hungry and we see food, we do not hesitate to consume it, expecting its nourishment to allay our hunger. This expectation is based on a presumption that past experience is a reliable guide to the future because the future will be like the past, a presumption belied by contingency. Thus Hume points out that our convictions about the reliability of our causal inferences rest upon mental custom, not rational argument. In a world of contingency there is no reason that the future should replicate the past. Custom, not reason, makes us expect a future that conforms to our expectations. A simple mental habit shores up our confidence in our fallible perceptions of constant conjunction, a mental habit with certain affinities to "wishful thinking."

By impugning the epistemological optimism of rationalists and empiricists, Hume sought to demonstrate that neither deductive nor inductive reasoning could provide an absolute foundation for human knowledge. Toward that end, he wielded skepticism as a formidable weapon against the views of other philosophers, but Hume did not believe that skepticism provided a viable epistemological basis for human life. On the contrary, he argued that the "chief and most confounding objection to excessive skepticism [is] that no durable good can ever result from it. . . . All human life must perish were . . . [Pyrrhonian or excessive skepticism] universally and steadily to prevail. All discourse, all action would immediately cease, and men remain in total lethargy till the necessities of nature, unsatisfied, put an end to their miserable existence" (168). In place of defective epistemological doctrines such as rationalism, empiricism, and skepticism, Hume celebrated "custom" as the great guide to human life. Although the "powers and forces by which nature is governed are wholly unknown to us," custom renders our experience useful to us, extends our knowledge beyond the narrow sphere of senses and memory, enables means-ends analysis so that we can survive in the world (68). As a political conservative, Hume was more than happy to vindicate custom and tradition as an alternative to epistemological foundationalism. While far less coercive than Hobbes's appeal to political force to support epistemic conventions, Hume's celebration of custom, freighted with male privilege and androcentric bias, may, however, give feminist scholars pause. Constructing the epistemological options in such stark terms, custom or reason, may not be the only alternative for feminist knowledge production.

Twentieth-Century Debates in the Philosophy of Science

Most discussions of feminist knowledge production have been framed by debates in the philosophy of science that developed over the course of the twentieth century. Some familiarity with these debates are particularly helpful in considering how to move beyond the stark alternatives that pit foundationalist appeals to absolute truth grounded in deductive or inductive logic against antifoundationalist appeals to conventions shored up by force or customs that entrench male domination. The final section of this chapter provides an overview of the positivist version of foundationalism and a postpositivist version of antifoundationalism.

POSITIVISM

The term positivism was first coined by the French sociologist Auguste Comte, who suggested that scientific understanding operates in the realm of the "positive," which denotes "real" or "actual" existence. Advancing a version of empiricism, Comte suggested that scientists must eschew the metaphysical and theological realms and restrict their investigations to observable facts and the relations that hold among observed phenomena. Within this finite sphere of the empirically observable, scientific inquiry could discover the "laws" governing empirical events. In the early twentieth century, a group of philosophers of science, known as the "Vienna Circle," developed "logical positivism," which further restricted the possibilities for valid knowledge by elaborating the "verification criterion of meaning." Focusing on how to establish the truth of specific statements about the empirical world, the verification criterion stipulated that a contingent proposition is meaningful if, and only if, it can be empirically verified, that is, if there is an empirical method for deciding the proposition's truth or falsity.

Within the natural sciences and the social sciences, positivist commitments generated a number of methodological techniques designed to ensure the truth, not of propositions, but of scientific investigations. Chief among these is the dichotomous division of the world into the realms of the "empirical" and the "nonempirical." The empirical realm, comprising all that can be corroborated by the senses, is circumscribed as the legitimate sphere of scientific investigation. As a residual category, the nonempirical encompasses everything else—religion, philosophy, ethics, aesthetics, and evaluative discourse in general, as well as myth, dogma, and superstition—and is relegated beyond the sphere of science. Within this frame of reference, science, operating within the realm of the observable and restricting its focus to descriptions, explanations, and predictions that are intersubjectively testable, can achieve objective knowledge. The specific techniques requisite to the achievement of objective knowledge have been variously defined by positivism and critical rationalism.

On the grounds that only those knowledge claims founded directly upon observable experience can be genuine, positivists deployed the "verification criterion of meaning" to differentiate not only between science and nonscience, but between science and nonsense (Joergenson 1951; Kraft 1952; Ayer 1959). In the positivist view, any statement that could not be verified by reference to experience constituted nonsense: it was literally meaningless. The implications of the verification criterion for a model of science were manifold. All knowledge was believed to be dependent upon observation; thus any claims—whether theological, metaphysical, philosophical, ethical, normative, or aesthetic—that were not rooted in empirical observation were rejected as meaningless. The sphere of science was thereby narrowly circumscribed, and scientific knowledge was accredited as the only valid knowledge. In addition, induction, a method of knowledge acquisition grounded upon observation of particulars as the foundation for empirical generalizations, was taken to provide the essential logic of science.

The task of science was understood to comprise the inductive discovery of regularities existing in the external world. Scientific research sought to organize in economical fashion those regularities that experience presents in order to facilitate explanation and prediction. To promote this objective, positivists endorsed and employed a technical vocabulary, clearly differentiating facts (empirically verifiable propositions) and hypotheses (empirically verifiable propositions asserting the existence of relationships among observed phenomena) from laws (empirically confirmed propositions asserting an invariable sequence or association among observed phenomena) and theories (interrelated systems of laws possessing explanatory power). Moreover, the positivist logic of scientific inquiry dictated a specific sequence of activities as definitive of "the scientific method."

According to this model, the scientific method begins with the carefully controlled, neutral observation of empirical events. Sustained observation over time enables the regularities or patterns of relationships in observed events to be revealed and thereby provides for the formulation of hypotheses. Once formulated, hypotheses were to be subjected to systematic empirical tests. Those hypotheses which received external confirmation through this process of rigorous testing could be elevated to the status of scientific laws. Once identified, scientific laws provided the foundation for scientific explanation, which, according to the precepts of the "covering law model," consisted in demonstrating that the event(s) to be explained could have been expected, given certain initial conditions ($C_1, C_2, C_3, \ldots$) and the general laws of the field ($L_1, L_2, L_3, \ldots$). Within the framework of the positivist conception of science, the discovery of scientific laws also provided the foundation for prediction, which consisted in demonstrating that an event would occur given the future occurrence of certain initial conditions and the operation of the general laws of the field. Under the covering law model, then, explanation and prediction have the same logical form, but the time factor differs: explanation pertains to past events; prediction pertains to future events.

Positivists were also committed to the principle of the "unity of science," that is, to the belief that the logic of scientific inquiry was the same for all fields. Whether natural phenomena or social phenomena were the objects of study, the method for acquiring valid knowledge and the requirements for explanation and prediction remained the same. Once a science had progressed sufficiently to accumulate a body of scientific laws organized in a coherent system of theories, it could be said to have achieved a stage of "maturity" that made explanation and prediction possible. Although the logic of mature science remained inductive with respect to the generation of new knowledge, the logic of scientific explanation was deductive. Under the covering law model, causal explanation, the demonstration of the necessary and sufficient conditions of an event, involved the deductive subsumption of particular observations under a general law. In addition, deduction also played a central role in efforts to explain laws and theories: the explanation of a law involved its deductive subsumption under a theory; and explanation of one theory involved its deductive subsumption under wider theories.

CRITIQUES OF POSITIVISM

The primary postulates of positivism have been subjected to rigorous and devastating critiques (Popper 1959, 1972a, 1972b). Neither the logic of induction nor the verification criterion of meaning can accomplish positivist objectives; neither can guarantee the acquisition of truth. As Hume demonstrated, the inductive method is incapable of guaranteeing the validity of scientific knowledge because of the "problem of induction." Because empirical events are contingent, that is, because the future can always be different from the past, generalizations based upon limited observations are necessarily incomplete and, as such, highly fallible. For this reason, inductive generalizations cannot be presumed to be true. Nor can "confirmation" or "verification" of such generalizations by reference to additional cases provide proof of their universal validity. For, as Hume made clear, the notion of universal validity invokes all future, as well as all past and present, occurrences of a phenomenon; yet no matter how many confirming instances of a phenomenon can be found in the past or in the present, these can never alter the possibility that the future could be different, that the future could disprove an inductively derived empirical generalization. Thus, a demonstration of the truth of an empirical generalization must turn upon the identification of a "necessary connection" establishing a causal relation among observed phenomena.

The notion of necessary connection raises serious problems for an empirical account of science, however. If the notion of necessity invoked is logical necessity, then the empirical nature of science is jeopardized. If, however, positivism appeals to an empirical demonstration of necessity, it falls foul of the standard established by the verification criterion of meaning, for the "necessity" required as proof of any causal claim cannot be empirically observed. As Hume pointed out, empirical observation reveals "constant conjunction"; it does not and cannot reveal necessary connection. As a positivist logic of scientific inquiry, then, induction encounters two serious problems: it is incapable of providing validation for the truth of its generalizations, and it is internally inconsistent; any attempt to demonstrate the validity of a causal claim invokes a conception of necessary connection that violates the verification criterion of meaning.

The positivist conception of the scientific method also rests upon a flawed psychology of perception. In suggesting that the scientific method commences with "neutral" observation, positivists invoke a conception of "manifest truth," which attempts to reduce the problem of the validity of knowledge to an appeal to the authority of the source of that knowledge (for example, "the facts 'speak' for themselves"). The belief that the unmediated apprehension of the "given" by a passive or receptive observer is possible, however, misconstrues both the nature of perception and the nature of the world. The human mind is not passive but active; it does not merely receive an image of the given, but rather the mind imposes order upon the external world through a process of selection, interpretation, and imagination. Observation is always linguistically and culturally mediated. It involves the creative imposition of expectations, anticipations, and conjectures upon external events.

Scientific observation, too, is necessarily theory-laden. It begins not from "nothing," nor from the "neutral" perception of given relations, but rather from immersion in a scientific tradition that provides frames of reference or conceptual schemes that organize reality and shape the problems for further investigation. To grasp the role of theory in structuring scientific observation, however, requires a revised conception of "theory." Contrary to the positivist notion that theory is the result of observation, the result of systematization of a series of inductive generalizations, the result of the accumulation of an interrelated set of scientific laws, theory is logically prior to the observation of any similarities or regularities in the world; indeed, theory is precisely that which makes the identification of regularities possible. Moreover, scientific theories involve risk to an extent that is altogether incompatible with the positivist view of theories as summaries of empirical generalizations. Scientific theories involve risky predictions of things that have never been seen and hence cannot be deduced logically from observation statements. Theories structure scientific observation in a manner altogether incompatible with the positivist requirement of neutral perception, and they involve unobservable propositions that violate the verification criterion of meaning: abstract theoretical entities cannot be verified by reference to empirical observation.

That theoretical propositions violate the verification criterion is not in itself damning, for the verification criterion can be impugned on a number of grounds. As a mechanism for validating empirical generalizations, the verification criterion fails because of the problem of induction. As a scientific principle for demarcating the "meaningful" from the "meaningless," the verification criterion is self-referentially destructive. In repudiating all that is not empirically verifiable as nonsense, the verification criterion repudiates itself, for it is not a statement derived from empirical observation nor is it a tautology. Rigid adherence to the verification criterion then would mandate that it be rejected as metaphysical nonsense. Thus, the positivist conflation of that which is not amenable to empirical observation with nonsense simply will not withstand scrutiny. Much, including the verification criterion itself, that cannot be empirically verified can be understood, and all that can be understood is meaningful.

CRITICAL RATIONALISM

As an alternative to the defective positivist conception of science, Karl Popper advanced "critical rationalism" (1972a, 1972b). On this view, scientific theories are bold conjectures that scientists impose upon the world. Drawing insights from manifold sources in order to solve particular problems, scientific theories involve abstract and unobservable propositions that predict what may happen as well as what may not happen. Thus scientific theories generate predictions that are incompatible with certain possible results of observation; that is, they "prohibit" certain occurrences by proclaiming that some things could not happen. As such, scientific theories put the world to the test and demand a reply. Precisely because scientific theories identify a range of conditions that must hold, a series of events that must occur, and a set of occurrences that are in principle impossible, they can clash with observation; they are empirically testable. Although no number of confirming instances could ever prove a theory to be true, owing to the problem of induction, one disconfirming instance is sufficient to disprove a theory. If scientific laws are construed as statements of prohibitions, forbidding the occurrence of certain empirical events, then they can be definitively refuted by the occurrence of one such event. Thus, according to Popper, "falsification" provides a mechanism by which scientists can test their conjectures against reality and learn from their mistakes. Falsification also provides the core of Popper's revised conception of the scientific method.

According to the "hypothetico-deductive model," the scientist always begins with a problem. To resolve the problem, the scientist generates a theory, a conjecture, or hypothesis that can be tested by deducing its empirical consequences and measuring them against the world. Once the logical implications of a theory have been deduced and converted into predictions concerning empirical events, the task of science is falsification. In putting theories to the test of experience, scientists seek to falsify predictions, for that alone enables them to learn from their mistakes. On this view, the rationality of science is embodied in the method of trial and error, a method that allows error to be purged by eliminating false theories.

In mandating that all scientific theories be tested, in stipulating that the goal of science is the falsification of erroneous views, the criterion of falsifiability provides a means by which to reconcile the fallibility of human knowers with a conception of objective knowledge. The validity of scientific claims does not turn on a demand for an impossible neutrality on the part of individual scientists, on the equally impossible requirement that all prejudice, bias, prejudgment, expectation, or value be purged from the process of observation or on the implausible assumption that the truth is manifest. The adequacy of scientific theories is judged in concrete problem contexts in terms of their ability to solve problems and their ability to withstand increasingly difficult empirical tests. Those theories that withstand multiple intersubjective efforts to falsify them are "corroborated," identified as "laws" that with varying degrees of verisimilitude capture the structure of reality, and for that reason they are tentatively accepted as "true." But, in keeping with the critical attitude of science, even the strongest corroboration for a theory is not accepted as conclusive proof. For Popperian critical rationalism posits that truth lies beyond human reach. As a regulative ideal that guides scientific activity, truth may be approximated, but it can never be established by human authority. Nevertheless, error can be objectively identified. Thus informed by a conception of truth as a "regulative ideal" and operating in accordance with the requirements of the criterion of falsifiability, science can progress by the incremental correction of errors and the gradual accretion of objective problem-solving knowledge.

Although Popper subjected many central tenets of logical positivism to systematic critique, his conception of "critical rationalism" shares sufficient ground with positivist approaches to the philosophy of science that it is typically considered to be a qualified modification of, rather than a comprehensive alternative to, positivism (Stockman 1983). Indeed, Popper's conception of the hypothetico-deductive model has been depicted as the "orthodox" positivist conception of scientific theory (Moon 1975, 143–187). Both positivist and Popperian approaches to science share a belief in the centrality of logical deduction to scientific analysis; both conceive scientific theories to be deductively related systems of propositions; both accept a deductive account of scientific explanation; both treat explanation and prediction as equivalent concepts; and both are committed to a conception of scientific progress dependent upon the use of the hypothetico-deductive method of testing scientific claims (Stockman 1983, 76; H. Brown 1977, 65–75). In addition, both positivist and Popperian conceptions of science are committed to the "correspondence theory of truth" and its corollary assumption: the objectivity of science ultimately rests upon an appeal to the facts. Both are committed to institutionalizing the fact/value dichotomy in order to establish the determinate ground of science. Both accept that, once safely ensconced within the bounds of the empirical realm, science is grounded upon a sufficiently firm foundation to provide for the accumulation of knowledge, the progressive elimination of error, and the gradual accretion of useful solutions to technical problems. And although Popper suggested that reason could be brought to bear upon evaluative questions, he accepted the fundamental positivist principle that, ultimately, value choices rested upon nonrational factors.

Most research strategies developed within the natural sciences and the social sciences in the twentieth century draw upon either positivist or Popperian conceptions of the scientific method. The legacy of positivism is apparent in behavioralist methods that emphasize data collection, hypothesis formulation and testing, and other formal aspects of systematic empirical enterprise, as well as in approaches that stress scientific, inductive methods, statistical models, and quantitative research designs. Likewise, the positivist legacy surfaces in conceptions of explanation defined in deductive terms and in commitments to the equivalence of explanation and prediction; it emerges in claims that social science must be modeled upon the methods of the natural sciences, for those alone are capable of generating valid knowledge. Moreover, evidence of positivism is unmistakable in the assumption that "facts" are unproblematic, that they are immediately observable or "given"; hence, their apprehension requires no interpretation. It is embodied in the presumption that either confirmation or verification provides a criterion of proof of the validity of empirical claims. And it is conspicuous in the repudiation of values as arbitrary preferences, irrational commitments, or meaningless propositions that lie altogether beyond the realm of rational analysis.

Popper's insistence upon the centrality of problem solving and incrementalism also resonates in many approaches to scientific inquiry and social analysis. Popperian assumptions surface in the recognition that observation and analysis are necessarily theory-laden, as well as in the commitment to intersubjective testing as the appropriate means by which to deflect the influence of individual bias from scientific studies. The Popperian assumptions are manifest in the substitution of testability for verifiability as the appropriate criterion for demarcating scientific hypotheses and in the invocation of falsification and the elimination of error as the strategy for accumulating knowledge. Popperian assumptions are obvious in the critique of excessive optimism concerning the possibility of attaining "absolute truth" about the world through the deployment of inductive, quantitative techniques, in the less pretentious quest for "useful knowledge," and in the insistence that truth constitutes a regulative ideal rather than a current possession of science. They are conspicuous in arguments that the hypothetico-deductive model is appropriate for scientific research and in appeals for developing a critical, nondogmatic attitude among researchers.

As we see in chapters 2 and 3, feminist scholars in the social and natural sciences, wrestling with positivist and critical rationalist conceptions of knowledge and scientific inquiry, have found them to be inaccurate accounts of actual research practices and obstructive to feminist efforts to generate scholarship that challenges androcentric bias. In attempting to break with the problematic assumptions of, and the limitations on, research practices associated with positivism and critical rationalism, feminist social scientists have gravitated toward a form of antifoundationalism explicated in recent post-positivist approaches in the philosophy of science.

POST-POSITIVIST PRESUPPOSITION THEORIES OF SCIENCE

Although Popper's critical rationalism significantly improves early positivist conceptions of science, it too suffers from a number of grave defects. The most serious challenge to critical rationalism has been raised by post-positivist presupposition theories of science (Polanyi 1958; Humphreys 1969; Suppe 1977; H. Brown 1977; Bernstein 1976, 1983; Hesse 1980; Longino 1990; Stockman 1983; Gunnell 1986, 1995, 1998). Presupposition theories of science concur with Popper's depiction of observation as "theory-laden." They agree that "there is more to seeing than meets the eye" (Humphreys 1969, 61) and that perception involves more than the passive reception of allegedly manifest sense-data. They suggest that perception depends upon a constellation of theoretical presuppositions that structure observation, accrediting particular stimuli as significant and specific configurations as meaningful. According to presupposition theories, observation is not only theory-laden but theory is essential to, indeed, constitutive of all human knowledge. Thus post-positivist presupposition theorists reject "instrumentalist" conceptions of theory, the view that theories are merely "tools" intentionally created to solve problems, consciously held, fully explicable, and easily abandoned when falsified. Instead, these theorists suggest that we live within theories, which structure our perceptions and understandings in ways that defy our conscious grasp. Operating at the tacit level, theories provide the criteria of intelligibility for the world and for ourselves.

Within recent work in the philosophy of science, the epistemological and ontological implications of the post-positivist understanding of theory have been the subject of extensive debate. Arguing that the theoretical constitution of human knowledge has ontological as well as epistemological implications, "antirealists" have suggested that there is no point in asking about the nature of the world independent of our theories about it (Laudan 1990). Consequently the truth status of theories must be bracketed. Echoing Hobbes, antirealists have insisted that theories need not be true to be good, that is, to solve problems (van Fraassen 1980; Churchland and Hooker 1985). Metaphysical "realists," however, have emphasized that, even if the only access to the world is through theories about it, a logical distinction can still be upheld between reality and how we conceive it, between truth and what we believe (Harre 1986). Hilary Putnam (1981, 1983, 1988, 1990) has advanced "pragmatic realism" as a more tenable doctrine. Putnam accepts that all concepts are theoretically constituted and culturally mediated and that the "world" does not "determine" what can be said about it. Nonetheless, it makes sense on pragmatic grounds to insist that truth and falsity are not merely matters of decision and that an external reality constrains our conceptual choices. Following Putnam's lead, "scientific realists" have argued that scientific theories are referential in an important sense and as such can be comparatively assessed in terms of their approximations of truth (Glymour 1980; Newton-Smith 1981; Miller 1987).

While the debates among realists and antirealists about the criteria of truth and the nature of evidence are intricate and complex, both realists and antirealists share convictions about the defects of positivism and critical rationalism and accept the broad contours of presupposition theories of science. On this view, science, as a form of human knowledge, depends upon theory in multiple and complex ways. Presupposition theories of science suggest that the notions of perception, meaning, relevance, explanation, knowledge, and method, central to the practice of science, are all theoretically constituted concepts. Theoretical presuppositions shape perception and determine what is taken as a "fact"; they confer meaning on experience and control the demarcation of significant from trivial events; they afford criteria of relevance according to which facts can be organized, tests envisioned, and the acceptability or unacceptability of scientific conclusions assessed; they accredit particular models of explanation and strategies of understanding; and they sustain specific methodological techniques for gathering, classifying, and analyzing data. Theoretical presuppositions set the terms of scientific debate and organize the elements of scientific activity. Moreover, they typically do so at a tacit or preconscious level, and for this reason they appear to hold such unquestionable authority.

The pervasive role of theoretical assumptions upon the practice of science has profound implications for notions such as empirical "reality" and the "autonomy" of facts, which posit that facts are "given," and that experience is ontologically distinct from the theoretical constructs advanced to explain it. The post-positivist conception of a "fact" as a theoretically constituted entity calls into question such basic assumptions. It suggests that "the noun, 'experience,' the verb, 'to experience,' and the adjective 'empirical' are not univocal terms that can be transferred from one system to another without change of meaning. . . . Experience does not come labeled as 'empirical,' nor does it come self-certified as such. What we call experience depends upon assumptions hidden beyond scrutiny which define it and which in turn it supports" (Vivas 1960, 76). Recognition that "facts" can be so designated only in terms of prior theoretical presuppositions implies that any quest for an unmediated reality is necessarily futile. Any attempt to identify an "unmediated fact" must mistake the conventional for the "natural," as in cases that define "brute facts" as "social facts which are largely the product of well-understood, reliable tools, facts that are not likely to be vitiated by pitfalls . . . in part [because of] the ease and certainty with which [they] can be determined and in part [because of] the incontestability of [their] conceptual base" (Murray 1983, 321). Alternatively, the attempt to conceive a "fact" that exists prior to any description of it, prior to any theoretical or conceptual mediation, must generate an empty notion of something completely unspecified and unspecifiable, a notion that will be of little use to science (Williams 1985, 138).

Recognition of the manifold ways in which perceptions of reality are theoretically mediated raises a serious challenge to not only notions of "brute data" and the "givenness" of experience but also the possibility of falsification as a strategy for testing theories against an independent reality. For falsification to provide an adequate test of a scientific theory, it is necessary that there be a clear distinction between the theory being tested and the evidence adduced to support or refute the theory. According to the hypothetico-deductive model, "theory-independent evidence" is essential to the very possibility of refutation, to the possibility that the world could prove a theory to be wrong. If, however, what is taken to be the "world," what is understood to be "brute data" is itself theoretically constituted (indeed, constituted by the same theory that is undergoing the test), then no conclusive disproof of a theory is likely. The independent evidence upon which falsification depends does not exist; the available evidence is preconstituted by the same theoretical presuppositions as the scientific theory under scrutiny (Moon 1975, 146; Brown 1977, 38–48; Stockman 1983, 73–76).

Contrary to Popper's confident conviction that empirical reality could provide an ultimate court of appeal for the judgment of scientific theories and that the critical, nondogmatic attitude of scientists would ensure that their theories were constantly being put to the test; presupposition theorists emphasize that it is always possible to "save" a theory from refutation. The existence of one disconfirming instance is not sufficient to falsify a theory because it is always possible to evade falsification on the grounds that future research will demonstrate that a counterinstance is really only an "apparent" counterinstance. Moreover, the theory-laden character of observation and the theory-constituted character of evidence provide ample grounds upon which to dispute the validity of the evidence and to challenge the design or the findings of specific experiments that claim to falsify respected theories. Furthermore, post-positivist examinations of the history of scientific practice suggest that, contrary to Popper's claim that scientists are quick to discard discredited theories, there is considerable evidence that neither the existence of counterinstances nor the persistence of anomalies necessarily lead to the abandonment of scientific theories. Indeed, the overwhelming evidence of scientific practice suggests that scientists cling to long-established views tenaciously, in spite of the existence of telling criticisms, persistent anomalies, and unresolved problems (Ricci 1984; Harding 1986).

Thus, it has been suggested that the "theory" that scientists themselves are always skeptical, nondogmatic, critical of received views, and quick to repudiate questionable notions has itself been falsified and should be abandoned.

The problem of falsification is exacerbated by the conflation of explanation and prediction in the Popperian account of science, for the belief that a corroborated prediction constitutes proof of the validity of a scientific explanation fails to recognize that an erroneous theory can generate correct predictions (Moon 1975, 146–47; H. Brown 1977, 51–57). The logical distinction between prediction and explanation thus further supports the view that no theory can ever be conclusively falsified. The problem of induction also raises doubts about the possibility of definitive refutations. In calling attention to the possibility that the future could be different from the past and present in unforeseeable ways, the problem of induction arouses the suspicion that a theory falsified today might not "stay" falsified. The assumption of regularity, which sustains Popper's belief that a falsified theory will remain falsified permanently, is itself an inductionist presupposition, which suggests that the falsifiability principle does not constitute the escape from induction that Popper had hoped (Stockman 1983, 81–82). Thus, despite the logical asymmetry between verification and falsification, no falsification can be any stronger or more final than any corroboration (H. Brown 1977, 75).

Presupposition theorists acknowledge that "ideally, scientists would like to examine the structure of the world which exists independent of our knowledge—but the nature of perception and the role of presuppositions preclude direct access to it: the only access available is through theory-directed research" (H. Brown 1977, 108). Recognition that theoretical presuppositions organize and structure research by determining the meanings of observed events, identifying relevant data and significant problems for investigation, and indicating both strategies for solving problems and methods by which to test the validity of proposed solutions, seriously challenges the correspondence theory of truth. Presupposition theory both denies that "autonomous facts" can serve as the ultimate arbiter of scientific theories and suggests that science is no more capable of achieving the Archimedean point or of escaping human fallibility than is any other human endeavor. Indeed, it demands acknowledgment of science as a human convention rooted in the practical judgments of a community of fallible scientists struggling to resolve theory-generated problems under specific historical conditions. Presupposition theory sustains an image of science that is far less heroic and far more human.

As an alternative to the correspondence theory of truth, presupposition theorists suggest a coherence theory of truth premised upon the recognition that all human knowledge depends upon theoretical presuppositions whose congruence with nature cannot be established conclusively by reason or experience.

Theoretical presuppositions, rooted in living traditions, provide the conceptual frameworks through which the world is viewed; they exude a "natural attitude" that demarcates what is taken as normal, natural, real, reasonable, or sane, from what is understood as deviant, unnatural, utopian, impossible, irrational, or insane. In contrast to Popper's conception of theories as conscious conjectures that can be systematically elaborated and deductively elucidated, the notion of theoretical presuppositions suggests that theories operate at the tacit level. They structure "pre-understandings" and "pre-judgments" in such a way that it is difficult to isolate and illuminate the full range of presuppositions that affect cognition at any given time (Bernstein 1983, 113–67). Moreover, any attempt to elucidate presuppositions must operate within a "hermeneutic circle." Any attempt to examine or to challenge certain assumptions or expectations must occur within the frame of reference established by the other presuppositions. Certain presuppositions must remain fixed if others are to be subjected to systematic critique. This does not imply that individuals are "prisoners" trapped within the framework of theories, expectations, past experiences, and language in such a way that critical reflection becomes impossible (Bernstein 1983, 84). Critical reflection upon and abandonment of certain theoretical presuppositions is possible within the hermeneutic circle; but the goal of transparency, of the unmediated grasp of things as they are, is not. For no reflective investigation, no matter how critical, can escape the fundamental conditions of human cognition.

A coherence theory of truth accepts that the world is richer than the theories devised to grasp it; it accepts that theories are underdetermined by "facts" and, consequently, that there can always be alternative and competing theoretical explanations of particular events. It does not, however, imply the relativist conclusion that all theoretical interpretations are equal. That there can be no appeal to neutral, theory-independent facts to adjudicate between competing theoretical interpretations does not mean that there is no rational way of making and warranting critical evaluative judgments concerning alternative views. Indeed, presupposition theorists have pointed out that the belief that the absence of independent evidence necessarily entails relativism itself depends upon a positivist commitment to the verification criterion of meaning. Only if one starts from the assumption that the sole test for the validity of a proposition lies in its measurement against the empirically "given" does it follow that, in the absence of the "given," no rational judgments can be made concerning the validity of particular claims (Bernstein 1983, 92; H. Brown 1977, 93–94; Stockman 1983, 79–101; Gunnell 1986, 66–68).

Once the "myth of the given" (Sellars 1963, 164) has been abandoned and once the belief that the absence of one invariant empirical test for the truth of a theory implies the absence of all criteria for evaluative judgment has been repudiated, then it is possible to recognize the rational grounds for assessing the merits of alternative theoretical interpretations. To comprehend the nature of such assessments it is necessary to acknowledge that, although theoretical presuppositions structure the perception of events, they do not create perceptions out of nothing. Theoretical interpretations are "world-guided" (Williams 1985, 140). They involve both the preunderstanding brought to an event by an individual perceiver and the stimuli in the external (or internal) world which instigate the process of cognition. Because of this dual source of theoretical interpretations, objects can be characterized in many different ways, "but it does not follow that a given object can be seen in any way at all or that all descriptions are equal" (Brown 1977, 93). The stimuli that trigger interpretation limit the class of plausible characterizations without dictating one absolute description.

Assessment of alternative theoretical interpretations involves deliberation, a rational activity which requires that imagination and judgment be deployed in the consideration of the range of evidence, and arguments that can be advanced in support of various positions. The reasons offered in support of alternative views marshal evidence, organize data, apply various criteria of explanation, address multiple levels of analysis with varying degrees of abstraction, and employ divergent strategies of argumentation. This range of reasons offers a rich field for deliberation and assessment. It provides an opportunity for exercising judgment and ensures that scientists reject a theory only because they believe they can demonstrate that the reasons supporting that theory are deficient. That the reasons advanced to sustain the rejection of one theory do not constitute absolute proof of the validity of an alternative theory is simply a testament to human fallibility. Admission that the cumulative weight of current evidence and compelling argument cannot protect scientific judgments against future developments, which may warrant the repudiation of those theories currently accepted, is altogether consonant with the recognition of the finitude of human rationality and the contingency of empirical relations.

Presupposition theorists suggest that any account of science, which fails to accredit the rationality of the considered judgments that inform the choice between alternative scientific theories, must be committed to a defective conception of reason. Although the standards of evidence and the criteria for assessment brought to bear upon theoretical questions cannot be encapsulated in a simple rule or summarized in rigid methodological principles, deliberation involves the exercise of a range of intellectual skills. Conceptions of science that define rationality in terms of one technique, be it logical deduction, inductive inference, or empirical verification, are simply too narrow to encompass the multiple forms of rationality manifested in scientific research. The interpretive judgments, characteristic of every phase of scientific investigations and culminating in the rational choice of particular scientific theories on the basis of the cumulative weight of evidence and argument, are too rich and various to be captured by the rules governing inductive or deductive logic. For this reason, the Aristotelian conception of *phronesis*, practical reason, manifested in the processes of interpretation and judgment, is advanced by some presupposition theorists as an alternative to logic as the paradigmatic form of scientific rationality (H. Brown 1977, 148–52; Bernstein 1983, 54–78).

Presupposition theorists suggest that a conception of practical reason more accurately depicts the forms of rationality exhibited in scientific research. In contrast to the restrictive view advanced by positivism that reduces the arsenal of reason to the techniques of logic and thereby rejects creativity, deliberative judgment, and evaluative assessment as varying forms of irrationality, *phronesis* constitutes a more expansive conception of the powers of the human intellect. Presupposition theorists suggest that a consideration of the various processes of contemplation, conceptualization, representation, remembrance, reflection, speculation, rationalization, inference, deduction, and deliberation (to name but a few manifestations of human cognition) reveals that the dimensions of reason are diverse. They also argue that an adequate conception of reason must encompass these diverse cognitive practices. Because the instrumental conception of rationality advanced by positivists is clearly incapable of accounting for these various forms of reason, it must be rejected as defective. Thus, presupposition theorists suggest that science must be freed from the parochial beliefs that obscure reason's diverse manifestations and restrict its operation to the rigid adherence to a narrow set of rules. The equation of scientific rationality with formal logic must be abandoned not only because there is no reason to suppose that there must be some indubitable foundation or some ahistorical, invariant method for scientific inquiry in order to establish the rationality of scientific practices, but also because the belief that science can provide final truths cannot be sustained by the principles of formal logic, the methods of empirical inquiry, or the characteristics of fallible human cognition. Phronesis constitutes a conception of rationality that can encompass the diverse uses of reason in scientific practices, identify the manifold sources of potential error in theoretical interpretations, and illuminate the criteria of assessment and the standards of evidence and argument operative in the choice between alternative theoretical explanations of events. As a conception of scientific rationality, then, phronesis is more comprehensive and has greater explanatory power than the discredited positivist alternative.

Presupposition theorists offer a revised conception of science that emphasizes the conventional nature of scientific practices and the fallible character of scientific explanations and predictions. Confronted with a world richer than any partial perception of it, scientists draw upon the resources of tradition and imagination in an effort to comprehend the world before them. The theories they devise to explain objects and events are structured by a host of presuppositions concerning meaning, relevance, experience, explanation, and evaluation. Operating within the limits imposed by fallibility and contingency, scientists employ creative insights, practical reason, formal logic and an arsenal of conventional techniques and methods in their effort to approximate the truth about the world. But their approximations always operate within the parameters set by theoretical presuppositions; their approximations always address an empirical realm that is itself theoretically constituted. The underdetermination of theory by data ensures that multiple interpretations of the same phenomena are possible.

When alternative theoretical explanations conflict, the judgment of the scientific community is brought to bear upon the competing interpretations. Exercising practical reason, the scientific community deliberates upon the evidence and arguments sustaining the alternative views. The practical judgment of the practitioners in particular fields of science is exercised in examining presuppositions, weighing evidence, replicating experiments, examining computations, investigating the applicability of innovative methods, assessing the potential of new concepts, and considering the validity of particular conclusions. Through a process of deliberation and debate, a consensus emerges among researchers within a discipline concerning what will be taken as a valid theory. The choice is sustained by reasons that can be articulated and advanced as proof of the inadequacy of alternative interpretations. The method of scientific deliberation is eminently rational: it provides mechanisms for identifying charlatans and incompetents, as well as for recognizing more subtle errors and more sophisticated approximations of truth. But the rationality of the process cannot guarantee the eternal verity of particular conclusions. The exercise of scientific reason is fallible; the judgments of the scientific community are corrigible.

The revised conception of science advanced by presupposition theorists suggests that attempts to divide the world into ontologically distinct categories of "facts" and "values," or into dichotomous realms of the "empirical" and the "normative," are fundamentally flawed (Hawkesworth 1988). Such attempts fail to grasp the implications of the theoretical constitution of all knowledge and the theoretical mediation of the empirical realm. They fail to come to grips with valuative character of all presuppositions and the consequent valuative component of all empirical propositions. In the theoretically mediated world description, explanation, and evaluation are inextricably linked. Any attempt to impose a dichotomous relation upon such inseparable processes constitutes a fallacy of false alternatives, which is as distorting as it is logically untenable. For the suggestion that "pure" facts can be isolated and analyzed free of all valuation masks the theoretical constitution of facticity and denies the cognitive processes through which knowledge of the empirical realm is generated. Moreover, the dichotomous schism of the world into "facts" and "values" endorses an erroneous and excessively limiting conception of human reason; this conception fails both to comprehend the role of practical rationality in scientific deliberation and to recognize that science is simply one manifestation of the use of practical reason in human life. Informed by flawed assumptions, the positivist conception of reason fails to understand that phronesis is operative in philosophical analysis, ethical deliberation, normative argument, political decisions, and the practical choices of daily life as well as in scientific analysis. Moreover, in stipulating that reason can operate only in a naïvely simple, "value-free," empirical realm, the positivist presuppositions that inform the fact/value dichotomy render reason impotent and thereby preclude the possibility that rational solutions might exist for the most pressing problems of the contemporary age.

Although the arguments that have discredited positivism are well known to philosophers, they have had far too little impact upon contemporary research practices in the natural and social sciences, where dominant paradigms remain positivist. This is especially unfortunate because the critique of positivism has wide-ranging implications, especially concerning the politics of knowledge. The post-positivist conception of knowledge suggests that theoretical assumptions have a pervasive influence upon our understandings of the world by accrediting contentious definitions of phenomena and validating particular strategies of inquiry while invalidating others. Moreover, positivist assumptions mask the controversial character of evidence adduced and the contestability of accredited strategies of explanation. Rather than providing a faithful method for the acquisition of truth, defective positivist assumptions themselves become a source of error shielded from scrutiny.

Post-positivist conceptions of science open new areas of investigation concerning sources of error within the presuppositions of particular research practices that have been particularly helpful to feminist researchers. Feminist scholars have explored androcentric presuppositions of particular research methods. They have probed the limitations imposed upon the constitution of knowledge within male-dominant disciplines. They have investigated the mechanisms by which androcentric accounts of the world have been accredited and rendered unproblematic. They have questioned the adequacy of standards of evidence, modes of analysis, and strategies of explanation privileged by dominant traditions. They have demonstrated how accredited methodologies subtly circumscribe our understanding of women's lives as well as raced and gendered practices within the world.

By illuminating the political implications of determinate modes of inquiry, feminist scholars have demonstrated that the politics of knowledge is a legitimate focus of analysis, for the analytic techniques developed in particular cognitive traditions have political consequences that positivist precepts render invisible. In circumscribing the subject matter appropriate to "science," restricting the activities acceptable as "empirical inquiry," establishing the norms for assessing the results of inquiry, identifying the basic principles of practice, and validating the ethos of practitioners, methodological strictures may sustain particular modes of life that entrench oppressive practices. Throughout the past three decades, feminist scholars have attempted to grapple with the politics of knowledge production across the disciplines. Chapters 2, 3, and 4 examine their efforts to debunk myths of neutrality, problematic conceptions of objectivity, and defective models of scientific method. They also explore feminist debates about the prospects for deploying an antifoundationalist conception of truth in interdisciplinary feminist research practices.

Chapter 2

Grappling with Claims of Truth

W omen's studies was introduced into the academy in the late 1960s as the academic arm of the women's movement. From the outset, feminist scholars proclaimed their politics: they sought to transform inequitable relations rooted in gender and race, to eliminate domination and end oppression. Feminist scholars who chose to launch intellectual contestations within academia were convinced that research and scholarship could contribute to emancipatory feminist ends. But in a period when positivist conceptions of value-neutral inquiry were ascendant in the social sciences and the natural sciences, especially in North America, it was no simple matter to explicate or vindicate the feminist assumption that a political stance concerning the promotion of women's liberation and empowerment could contribute to the discernment of truth.

What conception(s) of truth informed the early practices of feminist inquiry? How did feminist scholars begin to articulate their dissatisfactions with mainstream or "malestream" knowledge? How did they explain the errors about women that pervaded traditional disciplinary accounts? How did they attempt to justify alternative accounts devised by feminist scholars? This chapter provides an overview of three decades of debate within feminist scholarship about the nature of knowledge and the possibility of attaining truth. Examining vibrant debates among feminist scholars, chapter 2 traces gradual shifts from a notion that knowledge is "discovered" to an understanding that knowledge is "created," from an assumption that truth is a matter of correct perception to an argument that truths are theoretically constituted and underdetermined by data, and from a conception that truth involves an unmediated grasp of things-in-themselves to a recognition of the role of language, culture, and theory in mediating truth claims about the world. That most feminist scholars have converged on an antifoundationalist account of knowledge does not imply, however, that this convergence has eliminated all disagreement about the nature of truth or the criteria for truth established within disparate modes of intellectual inquiry. The final section of chapter 2 examines continuing feminist debates about these epistemological and methodological issues.

The Impetus to Feminist Epistemology

Feminist scholars across an array of disciplines were forced to grapple with epistemological issues. Recurrent tendencies within the dominant disciplines to marginalize feminist scholarship as a subject of interest to "women only" inspired a quest for epistemological arguments that could rescue feminist claims from trivialization by demonstrating their truth and importance. The discovery of a pervasive androcentrism in the definition of intellectual problems as well as in specific theories, concepts, methods, and interpretations of research fueled efforts to distinguish between knowledge and prejudice (Harding and Hintikka 1983; Spender 1981). Recognition that epistemological assumptions have political implications stimulated efforts to attain theoretical self-consciousness concerning the intellectual presuppositions of feminist analysis (Lowe and Hubbard 1983; Fox Keller 1984; Grimshaw 1986; Harding 1986; Pateman and Grosz 1986). Dissatisfaction with paternalistic politics premised upon malestream conceptions of "women's nature" sustained feminist epistemological challenges to men's claims to "know" women's nature or what constitutes "women's best interests" (Pisan 1405; Wollstonecraft 1792; Mill 1869; Daly 1978; Spender 1983). Objections raised by Third World women and women of color to the political priorities of white, Western feminists generated profound skepticism about the ability of any particular group of women to "know" what is in the interest of all women (Davis 1981; Joseph and Lewis 1981; Giddens 1984; hooks 1981, 1984, 1989; P. H. Collins 1990; Mohanty, Russo, and Torres 1991; Sandoval 2000; Duran 2001). The identification of conflicts experienced by many women between the contradictory demands of "rationality" and "femininity" stimulated a search for theoretical connections between gender and specific ways of knowing (Lloyd 1982; McMillan 1983; Belenky et al. 1986).

In a pathbreaking work that launched the field of "feminist epistemology," Sandra Harding (1986), synthesizing the wide range of assertions about knowledge in feminist scholarship, distinguished three major approaches: feminist empiricism, feminist standpoint theory, and feminist postmodernism. Harding's characterizations of these three main approaches can perhaps best be understood as "ideal types," for her primary goal was to illuminate the assumptions about knowledge and the implications for research that informed these diverse feminist approaches. Harding's characterizations became the subject of a rich and productive debate in feminist scholarship that has helped feminist researchers to clarify their epistemological assumptions. The following sections of the chapter briefly explicate Harding's ideal types of feminist epistemology and review important critiques of these early formulations.

Three Ideal Types of Feminist Epistemology

Feminist empiricism incorporates the tenets of philosophical realism, which posits the existence of the world independent of the human knower, and empiricist assumptions about the primacy of the senses as the source of all knowledge about the world. As characterized by Harding, feminist empiricists adhere to positivist assumptions about inquiry; they consider sexism and androcentrism to be identifiable biases of individual knowers that can be eliminated by stricter application of existing methodological norms of scientific inquiry. In this view, the appropriate method for apprehending the truth about the world involves a process of systematic observation in which the subjectivity of the observer is controlled by rigid adherence to discipline-specific methods designed to produce identical measurements of the real properties of objects. The eradication of misogynist bias is compatible with, indeed a necessary precondition for, the achievement of objective knowledge, for it promotes the acquisition of an unmediated truth about the world; it frees substantive knowledge about reality from the distorting lenses of particular observers.

Drawing upon historical materialism's insight that social being determines consciousness, feminist standpoint theories reject the notion of an "unmediated truth" and argue that knowledge is always mediated by a host of factors related to an individual's particular position in a determinate sociopolitical formation at a specific point in history. Class, race, and gender necessarily structure the individual's understanding of reality and hence inform all knowledge claims. Although they repudiate the possibility of an unmediated truth, feminist standpoint epistemologies do not reject the notion of truth altogether. On the contrary, they argue that, although certain social positions (the oppressor's) produce distorted ideological views of reality, other social positions (the oppressed's) can pierce ideological obfuscations and attain a correct and comprehensive understanding of the world. Thus, feminist analysis grounded upon the privileged perspective that emerges from women's oppression constitutes the core of a "successor science" that can replace the truncated projects of masculinist science with a more systematic and sophisticated conception of social and political life.

Informed by a Nietzschean conception of perspectivism, feminist postmodernism rejects the very possibility of *a* truth about reality. Feminist postmodernists use the "situatedness" of each finite observer in a particular sociopolitical historical context to challenge the plausibility of claims that any perspective on the world could escape partiality. Extrapolating from the disparate conditions

that shape individual identities, they raise grave suspicions about the very notion of a putative unitary consciousness of the species. In addition, feminist
postmodernists emphasize that knowledge is the result of invention, the imposition of form upon the world, rather than discovery of something pre-given, some
"natural order of being." As an alternative to the futile quest for an authoritative
truth to ground feminist inquiry, feminist postmodernists advocate a profound
skepticism regarding universal (or universalizing) claims about the existence,
nature, and powers of reason. Rather than succumb to the authoritarian impulses
of the "will to truth," they urge instead the development of a commitment to
plurality, multivocity, and the play of difference.

Harding's characterization of these alternative feminist epistemologies made
clear that there are major tensions among these approaches and that each
approach raises particular problems for feminist research. The elements of feminist empiricism and feminist standpoint epistemologies that sustain feminist
claims concerning a privileged perspective on the world are at odds with the insight generated by the long struggle of women of color within the feminist movement that there is no uniform "women's reality" to be known, no coherent
perspective to be privileged. Yet, the feminist postmodernists' plea for tolerance of
multiple perspectives is altogether at odds with feminists' desire to refute once and
for all the distortions of androcentrism. Recognizing the legitimacy of these
competing demands within feminist scholarship, Harding recommended that
feminists simply recognize and embrace the tensions created by these alternative
epistemologies:

> Feminist analytical categories *should* be unstable at this moment in his-
> tory. We need to learn how to see our goal for the present moment as a
> kind of illuminating "riffing" between and over the beats of the various
> patriarchal theories and our own transformations of them, rather than as
> a revision of the rhythms of any particular one (Marxism, psychoanalysis,
> empiricism, hermeneutics, postmodernism . . .) to fit what we think at
> the moment we want to say. The problem is that we do not know and we
> should not know just what we want to say about a number of conceptual
> choices with which we are presented—except that the choices them-
> selves create no-win dilemmas for our feminisms. (Harding 1986, 244)

Harding's depiction of these ideal types and her recommendation that feminist scholars opt for plurality rather than attempt to resolve incompatibilities
and contradictions in these competing approaches generated enormous debate.
During the next decade, critiques of these distinctive feminist epistemologies
identified troublesome shifts in feminist arguments about knowledge that contributed to the no-win dilemmas outlined by Harding and suggested strategies to
avoid them (Hawkesworth 1989; Longino 1990; Code 1991; Grant 1993; Wylie

2000a). Several scholars drew upon antifoundationalist arguments in an effort to reformulate feminist understandings of knowledge; they suggested that a change in the focus of feminist epistemological investigations from questions about knowers to claims about the known could enable feminist scholarship to preserve important insights of postmodernism, while advancing feminist efforts to correct a variety of inadequate conceptions of the world. Shifting from subjectivist to objectivist epistemic strategies and adopting a conception of cognition as a human practice would enable feminist inquiry to identify, explain, and refute persistent androcentric bias within the dominant discourses without privileging a putative "woman's" perspective and without appealing to problematic conceptions of "the given."

The next section explores the factors that contributed to the development of a subjectivist account of knowledge within early feminist scholarship and explicates the problems associated with that approach.

Knowers

In academic institutions and in interpersonal interactions, feminists often become acquainted with the claims of established knowledge from the underside. The classic texts of Western history, philosophy, literature, religion, and science, riddled with misinformation about women, are handed down as sacred truths. When individual women attempt to challenge the adequacy of such misogynist accounts, they are frequently informed that their "innate inabilities" preclude their comprehension of these classic insights. Hence, it is not surprising that brilliant feminists have agreed that reason has served as a weapon for the oppression of women, that it has functioned as "a kind of gang rape of women's minds" (Daly 1973, 9), that "in masculine hands, logic is often a form of violence, a sly kind of tyranny" (Beauvoir 1989, 201).

In response to such widespread abusive intellectual practices, feminist analysis often shifted very subtly from a recognition of misinformation about women to a suspicion concerning the dissemination of disinformation about women. The fact that the Western intellectual tradition has been conceived and produced by men was taken as evidence that this tradition exists to serve the misogynist interests of men. The existence of erroneous views was taken as proof of "sexual ideology, a set of false beliefs deployed against women by a conscious, well-organized male conspiracy" (Moi 1985, 28). The slide from misinformation to disinformation has a number of dire consequences for feminist approaches to epistemology. In focusing attention upon the source of knowledge, that is, men, rather than upon the validity of specific claims advanced by men, the terms of debate are shifted toward psychological and functionalist analyses and away from issues of justification. This in turn allows a number of contentious epistemological assumptions about the nature of knowledge, the process of knowing, standards of evidence, and criteria of assessment to be incorporated unreflectively into feminist arguments.

In feminist treatments of knowledge, one frequently encounters the curious claim that reason is gendered (Grant 1987). The claim takes a variety of forms. Some say that rationality—a tough, rigorous, impersonal, competitive, unemotional, objectifying stance—"is inextricably intertwined with issues of men's gender identities," such as obsession with separation and individuation (Harding 1986, 63; Chodorow 1978; Bordo 1986). Some also say that "distinctively (Western) masculine desires are satisfied by the preoccupation with method, rule, and law-governed behavior and activity" (Harding 1986, 229; Balbus 1982; Fox Keller 1984). Moreover, others say that the connections between masculinization, reification, and objectification are such that, should women attempt to enter the male realm of objectivity, they would have only one option: to deny their female nature and adopt the male mode of being (Lloyd 1982). Still others say that all dichotomies—objective/subjective, rational/irrational, reason/emotion, culture/nature—are products of the basic male/female hierarchy central to patriarchal thought and society (Fee 1984; Hekman 1987). Some say that reason is morphologically and functionally analogous to the male sex organ: linear, hard, penetrating but impenetrable (Irigaray 1985a, b; Cixous 1975, 1976). And finally, some say that representational conceptions of knowledge privileging evidence based upon sight/observation/"the gaze" are derived from men's need to valorize their own visible genitals against the threat of castration posed by women's genitalia, which exist as "nothing to be seen" (Irigaray 1985a, 48).

Underlying all these claims are speculative psychological notions about a fragile, defensive male ego that impels men constantly to "prove" their masculinity by mastering women, to affirm their own value by denigrating that which is "other." Whether one wishes to defend these psychological claims or to attack them, it is important to note that at issue are certain psychological theories, particular conceptions of psychosexual development, specific notions about the role of the body and of sexuality in the formation of individual identity, and speculations about the relationship between personal identity and sociability. Although all these questions are important and worthy of systematic investigation, they are not epistemological questions *per se*. The switch from consideration of claims about knowledge and about the truth of certain propositions about women contained in classical texts to concerns about the "will to power" embodied in the claims of "male reason" moves feminist inquiry to a set of highly complex psychological issues that in principle could be completely irrelevant to the resolution of the initial epistemological questions.

Feminist discussions of epistemology often devolve into modes of functionalist argument. Unlike psychological arguments that attempt to explain

phallocentric claims in terms of the psychic needs of male knowers, functionalist arguments focus attention upon the putative "interests" served by particular
beliefs, whether they be the interests of discrete individuals, groups, classes, institutions, structures, or systems. Thus, some say that "male reason" promotes the
interests of men as a sex-class by securing women's collusion in their own oppression by transforming each woman from a "forced slave into a willing one"
(Mill 1869; Greer 1971). Some argue that sexist beliefs serve the interests of individual men, for each man reaps psychological, economic, and political advantages in a society organized according to patriarchal imperatives (Ketchum and
Pierce 1979). Still others contend that sexist ideology serves the interests of capitalism: it reproduces the relations of dominance and subordination required by
capitalist production, facilitates the reproduction of labor power on a daily as
well as a generational basis, creates a marginal female labor force willing to work
for less than subsistence wages, and allows divisions within the working class on
the basis of gender that thwart the development of unified class consciousness
and revolutionary action (Seccombe 1974; Berger and Mohr 1975; Beechey
1977, 1978; Eisenstein 1979). Finally, some assert that "male rationality," functioning in accordance with the "logic of identity," operates as a mechanism of social control. In the interests of unrelenting domination, "thought seeks to have
everything under control, to eliminate all uncertainty, unpredictability, to eliminate otherness" (Young 1986, 384). Authoritarian reason imposes conformity
by policing thoughts, purging from the realm of the thinkable all that differs
from its own narrow presuppositions.

Functionalist arguments are frequently offered as causal explanations for the
existence of particular ideas on the assumption that the function served constitutes the *raison d'être* for the belief; for example, misogynist notions were/are invented precisely to serve as mechanisms of social control. Yet, this teleological
assumption, which equates function with first and final cause, overlooks the possibility that the origin of an idea may be totally unrelated to specific uses made
of the idea (Barrett 1980; Richards 1982). Functionalist explanations also tend
to gloss over complex sociological, political, and historical issues that arise when
one attempts to demonstrate that a particular idea or belief actually serves the la-
tent or manifest functions attributed to it in a contemporary setting and that it
served this function in different historical epochs. As feminists pursue the intractable problems associated with functionalist explanations, they are once
again carried away from questions concerning the validity of particular claims
about women. In the search for the putative purposes served by androcentric notions, arguments concerning the merits of these claims are abandoned.

Feminist analyses that focus on men as the source of knowledge and on the
psychological needs and social purposes served by androcentric rationality as *the*
central epistemological issues are premised on a number of highly problematic

assumptions about the nature of reason and the process of knowing. Rather than acknowledging that reason, rationality, and knowledge are themselves essentially contested concepts that have been the subject of centuries of philosophical debate, there is a tendency to conflate all reasoning with one particular conception of rationality, instrumental reason. Associated with Enlightenment optimism about the possibility of using reason to gain technical mastery over nature, with rigorous methodological strictures for controlled observation and experimentation, with impartial application of rules to ensure replicability, with the rigidity of the fact/value dichotomy and means-ends analysis that leave crucial normative questions unconsidered, with processes of rationalization that threaten to imprison human life within increasingly dehumanized systems, and with the deployment of technology that threatens the annihilation of all life on the planet, instrumental reason makes a ready villain (Weber 1958; Gadamer 1979; Horkheimer and Adorno 1972; Habermas 1981). When this villain is in turn associated with uniquely male psychological propensities, it is all too easy to assume that one comprehends not only that men have gotten the world wrong but also why they have gotten it wrong. The supposition that error is the result of willful deception dovetails patly with uncritical notions about unrelenting male drives for dominance and mastery.

The notion that instrumental reason is essentially male also sustains the appealing suggestion that the deployment of a uniquely female knowledge—a knowledge that is intuitive, emotional, engaged, and caring—could save humanity from the dangers of unconstrained masculinism (Daly 1978; French 1985; Ruddick 1980, 1983). To develop an account of this alternative knowledge, some feminists have turned to the body, to sexed embodiedness, to thinking in analogy with women's sexuality, to *eros*, and to women's psychosexual development (Code 1981; Cixous 1975; Flax 1983; Trask 1986). Some have focused upon the rich resources of women's intuition (Daly 1978; French 1985; Griffin 1980). Others draw upon insights from historical materialism, from theories of marginalization, and from the sociology of knowledge in an effort to generate an account of experiences common to all women that could provide a foundation for a women's standpoint or perspective. The unification of manual, mental, and emotional capacities in women's traditional activities, the sensuous, concrete, and relational character of women's labor in the production of use-values and in reproduction, and the multiple oppressions experienced by women that generate collective struggles against the prevailing social order have all been advanced as grounds for women's privileged epistemological perspective (Rose 1983; Hartsock 1983). In appealing to certain physical, emotional, psychological, and social experiences of women, all these approaches attempt to solve two problems—the source of knowledge and the validity of knowledge claims—simultaneously by conflating the disparate issues of knower and known.

They suggest that women's unique experience of reality enables them to pierce ideological distortions and grasp the truth about the world. Where men have gotten it wrong, women will get things right.

When stated so baldly, the claim that women will produce an accurate depiction of reality, either because they are women or because they are oppressed, appears to be highly implausible. Given the diversity and fallibility of all human knowers, there is no good reason to believe that women are any less prone to error, deception, or distortion than men. Appeals to the authority of the female "body" to substantiate such claims suffer from the same defects as appeals to the authority of the senses, which are central to the instrumental conception of reason that these feminists set out to repudiate. Both fail to grasp the manifold ways in which all human experiences, whether of the external world or of the internal world, are mediated by theoretical presuppositions embedded in language and culture (Wittig 1979). Both adhere to a romantic conception of transparency that enables a "natural" self to speak a truth free of all ambiguity. Both adhere to the great illusion that there is one position in the world or one orientation toward the world that can eradicate all confusion, conflict, and contradiction.

These problems are not eliminated by moving from embodiedness to intuition. The distrust of the conceptual aspects of thought, which sustains claims that genuine knowledge requires immediate apprehension, presumes not only that an unmediated grasp of reality is possible, but also that it is authoritative. Moreover, appeals to intuition raise the specter of an authoritarian trump that precludes the possibility of rational debate. Claims based on intuition manifest an unquestioning acceptance of their own veracity. When one assertion informed by the immediate apprehension of reality confronts another diametrically opposed claim, also informed by the immediate apprehension of reality, there is no rational way to adjudicate such a dispute. Of course, one might appeal to a notion of adjudication on "intuitive" grounds, but this is the beginning of a vicious regress. Thus, intuition provides a foundation for claims about the world that is at once authoritarian, admitting of no further discussion, and relativist, allowing no individual to refute another's "immediate" apprehension of reality. Operating at a level of assertion that admits of no further elaboration or explication, those who abandon themselves to intuition conceive and give birth to dreams, not to truth (Hegel 1977).

The theoretical monism that informs claims of truth rooted in both "body" and intuition also haunts the early arguments of feminist standpoint epistemologies. Although these proponents of feminist standpoint theories were careful to note that conceptions of knowledge are historically variable and contentious, certain aspects of their arguments tended to undercut the force of that acknowledgment. To claim a distinct women's "perspective" is "privileged" precisely because it possesses heightened insights into the nature of reality, a superior access to truth is to suggest some uniform experience common to all women generates this univocal vision. Yet, if social, cultural, and historical differences are taken seriously, the notion of such a common experience becomes suspect. In the absence of such a homogeneous women's experience, standpoint epistemologies must either develop complicated explanations of why some women see the truth while others do not, a strategy that threatens to undermine the very notion of a "women's standpoint," or collapse into a trivial and potentially contradictory pluralism that conceives of truth as simply the sum of all women's partial and incompatible views (Soble 1983). It might be suggested that this problem could be avoided by substituting the notion of a "feminist" perspective for that of a "women's perspective." Such a move could then account for the fact that some women grasp the truth while others do not by appealing to the specific experiences that make one a feminist. This move would also create the possibility that some men, those who are feminists, could also grasp the truth, thereby freeing this claim from the specter of biologism. But this strategy encounters other problems by assuming some unique set of experiences creates a feminist. The rich and diverse histories of feminism in different nations and the rivalry among competing feminist visions (for example, liberal feminism versus radical feminism versus Marxist feminism versus socialist feminism versus psychoanalytic feminism versus cultural feminism versus postcolonial feminism versus third wave feminism) raise serious challenges to the plausibility of claims concerning a uniform mode of feminism or an invariant path to feminist consciousness.

Starting from a subjectivist approach to epistemology that focuses on issues pertaining to the faculties and sentiments of knowers as the source of knowledge, feminist inquiry arrives at an impasse. Presuppositions concerning a romantic notion of a "natural" subject/self capable of grasping intuitively the totality of being and a homogeneous "Woman's" experience that generates a privileged view of reality fail to do justice to the fallibility of human knowers, to the multiplicity and diversity of women's experiences, and to the powerful ways in which race, class, ethnicity, culture, and language structure individuals' understandings of the world. Claims concerning diverse and incompatible intuitions about the nature of social reality premised upon immediate apprehensions of that reality overlook the theoretical underpinnings of all perception and experience and consequently devolve into either authoritarian assertion or uncritical relativism. Moreover, the pervasive tolerance for and indulgence in "gender symbolism" (the attribution of dualistic gender metaphors to distinctions that rarely have anything to do with sex differences [Harding 1986, 17]) within these early feminist discussions of epistemology reproduced patriarchal stereotypes of men and women, while flirting with essentialism, distorting the diverse dimensions of human knowing, and falsifying the historical record of women's manifold uses of reason in daily life.

Knowing

If the complex epistemological problems confronting feminist inquiry cannot be resolved by appeals to the authority of the body, intuition, or a universal "Woman's" experience, neither can they be solved by reference to neutral scientific or philosophical methods. Foundationalist versions of feminist empiricism, which relied upon scientific techniques designed to control for subjectivity in the process of observation, and foundationalist versions of feminist standpoint theories, which relied upon historical/dialectical materialism as a method for achieving an objective grasp of reality, depend upon problematic conceptions of perception, experience, knowledge, and the self. An antifoundationalist account of human cognition illuminates the defects of these conceptions.

Critiques of foundationalism have emphasized that the belief in a permanent, ahistorical, Archimedean point that can provide a certain ground for knowledge claims is incompatible with an understanding of cognition as a human practice (Albert 1985; Bernstein 1983; Cavell 1979). They have suggested that the belief that particular techniques of rational analysis can escape finitude and fallibility and grasp the totality of being misconstrues both the nature of subjective intellection and the nature of the objective world. Attacks on foundationalism, therefore, raise questions concerning specific forms of knowing, particular conceptions of subjectivity, and various theories of the external world. Insights drawn from antifoundationalism have delineated the contours of a critical feminist epistemology that avoids the limitations of foundationalist versions of feminist empiricism and feminist standpoint theories.

As discussed in chapter 1, standard critiques of foundationalism question the adequacy of deductive and inductive logic as the ground of objective knowledge. To challenge rationalists' confidence in the power of logical deduction as a method for securing the truth about the empirical world, critics typically point out that the truth of syllogistic reasoning is depends altogether upon the established truth of the syllogism's major and minor premises. Yet, when one moves from relations of ideas governed by logical necessity to a world of contingency, the "established truth" of major and minor premises is precisely what is at issue. Thus, rather than providing an impeccable foundation for truth claims, deduction confronts the intractable problems of infinite regress, the vicious circle, or the arbitrary suspension of the principle of sufficient reason through appeals to intuition or self-evidence (Albert 1985).

Attacks on empiricist exuberance have been equally shattering. It has been repeatedly pointed out that inductive generalizations, however scrupulous and systematic, founder on a host of problems: observation generates correlations that cannot prove causation; conclusions derived from incomplete evidence sustain probability claims but do not produce incontestable truth (Albert 1985; Popper 1962). Moreover, where rationalism tends to overestimate the power of theoretical speculation, empiricism errs in the opposite extreme by underestimating the role of theory in shaping perception and structuring comprehension (Albert 1985). Thus, "objectivity," according to positivist versions of the empiricist project, turns upon the deployment of an untenable dichotomy between "facts" and "values"—a dichotomy that misconstrues the nature of perception, fails to comprehend the theoretical constitution of facticity, and uncritically disseminates the "myth of the given" (Sellars 1963, 64).

As an alternative to conceptions of knowledge that depend upon the existence of an unmediated reality that can be grasped directly by observation or intellection, antifoundationalists suggest a conception of cognition as a human practice. In this view, "knowing" presupposes involvement in a social process replete with rules of compliance, norms of assessment, and standards of excellence that are humanly created. Although humans aspire to unmediated knowledge of the world, the nature of perception precludes such direct access. The only possible access is through theory-laden conventions that organize and structure observation by according meanings to observed events, bestowing relevance and significance upon phenomena, indicating strategies for problem solving, and identifying methods by which to test the validity of proposed solutions. Knowledge, then, is a convention rooted in the practical judgments of a community of fallible inquirers who struggle to resolve theory-dependent problems under specific historical conditions.

Acquisition of knowledge occurs in the context of socialization and enculturation to determinate traditions that provide the conceptual frameworks through which the world is viewed. As sedimentations of conventional attempts to comprehend the world correctly, cognitive practices afford the individual not only a set of accredited techniques for grasping the truth of existence, but also a "natural attitude," an attitude of "suspended doubt" with respect to a wide range of issues based upon the conviction that one understands how the world works. In establishing what will be taken as normal, natural, real, reasonable, expected, and sane, theoretical presuppositions camouflage their contributions to cognition and mask their operation upon the understanding. Because the theoretical presuppositions that structure cognition operate at the tacit level, it is difficult to isolate and illuminate the full range of presuppositions informing cognitive practices. Moreover, any attempt to elucidate presuppositions must operate within a "hermeneutic circle." Any attempt to examine or to challenge certain assumptions or expectations must occur within the frame of reference established by mutually reinforcing presuppositions. That certain presuppositions within a conceptual framework remain fixed when others are subjected to systematic critique does not imply incommensurability, the idea that one is locked within a conceptual scheme and that it is impossible to understand or communicate across different cognitive frameworks (Bernstein 1983). Critical reflection upon and abandonment of certain theoretical presuppositions is possible within the hermeneutic circle; but the goal of transparency, of the unmediated grasp of things as they are, is not; for no investigation, no matter how critical, can escape the fundamental conditions of human cognition.

Thus, the conception of cognition as a human practice challenges the possibility of unmediated knowledge of the world, as well as notions such as "brute facts," the "immediately given," "theory-free research," "neutral observation language," and "self-evident truths," which suggest that possibility. Because cognition is always theoretically mediated, the world captured in human knowledge and designated "empirical" is itself theoretically constituted. Divergent cognitive practices rooted in conventions such as common sense, religion, science, philosophy, and the arts construe the empirical realm differently by identifying and emphasizing various dimensions as well as accrediting different forms of evidence, different criteria of meaning, different standards of explanation, and different tokens of truthfulness. Such an understanding of the theoretical constitution of the empirical realm in the context of specific cognitive practices requires a reformulation of the notion of "facts." A "fact" is a theoretically constituted proposition, supported by theoretically mediated evidence, and put forward as part of a theoretical formulation of reality. A "fact" is a contestable component of a theoretically constituted order of things (Foucault 1973).

The recognition that all cognition is theory-laden has also generated a critique of many traditional assumptions about the subject/self that undergird rationalist, empiricist, and materialist conceptions of knowing. Conceptions of the "innocent eye," the "passive observer," and the mind as a tabula rasa have been severely challenged (H. Brown 1977; Stockman 1983). The notion of transparency—the belief that the individual knower can identify all his/her prejudices and purge them in order to greet an unobstructed reality—has been rendered suspect (Albert 1985; H. Brown 1977; Stockman 1983). Conceptions of an atomistic self who experiences the world independent of all social influences, of the unalienated self who exists as a potentiality awaiting expression, and of a unified self who can grasp the totality of being have been thoroughly contested (Benhabib 1986; C. Taylor 1984; Connolly 1985). The very idea of the "subject" has been castigated for incorporating assumptions about the "logic of identity," positing knowers as undifferentiated, anonymous, and general, possessing a vision independent of all identifiable perspectives (Megill 1985; Young 1986). Indeed, the conception of the knowing "subject" has been faulted for failing to grasp that, rather than being the source of truth, the subject is the product of particular regimes of truth (Foucault 1977, 1980). In postmodernist discourses, the notion of a sovereign subject who possesses unparalleled powers of clairvoyance affording direct apprehension of internal and external reality has been supplanted by a conception of the self as an unstable constellation of unconscious desires, fears, phobias, and conflicting linguistic, social, and political forces.

In addition to challenging notions of an unmediated reality and a transparent subject/self, the conception of cognition as a human practice also takes issue with accounts of reason that privilege one particular mode of rationality while denigrating all others. Attempts to reduce the practice of knowing to monadic conceptions of reason fail to grasp the complexity of the interaction between traditional assumptions, social norms, theoretical conceptions, disciplinary strictures, linguistic possibilities, emotional dispositions, and creative impositions in every act of cognition. Approaches to cognition as a human practice emphasize the expansiveness of rationality and the irreducible plurality of its manifestations within diverse traditions. Perception, intuition, conceptualization, inference, representation, reflection, imagination, remembrance, conjecture, rationalization, argumentation, justification, contemplation, ratiocination, speculation, meditation, validation, deliberation—even a partial listing of the many dimensions of knowing suggests that it is a grave error to attempt to reduce this multiplicity to a unitary model. The resources of intellection are more profitably considered in their complexity, for what is involved in knowing is heavily dependent upon what questions are asked, what kind of knowledge is sought, and the context in which cognition is undertaken (Cavell 1979).

The conception of cognition as a human practice affords feminists an explanation of androcentric bias within dominant discourses that is free of the defects of psychological and functionalist arguments. Rather than imputing contentious psychological drives to all males or positing speculative structural interests for all social formations, feminists can examine the specific processes by which knowledge has been constituted within determinate traditions and explore the effects of the exclusion of women from participation in those traditions. Feminists can investigate the adequacy of the standards of evidence, criteria of relevance, modes of analysis, and strategies of argumentation privileged by the dominant traditions. By focusing on the theoretical constitution of the empirical realm, feminists can illuminate the presuppositions that circumscribe what is believed to exist and identify the mechanisms by which facticity is accredited and rendered unproblematic. In raising different questions, challenging received views, refocusing research agendas, and searching for methods of investigation adequate to the problems of feminist scholarship, feminists contribute to the development of a more sophisticated understanding of human cognition.

The conception of cognition as a human practice suggests that feminist critique is situated within established traditions of cognition even as it calls those traditions into question. Defects in traditional accounts of knowledge engender critical feminist reflection that relies upon a range of traditional philosophical and analytical techniques to criticize the limitations of received views. Thus, feminists must deal deftly with the traditions that serve both as targets of criticism and as sources of norms and analytic techniques essential to the critical project. The conception of cognition as a human practice also suggests that feminist analysis can itself be understood as a rich and varied tradition. Feminist epistemology understood within the framework of cognition as a human practice, then, requires careful consideration of the diverse cognitive practices that already structure feminist inquiry. Rather than privileging one model of rational inquiry, feminists must consider multiple issues pertaining to the level of analysis, the degree of abstraction, the type of explanation, the standards of evidence, the criteria of evaluation, the tropes of discourse, and the strategies of argumentation that are appropriate to feminist investigations of concrete problems.

Awareness of the structuring power of tacit theoretical presuppositions requires detailed investigation of the political implications of determinate modes of inquiry. The politics of knowledge must remain a principle concern of feminist analysis, in the course of not only examining malestream thought but also determining the most fruitful avenues for feminist research. The analytic techniques developed in particular cognitive traditions may have unfortunate political implications when applied in different contexts. Cognitive practices appropriate for psychological analysis may not be appropriate for political and sociological analysis; hermeneutic techniques essential for an adequate interpretation of human action may be wholly inadequate to the task of structural analysis; statistical techniques crucial for the illumination of discrimination and structural inequalities may be powerless to address problems relating to ideological oppression; semiotic analyses central to the development of feminist literary criticism may be insufficient to the task of feminist historical investigations; hormonal and endocrinological studies necessary for the creation of feminist health care may be altogether inapplicable as accounts of motivation or explanations of action. Causal, dialectical, genealogical, hermeneutic, psychological, semiotic, statistical, structural, and teleological explanations may all be important to specific aspects of feminist inquiry. But knowing which mode of analysis is appropriate in specific research contexts involves a host of complex evidentiary questions, which I discuss in chapter 4.

A feminist theory of knowledge must be sufficiently sophisticated to account for the complexity and for the political dimensions of diverse cognitive practices. To equate feminist epistemology with any particular technique of rationality is to impose unwarranted constraints on feminist inquiry, impairing its ability to develop and deploy an arsenal of analytic techniques to combat the distortions permeating the dominant malestream discourses.

Known

Understanding cognition as a human practice does not, in itself, resolve the question of what, if anything, can be known. Skeptics, relativists, deconstructionists, structuralists, hermeneuticists, and critical theorists might all concur about the social construction of cognition yet come to different conclusions about the nature of truth claims. Although contemporary feminist scholars share commitments to value-critical research, antifoundationalism, and plurality, a good deal of contestation continues to exist among feminist scholars concerning the nature of truth and the possibility of achieving it.

POSTMODERN FEMINISM

Postmodern feminists remain the most skeptical about the concept of truth. They use the "situatedness" of each finite knower in a particular sociopolitical historical context to challenge the possibility that any perspective could escape partiality. Indeed they emphasize that the perspective of each knower contains blind spots, tacit presuppositions, and prejudgments of which the individual is unaware, which make it impossible for the individual to gain an accurate perception of the world (Moi 1985; Buker 1990). The partiality of individual perspectives stems from not only idiosyncratic distortions in individual perception but also "invention." Every claim about the world, "every account can be shown to have left something out of the description of its object and to have put something in which others regard as nonessential" (White 1978). Recognition of the selectivity of cognitive accounts, in terms of conscious and unconscious omission and supplementation, has led some postmodern thinkers to characterize the world in literary terms, to emphasize the fictive elements of "fact," the narrative elements of all discourse—literary, scientific, historical, social, political—and the nebulousness of the distinction between text and reality. The move to "intertextuality" suggests the world be treated as text, as a play of signifiers with no determinate meaning, as a system of signs whose meaning is hidden and diffuse, as a discourse that resists decoding because of the infinite power of language to conceal and obfuscate. Postmodernist discourses celebrate the human capacity to misunderstand, to universalize the particular and the idiosyncratic, to privilege the ethnocentric, and to conflate truth with those prejudices that advantage the knower. Postmodernist insights counsel the abandonment of the very notion of truth as a hegemonic and, hence, destructive illusion.

Feminist postmodernists call attention to the hubris of scientific reason and the manifold ways in which scientism sustains authoritarian tendencies. By merging the horizons of philosophical and literary discourses, feminist postmodernists loosen the disciplinary strictures of both traditions and produce creative deconstructions of the tacit assumptions that sustain a variety of unreflective beliefs.

By taking discourse—structures of statements, concepts, categories, and beliefs that are specific to particular sociohistorical formations—as its primary object of analysis, postmodernists seek to heighten our understanding of the integral relations between power and knowledge and the means by which particular power/knowledge constellations constitute us as subjects in a determinate order of things (Scott 1988, 1992).

Two analytic techniques have been central to postmodern feminist inquiry, deconstruction and genealogy. Both seek to disrupt widely accepted understandings of the world by denaturalizing categories, destabilizing meaning, unmasking the "will to truth" that informs particular discursive formations, and exposing the operation of power in knowledge production itself. Deconstruction is a method of discursive analysis developed by French philosopher Jacques Derrida (1979, 1980, 1981a, 1981b), which challenges the idea that language merely describes or represents what exists; he suggests instead that language is constitutive of reality. Within this framework, meaning is created through implicit and explicit contrasts structured by language. Binaries, such as man/woman, define terms by creating oppositions that are hierarchically ordered and that privilege the first term, insinuating that priority implies primacy and that the residual term is derivative or inferior. As an analytical technique, deconstruction involves the interrogation of binaries, examining how meaning is constrained, how mistaken assumptions of homogeneity inform each term of the binary, and how the binary form exudes faulty notions that it exhausts the full range of categorical possibilities.

Informed by the works of Nietzsche (1969) and Foucault (1977), genealogy is a unique form of critique premised on the assumption that what is taken for granted—objects, ideas, values, events, and institutions—have been constituted contingently, discursively, practically. Described as diagnostic histories of the present, genealogies seek to undermine the self-evidences of the present and to open possibilities for the enhancement of life. Unlike traditional techniques of historical analysis, genealogy rejects any search for origins, notions of progress or unilinear development, and assumptions concerning definitive causes and unbroken continuity. Genealogy's unit of analysis is not "the past" as it was lived (which is taken to be unknowable), but the historical record, the arbitrary assemblage of documents and narratives with which people make sense of their pasts. Following Nietzsche, genealogists problematize such established discourses; they insist that historical narratives are framed by questions that reflect the preoccupations and concerns of the writers. Thus the genealogist attempts to identify the conditions under which particular discourses arise, illuminate multiplicity and randomness at the point of emergence; interrogate the interests that inform the narrative, and question the values that sustain the discursive formation. In an effort to trace complexity and disparity, genealogists begin their analysis with particularity, chance, disjuncture, accidents, dredging up forgotten documents and apparently insignificant details in order to recreate forgotten historical and practical conditions for contemporary existence. In seeking to reveal the arbitrariness of what appears "natural" and "necessary," the genealogist aspires to open possibilities, by disrupting dominant discourses, stimulating reflection on and resistance against what is taken for granted about world and about ourselves. In this sense, genealogical narratives are oriented toward the enhancement of life. Postmodernists caution, however, that all new discursive formations produce new power/knowledge constellations; it is impossible to escape aspects of domination even within liberatory discourses.

While proponents of postmodern feminist modes of analysis explicitly challenge the legitimacy of all truth claims, some scholars have pointed out that the modes of critique they embrace presuppose the possibility of evaluating the comparative merits of various forms of knowledge (Walby 2001). Thus their analytic practices suggest implicit criteria for assessing "better, not merely different" knowledge claims. Indeed, the assertion that postmodern research strategies alone are appropriate for the analysis of the "will to power" in knowledge production can itself be interpreted as a claim to truth about the nature of intellectual inquiry and the analytic techniques best suited to engage that reality.

Other feminist scholars, arguing against an uncritical adoption of postmodernist assumptions, suggest that there are undesirable consequences of the slide into relativism that results from too facile a conflation of world and text (Hawkesworth 1989; Hartsock 1990; Grant 1993; Code 1991; Tanesini 1999; Wylie 2000b; Kruks 2001). Relativism provides no basis for criticizing oppressive ideas. It also has the unsavory consequence of placing feminist claims and misogynist claims on equal footing: both are simply "partial perspectives" or, worse, articulations of an individual's "will to power." Moreover, postmodernists tend to posit an untenable version of social constructionism as the "truth" about reality. In contrast to the antifoundationalist claim that all our ideas about the world and our experiences of it are mediated by theories, which are humanly created or "socially constructed," some postmodernists suggest that all reality is socially constructed. As Ian Hacking (1999, 24) has pointed out, a "universal constructivist," someone who claims that "every object whatsoever—the earth, your feet, quarks, the aroma of coffee, grief, polar bears in the Artic—is in some nontrivial sense socially constructed," embraces a form of "linguistic idealism," which posits that "only what is talked about exists, nothing has reality until it is spoken of or written about."

Central to these critiques of postmodernism is a central tenet of philosophical realism: the world is more than a text. Although both theories of life and theories of literature are necessarily dependent upon conceptual schemes that are themselves structured by language and, hence, contestable and contingent, theories of life must deal with more than the free play of signifiers. There is a modicum of permanence within the fluidity of the life-world: traditions, practices, relationships, institutions, and structures persist and can have profound consequences for individual life prospects, constraining opportunities for growth and development, resisting reconstitution, frustrating efforts at improvement or change. For this reason, it can be a serious mistake to neglect the more enduring features of existing institutional structures and practices while indulging the fantasies of freedom afforded by intertextuality. Contentment with relativist perspectivism does not do justice to the need for systematicity in analyses of the structural dimensions of social and political life. Although much can be gained from the recognition that there are many sides to every story and many voices to provide alternative accounts, the escape from the monotony of monologue should not be at the expense of the very notion of truth. The need to debunk scientistic pretensions about the unproblematic nature of the objective world does not require the total repudiation of either external reality or the capacity for critical reflection and rational judgment.

ANTIFOUNDATIONALIST REFORMULATIONS OF FEMINIST EMPIRICISM AND FEMINIST STANDPOINT THEORIES

FEMINIST EMPIRICISM. During the past two decades, feminist scholars concerned about the limitations of postmodern strategies of inquiry, have helped to develop a post-positivist, antifoundationalist version of empiricism, attuned to the value-ladenness of perception. the theoretical constitution of facticity, and the underdetermination of theory by evidence (Longino 1990; Nelson 1990; Oakley 2000; Wylie 2000a; Walby 2001). Within this frame, feminist empiricists emphasize the complexity and diversity of empirical strategies of knowledge production and note that conflict, contestation, argument, and disagreement are both central to and productive for the practices of scientific inquiry. Through such intersubjective contestations truth claims are adjudicated.

Feminist empiricists suggest that systematic inquiry to "unbury" the data of women's lives is crucial, precisely because women have so often been omitted from scientific studies. Through empirical investigation, feminist scholars seek to discover and articulate patterns in women's experiences, judge the strength and scope of these patterns, locate particularity and deviations from these patterns, and attempt to understand the patterns as well as the variations from them in all their complexity (Frye 1993, 108). Keenly attuned to problems of bias and distortion that result from inadequate evidence and overgeneralization, feminist scholars have been remarkably innovative in devising concepts and research strategies to describe and explain dimensions of women's realities that encompass questions of embodied existence, health, sexualities, divisions of labor and power, structures of inequality, violence, reproduction, and mothering.

Within the frame of feminist empiricism, scholars working with specific methods have identified different tokens of truthfulness. Ethnographers, for example, generate "thick descriptions" (Geertz 1994), detailed descriptions of a particular mode of life that attempt to situate social practices within the cultural norms and values of a particular group. To test the validity of their accounts, ethnographers, often appealing to the judgment of the group being studied, present their analysis to their research subjects to see if they find the account adequate to their understanding of their cultural practices (Wolf 1996). Feminist sociologists interested in analyzing the interaction of multiple forms of structured inequality, such as race, class, and gender in particular regions of the United States, have developed sophisticated quantitative techniques to investigate multiple groups, examine the relations among them, control for a range of interaction effects, and develop systematic comparisons that help to identify dimensions and causes of inequality (McCall 2001). To heighten the validity of their causal claims, some feminist scholars in the social sciences and the natural sciences use experimental methods that allow sustained observation under controlled conditions. Randomized controlled trials, which investigate the causal effects of particular interventions, such as the effects of tamoxifen on breast cancer or the effects of increased welfare payments on the work incentives of the poor, involve the comparison of particular groups of randomly selected research subjects in order to isolate particular cause-effect relations while controlling for the effects of chance (Oakley 2000). While the specific method of empirical inquiry chosen by these scholars depends upon the specific research question they seek to answer, feminist empiricists concur in their judgment that these diverse methods can generate reliable knowledge about the world by identifying truths of critical importance to the health, livelihoods, and well-being of women and men in the contemporary world.

FEMINIST STANDPOINT THEORIES. As we have seen, early versions of standpoint theory were criticized for falling prey to essentialist assumptions about women that failed to recognize hierarchical structures of difference among women. They also presupposed too simple a relation between oppression and truth and suggested therefore that certain forms of adversity afford epistemic privilege, which could free the oppressed from confusion, error, distortion, contradiction and fallibility (Hawkesworth 1989; Grant 1993; Longino 1993; Hekman 1997).

Over the past two decades more sophisticated and nuanced accounts of standpoint theory have been developed, which scrupulously avoid "essentialist definitions of the social categories or collectivities in terms of which epistemically relevant standpoints are characterized . . . [and] any thesis of automatic epistemic privilege, any claim that those who occupy particular standpoints (usually subdominant, oppressed, marginal standpoints) automatically know more, or know better, by virtue of their social, political location" (Wylie 2000a, 2). Within this frame, feminist scholars deploy a conception of standpoint to investigate "how power relations inflect knowledge; what systematic limitations are imposed by the social location of different classes or collectivities, or groups of knowers; and what features of location or strategies of criticism and inquiry are conducive to understanding this structured epistemic partiality" (Wylie 2000a, 7). Thus proponents of standpoint inquiry acknowledge that "it is an empirical question exactly what historical processes create hierarchically structured relations of inequality and what material conditions, socio-political structures, and symbolic or psychological mechanisms maintain them in the present" (Wylie 2000a, 4).

Standpoint theory on this construal serves as an analytical tool, a heuristic device that illuminates areas of inquiry, frames questions for investigation, identifies puzzles in need of solution and problems in need of exploration and clarification. Standpoint theory also provides concepts and hypotheses to guide research, as chapter 7 will explore in greater detail. Accepting plurality as an inherent characteristic of the human condition, inquiry guided by standpoint theory recognizes that scholars must attend to the views of people in markedly different social locations. Investigation of multiple interpretations of the same phenomenon helps to illuminate the theoretical assumptions that frame and accredit the constitution of facticity within each account. Analyzing and comparing competing claims requires the researcher to engage questions concerning the adequacy, internal consistency, and explanatory power of alternate accounts as a way to adjudicate the truth of competing interpretations.

Concerns with ideological distortion and ideology critique have been central to projects that involve standpoint analysis. While conceptions of ideology are themselves a subject of contestation, proponents of standpoint theory agree that ideologies involve systems of representation and material practices that structure beliefs and that legitimate systemic inequalities. By advocating modes of research that challenge dominant ideologies, proponents of standpoint theory suggest that feminist knowledge production can do more than describe and explain the empirical world; it can contribute to human emancipation, by generating insights that can enable people to free themselves from ideological distortion and various modes of domination. Thus the conception of truth embedded in feminist standpoint theory links claims about existing structures of inequality to modes of critical reflection that can empower people to transform existing social relations.

Antifoundationalist versions of feminist empiricism and feminist standpoint theory concur that feminist inquiry must avoid both the foundationalist tendency to reduce the multiplicity of reasons to a monolithic "Reason" and the postmodernist tendency to reject all reasons *tout court*. Keenly aware of the complexity of all knowledge claims, antifoundationalist strategies of inquiry defend the adoption of a minimalist standard of rationality requiring that belief be apportioned to evidence and that no assertion be immune from critical assessment. Deploying this minimalist standard, feminist analysis can demonstrate the inadequacies of accounts of human nature derived from an evidentiary base of only half the species, refute unfounded claims about women's "nature" that are premised upon an atheoretical naturalism, identify androcentric bias in theories, methods, and concepts and show how this bias undermines explanatory force, and demonstrate that the numerous obstacles to women's full participation in social, political, and economic life are humanly created and hence susceptible to alteration. In providing sophisticated and detailed analyses of concrete situations, feminist inquiry can dispel distortions and mystifications that abound in malestream thought.

Based on a consistent fallibilism consonant with life in a world of contingencies, feminist scholars need not claim universal, ahistorical validity for their analyses. They need not assert that theirs is the only or even the final word on complex questions. In the absence of claims of universal validity, feminist accounts derive their justificatory force from their capacity to illuminate existing social relations, demonstrate the deficiencies of alternative interpretations, and debunk opposing views. Thus feminists researchers provide concrete reasons in specific contexts for the superiority of their accounts. Such claims to superiority are derived not from some "privileged" standpoint of the feminist knower nor from the putative merits of particular intuitions, but from the strength of rational argument and the ability to demonstrate point by point the deficiencies of alternative explanations. At their best, feminist analyses engage both the critical intellect and the world; they surpass androcentric accounts because in their systematicity more is examined and less is assumed.

Chapter 3
Reconceptualizing Objectivity

W HAT IS OBJECTIVITY? Is it a matter of ethical research practices or of adherence to standard scientific methods? Does it pertain to the researcher's attitude or to the process of inquiry? Is it a gendered phenomenon? Is objectivity compatible with feminist arguments concerning the politics of knowledge? If so, what is the relation between cultural values and objective analysis? Can feminist political convictions enhance the objectivity of academic inquiry?

This chapter examines a variety of feminist critiques of objectivity, including critiques grounded in ethical concerns and critiques that derive from the failure of scientific research practices to produce the forms of objectivity they promise. After explaining why feminist scholars have been concerned about objectivity, the chapter probes a fundamental feminist ethical concern that objectivity in research necessarily requires morally objectionable objectification of research subjects. It then analyzes three efforts to demonstrate the connection between objectivity and objectification and identifies problematic assumptions in each model. Having shown that the concept of objectivity is not inherently unethical, the chapter concludes with an examination of feminist efforts to reclaim the conception of objectivity, which link objective inquiry to arguments for inclusive and accountable research practices. This feminist reconceptualization of objectivity then provides one example of the means by which feminist political principles contribute to strategies for improved knowledge production.

Against Objectivity

FEMINIST ETHICAL CONCERNS

In addition to contestation over the nature and possibility of truth, the "product" of feminist inquiry, feminist scholars have also engaged in strenuous debates about processes of inquiry. They have been particularly concerned about the prospects for developing forms of research that establish an ethical relationship between the researcher and the human subjects who are being researched. Attuned to manifold dimensions of inequality between researchers and their research subjects, feminist anthropologists and sociologists have catalogued an array of dangers that can beset feminist inquiry, despite the good intentions of the researcher. Research that reveals dimensions of racism, sexism, ethnocentrism, or homophobia within a community, for example, may be construed as "an act of betrayal" by the members of that community (Islam 2000, 35). Minimally, scholarship "publicizes as it scrutinizes," portraying the beliefs, values, and opinions of the researched before the world and violating the privacy of research subjects (Blee 2000, 100). Extrapolating from the "Hawthorne effect," which demonstrated that changes documented in social science research may have been caused by the research itself (Oakley 2000, 182–83), some feminist researchers have been concerned that their research is an intervention that "destroys the evidence," changing the social relations that it only meant to document (Kenny 2000, 127). Other scholars have noted that field work should be understood as a "foreign or neocolonial intrusion" on researched populations (Wolf 1996, 26); they suggest that researchers "fabricate data," substituting their representations for the real. Indeed, Phillipe Bourgeois (2000, 207) has noted that regardless of the intention of the researcher, academic discourses are "inferiorizing narratives," for "when you study the poor and powerless, everything you say is used against them." Although many of these examples could be considered "unintended harms," Diane Wolf (1996, 207) has pointed out that there have also been instances in which a feminist researcher uses her academic advantages to gain her own objectives, at real costs to particular women studied, and she cautions that the notion that feminist research generates "empowerment" may be another "missionary fantasy" (Wolf, 1996, 26).

These important ethical concerns question the possibility of objectivity in research. Related challenges have been raised by feminist scholars who have developed critiques of positivist conceptions of scientific method and analytic techniques in philosophical method, which promise but fail to produce objective analysis. These issues are taken up in the next section.

Objectivity in Scientific Research Methods

Objectivity surfaces as a regulative ideal in philosophical investigations, scientific debates, ethical deliberations, judicial proceedings, and bureaucratic practices. Objectivity gains its purchase within these diverse domains on the basis of specific promises. In the context of philosophical and scientific investigations, an objective account implies a grasp of the actual qualities and relations of objects as they exist independent of the inquirer's thoughts and desires regarding them (Cunningham 1973). In the spheres of ethics, law, and administration, objectivity suggests impersonal and impartial standards and decision-procedures that produce disinterested and equitable judgments. Objectivity, then, promises to free us from distortion, bias, and error in intellectual inquiry and from arbitrariness, self-interest, and caprice in ethical, legal, and administrative decisions.

Feminist critiques of objectivity have been triggered by breach of promise. Feminist scholars have demonstrated that observations, beliefs, theories, methods of inquiry, and institutional practices routinely labeled "objective" fall far short of the norm. A significant proportion of feminist scholarship involves detailed refutations of erroneous claims about women produced in conformity with prevailing disciplinary standards of objectivity. The pervasiveness of the mistakes about the nature of women and their roles in history, politics, and society, as well as the imperviousness of mistaken views to refutation, have lead some feminist scholars to examine the conception of objectivity accredited within positivist conceptions of knowledge production.

Within the natural sciences and the social sciences, positivist commitments generated a number of methodological techniques to produce objective knowledge. Chief among these were the fact/value dichotomy and hypothetico-deductive model of scientific inquiry. As we have seen in previous chapters, positivist precepts require that factual claims be distinguished from evaluative judgments as the first step in a scientific investigation designed to culminate in the vindication of empirical propositions as objective representations of the world. Categorizing claims as empirical, that is, as statements that can be verified by sensory inspection, and separating them from those which are normative, constitutes a crucial precondition for the acquisition of valid knowledge, for it demarcates the range of propositions amenable to scientific investigation. According to the positivist model, the scientific method begins with the carefully controlled, neutral observation of empirical events. Sustained observation over time reveals regularities or patterns of relationships in observed events, which provide the evidence for the formulation of hypotheses. Once formulated, hypotheses are subjected to systematic empirical tests. Those hypotheses which receive external confirmation or withstand falsification through this process of rigorous testing are then elevated to the status of "scientific laws."

Ruth Berman (1989, 236) has identified three core assumptions of objectivity within positivist approaches to scientific inquiry: "that a rational method of investigation, the scientific method, exists, which can be utilized regardless of social context or the phenomenon being investigated; that any 'good,' well-trained, honest scientist can apply this well-defined, neutral method to the object being investigated and obtain objective, unbiased data; and that the 'facts' (data) are the facts: the results reported are hard, immutable and unaffected by personal concerns." Numerous feminist scholars have taken issue with each of these assumptions.

In contrast to broad construals of the scientific method in terms of formulating, testing, and falsifying hypotheses, feminist scholars have pointed out that "science has many methods," all of which are discipline specific and most of which are closely linked to the nature of the phenomenon under study (Fee 1983; Harding 1986; Longino 1990). Moreover, whether the specific method of investigation involves induction, deduction, or controlled experimentation, no method can guarantee the validity of its results. The attainment of truth cannot be assured by adherence to a simple procedural formula. Thus, conceptions of objectivity that turn on adherence to an appropriate disciplinary method are seriously defective. Nor can positivists save the belief that the scientific method guarantees the objectivity of results by appealing to replicability. Intersubjective testing and confirmation cannot be taken as reliable tokens of truthfulness. For, as the history of scientific and philosophical claims about women so clearly demonstrates, conventional misogyny sustains verifications of erroneous views (Ruth 1981). Multiple investigators deploying identical techniques may produce the same conclusions, but such intersubjective consensus cannot attest to the veracity of the claims.

It could, of course, be argued that belief in an invariant scientific method is not a criterion of objectivity in science but rather an artifact of certain reconstructions of science characteristic of the philosophy of science. Central to scientific objectivity is the neutrality of precise methods within the various scientific disciplines. Adherence to a neutral, public methodology devised to control for the idiosyncrasies of the individual inquirer produces credible scientific results. In response to this kind of claim, many feminist scholars have devoted much attention to the examination of methodological "neutrality" in the natural and social sciences. Their investigations have revealed extensive androcentrism in diverse scientific methods manifested in the selection of scientific problems deemed worthy of investigation, research design, definition of key terms and concepts, decisions concerning relevant evidence and counterexamples, data collection and analysis, interpretations of results, and assessments of practical falsifications (Bleier 1979, 1984; Fausto-Sterling 1986; Hubbard, Hennifin, and Fried 1982; Eichler 1980; Westkott 1979; Stanley and Wise 1983). Contrary to claims of neutrality, their researches have demonstrated a pervasive level of sexism in scientific research that renders women invisible, ignores women's concerns, precludes elicitation of certain kinds of information about women, reproduces gender stereotypes in the operationalization of terms, denies that gender might serve as an explanatory variable in any instance, and reverts to functionalist explanations that accredit the status quo (Kelly, Ronan, and Cawley 1987; Benston 1982; Vickers 1982; Farganis 1989). Sandra Harding has suggested that not only are the concepts, methods, and conclusions of inquiry permeated by androcentrism, but sexism also influences the recruitment of personnel in science and the evaluation of the significance of scientists' research. "If women are systematically excluded from the design and management of science and their work devalued, then it appears that neither the assignment of status to persons within science nor the assessment of the value of the results of inquiry is, or is intended to be, value-neutral, objective, socially impartial" (Harding 1986, 67). And Margaret Benston (1982, 59) has concluded that "present science practices a kind of 'pseudo-objectivity' where, because they are not taken explicitly into account, subjective factors are uncontrolled and unaccounted for."

If the disciplinary techniques devised to investigate the natural and social worlds are value-permeated rather than value-neutral, then perhaps the best hope for objectivity lies in the attitude of the investigator. Berman's reference to any "honest scientist" reflects the belief that the critical, nondogmatic, skeptical stance of scientists themselves can serve as a guarantor of objectivity. In disciplinary discussions of objectivity, it is not uncommon to find a peculiar displacement. Absent a neutral method, descriptions of the qualities of "objective knowledge" are offered as clues to the appropriate means to its attainment. Disinterestedness, dispassionateness, detachment, impersonality, universality have been put forward as model deportment for researchers on the assumption that if the inquirer emulates the qualities attributed to objective knowledge, then the results of inquiry will be imbued with those characteristics. Feminist investigations have raised logical and empirical objections to this construal of objectivity as well. Logically, displacing the characteristics of objective knowledge onto the attitudes of "objective" inquirers can no more guarantee the attainment of truth than can a clearly elucidated research method. Empirically, there are good reasons to doubt that scientists conform to these model traits. In contrast to systematic skepticism, many scientists not only never question popular gender stereotypes, but they actually incorporate culturally specific gender roles in their hypotheses about various animal species, cellular organisms, and social systems (Martin 1990; Haraway 1989; Strum and Fidigan 2000). Claims of detachment, disinterest, distance, and universality merely serve as mechanisms for male hegemony, substituting certain men's perspectives for the "view from nowhere" (Nagel 1986).

Like many post-positivist critics, feminist scholars have pointed out that norms of value-neutrality pertaining to either methods of inquiry or attitudes of inquirers seriously misconstrue the nature of cognition, create a false dichotomy between emotion and rationality, overlook the theoretical presuppositions that shape perception and interpretation, mask individual creativity, and conceal the politics of disciplinary practices (Jaggar 1989; Hawkesworth 1989; Longino 1990; Grant 1993). They have also pointed out that the continuing invocation of conceptions of objectivity rooted in erroneous notions of value-neutrality can have pernicious consequences. "Commonly, women's perspectives of social reality have been denied, suppressed, or invalidated and women have been labeled 'deviant' or 'sick' if they have refused to accept some dominant definition of their situation. Commonly, too, theories have been put forward in the name of 'science' or 'objectivity' which have not only denied or distorted female experience but have also served to rationalize and legitimize male control over women" (Grimshaw 1986).

Several feminist scholars have suggested that rather than producing accurate depictions of natural and social worlds, allegedly objective scientific inquiry has produced propaganda that serves purposes of social control (Harding 1986, 67). Scientifically accredited "facts" are not the hard, incontrovertible, immutable givens they are purported to be, but rather ideological fragments that promote male dominance (Fox Keller 1985; Mies 1984). Rather than capturing things as they are, appeals to objectivity "bolster the epistemic authority of the currently dominant groups, composed largely of white men, and discredit the observations and claims of the currently subordinate groups including, of course, the observations and claims of many people of color and women" (Jaggar 1989, 158). On this view, dominant conceptions of objectivity serve "as a potent agent for maintaining current power relationships and women's subordination" (Berman 1989, 224), precisely because they accord authority to androcentric claims not merely by masking their bias, but by certifying their "neutrality."

In stark contrast to claims of neutrality, feminist scholars have demonstrated that dominant disciplinary conceptions of objectivity circumscribe the scope of legitimate inquiry, constitute the object of investigation within narrow parameters, accredit specific modes of analysis and explanation, demarcate standards of evidence and strategies of argumentation, and identify the criteria for credible findings. In addition to certifying what will be accepted as valid knowledge, specific conceptions of objectivity establish characteristics deemed desirable in investigators. Objectivity not only defines the field and methods of inquiry and the qualities and attitudes of investigators but also provides rhetorical strategies that insulate accredited findings from refutation. The language of objectivity privileges the accounts that fall within its mantle and condones the repudiation of opposing views without detailed consideration of the arguments adduced. Thus when feminist scholars have attempted to demonstrate the falsity of philosophical and scientific claims about women, their cogent arguments frequently have been dismissed on the basis of *ad hominem* arguments concerning the irrational, emotional, engaged, or biased perspective of the woman investigator (Kelly, Ronan, and Cawley 1987).

Feminist critiques of objectivity have produced divergent recommendations. Some feminist scholars have identified flaws in dominant conceptions of objectivity in order to reformulate a conception of objectivity that avoids such defects (Hartsock 1983; Jaggar 1983; Grimshaw 1986; Longino 1990; Harding 1992, 1993; Wylie 2000a). Other feminist scholars have argued that objectivity lies beyond reclamation. It represents a peculiarly male mode of knowing, a "specular epistemology" that necessarily objectifies women and contributes to their exploitation (Irigaray 1985b). Catharine MacKinnon (1987, 50) has argued that "the non-situated, distanced standpoint . . . is the male standpoint socially. . . . The relationship between objectivity as the stance from which the world is known and the world that is apprehended in this way is the relationship of objectification. Objectivity is the epistemological stance of which objectification is the social process, of which male dominance is the politics, the acted-out social practice." Central to the arguments for the rejection of objectivity is the charge that far from being remote and insular, philosophical and scientific debates and practices have pernicious consequences for women. Under the guise of objectivity, philosophy and science objectify women, deny their agency, silence their alterity, and condemn them to "objectively" certified inferiority. The authority of these "objective" pronouncements then provides the foundation for excluding or marginalizing women in culture and society.

What should the feminist stance toward objectivity be: reclamation or rejection? Can any conception of objectivity withstand scrutiny? If all conceptions of objectivity are systematically flawed and if the very notion of objectivity is complicitous in the subordination of women, then there are strong intellectual and moral grounds for abandoning the concept. Before accepting that conclusion, however, it is important to investigate the merits of the moral charge that the pursuit of objectivity necessarily objectifies women and thereby contributes to their subordination. The next section traces the movement within certain feminist critiques from objectivity to objectification, that is from epistemological process to a morally suspect reification of difference that dehumanizes women.

The following section examines the notions of necessity that sustain three models linking objectivity to objectification: (1) a combination of psychological necessity and semiotic connections underlying a contamination model; (2) a commodification model that ties the depersonalization of knower and known to the imperatives of a capitalist economy; and (3) a reductionist model that construes objectification as a concomitant of methodological techniques that privilege the quantifiable, the measurable, and the replicable. Although I shall argue that no model adequately establishes an inherent link between objectivity and objectification, specific aspects of these critiques reveal important insights about the nature and limits of dominant conceptions of objectivity. Thus I suggest that feminist analysis advances a more sophisticated conception of objectivity than many traditional philosophical and scientific conceptions. In this, as in many other areas of feminist scholarship, feminist critique serves as a corrective to erroneous views. The ultimate objective of feminist objections, then, is not the repudiation but the reformulation of the conception of objectivity and the transformation of the social practices that instantiate its precepts.

Objectification

Like objectivity, objectification is a complex philosophical concept that has an array of different meanings. In the context of mental operations, objectification can mean merely to make something an object of consciousness. In this epistemologcial sense, to "objectify women" would have no pejorative connotation, for it means simply to contemplate women, to engage in reflection about them. Within Hegelian philosophy, to objectify is to externalize, to give concrete form to what previously existed only as an idea. Whether one explicates this notion by referring to the production of works of art, the artifacts and relations of the social world, or the reproduction of human beings, creativity remains central to this conception of objectification. Through their creative activity, humans may give concrete form to benign or malicious ideas. Misogyny can be objectified in this sense: noxious representations of women can be given concrete existence through philosophical, literary, or scientific texts. Under this construal, objectification approximates reification, a process that distorts as it concretizes. To reify a human being is to view a person as a thing, devoid of consciousness and agency. When objectification is conceived in terms of reification, the morally objectionable aspects of the process begin to surface. It seems a small step from envisioning a person as a thing to treating a person as a thing. Thus, reification provides a link to objectification in the most pejorative sense—a morally objectionable practice of treating a person as a means rather than as an end, as inert matter rather than as autonomous subject.

Objectification may involve an unobjectionable thought process, a creative activity that can be used for good or ill, or a moral offense. When some feminists charge that objectivity and objectification are linked, they seem to be suggesting that in both history and contemporary life efforts to objectify women in the epistemological sense give way to a morally suspect reification of difference that dehumanizes women. This charge has surfaced in a number of feminist arguments. Elizabeth Fee (1983, 24) has noted that philosophical, scientific, and historical "investigations of the 'woman problem' have considered women as natural objects and as passive in relation to the creation of knowledge." Alan Soble (1983, 298) has argued that "concentration of the properties of women qua women reifies women's experiences, interests, and social ties . . . [culminating] in an enforced homogenization of women as objects of research." Jill McCalla Vickers (1982, 40) has suggested that commitments to dominant disciplinary conceptions of objectivity mandate that scientists distance themselves from those under investigation and treat the women who are being studied as objects, "objectify-ing their pains in words which hide the identity of their oppression." Maria Mies (1984, 359) has argued that the postulate of value free research endorses a form of "'spectator-knowledge' which is achieved by showing an indifferent, disinter-ested, alienated, and reified attitude towards the 'research objects.'" Susanne Kappeler (1986, 49–50) has suggested that representational discourses attribute a pure subjectivity to men that simultaneously objectifies women, which robs them of their own subjectivity. The male gaze permits no reciprocity, mutuality, or crossgender intersubjectivity: "He is pure subject in relation to an object, which means that he is not engaging in exchange or communication with that objectified person who by definition cannot take the role of a subject." And Catharine MacKinnon (1987, 54–55) has claimed that the legacy of patriarchy makes objectivity and objectification indistinguishable modes of male appre-hension: "Objectivity as a stance is specifically male. . . . It is only a subject who gets to take the objective standpoint . . . it is men who are socially subjects, women socially who are other, objects." As further corroboration of this claim, MacKinnon notes that "in language as well as in life, the male occupies both the neutral and the male position. This is another way of saying that the neutrality of objectivity and of maleness are coextensive linguistically. . . . Another ex-pression of the sex specificity of objectivity socially is that women have been na-ture. That is, men have been knowers, mind; women have been 'to be known,' matter, that which is to be controlled and subdued, the acted upon" (55).

When claims such as these surface in feminist analyses, they are seldom de-fended in any systematic fashion. Are they defensible? What evidence might be adduced to support such claims? Feminist scholars have drawn attention to a wide range of discourses that depict women as objects. Claiming objectivity for both their methods of inquiry and for their substantive conclusions, the classic texts of philosophy and science advance conceptions of "femininity," "female-ness," and "womanhood" that eclipse the human agency and individuality of women. Universal claims about "Woman" supplant the enormous range of dif-ferences that characterize women in particular cultures, classes, races, nations. For example, "Woman" as an object of desire is conceived in terms of a profound passivity. Possessing no autonomous needs or interests, "Woman" as object of de-sire is amenable to any fantasy or projection. But the condition for such versatil-ity is the denial of the fundamental characteristics of a desiring subject. "Woman" as an object of desire lacks imagination, agency, autonomy, or even the capacity for action (de Lauretis 1984; Doane 1987).

"Woman" *qua* reproductive body is portrayed as a means for generating life, not as a living being. Whether the metaphors are drawn from nature or from technology—the soil that nourishes the seed, the matter awaiting the imposi-tion of form, the fetal environment, the incubator—the images produced are of inert, lifeless things that require monitoring and control. When the reproductive body becomes an object of investigation, women who reproduce become objects of regulation, with particularly harsh mechanisms of control imposed upon poor women of color. Forced caesarian sections, incarceration to insure proper diet, physical restraints to preclude ingestion of substances deemed harmful to the developing fetus, mandatory exercise to insure proper fetal oxygen supply, exclusion from occupational categories suspected of posing genetic risks are just a few of the concomitants of conceptions of womanhood that occlude women's rationality, moral judgment, and humanity (Holmes, Hoskins, and Goss 1981; Arditti, Klein, and Mindon 1984; Corea 1985; Roberts 1997; Morgan 2004).

"Woman" as defective male is constructed as an object for improvement. When the male is taken as norm, women are subjected to detailed surveillance to insure that every aspect of their "deficiency" is measured and catalogued. The "objective analyst" seeks a complete inventory of imperfections or deviations from the norm in order to remedy or control them. Whether "Woman's lack" is construed in terms of rationality, spirituality, morality, psychology, or biology, corrective strategies are imposed for the "Woman's own good." The paternalism central to these efforts to help woman overcome her "objective" deficiencies is inherently tied to a construal of woman as inferior and in need of molding, according to the dictates of the male gaze.

As slightly more than half of the world population, women are a majority of every ethnic and national group that does not practice female infanticide or abortion for purposes of sex-selection. Differing from one another by culture, language, religion, class, ideology, education, personality, personal history, aspiration, and capability, women have been objectified by allegedly objective philosophical and scientific investigations. All their individuating characteristics have been subordinated to an imputed ideal of femininity. Their individual identities have been effaced by norms of womanhood that operate within an extremely narrow range of possibility. By defining the female as inferior, philosophy and science have denied the vast range of characteristics that men and women share as members of the same species; instead, they impose an artificial dichotomy on the sexes that glorifies the male and denigrates the female. Treating women as undifferentiated mass, confining them to categories from which they cannot escape, denying their talent and their crucial contributions to culture and history have been staples of "objective" intellectual investigations and social practices.

Male researchers are not alone in constructing their research objects as inferior, however. Feminist scholars of color in the United States have called attention to similar objectifying practices in the research of white women, who depict Black women in terms that reiterate racist stereotypes of the "mammy," "matriarch," the "Jezebel"; or these scholars fall prey to the twin perils of treating women of color as invisible or hypervisible (hooks 1981, 1984; Hull, Bell

Scott, and Smith 1982; P. H. Collins 1990; Hurtado 1996). Postcolonial feminist scholars have traced colonizing, orientalizing, and othering practices in the depictions of "Third World Women" advanced by middle-class, white, Western women (Mohanty, Russo, and Torres 1991; Narayan 1997; Narayan and Harding 2000; Wing 2002). Poignant discussion of the "politics of representation" emphasize that privileged researchers with access to the media and scholarly venues for publication often frame discourses according to their own understandings of what is at issue and what must be done. Substituting their own thoughts and words for those of women of color or women of the global South, these researchers produce "authentic" representations of "the oppressed," portrayals in which "the oppressed" conform to the expectations the dominant have of the oppressed. The very act of rhetorical substitution exacerbates inequalities: silencing the views of the oppressed, distorting the thoughts of the subaltern speaker, denying her ability to analyze her situation and prescribe appropriate remedies. The objectification within these research efforts manifests a colonizing impulse that casts the white Westerner as savior even as it masks the colonizer's production of the structures and relations of oppression.

How can we best understand the connections between allegedly "objective" claims about women and morally objectionable, dehumanizing practices of objectification? Is it a matter of historical accident that numerous attempts to study women "objectively" produce objectifying representations of women? Does the relationship between objectivity and objectification stem from equivocation involving two distinct meanings of objectification—an unwarranted slide from the epistemological process to the moral offence? Does the connection result from the pervasive sexism and racism that underlies Western culture? Is the connection contingent and as such eliminable once sexism and racism are eradicated? Or does something inherent in the quest for objectivity produce objectification? Does some form of logical entailment or causal necessity render morally offensive objectification the inevitable outcome of strategies of objective investigation? To answer such questions, it is helpful to examine three cases in which feminist scholars have attempted to identify clearly the processes that link objectivity to objectification. Each of these instances focuses on the objectification of women in "objective" research conducted by men. We return to the problem the politics of representation within feminist efforts to conduct research on women in chapter 5.

Linkages

Some feminists have noted that conceptions of objectivity that emphasize "disinterested," "dispassionate," "disengaged" inquiry incorporate behaviors and mannerisms characteristic of a particular race, gender, and class into the requirements for scholarly research. To be a researcher, on this view, one must possess certain traits and comport oneself in a particular way (Schott 1988, 105). A "critical analytical attitude," a "distant and dispassionate stance," an "impersonal and universalizable perspective"—these are traits that have been particularly prized by elite European and American men. Associating these traits with the "essentials" of objectivity, then, prescribes that those who wish to engage in "objective" research mimic elite European and American men, thereby adopting particular modes of interaction with research objects. Thus, it is suggested that conceptions of objectivity developed within various disciplines mandate not only particular traits, attitudes toward the subject matter under investigation, and specific techniques of analysis, but they also sanction thoroughly value-laden modes of life. Lynne Arnault (1989, 201), for example, has called attention to the manner in which particular conceptions of objectivity create social biases in the forms of discourse that disadvantage particular groups: "In a society that values dispassionate, abstract argumentation and principled reasoning, those who argue in an emotional, vibrant, physically expressive way or who make appeals from the heart and personal experience are easily discredited and readily excluded from defining the terms of debate." Following this line of argument, some feminist scholars have attempted to comprehend the complex nexus between objectivity and objectification by searching for clues in the attitudinal and behavioral prescriptions associated with particular conceptions of objectivity.

THE CONTAMINATION MODEL

"Intellectual purity" constitutes one recurrent motif in discussions of objectivity from Plato through positivism. Within this frame of reference, objective knowledge is said to depend upon a series of operations through which investigators purge unreliable sensory perceptions, idiosyncratic distortions, distracting appetites, desires, and emotions in order to arrive at a class of privileged representations "so compelling that their accuracy cannot be doubted" (Bordo 1987, 75). The notion of objectivity as pure intellect suggests that "if reason is to provide trustworthy insight into reality, it has to be uncontaminated" (Jaggar 1989, 146). To attain a decontaminated intellect presupposes that unwanted contaminants can be clearly identified. As I discussed in chapter 1, those interested in achieving objective knowledge have disagreed about the precise forces that contaminate knowledge. The possibilities have ranged from ambiguity and contradiction, in general, to the senses, desires, passions, emotions, values, individual subjectivity, and to the body itself. But despite notable disagreement about the nature of contaminants, concern for intellectual purity warrants strategies to neutralize or negate the effects of perceived contaminants.

Preoccupations with purity and the resulting quest to identify and purge possible contaminants of knowledge provide the rudiments of what might be

called a "contamination model" that links the quest for objectivity to objectification. Susan Bordo has suggested that techniques designed to marginalize or
exclude threats to the purity of knowledge necessitate a reconceptualization of
the nature of those threats. They must be conceived as alien, inessential, and
hence fundamentally eliminable (Bordo 1987, 81). Whether the potentially
confounding factor be the body, the senses, the passions, or values, the quest for
pure knowledge requires that these aspects of human existence be conceived "as
a waste element, to be sloughed off . . . diseased, inferior, excrementious stuff"
(Bordo 1987, 129).

     According to the contamination model, psychological necessity links objec-
tivity to objectification. If the objective analyst is to exercise the discipline required to attain truth, he/she must deploy a psychological defense mechanism that
denigrates the importance of that which must be repudiated for the sake of truth.
To bear the pain of the renunciation of these aspects of human existence, the
knower must devalue the contaminants, construe them as objects, deny their essential relations to humanity. Typically, this analysis of the relation between objectivity and objectification turns on a particular psychoanalytic theory. On this
view, objectivity *requires* objectification on Freudian grounds concerning the
ego's reliance upon defense mechanisms to mediate reality and mitigate frustration, in general, with a particular nod to Kristeva's theory of abjection (1982).

     If one is willing to grant the adequacy of psychoanalytic arguments about
defense mechanisms, then the contamination model demonstrates that objectivity "requires" objectification, but not necessarily the objectification of women.
The move from the objectification of the body, the passions, the senses, emotions,
or values to the objectification of women in particular requires an additional
step. The connection between possible sources of contamination and women is
typically established via semiotics. Women are said to symbolize the body, sexed
embodiedness, sensuality, emotion (Irigaray 1985; Kristeva 1982; Trask 1986).
Indeed, it is said that women symbolize the very idea of pollution (Schott 1988,
32). The objectification of women, then, is necessitated by a symbolic transfer-
ence that links women to a range of physical contaminants that are believed to
threaten or impede the acquisition of truth.

     Under the contamination model, psychological necessity is posited as the
link between objectivity and objectification. But the objectification of women is
at two removes from the initial claims concerning objectivity. The first mediation
relies upon a particular psychoanalytic theory that asserts a necessary relation
between efforts to control sources of error and certain defense mechanisms. The
second mediation involves claims concerning the necessary symbolic relation
between women and the body, women and emotion, and women and pollution.
What is alleged to be inevitable could then founder in various ways. If psychoanalytic claims about inquirers' responses to obstacles to knowledge are mistaken,

then the very notion of psychological necessity collapses. Moreover, if the symbolic connection between women and the body/emotion/pollution can be shown to be an artifact of misogyny that can be eliminated through feminist efforts to purge sexist assumptions, then what may once have been an "automatic" association would no longer be such. What had appeared to be a necessary connection between objectivity and objectification, would be shown to be contingent and alterable. Rather than a necessary connection between objectivity and objectification, one finds anachronistic error that can in principle be eradicated by feminist scholarship, which would allow the concept of objectivity to be retrieved from association with morally objectionable objectification.

THE COMMODIFICATION MODEL

The second model of linkage between objectivity and objectification challenges both the autonomy and the integrity of scientific and philosophical investigations. In contrast to claims that objective inquiry develops according to its own inherent logic and that accredited techniques of analysis reflect unique problems of knowledge acquisition and nothing more, some feminists have charged that both research problems and strategies of inquiry mirror prevailing social and cultural values. Robin Schott (1988, 115) has argued that the Kantian paradigm of objectivity, which has had such importance in structuring contemporary conceptions of objectivity, both reflects and "justifies a particular form of suppression [of sensuality] that developed in an emerging system of commodity production and exchange." Schott argues that the Kantian insistence that there is only one mode of human reason, that all knowers are the same, that objective knowledge is therefore anonymous and impersonal, reflects an "exchange mentality" characteristic of bourgeois society. On Schott's view, "the abstract equivalence among diverse consciousnesses mirrors the quantitative equivalence of labor in a market economy" (124). The faculties of the individual knower are not the only target of depersonalization. The imperatives of commodification strip all objects of their unique properties in order to facilitate their exchange. "'Pure' reason reflects and idealizes the objectification that occurs in bourgeois society. Kant's systematic purification divests both the subject and the object of all immediate, sensuous, qualitative features" (Schott 1988, 168).

The "commodification model" delineated by Schott suggests that the quest for objectivity objectifies both knower and known. To acquire knowledge, the knower must distance himself/herself from "the multitude of sensuous, erotic, and emotional concerns" (Schott 1988, 118). "Depersonalization of the self" is a requirement of the most basic processes of knowing. Thus, the Kantian model of objectivity prescribes a strategy for knowledge acquisition that produces a markedly desensualized human knower. According to Schott, this model of objectivity endorses the repudiation of individuality, uniqueness, and passion. The

Kantian ideal of stoic apathy also has consequences for the objects of investigation, for it desensualizes apprehension to such an extent that the material world becomes devoid of personal meaning and value (Schott 1988, 106, 171). As objects of consciousness, human beings are reified; their multidimensionality is reduced either to a denuded conception of the person as an embodiment of moral law, or to a notion of the body as an array of physical properties of interest to scientific investigation (Schott 1988, 146, 177).

The commodification model suggests that the quest for objectivity produces a pervasive objectification necessitated by the imperatives of capitalist society. The objectification of women is not unique; it is simply a part of a larger process of alienation and reification mandated by the demands of capitalist existence. But if the objectification of women is no different conceptually than the objectification of men, why do women come out so much the worse from the process? The commodification model alone cannot explain why the depictions of women emanating from "objectifying consciousness" are more noxious than the depictions of men. To bridge this gap in the commodification model, Schott introduces both semiotic claims concerning women's symbolism of the body and pollution and psychoanalytic claims concerning conceptual analysis per se: "There is no strictly conceptual representation of an object. When an object is represented as strictly conceptual, this idealization itself serves purposes of defense. . . . The conceptual structure reflects the suppression of the erotic feelings demanded by the ascetic ideal" (Schott 1988, 221). Reliance upon psychological necessity and semiotic connections to link objectivity to objectification has been criticized above in the context of the contamination model, but the commodification model also raises a number of distinct issues.

The precise nature of the "necessity" that sustains the commodification model's link between objectivity and objectification is problematic. Like other instances of the sociology of knowledge, the commodification model construes objectivity in terms of ideology, which either intentionally or unwittingly advances the interests of the ruling class. But whether such functionalist arguments link objectification to either the demands of commodity exchange, the alienation requisite for the sale of labor power as a commodity, or the suppression of eros necessary to sustain industrial production, the conception of necessity fueling the link is remarkably loose. References to "determination," "correspondence," "reflection," "outgrowth," and "dependence" cannot mask the absence of any relation of strict determinism between economic conditions and abstract ideas (Speier 1938; Wright Mills 1939; Merton 1945). In lieu of strict determinism, one finds claims concerning pertinent parallels between structures of thought, strategies of inquiry, and economic relations. Such parallels, however, must admit of deviations from the posited necessity in order to explain the possibility of ideology-critique. Notions of strict determinism must give way to more complex accounts if we are to make sense of the practices of feminist critique. As Toril Moi (1985, 26) has pointed out: "Only a concept of ideology as a contradictory construct, marked by gaps, slides, and inconsistencies, would enable feminism to explain how even the severest ideological pressures will generate their own lacunae," thereby creating openings for women to resist the force of the dominant ideology and voice opposition. At a time when capitalism has become hegemonic in the global system, the very existence of feminist critiques that challenge the commodification inherent in the Kantian conception of objectivity and outline alternative conceptions of cognition undermines those claims about a necessary or inherent connection between objectivity and objectification on the terms set by the commodification model.

THE REDUCTIONIST MODEL

The third bridge between objectivity and objectification advanced by some feminists supplants discussions of defensive psychological mechanisms and unwitting ideological distortions with the claim that the objectification of women emerges as an unavoidable consequence of reductive intellectual strategies that abstract from particulars to such an extent that they fall into caricatures of the object under study. The reductionist model suggests that the link between objectivity and objectification combines intellectual and perceptual processes with dire psychological consequences. On this view, the objective analyst begins with the conviction that inquiry is value-neutral and that the appropriate techniques for knowledge acquisition are analytical and experimental. The task of the objective inquirer is to "step back," "gain distance," and "develop perspective" in order to cultivate an understanding of the phenomenon under investigation, which is sufficiently abstracted from the murky complexities of daily existence that causal relations may be isolated. Frequently associated with physicalism, mechanism, positivism, and behaviorism, this approach is premised upon a presumption that the concepts and categories that explain the physical world can explain human action. To glean adequate explanations, then, the investigator must bracket issues pertaining to agency, to thinking, willing subjects who have reasons for their actions. This analytical strategy does not deny that individuals have intentions for their actions; it merely doubts the causal adequacy of purposive claims. As manifested in research paradigms as diverse as cognitive science, neurophysiology, and sociobiology, "objective" explanation is assumed to require detailed investigation of underlying causes, such as neurological processes, endocrinological influences, or biochemical determinants of behavior.

According to the reductionist model, denial of personhood is an artifact of methodologies that fail to take consciousness seriously. By excluding certain dimensions of human experience from investigation, the methods of inquiry subtly denigrate those aspects of human life. The quantifiable, the measurable, and the replicable are privileged to the long-term detriment of the idiosyncratic, the intangible, and the developmentally complex (Fee 1983; Mies 1984; Kelly, Ronan, and Cawley 1987; Berman 1989). In a classic manifestation of metonymic consciousness, the parts of human existence deemed amenable to scientific study are mistaken for the whole. Efforts to "control" extraneous variables devolve into control over the objects of study. Human beings are reduced to objects of investigation whose characteristics are conceived solely in terms of properties of scientific interest.

Proponents of this model acknowledge that the objectification inherent in reductionist methodologies caricature men as well as women, but they suggest that the psychological concomitants of the objectifying stance generate particularly pernicious consequences when applied to women. Central to objectification is a distancing between the investigator and the phenomenon being investigated. The intellectual distance cultivated to gain an "objective" view produces psychological distance, which precludes the investigator's identification with or empathy for the objects of study. When both the investigator and the objects of investigation are men, the full force of this psychological distance is mitigated. When the investigator is a man and the objects of inquiry are women, the effects of psychological distance are potent. By tacitly taking himself as norm, the male investigator perceives women as "other." Precisely those characteristics that can be construed as anomalies or deviations from the (male) norm are taken to be the prime targets for scientific investigation. The scientific study of women is thus reduced to the study of "sex differences." Exaggerated attention to differences eclipses commonality. As the reality of those things that have been excluded from investigation is occluded, "Woman" is reduced to reproductive organs, female hormones, or specific chromosomal configurations. Psychological distance is magnified through this reification of difference. The inability of the "objective" analyst to empathize with the female research object cements the relation between objectification as intellectual process and objectification as moral offense. Understood in terms of reified differences and excluded from empathic recognition as human beings, women are easily mistaken for sexual objects, reproductive objects, or objects of manipulation and control.

The reductionist model posits a complex process through which intellectual techniques designed to attain objectivity deteriorate into morally objectionable objectifications of women. Is the deterioration inevitable? Must metaphors of distance, space, or perspective degenerate into practices that treat women as objects? Do reductionist strategies necessitate dehumanizing caricatures? To argue that a conception of objectivity that sustains notions of value-free inquiry contributes to a process of objectification is not to prove the existence of iron-clad connections. The move from intellectual operation to moral offense involves numerous mediations and decision points. Although there are good reasons for challenging the adequacy of reductionist accounts of human action (Bernstein 1976), claims concerning an inevitable dehumanization are not prominent among them. Neither abstracting from particulars nor bracketing questions of human agency logically entails dehumanization. Decontextualized analysis does not necessarily generate caricatures. The gap between procedure and substantive outcome is as relevant here as it is in the discussion of objectivity per se. An analytical strategy in and of itself can no more guarantee dehumanization than it can guarantee the acquisition of truth.

The notion of psychological distance introduced in this model is also troublesome. The model invokes psychological distance to explain why the same techniques produce more pernicious consequences for women than for men. Appealing to the psychological orientation of the male investigator as the fundamental explanans for the objectification of women, however, raises the possibility that the problem lies with not the method but the men. In many of these accounts of objectification, the blame associated with certain strategies of inquiry is closely tied to claims about male inquirers. If the core of feminist claims about the objectification of women is a set of assumptions about the limitations of "male" reason, however, they can be rejected for the reasons laid out in chapter 2. Whether the problematic grounds involve unacceptable levels of gender symbolism, essentialism, biologism, or ad hominem fallacies, the change in the problem site from intellectual operation to male intellects undermines the original claims concerning an inherent link between objectivity and objectification. Once more, objectivity as such does not appear to be the culprit.

Lessons

If attempts to demonstrate a necessary connection between objectivity and the objectification of women fail, how can one explain the relation between allegedly objective inquiry and the persistent production of noxious representations of women? Markedly defective accounts of women surface too frequently and too consistently within "objective" philosophical and scientific discourses to be dismissed as either historical accident or "bad" science (Harding 1986, 102–110). What lessons can be drawn from an examination of the evidence that suggests that the relation between allegedly objective inquiry and the resulting objectifications of women are not necessary, yet are routine?

Feminist scholarship across the disciplines has revealed that misogyny routinely blinds "objective" investigators. In addressing the "Woman Question," philosophers and scientists often ignore or violate the methodological constraints of their fields, generate contradictory claims about women that undermine the internal consistency of their arguments about human beings, and fail to notice that the hypotheses they advance about women are inadequately warranted.

The frequency with which such problems arise in the context of "objective" modes of inquiry implies both that existing strictures of objectivity are insufficient to attain truth and that there are serious deficiencies in the dominant conceptions of objectivity.

Feminist scholarship offers a critique of dominant, disciplinary conceptions of objectivity that illuminates the role of social values in cognition and that has important implications beyond investigations in which women are the objects of inquiry. It has already been noted that feminists have identified a number of faulty inferences that can explain how investigators committed to objective inquiry and acting in good faith can generate erroneous claims. The assumption that emulation of the qualities of objective knowledge can assure its attainment and the belief that adherence to specific research techniques can guarantee the validity of the results both reflect mistakes about the requirements of objectivity. Although they arise in different problem contexts, both also manifest an erroneous understanding of the social constitution of knowledge and its implications for objective inquiry.

Conceptions of objectivity premised upon self-purging of bias, value, or emotion and conceptions of objectivity dependent upon intersubjective correction of the same sources of error imply that the fundamental threat to objectivity is idiosyncrasy. Both share the Baconian view of subjectivity as an obscuring, "enchanted glass, full of superstition and imposture, if it be not delivered and reduced" (Bacon 1861, 276). Both locate the chief obstacle to the acquisition of truth within the individual researcher. Thus the techniques of objective inquiry, whether conceived in terms of acts of pure intellect or intersubjective emendation, are designed to protect against "the capacity of the knower to bestow false inner projections on the outer world of things" (Bordo 1987, 51).

The feminist discovery of persistent patterns of sexist error in "objective" inquiry suggests that the target of the various corrective strategies has been mislocated. The conviction that the central problem of objectivity lies with the emotional and perceptual quirks of the subjective self that distort, confuse, and interfere with objective apprehension of phenomena neglects the social dimensions of inner consciousness. Situating the issue of objectivity in a contest between the inner self and external reality masks the social constitution of subjectivity. The recurrence of a profound degree of sexism and racism that filters perceptions, mediates philosophical arguments, structures research hypotheses, and "stabilizes inquiry by providing assumptions that highlight certain kinds of observations and experiments in light of which data are taken as evidence for hypotheses" (Longino 1990, 99) indicates a remarkable uniformity in the kinds of distortion that impede the acquisition of truth. Such uniformity challenges the myth of radical idiosyncrasy. One need not be committed to the full implications of Foucault's view of subjectivity as normalizing practice to accept the feminist argument that even one's innermost consciousness is culturally freighted.

If social values incorporated within individual consciousness present an important obstacle to objective knowledge, then norms of objectivity that blind the individual to their role or assure the individual that intersubjective consensus is a sufficient remedy will fail to produce objective accounts of the world. For if certain social values structure conceptions of self and perceptions of the social and natural worlds, then neither isolated acts of pure intellect nor intersubjective testing will suffice to identify them. On the contrary, the belief that idiosyncracy is the fundamental obstacle to objectivity will preclude detailed investigations of shared assumptions and observations as well as intersubjectively verified theories. Rather than being perceived as a potential source of error, values such as sexism and racism that are widely held will escape critical reflection. Their very popularity will be taken to certify their validity, thereby truncating further inquiry into their merits.

Feminist scholars have illuminated the numerous points at which social values infiltrate discourses on women. Helen Longino (1990) has drawn upon these insights to develop an account of objectivity that can coexist with a clear understanding of the social and cultural construction of science. Longino identifies the crucial role played by social values in framing research questions, characterizing the objects of inquiry, accrediting forms of explanation, demarcating credible evidence, structuring modes of argumentation, and reducing a discipline's vulnerability to maverick claims. The point of Longino's investigation is not to demonstrate the impossibility of objectivity, but rather to illuminate the complexity of attaining it. Only heightened awareness of the multiple sources of error and the complexity of problems of knowledge can sustain adequate strategies to achieve objectivity. And only repudiation of naive faith that adherence to a simple method can guarantee the acquisition of truth can help cultivate the sophistication essential to objective inquiry.

At the heart of this feminist conception of objectivity is a conception of cognition as a human practice, a conception that recognizes the complex interaction among traditional assumptions, social norms, theoretical conceptions, disciplinary strictures, linguistic possibilities, emotional dispositions, and creative impositions in every act of cognition. Operating in the context of cognition as complex social practice, the quest for objectivity entails the cultivation of the intellect. To track the multiple sources of error in a specific field of inquiry requires far more than intellectual engagement within a narrow sphere of specialization. Sensitivity to distortion and bias presupposes an intellect informed by systematic study of a chosen field, familiar with strengths and weaknesses of a wide range of methodological tools and sufficiently knowledgeable across disciplines to analyze the role of social values in constituting the research object (Hawkesworth 1989; Alcoff 2000).

A capacity for critical reflection is central to this feminist conception of objectivity, but it is not the sole requirement. Intersubjectivity also plays a key role. "A method of inquiry is objective to the extent that it permits transformative criticism" (Longino 1990, 75). The point of intersubjectivity within this framework is not the confirmation of shared assumptions about what is normal, natural, or real, but rather to subject precisely what seems least problematic to critical scrutiny. Awareness of the role of social values in naturalizing oppressive practices, leads feminists to emphasize the importance of critical intersubjectivity in probing tacit assumptions and foundational beliefs of various disciplines.

If objective inquiry is dependent upon systematic probing of precisely that which appears unproblematic, then who does the probing may be a matter of central concern to those committed to objective inquiry. For what is taken as given, what appears to be natural, what seems to fall outside the legitimate field of investigation may be related to the gender, race, class, and historical situatedness of the investigator. Feminist scholars have argued that the attainment of objectivity by means of probing and sophisticated intersubjective critique has implications that transcend the quest for an appropriate intellectual procedure. Convinced that "methodological constraints are inadequate to the task of ruling values out of scientific inquiry" (Longino 1990, 15), feminists have argued that objectivity demands inclusivity. Objective inquiry cannot be attained within the preserve of privilege—whether it be the privilege of whites, Westerners, the middle class, or men. The feminist argument for the inclusion of women and people of color within academic disciplines can thus be understood in terms of the demands of objectivity. To the extent that social values mediate perception and explanation, exclusionary practices can only help insulate questionable assumptions from scrutiny. A commitment to objectivity conceived as sophisticated intersubjective critique embraces diversity as a means. More and different "guides to the labyrinths of reality" (Stimpson 1991) may help us to confront the contentious assumptions most deeply entrenched in our conceptual apparatus. The inclusion of people from different social backgrounds, different cultures, different linguistic communities, and different genders within science and philosophy cannot guarantee, but it might foster, sustained critique of problematic assumptions long entrenched in the academic disciplines (Alcoff 2000).

A feminist conception of objectivity does not offer an authoritative technique that can guarantee the production of truth. In lieu of a simple method, it calls for cultivating sound intellectual judgment. It demands a level of sophistication that can be cultivated only by sustained study across an array of disciplines. It presupposes a reconceptualization of the relation between inner self and external world. Moreover, it demands the expansion of the scientific and philosophical communities to encompass formerly excluded groups. Thus this feminist conception of objectivity cannot be easily attained. It remains at odds with the excessive specialization of contemporary academic training, with the naive conviction that truth lies in the application of an accredited method, and with the renewed commitment to preserve white, middle-class, male hegemony in philosophy, science, and society at large. Despite such marked differences from dominant trends, the strength of this feminist conception of objectivity lies in its promise of fostering the benign aspirations and objectives of objectivity where traditional conceptions have failed.

Chapter 4   Evidence

THE FIRST THREE chapters have suggested that an antifoundationalist account of knowledge lies at the heart of feminist practices of inquiry. Feminist antifoundationalism is attuned to the role of theory, language, culture, and disciplinary training in the production of knowledge. It also recognizes the role of particular communities of scholars in accrediting theories, which in turn circumscribe what counts as "facts." An understanding of facts as theoretically mediated requires a reconsideration of the nature and meaning of "evidence."

Etymologically the meaning of evidence is linked to visual metaphors for knowledge, which construe knowing as a kind of seeing. The "evident" is that which is "distinctly visible" and, as such, "clear to the understanding." Within this frame, evidence refers to proofs that grow out of seeing, as in the case of eyewitness testimonies. If antifoundationalism moves beyond mistaken notions that the truth is "manifest," or "conspicuous" in the "given," what then counts as evidence? How do theories identify relevant evidence? What standards can be used to assess theoretically constituted evidence? When conflicting theories construe evidence differently, how can these conflicts be adjudicated? This is a particularly pressing concern given the frequency with which feminist scholarship is challenged by traditional scholars with distinctly antifeminist agendas.

Throughout the past three decades, feminist researchers have created an interdisicplinary epistemic community linked by political commitments to eliminate oppressive social conditions, formations, and relations. Beyond this shared political commitment, feminist inquiry involves extensive networks of scholars, who have developed diverse strategies of knowledge production tied to particular research questions. Standards of evidence, levels of analysis, types of explanation, and forms of argumentation deemed appropriate vary across diverse forms of feminist analysis and investigation. To develop the sophistication that objective feminist inquiry requires, interdisciplinary feminist scholars must grapple with the strengths and weaknesses of a wide range of methodological tools, which can help them to track multiple sources of error and to illuminate bias and distortion. Feminist research within established disciplines is demanding. Interdisciplinary feminist research is even more so. Drawing upon the rich resources provided by thirty-five years of feminist inquiry, this chapter investigates how evidence is constructed within a variety of theoretical frameworks deployed across humanities, social science, and natural science disciplines.

Evidence

Popular television shows that feature courtroom dramas have familiarized audiences with two legal standards for evidence used in assessing responsibility for criminal conduct, "a preponderance of evidence" and "evidence beyond a reasonable doubt." In these fictionalized treatments of courtroom proceedings, viewers are often privy to additional information so that they can assess how well a jury is doing its job. Through a variety of cinematic techniques, viewers may be shown the "actual crime" as it is committed. They may see police interrogation of suspects or lawyers interviewing their clients. They may observe prosecuting and defense attorneys mapping their legal strategies or preliminary hearings on motions to exclude evidence or "side-bars" in which the judge rules on specific objections. Allowing audiences to possess such supplementary information is akin to a bestowal of omniscience. The viewers know what really happened, so they can see when witnesses lie or how legal adversaries distort evidence or how jurors allow their own biases to affect their deliberations on the case. Being aware of the truth in a particular case, viewers can see the gulf between legal evidence, the constraints of court proceedings, and the actual happening.

When one moves from portrayals of trials in television and film to institutional practices, the relation between evidence and truth is far more complicated. Law students are required to take courses to familiarize themselves with complex rules of evidence, but citizens impaneled as jurors are expected to be able to assess conflicting evidentiary claims simply on the basis of common sense, everyday understandings of how the world works and what kinds of beings humans are. The legal system in the United States structures an adversarial process in the courts designed to screen out partiality on the part of the jurors, while institutionalizing partiality in the presentation of evidence and arguments by prosecuting and defense attorneys. Through the process of voir dire, prospective jurors are asked a series of questions and are eliminated from the jury pool if they have any relation to the case or knowledge about related matters that might impugn their impartiality in hearing evidence. The structure of the trial requires lawyers for the prosecution and for the defense to act as adversaries who passionately argue "their side" of the case. In the U.S. legal system, each lawyer is expected to act as a partisan. The law does not expect self-interested, short-sighted, and contentious beings to be capable of neutrality. On the contrary, the adversarial process assumes that impassioned presentations on both sides enable jurors to arrive at a judgment of truth in a particular case.

In the context of a trial, the jury is asked to weigh and assess multiple kinds of evidence. Jurors are asked to judge the credibility of the testimony of eyewitnesses and principals in the case, to decide whose character and whose words to trust. They are asked to consider corroborating witnesses who afford the defendant an exculpating alibi. The jury assesses circumstantial evidence, a range of observable, material items that allegedly tie the accused to the crime. Jurors are also asked to assess unobservables: questions of intention and motive that reside wholly within the mind of the perpetrator and are not available for inspection. After hearing all the evidence presented and cross-examined by the prosecution and the defense, the jury is instructed by the judge on the relevant issues of law that should guide their deliberations, and then they are sent to a quiet room to decide the guilt or innocence of the accused.

A jury trial establishes a procedural mechanism for the determination of truth. All the members of the jury are acknowledged to be fallible individuals. Yet the procedure of collective deliberation relies on a participatory process to generate a good faith judgment of guilt or innocence. Within this deliberative process, jurors go over the evidence, rehash arguments, exchange their recollections of the details of the case, share their judgments concerning "the facts," and try to persuade one another to agree to a particular verdict of guilt or innocence. In the course of their discussion, jurors often reveal a range of prejudgments, beliefs, and values with which they entered the courtroom. If the members of the jury can arrive at a collective determination, a verdict—literally a statement of truth—is rendered; if they cannot reach agreement, a mistrial is declared. Within the procedures established by the legal system, the decision of a jury of one's peers is not accredited as infallible, it is simply accepted as the best that fallible knowers can do when confronting conflicting claims about the facts of a case. Recognizing that a deliberative procedure cannot guarantee a correct verdict, the legal system also allows for the possibility of appeals through which judges, better versed in the technical requirements of the law, may overturn a jury verdict.

In beginning to think about evidence in the context of feminist inquiry, it is useful to keep fictional depictions of courtroom procedures as well as trials by jury in mind, for they help to illuminate some similarities and some critical differences in assumptions about the nature of evidence in scholarly investigations. Like jury verdicts, feminist knowledge production involves deliberative processes that require individual and collaborative efforts to assess the merits of contending views. In keeping with its antifoundationalist premises, feminist research accepts fallibilism and proceduralism, both of which call into question the "omniscience" that television so benignly accords the viewer. There is no position from which to know the truth of the world independent of the practices of inquiry accredited by particular networks of scholars. Moreover, the role that theories play in constituting facts and accrediting relevant evidence challenges the assumption that there are only two sides to any story, that an adversarial process is the best way to adjudicate complex issues of evidence and interpretation, and that common sense alone is sufficient to weigh evidence.

Emerging from millennia of patriarchal claims about women and the world, feminist inquiry begins by acknowledging that nothing is manifest or self-evident. To grapple with complex claims of truth, feminist scholars must begin by attending to the theoretical frameworks that construct and accredit evidence within particular research practices. Knowing how particular theories structure perception and construe relevant evidence is crucial for evaluating evidentiary claims. Familiarity with existing theoretical frameworks is not sufficient for feminist scholarship, however, for feminist critique often renders these dominant paradigms suspect. Unlike the courtroom situation in which the judge instructs the jury about the specific matters of law relevant to the case, feminist researchers often contest the parameters of debate within and across academic disciplines. They interrogate existing categories, question how boundaries have been drawn between one phenomenon and another, challenge the "operationalization" of terms, probe omissions and distortions, examine metaphors and analogies that structure understanding, develop new concepts, introduce new modes of argument, and appeal to different registers of experience. Deliberating on the evidence in feminist inquiry, then, is a markedly creative endeavor that involves the collective efforts of networks of scholars who engage one another in the identification and justification of, as well as contestations about, innovative analytic strategies.

If evidence is complex, multifaceted, and accredited within particular theoretical frameworks, then consideration of how a range of theories construe evidence differently can be a useful exercise. The following sections explore examples of theoretical presuppositions that inform conceptions of evidence in the humanities and the social sciences.

TEXTUAL ANALYSIS

One staple of scholarship in the humanities and the social sciences is the analysis of texts. But what exactly counts as a text? Different disciplinary and theoretical frameworks afford different answers to this basic question. Historically, the humanities emerged in the context of biblical interpretation, and the Bible was the text for which textual scholarship was invented. Hermeneutics originated as a mode of biblical interpretation. With the secularization of the humanities, the Bible lost its place of privilege, and the great works of philosophy and literature were deemed the texts worthy of scholarly attention. Historians expanded the range of texts appropriate for analysis to include historical documents, speeches, diaries, letters, newspapers, interviews, pamphlets, and inventories— the whole range of historical artifacts that have survived from earlier eras. Psychoanalysis conceived the texts warranting analysis to include everyday speech, digressions, "slips-of-the-tongue," dreams, desires, recollections from childhood. Discursive analysis extended the meaning of "texts" beyond books and documents to utterances of any kind, structures of statements, terms, categories, beliefs, cultural practices, and institutions. Inspired by Derrida's famous quip that "there is nothing outside of the text," postmodernists suggested that everything— art, architecture, culture, films, bodies, institutions, social practices—was ripe for deconstructive textual analyses.

If the nature of a text appropriate for interrogation is a subject of contestation, so too is the question of how to interpret texts. Debates about interpretive strategies have been a staple of scholarship in the humanities and the social sciences, and the stand one takes concerning modes of interpretation dictates what counts as textual evidence. Consider, for example, the differences: intentionalists stipulate that the meaning of a text is determined by the intention of the author; formalists insist that interpretation of literature focus exclusively on the formal characteristics intrinsic to the "literariness" of texts; historicists argue that the meaning of any text can only be understood in the context of the historical, cultural, and linguistic practices and connotations at the time of its creation; psychoanalysts suggest that meaning is linked to painful or frustrated longings, desires, and impulses that have been repressed and as such are no longer available for conscious inspection; semioticians construe meaning in terms of cultural codes or myths through which ideologies and counter-ideologies circulate in a particular society; reader-response theorists argue that meaning must be understood in terms of popular culture and a particular audience's reception of a text; and deconstructionists posit the ambiguity and indeterminacy of meaning in all texts.

To analyze a text, then, requires very different kinds of evidence depending upon the interpretive theory that guides the analysis. For an intentionalist, evidence of authorial intent might be found in the structure of argument in the text itself, in autobiographical and biographical writing, the author's letters, diaries, notes, marginalia, or other published works, interviews with the author, or even students' notes of lectures given by the author. Formalists bring markedly different concerns to their analyses of texts. Seeking to understand and explain the aesthetic qualities of literature, formalists look for evidence in the particular literary devices (figures of speech, genres, rhetoric, symbology) deployed by an author to achieve novelty, creativity, originality. For historicists, texts provide a window into specific cultures at determinate points in history. Correct interpretation of texts, then, requires immersion in historical specificity: evidence drawn from other writings of the period such as religious, philosophical, political, literary, and scientific documents illuminate the worldview or "spirit of the age," which shapes the connotation of language used in a particular text.

In marked contrast to historicists' call for sociocultural specificity in the understanding of evidence, psychoanalytic interpretations presuppose a structure of the human psyche impervious to history. Freud's theory posits a primordial realm of "instinctual impulses" for pleasure and for death (the "id") that drives individual conduct, encountering multiple sources of frustration from the frailty of the human body, relations with other people, and the intransigence of the material world. The "ego" or reality principle emerges to mediate the id's frustration from unsatisfied desire by developing a complex range of "defense mechanisms" that repress, redirect, or revalue the original desires and their objects. The "superego" emerges as an internal mechanism of social control to thwart individual impulses that threaten the projects of community existence and the demands of civilization. Whether embedded in Freud's theory of psychosexual development, Winnicott's theory of object-relations, or Lacan's account of the subject's entry into the Symbolic Order (a reformulation of Freudian theory in the context of structural linguistics), psychoanalytic interpretation claims a certain universality, suggesting that it can provide interpretive mechanisms that transcend cultural specificity. Powerful images drawn from Greek tragedies, such as Oedipus and Electra, label psychological complexes that afford insights into human conduct, sociocultural practices and literary texts across historical eras and epochs. Because these are insights into unconscious psychological processes insulated from conscious reflection, evidence within this theoretical framework is always indirect. Psychoanalytic theory maps the range of defense mechanisms (repression, sublimation, projection, introjection, displacement, reaction formation), and the task of the analyst is to search texts for symptoms that provide clues to these unconscious psychological processes.

The term, semiotics, is derived from the Greek *semeiosis*, the "observation of signs." Although Locke referred to semiotics as "the science of signs and signification," contemporary theories of semiotics are more typically drawn from the pragmatic philosophy of Charles Peirce, the linguistic structuralism of Ferdinand de Saussure, and the literary and cultural theory of Roland Barthes. Peirce ([1883] 1982) identified three dimensions of semiotics that constitute evidence somewhat differently: pragmatics investigates the ways that humans, animals, or machines, such as computers, use linguistic signs; semantics examines the relation between signs and their meanings by abstracting from their use; and syntax explores the relation among signs themselves, abstracting both from use and meaning. Saussure ([1916] 1974) focused on the latter dimension in developing his account of structural linguistics. Challenging notions that there is an essential relation between words and things, "signifiers" and "signified," Saussure argued that meaning is established by relationships of difference and distinction within a linguistic system, which is itself a system of opposites and contrasts. Rejecting referential theories of language that suggest that words are labels for independently existing things, Saussure suggested that language is constitutive: signifying processes create meaning through the interplay of relationships of selection and combination, through the juxtaposition of similarities and differences within a grammatical structure without necessarily referring to anything outside the language. For Saussure, the task of structural analysis was to reveal the rules and conventions that structure meaning within particular linguistic systems. Barthes (1967, 1973) appropriated Saussure's structural account of signification to probe the means by which dominant meanings or "myths" are produced and circulated in culture. Barthes construed myth or ideology as a body of ideas and practices that defend and legitimate the status quo, actively promoting values that serve the interests of the dominant groups in society while operating outside the intentions of any particular writer or author. Indeed, in "The Death of the Author," Barthes (1977, 146) insisted that the meaning of texts cannot be conflated with authorial intention, for a text is "a multidimensional space in which a variety of writings, none of them original, blend and clash. The text is a tissue of quotations drawn from innumerable centers of culture." Within Barthes's (1973, 11) theoretical framework, evidence emerges from interrogation of "the falsely obvious" and the unmasking of the "Bourgeois norm" (1973, 9) to reveal the cultural codes that sustain modes of domination. The analytic task of the "mythologist" is to demonstrate the means of ideological production, to reveal how oppressive images and meanings are naturalized and rendered morally unproblematic.

Providing a bridge from structuralism to post-structuralism, Barthes's proclamation of the "death of the author" laid the foundation for reader-response theory, which posits that the reader defines the meaning of a text. In the act of reading, the reader brings a temporary unity to the text, momentarily fixing meaning that is otherwise fluid. Celebrating the free play of signifiers in the contradictory readings of texts by multiple readers, proponents of reader-response theory emphasize that there can be no such thing as an "authoritative interpretation" of a text. The methodological consequence of this relativist stance is manifest in the conception of evidence that surfaces in reader-response theory. As the focus of analysis shifts from the text to individual interpretations of a text, relevant evidence becomes sociological. The reader-response researcher must gather evidence of how readers are actually interpreting texts. The boundary between humanities and social science blurs as reader-response theorists adopt methods, such as focus groups, interviews, and surveys to generate quantitative data about popular reception of particular texts.

Derrida's theory of deconstruction moves the site of fluidity in meaning from multiple readers to the ambiguity of language itself. Deploying a notion of *"différance,"* Derrida suggests that meaning is elusive, always deferred, never fully present, but rather simultaneously absent and present. In contrast to the structuralist focus on the relation between the signifier and the signified, Derrida's (1978, 25) post-structuralism suggests that the continual deferment of meaning establishes relations only among signifiers: "the indefinite referral of signifier and signifier . . . gives the signified meaning no respite . . . so that it always signifies again." Neither context nor connotation can fully control the meaning of signifiers, which carry with them traces of meanings from other contexts. If meaning is always unstable, the task of deconstruction cannot be a futile effort to fix meaning. On the contrary, critical interrogation of binaries is intended to supplement meaning by illuminating flawed attempts to constrain interpretation within the binary formation, decontextualizing and recontextualizing terms in order to disrupt dominant frames of reference. Within this deconstructive framework, evidence itself is linguistic, unstable and unfixed, but attention to contradictions, lacunae, false totalities, and homogenizations within particular relations of signification can provide an opening for efforts to trace multiplicities of meaning, deconstruct binary oppositions, and overthrow the hierarchies and privilege they attempt to establish.

Feminist scholars have appropriated and continue to deploy these diverse theories and the conceptions of evidence they accredit in creative interpretations of textual, discursive, and material practices. They have also devised certain distinctive modes of feminist textual analysis. Elaine Showalter (1987) provided an overview of the first two decades of feminist literary criticism that distinguished between two innovative approaches. She coined the term "gynocriticism" to characterize feminist interpretive strategies that focus on the works of women writers. In contrast to an earlier feminist analytic tactic that interrogated the texts of male writers, illuminating their problematic representations of women, gynocriticism sought to retrieve and analyze the literary and philosophical works of women, who had been excluded from the Western canon. Gynocriticism was simultaneously an exercise in feminist canon formation, an historical study of women writers as a distinct literary tradition, and a comparative exploration of genres of women's writing that differed in significant ways from genres associated with classic male texts. While feminist scholars used a wide range of theoretical frameworks in analyzing women's writing, they supplemented these diverse theoretically constituted conceptions of evidence with an additional feminist evidentiary requirement, engagement with texts written by women.

Borrowing a term coined by Alice Jardine (1982, 1985), Showalter labeled a second distinctly feminist, analytical approach, "gynesis." Where gynocriticism places women's writing at the center of analysis, gynesis probes language itself as its fundamental evidentiary base. Drawing upon post-structuralist linguistic theory and psychoanalytic theory, gynesis explores certain gendered binaries that are posited as constitutive of language, modernity, or the Symbolic Order. Informed by the works of French psychoanalytic feminist theorists such as Luce Irigaray, Helene Cixous, and Julia Kristeva, proponents of gynesis suggest that understanding the "feminine" as a particular kind of discursive effect or as the "radically repressed" provides insights into the gendered nature of subjectivity and culture. Devising analytic strategies grounded in the "feminine" also affords mechanisms to disrupt the master narratives of the Western tradition.

As an alternative to gynocriticism and gynesis, Susan Stanford Friedman (1998) draws upon the work of Latina feminist theorists such as Gloria Anzaldua, Maria Lugones, and Sonia Alvarez to develop "hybridity theory" as a frame for feminist inquiry. Particularly attuned to the matrix of differences that structures subjectivity and social formations in a globalizing world, Stanford Friedman suggests that feminist analysis informed by hybridity is better able to capture complexity and fluidity. According to Stanford Friedman (1998, 84):

> The core meaning of hybridity in contemporary cultural studies shifts among three distinct but not mutually exclusive types of cultural mixing: fusion of differences, intermingling of differences; and mixing of the always already syncretic. The first alludes to the creation of something entirely new out of the mixing of two or more distinct phenomena. The second suggests that the differences that make up the hybrid remain in play retaining some of their original character, although altered in the weaving. The third questions fundamentally the existence of pure difference and regards hybridity as the ongoing precondition of all cultural formations.

Evidence informed by hybridity theory, then, is "in process" rather than complete, interactive rather than static, shifting rather than constant, multidimensional rather than reductionist.

To capture the dynamism suggested by hybridity, Stanford Friedman (1998, 8) suggests that the unit of feminist analysis should be "narratives—whether verbal, visual, oral or written, fictional or referential, imaginary or historical—[which] constitute the primary documents of cultural expressivity." As "multiplicitous forms of meaning making," narratives are simultaneously a "window into, mirror, constructor, and symptom of culture. Cultural narratives encode and encrypt in story form the norms, values, and ideologies of the social order" (8–9). Narrative analysis then can provide insights into "the political unconscious" and the "cultural scripts around which institutions of gender, race, class, and sexuality are organized" (9). Capturing on-going contestation within cultures, narratives informed by hybridity theory also track "strategic plots of interaction and resistance as groups and individuals negotiate with and against hegemonic scripts and histories" (9). On Stanford Friedman's view, concern with narratives also reminds feminist researchers that any analysis of evidence must also be attuned to the "narrator" who relates the evidence. Awareness of narrative as "a mode of knowing that selects, organizes, orders, interprets, and allegorizes" (200–201) orients the feminist researcher toward critical interrogation of the assumptions that structure the tale. For, as feminist critics have long noted, careful attention to clues in a narrative can enable an analyst to track dimensions of bias incorporated by an "unreliable" narrator.

PHENOMENOLOGICAL ANALYSIS

Although it is undeniably the case that language is the medium through which we know and communicate our knowledge about the world, many theories guiding feminist inquiry insist that it is possible to know dimensions of existence "outside" the text. It is important to consider how these diverse theories structure perception and construe evidence.

Phenomenologists note that certain characteristics distinguish human existence from the existence of inanimate objects and other forms of organic life. Chief among these is intentional consciousness, the source of the concepts and categories that humans produce to bestow meaning on our existence. Thrown into a world of ambiguity and contingency, humans create *lebenswelt*, intersubjective "life worlds," that organize our experience, make sense of our conscious sensations, and provide the categories through which we make our action meaningful. Phenomenological analysis seeks to identify and explicate the structures of the life world constituted in and through intentional consciousness. Insisting that the life world is the domain of the "lived body" or "embodied consciousness," phenomenologists reject the mind/body dualism of Cartesian philosophy. Acknowledging the intersubjective constitution of the life world, they also reject forms of radical individualism and solipsism that deny the social constitution of lived experience.

Phenomenologists have developed a range of techniques with which to analyze the structures of meaning constitutive of the life world and embodied consciousness. *Verstehen*, the complex process by which we interpret our own actions and the actions of those with whom we interact, is perhaps the best known of these. Verstehen, a hermeneutic technique, differs from introspection and from psychological inference in important respects. As a way of understanding the "stock of knowledge at hand" that each person uses to make sense of the world, verstehen excavates the socially constituted, intersubjective conceptual frameworks acquired in the course of socialization. Because the life world is shared, it is amenable to interpretive efforts to unearth its most basic modalities. Thus phenomenologists explore how common sense is constructed and naturalized, how it structures expectations and typifications (attributions of particular properties to categories of objects), and how it lends an air of inevitability to particular modes of action. Beliefs, values, intentions, motivations, explanations that we offer for our actions and the complex assumptions that inform these forms of intentionality constitute the evidence in phenomenological analysis.

In addition to the works of certain feminist philosophers, such as Iris Young (1989), Judith Butler (1989, 2003) and Sonia Kruks (2001), who have used phenomenological analysis to explore dimensions of women's embodiment and sexuality, feminist scholars working with ethnography, ethnomethodology, interpretive sociology, and symbolic interactionism have used phenomenological techniques to examine the interactive processes through which women and men make meaning in specific social contexts, negotiate raced and gendered meanings within particular institutions and practices, and reflect upon, contest and transform naturalized assumptions of gendered embodiment and social life (Kessler and McKenna 1978; West and Fenstermaker 1995; Wolf 1996; Devault 1999).

SYSTEMIC ANALYSIS AND STRUCTURAL ANALYSIS

Certain kinds of questions cannot be answered with interpretive methods that take individual intention, intersubjective meanings, or social consciousness as their objects of analysis. For example, explanations tied to individual intentions, intersubjective meanings, or the life world of particular groups do not and cannot address unintended consequences that result from the uncoordinated actions of large numbers of people who are acting on their own concerns. Certain regularities result from individual action even though they are not intended. Consider rush hour traffic, for example, a routine and predictable effect of hundreds of thousands of workers driving to and from work on an average week day. No one intends to contribute to gridlock on the streets when getting into a car. The only intention is to get to work, but horrific traffic jams nonetheless result on a painfully regular basis. To analyze "systemic effects," such as unintended consequences, researchers must move to a different level of analysis, a level that describes large numbers of people or even whole populations.

Statistical evidence is designed to provide descriptions of populations, either on the basis of a complete count ("enumeration") or on the basis of "sampling techniques" that can be generalized to the population. Drawing upon the theory of probability, statistical analysis allows researchers to supplement their descriptive claims about populations with information concerning "levels of significance," which indicate the likelihood that the findings could have occurred by chance. Using sophisticated sampling techniques, statisticians can also provide "confidence levels" that indicate how accurately their findings can be generalized to the whole population. When statistical data is characterized as "descriptive," it is easy to assume that it provides unbiased depictions of the objective "facts." Like the other kinds of evidence considered in this chapter, however, statistical data result from a host of assumptions about what and how to count, as well as multiple interpretive judgments concerning the nature and meaning of measurement in general and the meaning of statistical results of particular studies.

Statistical analysis has enabled feminist scholars to demonstrate the existence of serious problems that traditional scholars failed to notice. Consider, for example, the Nobel Prize winning economist, Amartya Sen's "discovery" of more than one hundred million missing women around the world. Sen (1988, 1990, 1992) compared demographic data involving gendered birth rates (on average, 106 male infants are born for every 100 female infants) with current sex ratios of the population in African and Asian nations to demonstrate that there are one hundred million fewer women alive than would be expected. Sen hypothesized that the "missing women" could be explained by "mortality inequality" and "natality inequality," practices such as inadequate health care and nutrition for girls and women and female infanticide and abortion for purposes of sex selection, which grow out of and reflect cultural values that denigrate women.

Feminist scholars have also used statistical analysis to demonstrate systemic differences tied to race, class, and gender. "Structural analysis" seeks to show how race, class, and gender operate within the social systems as structural constraints, independent of the intentions of any particular agents. Consider, for example, feminist political economists' analysis of gendered aspects of changing employment patterns within the United States. During the last three decades of the twentieth century, the nature of the U.S. economy changed dramatically. Deindustrialization shifted the U.S. economy from a manufacturing powerhouse to a service economy. At the outset of the twenty-first century, 72 percent of the jobs in the United States were in the service sector; only 2.5 percent of the jobs were in farming, fishing, and forestry. While the nature of both male and female employment has changed with deindustrialization, job segregation by sex persists, and the kinds of service work that women do (for example, nursing, secretarial and clerical work, childcare, fast food) differ from the kinds of service work that men do (for example, finance and investments, marketing and public relations, funeral directors and morticians). Studies of comparable worth have documented that jobs traditionally performed by women pay 32 percent less than jobs traditionally performed by men that require comparable levels of education, responsibility, and skill. Thus feminist analysis of huge data sets involving employment in hundreds of occupational categories makes it possible to document a kind of gender-based pay inequity, which severely effects the economic well-being of women.

Statistical analysis also makes it possible to demonstrate how race and gender interact to structure inequality in the contemporary United States. For example, discussions of gender-based pay inequity are radically incomplete, if they fail to consider how race exacerbates inequalities among women as well as inequalities between women and men. According to the Bureau of Labor Statistics, white women's earnings were 78 percent of white men's earnings in 2002, while African American women's earnings were 67 percent and Latina's earnings were 54 percent of white men's earnings. For feminist scholars who seek to identify inequities so they can be redressed, evidence concerning the "intersection" of race and gender is essential for correct diagnosis of structural inequalities, and this evidence requires systematic analysis of statistical data. Demonstrating the existence of racial and gender inequalities, however, does not explain the causes of these inequalities. How much of the difference in pay is the result of racial segregation of the job force and the different kinds of work done by women of color and white women? How much can be traced to forms of racial discrimination against women of color who are working in the same occupations as white women? How much is related to region? How much pertains to part-time and temporary work as opposed to full-time, permanent employment? Do education and seniority play roles in income differences? Feminist scholars working on issues of inequality have developed sophisticated statistical models to allow detailed comparisons among women that control for the effects of a wide range of factors in order to explain dimensions of income inequality (Blau 1983, 1984; McCall 2001). Testing competing hypotheses enables these scholars to refine their diagnosis of the causes of inequality and to begin to identify strategies for social change.

The term, "feminization of poverty," was coined by feminist economists to make visible the growing concentration of poverty among women and their children in the late twentieth century (Pearce 1993). Since 1969, the incidence of poverty among adult women has grown dramatically as the incidence of poverty among adult men has declined. In 2004, 36 million U.S. citizens (7 million families), 13 percent of the population, live below the poverty line: 80 percent of the adult poor are women. As in the case of pay inequity, the analysis of poverty is radically incomplete if it fails to take race as well as gender into account. According to the U.S. Census (2002), poverty is not equally distributed across the U.S. population: 9 percent of white Americans, 23 percent of African Americans, 21 percent Latino/as, 10 percent Asian Americans, and 30 percent of Native Americans live in poverty. Poverty is particularly concentrated among single women heads-of-household, that is, among women who are raising children alone: 22 percent white, 35 percent black, 37 percent Latina, and 15 percent Asian American women heads-of-household live on incomes below the poverty line, which the federal government set at $8,890 for a single individual and $18,400 for a family of four in 2004. As in the case of pay differentials, feminist scholars use this demographic data as a starting point for investigating the factors that contribute to the concentration of poverty among single women of color who are heading households. As we will see in chapters 7 and 8, their research has dispelled multiple pernicious stereotypes and provided important information for feminist policymakers. The evidence that they have produced from systemic studies of the poor question the most fundamental assumptions about welfare recipients that have informed U.S. policymakers' decisions to abolish welfare. That this evidence did not succeed in changing the misperceptions of policymakers raises important questions about evidence blindness, which I discuss in chapter 5.

Statistical "facts" are no more "self-evident" than are the meanings of texts. Statistical evidence is constructed within theoretical frames that accredit what to count, how to count, how to measure, how to assess the validity of measurements, and the reliability and generalizability of the data collected. Supplementing traditional approaches to structural analysis that focus exclusively on class, feminist scholars have introduced race and gender as categories of structural analysis to illuminate constraints on women's lives that traditional scholarship failed to address. Although the production and analysis of statistical evidence requires very different skills than textual analysis, these skills afford feminists a means to demonstrate systemic bias, discrimination, and inequalities that have profound effects on the lives and livelihoods of contemporary women.

BEHAVIORAL ANALYSIS

Some feminist scholars use quantitative methods to investigate the beliefs, values, attitudes, and behaviors of individuals rather than to examine the demographic characteristics of whole populations. Survey research is perhaps the most popular instrument for feminist behavioral inquiry. At the most elementary level, individuals' responses to questions constitute the evidence in survey research, but that evidence can vary depending on the wording of questions, the organization of the questionnaire, the race, gender, and class of the interviewer, the manner in which the questionnaire is administered (written survey, phone survey, face-to-face interview), the salience of the questions to the respondents, and the size and randomness of the sample of respondents.

Consider, for example, attitudes toward abortion. Listening to the political rhetoric of pro-choice and anti-choice advocates, one might be led to believe that there are majorities supporting a women's right to choose to have an abortion and majorities opposed to abortion. Both sides claim to be citing surveys of "the American people." Both sides cannot possibly be right in their characterizations of public opinion on abortion, but how do listeners know whom to believe?

Two major academic surveys, the General Social Survey and the National Election Study, conducted annually in the United States for nearly thirty years, have demonstrated that attitudes toward abortion have remained largely unchanged for three decades: 22 percent believe that abortion should be legal under any circumstances; 62 percent believe that it should be legal under certain circumstances (for example, medical reasons such as fetal defect, health of the mother, and so on), and 15 percent believe that it should be illegal in all circumstances (Rand 2004; Cook, Jelen, and Wilcox 1992; Wilcox and Norrander 2001; Jehlen and Wilcox 2003). Despite the general stability of attitudes toward abortion, other research has shown that the wording of questions in particular studies does influence survey results. Jehlen and Wilcox (2003, 4) have pointed out that most abortion questions measure attitudes toward abortion in relation to the reasons a woman might seek an abortion (for example, health risks, pregnancy resulting from rape or incest; inability to support a child financially or emotionally):

> The questions ask "why" but do not ask "who, what, when, where, or how." Yet there are reasons to think that some of these other dimensions matter. One poll showed that respondents were much more willing to permit abortions for teenagers than for married career women, suggesting that citizens draw distinctions based on "who" is seeking abortion. Data from the Los Angeles Times surveys suggest that many of those who would support abortion for most circumstances in the first trimester may oppose abortions for most reasons in the second trimester, and support an outright ban in the third trimester, suggesting that "when" an abortion is performed matters. There is evidence that the public distinguishes between types of abortions, including a new distinction between medical and surgical abortions, suggesting that "how" an abortion is performed is significant. (Jehlen and Wilcox 2003, 4)

When proponents and opponents of abortion rights cite surveys, then, it is important to know exactly what question has been asked. If anti-abortion activists are citing responses to questions concerning third trimester abortions and pro-abortion activists are citing responses about first trimester abortions, they may be extracting data from the same study, but they are not measuring the same thing. It is also important to know how the survey respondents have been selected and how many have been surveyed. If anti-abortion activists are conducting surveys of church-going Americans who self-identify as Christian fundamentalists and pro-choice activists are surveying women on college campuses who call themselves feminists, then their results will vary significantly, but neither can claim that their sample represents "the American people."

Public Agenda (www.publicagenda.org), a nonpartisan opinion research organization, tracks opinion polls and provides background information to help sort out differences in public opinion due largely to wording of questions. Their data illustrate how much difference the wording of abortion questions can make. A Gallop/CNN/USA Today poll conducted in January 2003 asked the following question: "Now I am going to read some specific situations under which an abortion might be considered. For each case, please say whether you think abortion should be legal in that situation, or illegal." The following responses generated a headline entitled, "Majorities Say Abortion Should Be Legal in Some, But Not All, Circumstances": 85 percent of Americans think abortion should be legal when the woman's life is endangered; 76 percent think abortion should be legal when the pregnancy was caused by rape or incest; 56 percent think abortion should be legal when there is evidence that the baby may be physically impaired; 35 percent think abortion should be legal when the woman or family cannot afford to raise the child. By contrast, the headline "Large Majorities Favor Proposed Laws to Restrict Abortions" was published to summarize responses to the question, "Do you favor or oppose each of the following proposals?" where 88 percent of the respondents favored a law requiring doctors to inform patients about alternatives to abortion before performing the procedure; 78 percent favored a law requiring women seeking abortions to wait twenty-four hours before having the procedure done; 73 percent favored a law requiring women under eighteen to get parental consent for any abortion; 70 percent favored a law making it illegal to perform an abortion procedure conducted in the last six months of pregnancy, known as "partial birth abortion," except when necessary to save the mother's life; 38 percent favored a constitutional amendment to ban abortion in all circumstances except when necessary to save the mother's life.

Since its introduction in the 1930s, public opinion polling has developed increasingly sophisticated techniques to select representative samples of the population and to minimize bias in construction and administration of questionnaires. Responsible pollsters provide detailed information about their sampling techniques, the wording of survey questions, and the form of survey administration. Such information is essential to assessing the validity of the evidence generated by survey research.

Since the mid-1990s, one of the most charged debates about the validity of statistical evidence within feminist inquiry has focused on rape statistics. Two books published in 1994, Christine Hoff Summers's *Who Stole Feminism* and Katie Roiphe's *The Morning After*, attacked feminist research on acquaintance rape as part of larger efforts to discredit feminism. The subject of enormous media attention at the time of their publication, these texts continue to circulate and to be deployed by journalists to impugn feminist anti-rape activism. Ten years after the publication of Hoff Summers's book, for example, a student journalist at the

University of Kansas used her statistical claims to repudiate feminism. Under the headline, "Feminist Statistics Skew Issues," Arrah Nielsen (2004) proclaimed: "Feminists are good at many things: hysterical exaggeration, parroting bogus statistics, and promoting ridiculous productions like the Vagina Monologues. However, facts are not their forte." Nielsen then goes on to cite Hoff Summers's attack on the feminist "factoid" that one in four college women is raped during her college experience.

What counts as evidence lies at the heart of this controversy, which pits data collected by government agencies, the Federal Bureau of Investigation (FBI), and U.S. Bureau of Justice Statistics, against feminist survey research investigating sexual behavior on college campuses. An examination of the evidentiary bases that support the conflicting sides in this controversy can illuminate how different theoretical assumptions produce markedly different "facts."

"Forcible rape" is one of seven crime categories included in the FBI's "Crime Index," which was devised to measure trends and distribution of crime in the United States. Police Departments across the nation submit data annually for the seven crimes indexed in the Uniform Crime Reporting Program. The FBI defines "forcible rape" as "the carnal knowledge of a female forcibly and against her will." According to this definition, rape is restricted to the forced penetration of a woman's vagina by a man's penis. Penetration of other orifices (mouth or anus) does not count as rape. Penetration by objects other than a penis (bottles, broom handles, sticks) does not count as rape. Statutory rape, which the law defines as sexual intercourse involving an individual under the age of consent, does not count as rape. Moreover, according to this definition, only women can be raped.

The Uniform Crime Reporting Program collects information only about crimes that are either reported to the police at the time they are committed or witnessed by a police officer. In instances of reported crimes, police are asked to submit data to the FBI only on crimes that are "founded." If the police do not believe a victim's claim or consider it impossible to prove the victim's claim, then the report is considered "unfounded" and is not included among the official statistics submitted to the FBI. The Uniform Crime Reporting Program is voluntary, and some police departments choose not to submit data. For this reason, the FBI generates "estimates" for its index crimes by extrapolating from the data submitted to the national population.

On the basis of Uniform Crime Report data, the FBI estimated that 72 of every 100,000 women in the U.S. was raped in 1994, the year that Hoff Summers and Roiphe launched their attack on feminist rape statistics. But the FBI also acknowledged that this figure was unlikely to be an accurate count of rapes because the Uniform Crime Report data defines rape more narrowly than most state laws do and because rape is one of the least reported crimes. Indeed, the FBI estimates that only 37 percent of rapes are reported to the police; the Department of Justice estimates that only 26 percent of rapes are reported to law enforcement officials; and the National Women's Study conducted by the National Victim Center and the Crime Victim Research and Treatment Center found that only 16 percent of rape victims reported their assault to the police.

The extent of the inaccuracy in the FBI statistics caused by underreporting of rape and the excessively narrow definition of rape used in the Uniform Crime Reports can be illuminated by a comparison with data gathered in the National Crime Victimization Survey conducted by the Bureau of Justice Statistics in the U.S. Department of Justice in conjunction with the U.S. Census Bureau. Last conducted in 2000 through a telephone survey of 159,420 individuals over twelve years of age, the National Crime Victimization Survey also gathers information about a range of crimes, including rape. The definition of rape used in this survey is considerably broader than that used by the FBI and is not restricted to women: "carnal knowledge through the use of force or threat of force, including attempts." In 1994, the National Crime Victimization Survey calculated that 433,000 rapes were committed (Greenfield 1997). Whereas FBI estimates suggested one of every 1,388 American woman was raped; the National Crime Victimization Survey indicated one of every 270 women and one of every 5,000 men over the age of twelve was raped in 1994. According to the National Crime Victimization Surveys, the incidence of rape has been declining in the U.S., falling from 433,000 in 1994 to 383,000 in 1999 and to 261,000 in 2000. During the same period, the FBI reports that the incidence of forcible rapes has been increasing, while other violent crimes have been decreasing.

Although the National Crime Victimization Survey (NCVS) data calls the accuracy of the FBI data into question, other researchers have raised questions about the reliability of the rape statistics generated by the NCVS. Reliance upon telephone interviews has been a particular concern. How likely is it that a rape victim will be willing to confide intimate information to a stranger over the phone when other members of the household may be present? Absence of privacy and trust may contribute to underreporting (Koss 1996). Some researchers have also questioned whether the sample size of the National Crime Victimization Survey is large enough to support generalizations to the whole population (RAINN 2004).

Feminist discussions of rape initially emerged in the context of consciousness raising groups in the early 1970s, where women began sharing stories of coercion in intimate relationships. Keenly aware that the dynamics of coercion they discussed differed significantly from popular conceptions of stranger rape, which often occurred in public spaces (streets, parking lots, libraries, stores, bars) at gunpoint, knifepoint, or accompanied by severe physical brutality, feminists generated a new definition of rape: intercourse without consent. Occurring within marriages and long-term relationships as well as in the context of short-term dating relations and "one-night stands," nonconsensual sex typically took place in the home, in workplaces, and in college residence halls. Feminist activists politicized this form of violation by situating it in a larger context of male power and domination. They created rape crisis centers and rape hot lines to afford women new ways to find assistance. Feminist "rape relief" efforts began to generate new kinds of evidence about rape and about the treatment of rape in the criminal justice system. "Acquaintance rape" appeared far more prevalent than stranger rape, and police seemed far less inclined to take reports of acquaintance rape seriously. As evidence of acquaintance rape grew, feminists mobilized to change the definition of rape in state criminal statutes and to change police, hospital, and court procedures to ensure victims of acquaintance rape access to the criminal justice system.

Feminist anti-rape activism on college and university campuses developed in the context of larger feminist mobilizations to change the legal system to reflect women's needs, interests, experiences, and concerns and to change cultural values to recognize women's bodily integrity. Feminists working in campus counseling centers, student life offices, residence halls, and on faculty began to collect data on reports of acquaintance rape from students. Early studies conducted at Auburn University and Cornell University generated alarming figures. When asked "Have you ever had sexual intercourse without your consent?" 21 percent of undergraduate women students said "Yes"; 25 percent reported that they had been "subjected to forms of restraint to get sex"; and 25 percent reported that they had been slapped, hit, beaten, or threatened with a knife to get sex (Burkhardt 1983; Sherman 1985). National studies of college women produced similar findings (Russell and Howell 1983; Koss, Harvey, and Butcher 1987; Koss 1992a, 1992b, 1993). As awareness of the high incidence of rape on college campuses grew, so too did feminist efforts to change university policies concerning reporting procedures, on-campus investigations of rape allegations, student judiciary board procedures for handling complaints, and appropriate punishments for students guilty of rape. Many feminists also developed rape prevention programs for students.

Evidence from campus counseling centers, rape hot lines, and rape prevention programs, and survey research also indicated that college-age women often struggled to make sense of their experiences of coerced sex. Knowing that their encounters had not involved a stranger or a severe beating, many young women did not think that their experience fit the cultural script for the crime of rape. While they were quite certain that they had not consented to have sex and that their partners ignored their wishes, they did not think that police or university officials would take their word seriously if they filed a rape charge. After all, they had agreed to go out with the man who attacked them. To test how widespread such confusion about coerced sex was, some feminist researchers began including two different questions on their surveys of college students: Have you ever been raped? Have you ever been forced to have sex against your will? Responses to these surveys routinely indicate that far more students (19–27 percent) report having had sex against their will than report having been raped (2–5 percent) (Burkhardt 1983; Russell and Howell 1983; Koss, Harvey, and Butcher 1987). In accordance with the feminist definition of rape as intercourse without consent, both groups of respondents have experienced rape.

When feminist rape statistics are discredited by simple appeal to government statistics, competing theories of women, power, and social relations are at stake. In a period when cynicism about the government runs particularly high, the notion that government evidence is reliable and feminist evidence suspect is fueled by far more than trust in government. Beyond the specific interest of conservative groups (like the Olin Foundation, which funded Hoff Sommers research) to roll back the clock to a prefeminist era, many popular misconceptions about knowledge sustain the support for "official" statistics. Traditional claims concerning "value-neutral" inquiry collide with feminist avowals of emancipatory politics. Naïve assumptions about the "self-evidence" of "facts" collide with post-positivist understandings of the theoretical constitution of facticity. Lack of familiarity with complex strategies of knowledge production leaves the public unaware of the manifold interpretive decisions that inform every statistical measurement. "Evidence blindness," then, can be bolstered by multiple factors, a topic that is taken up in chapter 5.

Awareness of the complex questions surrounding evidence is vitally important for feminist scholars. As the discussions of textual analysis, phenomenological analysis, structural analysis, and behavioral analysis in this chapter make clear, competing theoretical assumptions accredit markedly different tokens of truthfulness. If right-wing pundits are not to succeed in their efforts to dismiss feminist scholarship as "femi-nazi" propaganda, then feminist researchers must develop enormous theoretical sophistication. If, as Alessandra Tanesini (1999, 243) has suggested, "the fight against oppression requires that we distinguish between knowledge and what people mistakenly believe to be knowledge," a thorough grasp of antifoundationalist understandings of evidence is a critical part of feminist researchers' arsenal.

Chapter 5   Evidence Blindness

W HAT EXACTLY IS "evidence blindness"? Is evidence blindness, as the analogy with sightlessness suggests, a matter of physical incapacity? Or, as Anthony Appiah (1992) has argued, is it a matter of "cognitive" incapacity? Do certain methodological assumptions actively foster evidence blindness? Following the efforts of antifoundationalists to move away from visual metaphors for knowledge, is evidence blindness better understood as a failure to grasp the complex relation between theories and the evidence they accredit? Is evidence blindness among feminist scholars and activists different from evidence blindness among nonfeminists or antifeminists? Can an astute understanding of evidence blindness reveal additional dimensions of the politics of knowledge? Can feminist scholars devise analytic strategies to counter evidence blindness?

The problem of evidence blindness is seldom addressed in mainstream discussions of methodology within the social sciences and the natural sciences. Notions that knowledge is "discovered" and truth "revealed" through systematic observation and testing mitigate against the possibility that some people might actively resist "evidence." Conversely, some postmodernist arguments, which suggest that knowledge is sheer "invention," rule out the possibility that "compelling evidence" exists; hence there is no need for resistance. This chapter seeks to demonstrate that, for good reason, feminists attend to the problem of evidence blindness. Awareness of the contentiousness of theories, coupled with an understanding of the role that theories play in structuring perception, analysis, and explanation, provides feminist researchers clues about the nature of evidence blindness and strategies to begin to redress it. In addition, the political commitments of feminist scholarship, combined with ethical concerns to avoid objectifying research practices, make it imperative that feminist researchers carefully track the circulation of power in theoretically structured accounts of the world.

To illustrate the scope of the problem, this chapter considers a number of examples of evidence blindness. It also examines various explanations of evidence blindness advanced in the context of critical race theory, social science claims concerning competing levels of analysis, sociology of knowledge, and arguments concerning strategic discourse. After identifying problems with these diverse explanatory efforts, chapter 5 explores how the antifoundationalist conception of knowledge provides richer resources for comprehending and countering evidence blindness. Exploring forms of evidence blindness that have surfaced in feminist scholarship, as well as in nonfeminist research, the chapter attempts to show how theoretically accredited concepts and frames of analysis can mask dimensions of power. Openly contesting tacit theoretical assumptions, then, should be a standard methodological practice for feminists who want to disrupt dominant power hierarchies.

Competing Explanations of Evidence Blindness

In his discussion of extrinsic racism, Anthony Appiah (1992) introduces the problem of evidence blindness as a manifestation of a "cognitive incapacity," an inability to perceive evidence contrary to one's beliefs. Extrinsic racism, one form of racism, involves empirical claims about the physical characteristics as well as the intellectual and moral abilities of members of particular races, which should be amenable to empirical refutation. The issue that Appiah probes in his discussion of evidence blindness is the apparent refusal of many racists to accept empirical evidence that impugns their racist beliefs. Feminist scholars have pointed to a similar problem with people who seem incapable of accepting refutations of sexist claims about women and men.

Recent policy debates concerning affirmative action and welfare "reform" provide useful examples of evidence blindness. Despite the continuing underrepresentation and underutilization of women and people of color in positions of high power, pay, and prestige, despite numerous studies documenting race and sex bias in evaluation, and despite "job audits" that demonstrate discrimination in hiring, opponents of affirmative action insist that no discrimination exists in the contemporary United States. (See chapter 7 for a fuller elaboration of this view.) Despite demographic data from the U.S. census indicating that the majority of the poor in the United States are under age eighteen, over age sixty-five, or working in paid employment outside the home, and despite more than twenty-five years of studies that prove that poor Americans are as firmly committed to the work ethic as are middle-class Americans, welfare "reformers" continue to appeal to the pathological theory of poverty as the "problem" that social welfare policy needs to address. On this view, the real "cause" of poverty lies in the attitudes and characteristics of the poor, in a "mindset" that seeks a "prepaid life-time vacation plan," to borrow the words of former President Ronald Reagan. (See chapters 7 and 8 for additional dimensions of this debate.)

How can we make sense of such evidence blindness? Although he worries about the policy implications of his view, Appiah hints at a psychological explanation; he suggests that racism so systematically deforms the psyche that a racist's ability to integrate new information into his or her cognitive framework is literally impaired. While the intransigence of racism pushes Appiah to ponder psychological impairment, he is keenly aware of the difficulties with such an explanatory framework. If the racist's evidence blindness is construed as a form of mental incapacity, how does one explain people who repudiate virulent racism after years of propounding it? If some people can repudiate racism, why can't others? What would be the appropriate policy response to racists who appear incapable of changing their mistaken views? Are they a threat to society? Should they be placed within institutions to shield the public from the harms they could do? Is this form of cognitive incapacity a crime? How would criminalizing a cognitive incapacity fit with constitutional guarantees of freedom of thought and freedom of speech? If juridical solutions for evidence blindness seem incompatible with basic liberties, does medicine offer better options for addressing this putative psychological defect? Should those who manifest evidence blindness be subjected to mandatory treatment? If so, what treatment will fix a cognitive incapacity? Medicalization of evidence blindness seems every bit as problematic as criminalization. That both strategies are fraught with dangers associated with "normalization" constitutes sufficient reason for searching for other explanations of evidence blindness that move away from medico-juridical accounts (Foucault 1977).

Mainstream approaches to social science provide a number of possible explanations for evidence blindness. Some social scientists might suggest that evidence blindness stems from a classic problem involving differing levels of analysis. For example, proponents of the pathological theory of poverty appeal to anecdotal evidence. Claims about the "welfare queen" and her omnipresent "cadillac" may be drawn from isolated instances that capture the imagination so powerfully that they overwhelm impersonal quantitative data. When coupled with acknowledgment that aggregate statistics do not govern any individual case, proponents of the pathological theory of poverty have the makings of a reasonable explanation for refusing to "perceive" evidence that challenges their views about the poor. The problem with the conflicting levels of analysis hypothesis, however, is that it accredits the existence of the anecdotal welfare queen. Thus it may be an instance of, rather than an explanation of, evidence blindness.

Karl Mannheim's (1936) conception of the sociology of knowledge provides an alternative account of evidence blindness. The sociology of knowledge accepts the post-positivist premise that all knowledge is socially and linguistically mediated, but it adds to that premise a theory of social determination. Indeed the sociology of knowledge suggests that all knowledge—ideas, ideology, ethical beliefs, philosophical, scientific, historical claims—is determined by particular social relations, which Mannheim tied to membership in specific class-based, occupational, generational, religious, racial, and ethnic groups. Within this framework, evidence blindness might be understood as a form of cognitive immunity afforded by membership in a particular race and class at a particular moment in time. Literally, one's group membership would make it impossible for one to perceive certain evidence. Even if one is willing to ignore the epistemic relativism that plagues the sociology of knowledge, there are reasons to question this account of evidence blindness. Many proponents of diametrically opposed views on affirmative action, for example, have virtually identical race and class backgrounds (African American twin brothers, Shelby and Charles Steele, for example), while some who share the same view have radically different race and class backgrounds (Clarence Thomas and George Will, for example). The sociology of knowledge cannot explain either such profound differences in opinion within a membership group or the shared views across disparate groups. Nor can it explain how group membership "blinds." The actual mechanics of the posited cognitive immunity remain untheorized and unspecified. Moreover, the notion that ideas are "determined" by group characteristics suffers from all the defects discussed in relation to the "commodification model" in chapter 3.

Evidence blindness might also be explained as an instance of strategic discourse. On this view, differing political views, policy stances, and racist and sexist ideas are articulated for partisan political advantage; as such, they should be understood as nothing more than manipulative ploys. If this cynical explanation is correct, then the "problem of evidence blindness" disappears. At issue are not conflicting beliefs and knowledge claims, but exercises in strategic manipulation. To shore up this hypothesis, some might appeal to Tanya Melich's (1996) account of the U.S. Republican Party's thirty-year "Southern strategy," a campaign that used racism as a wedge to woo white, blue-color voters to Republican ranks. While such a cynical interpretation may afford some solace to critics, it remains at great remove from the self-understandings of many involved in recent policy debates, those who are convinced of the validity of their views and who would bristle at the charge of strategic manipulation.

Certain conceptions of knowledge push analysts toward cynical explanations, which make the problem of evidence blindness disappear. As we have seen, naïve versions of empiricism suggest that the mind as a mirror accurately reflects objects in the external world (Watkins 1957; Rorty 1979). But if minds faithfully record and store objective depictions of all that happens, error becomes difficult to explain without resorting to a cynical imputation of manipulative motives. J.W.N. Watkins (1957, 95) pointed out long ago that certain versions of empiricism give rise to a "conspiracy theory of error." "A certain intolerance of error is implicit in . . . empiricism as classically formulated. . . . It implies that if two people are in serious factual or moral disagreement, at least one of them must be either the direct or indirect victim of someone else's willful deception or a willful deceiver." On this view, evidence blindness, a ruse for deceit, marks the "will to power" that manipulates, lies, distorts, and misrepresents in order to promote a particular agenda. While the intransigence of evidence blindness may make a conspiracy theory of error attractive, it also offers too facile an account. Relying on a mistaken account of knowledge, the conspiracy theory of error explains away a problem that it is important to take seriously. It also shifts debate away from investigation of the substantive merits of particular claims and interrogation of the assumptions and reasons that support particular views to the unmasking of the motives of claimants, assertions of the putative social, psychological, economic, sexual, racial forces that "cause" belief, or allegations concerning the individual, group, or social functions the belief serves. Although questions concerning motives, functions, and interests are worthy of investigation, they do not exhaust the possible explanations for evidence blindness.

Previous chapters have enumerated the defects of naïve empiricist accounts, which mistakenly assume that the mind is passive and that observation is direct and unmediated. They have pointed out the critical role of language, culture, and theory in structuring perception and cognition. The multiple mediations of knowledge that stem from language, culture, society, history, and complex theories about the world provide much richer resources for understanding problems of evidence blindness. The antifoundationalist conception of cognition as a human practice suggests that evidence blindness may stem from tacit assumptions that structure perceptions, tacit assumptions that make some things appear normal, natural, unquestionable, given. Precisely because these assumptions are widely shared, they insulate beliefs from critical scrutiny.

Efforts to "denaturalize" conventional modes of thinking and interrogate what is most taken for granted have been hallmarks of feminist inquiry. These analytic strategies also provide a means to engage evidence blindness constructively. Rather than assuming that evidence is manifest, that facts speak for themselves; feminist analysis begins from the premise of plurality by acknowledging the existence of multiple perspectives, the partiality and incompleteness of accounts, and the role of theories in structuring perception and cognition. By examining tacit presuppositions of alternative accounts, feminist inquiry helps make visible sources of error overlooked by mainstream approaches and probes how such errors may preclude perception of evidence advanced within alternate theoretical frameworks.

Approaching evidence blindness with a sophisticated understanding of the complex interaction of theoretical assumptions, social values, and discipline-specific methods in the constitution of facticity enables feminist inquiry to examine dimensions of contention over evidence within interdisciplinary feminist scholarship, as well as problems of evidence blindness that surface outside feminist scholarship. Attention to value-laden presuppositions that structure perception and cognition, but which are open to interrogation, critical reflection, and change, provides an alternative way to understand and to begin to address problems of evidence blindness. This approach is of particular import in addressing issues of racism, ethnocentrism, and "the politics or representation" within feminist scholarship. It also helps chart dimensions of the politics of knowledge that mainstream approaches render invisible.

The following sections examine particular aspects of evidence blindness that surface within and outside feminist research. Rather than resting content with reductionist accounts of evidence blindness that allude to an "inability to perceive," which lies beyond possible redress, the following sections identify feminist techniques to dispel evidence blindness. To return to the "blindness" metaphor one more time, the remaining sections suggest that exclusive reliance on physical explanations may actually preclude identification of corrective analytic strategies. Very different causes can produce sightlessness. An individual may not be able to perceive something because retinal damage or nerve damage to the eye makes it physically impossible to do so. Contextual factors may also interfere with sight, however. Absence of light may make it impossible to see; or too much light may "blind" one, as in the case of brilliant sunlight occluding other stars in the sky. Angle of vision may block perception as does the driver's "blind spot" in an automobile. Lack of relevant background information may make it impossible to make sense of certain visual stimuli. Lack of attentiveness may keep one from noticing things that seem manifest to others. Politically freighted theoretical assumptions may direct one's perception in a particular way, by accrediting some evidence, while masking other facets of events. Keeping multiple explanatory possibilities in play and considering the different implications of each for strategies of redress can help feminist researchers think creatively about the complexities of evidence blindness, while avoiding unnecessary resignation to intractable problems of knowledge.

Theoretical Expectations and the Politics of Representation

The politics of representation has been and continues to be central to feminist activism and scholarship. Political contestations concerning the claims made on behalf of women, the conditions under which such claims are made, who makes the claims, for whom they are made, and whose interests are served by particular

articulations of women's needs and interests have been a staple of feminist debates both inside and outside of the academy. Consider, for example, the continuing contestation over the term, "Third World women." The depiction of
Third World women as a "singular monolithic subject" by Western feminist
scholars has been problematized by postcolonial feminist theorists who rightly
point out that the "Third World" includes more than one hundred nations with
very different histories, traditions, languages, and cultures (example, Mohanty
1991; Grewel and Kaplan 1994; John 1996). Concern with accuracy and analytic
rigor, then, would seem to warrant abandoning such a vague and homogenizing
rubric for the majority of the world's population. Other scholars, particularly in
the social sciences, have also argued for abandoning references to the "Third
World," but for very different reasons. In the aftermath of the Cold War and the
end of a clear demarcation between capitalist ("First World") and socialist
("Second World") spheres of influence, the nonaligned movement of nations advocating a "third alternative" has lost its geographic and ideological purchase.
Alternative efforts to classify significant differences among nations have generated distinctions between North/South, minority world/majority world, and the
West/LACAAP countries (Latin America, Caribbean, Africa, Asia, and the Pa-
cific). Although some categories are needed to capture important regional economic and political differences, these scholars suggest that the category, Third
World, no longer serves a useful analytical purpose. Fully cognizant of these two
sets of critiques, some feminist scholars have nonetheless attempted to defend
the category, "Third World Women." The term has been embraced by some feminist scholars and activists as their preferred descriptor for an "imagined community," comprising women of color in the global South, as well as "internally
colonized" women of color within the North (Sandoval 2000; Corradi 2001;
Kabeer 2003). As a self-chosen identification then, Third World women can
imply both postcolonial politics and transnational solidarity. Indeed, some
scholars have argued that "the use of the term Third World women helps Westerners to recognize the nature of women's struggle against poverty and oppression and stimulates efforts to theorize pernicious social processes that
differentiate women" (Chapoval 2001, 148).

     Whether feminist scholars abandon or reclaim the Third World women cat-
egory, their choices reflect political decisions. Each descriptive locution noted
above is enmeshed in a politics of representation of enormous import to knowledge production. The discursive choices made by particular scholars encompass
complex political issues about how to demarcate diversity and commonality,
how to circumscribe "center" and "periphery," how to make certain power relations visible, how to render other power relations invisible. Far from capturing a
manifest truth, differently constructed categories lie at the heart of the politics
of knowledge. Familiarity with the theoretical issues that fuel these contestations

is important for feminist scholars who wish to avoid replicating errors that have haunted feminism since the nineteenth century.

The politics of representation was initially introduced to the feminist agenda by voices from the margin speaking in their own behalf. African American women contested the priorities and lack of inclusiveness of movements led by white women's rights activists in the nineteenth and twentieth centuries in the United States. Feminists of color within the academy challenged pervasive biases in scholarship done by white women about white women that failed to mark the specificity of their analyses. Lesbian feminists challenged homophobia and heteronormativity in second wave feminism and in women's studies research. "Third World women" repudiated the racial, ethnic, nationalist, and class biases circulating in transnational feminist networks and in academic analyses of women in the global South.

These frequent and recurrent contestations might be considered classic instances of "subaltern speech." As articulations of those who have been oppressed by particular forms of racist, colonizing practices, they raise questions of power and privilege, inclusion and exclusion of great import for feminist activism and inquiry. According to Gayatri Spivak (1988), one defining characteristic of subaltern speech is that it has not been heard by the privileged and the powerful who participate in colonization. Although evidence blindness deploys visual metaphors to illuminate a particular problem of knowledge, Spivak's conception of subaltern speech uses an aural metaphor to somewhat similar effect. But Spivak draws explicit attention to theoretical frameworks such as orientalism and colonialism that allow those in power not to listen by sustaining a conviction that the subaltern have nothing to say. Thus Spivak identifies a methodological concern and a strategy to engage it. She asks feminists to consider the most basic theoretical underpinnings of our research, to explore how tacit assumptions can make it difficult to grasp alternative worldviews. By engaging theoretical frameworks that call privilege into question, Spivak suggests that feminist researchers may be able to heighten the sophistication of their knowledge production.

"AR'N'T I A WOMAN?"

Working within very different analytic traditions, feminist scholars Helen Longino (1990) and Gayatri Spivak (1988) call attention to the manifold ways that social values infiltrate theoretical frameworks. Precisely because these social values are shared, they are deeply camouflaged within theories that are used to describe and explain the world. Shielded from scrutiny by their very familiarity, such contentious assumptions might be said to be "hidden" in plain sight. Feminist scholarship is not insulated from this problem, but the transformative objectives of feminist inquiry make efforts to address it particularly important. An example drawn from Nell Painter's historical investigations of abolitionist and "woman rights" activist, Sojourner Truth, may help to illuminate the stakes in the methodological challenges raised by evidence blindness.

Feminist activists and scholars seeking to illuminate the politics of representation have often taken the words of Sojourner Truth, "Ar'n't I a Woman?" as their point of departure (hooks 1981; Riley 1988; Maracle 1996; G. Mink 1999). The figure of a strong, formerly enslaved, black woman who embodies the simultaneity of oppressions seems the perfect icon to challenge racist and classbased norms of womanhood and to interrogate the comprehensiveness of an agenda articulated by privileged white women. Nell Painter (1996, 174) has pointed out that Sojourner Truth exemplifies the politics of representation at another level as well. For "every word about Truth comes from a white person." Tracing the production of Sojourner Truth as a cultural symbol, Painter demonstrates that various white authors generated representations of Truth at great remove from the historical subject who was named Isabella Van Wagenen at birth and who later reinvented herself as Sojourner Truth. Certain racist characteristics of the nineteenth-century depictions of Truth within abolitionist and feminist circles are particularly noteworthy, for they foreshadow dynamics that continue to haunt Western feminist discourses, namely, the production of racialized otherness through white ventriloquism that silences the voices of women of color.

Sojourner Truth (1797–1883) was a native-born American whose experience of slavery occurred on a farm in upstate New York. Although her first language was Dutch, she took pride in her mastery of English, which served as the vehicle for her success in her chosen profession, itinerant preacher. Harriet Beecher Stowe had met and conversed with her fellow American, Sojourner Truth, yet when she published the article in *Atlantic Monthly* that made Sojourner a celebrity, she chose to portray Sojourner Truth as "a native African," a "product of the desert, Sahara." She also characterized Sojourner as a "wild savage," who had been tamed by the power of Christianity. Contrasting Sojourner with former slaves like Frederick Douglass, who called upon blacks to fight for their freedom, Beecher Stowe depicted Truth as a proponent of nonviolence, who followed the Christian doctrine of forgiveness and left it to "God to right the most heinous wrongs" (Painter 1996, 154–160). Stripped of her nationality, her native tongue, and her anger, Beecher Stowe's fictive Sojourner is at once exoticized and domesticated, produced as a comforting black presence that bears no animosity toward her oppressors and prefers to trust in the inherent goodness of a "Christian people."

Frances Dana Gage also participated in the production of the Sojourner Truth of feminist fame. Indeed, according to Nell Painter (1996, 169–173), Gage, writing from South Carolina, accorded Truth a pronounced Southern accent and penned the phrase, "Ar'n't I a Woman," which has become synonymous with Sojourner's name. In appropriating and embellishing a speech that Sojourner Truth delivered in Ohio, Gage sought to link the causes of abolitionism and feminism, causes that Sojourner supported. But by recasting Sojourner's words in a black dialect typical of South Carolina, Gage also molded Truth to fit a form of Blackness particularly suited to northern U.S. interests. In contrast with Truth's experience of slavery in a northern state, Gage's rendition of Sojourner's voice locates slavery as a southern institution, thereby exculpating the North from its complicity in the creation and preservation of slavery and positioning northern abolitionists as the saviors of enslaved peoples.

The transformations of Sojourner Truth's life and words at the hands of white women writers, whose racialized depictions produce a black woman acceptable to white audiences, manifest many of the most problematic characteristics of the politics of representation within feminism. Privileged white women with access to the media frame a discourse according to their understanding of what is at issue and what must be done. Substituting their own thoughts and words for those of a black itinerant preacher, they produce an "authentic" oppressed character, that is, one who conforms to the expectations the dominant have of the oppressed. The very act of rhetorical substitution exacerbates inequalities, silences the views of the oppressed, distorts the thoughts of the subaltern speaker, denies her ability to analyze her situation and prescribe appropriate remedies. The colonizing impulse that casts the white Westerner as savior even as it masks the colonizer's production of the structures and relations of oppression is also very much in evidence.

How do feminists begin to deal with the weight of evidence provided by Nell Painter's careful scholarship? How do we respond to the racism in the appropriations of Truth by white abolitionists and feminists? The response has not been what Nell Painter expected. She reports multiple instances of evidence blindness on the part of her audiences and students when she delivered lectures on the racist production of claims about Sojourner Truth. Rather than outrage at the racism, she more often encounters a willed refusal to accept her evidence and arguments.

In *Sojourner Truth: A Life, A Symbol*, Painter combines scrupulous historical analysis with discursive and semiotic analysis to distinguish certain features of the life of the nineteenth-century historical subject, Sojourner Truth, from the manifold cultural appropriations of that life by political activists in the nineteenth and twentieth centuries. She demonstrates how it is possible to identify errors and distortions in assertions by Gage and Beecher Stowe, even if it is not possible to know "what Truth might actually have said" (1996, 281). Painter points out that "historians have criteria for deciding which documents to trust" (282), and she carefully explicates the complex criteria she used to separate Truth's biography from iconographic narratives that circulated about her. By tracing the cultural appropriations of Truth to specific abolitionist and feminist campaigns in the nineteenth century and to black power and feminist campaigns in the twentieth century, Painter also offers some rich speculations concerning an enduring preference for the symbol over the historic person among some students of color and some feminist students and scholars. Grappling with a profound form of evidence blindness that leads some students and scholars to prefer a racialized representation tied to the political interests of white activists over compelling claims about an historic figure who engaged in self-invention as well as political activism, Painter alludes to the complex role that symbols play in the racist ideologies and antiracist counterideologies that circulate in American culture.

This instance of evidence blindness involves far more than "facts" or human perceptual equipment. At issue are worldviews absorbed in childhood, which include theories about race, gender, religion, class, and the prospects for social change spearheaded by a lone, "self-made" individual who struggles against the dominant system. At issue are competing theories about how racism works, how it can be combated, and how convictions about these issues help one "to get through life" (Painter 1996, 287). To treat evidence blindness in the context of the politics of representation as a matter of misperception, deception, or as a function of the will to power is to miss the underlying theoretical issues about race, racism, and the American mythos in contemporary life. One great virtue of Nell Painter's scholarship is that she illuminates the complexity of the issues at stake, demonstrates how differing methodological approaches (historical, discursive, semiotic) inform markedly different interpretations of Sojourner Truth, and creates the opportunity for critical reflection on the difficult methodological, theoretical, and social issues that underlie an apparent perceptual malfunction. Painter's scholarship also makes clear why feminist scholars must attend to discourse, to the registers of language and value that structure theoretical arguments. While naivete about "value-free" inquiry or purely "descriptive" language allows the politics of knowledge production to proceed unmarked and unchecked, Painter's excavation of and direct engagement with the underlying theoretical issues shows feminist researchers how to begin to address the "whole set of defects left over from childhood" (Fanon 1967, 10).

Ignorance, Sanctioned Ignorance, and Ventriloquism

Nell Painter's analysis of the writings of Harriet Beecher Stowe and Frances Dana Gage documents two instances in which white women writers put words into the mouth of Sojourner Truth in order to advance causes that they mutually supported. Feminist activists and scholars from the global South have suggested that similar forms of "ventriloquism" have been a staple of interactions between women from the North and women from the South during the decades of transnational feminist mobilization since 1975. This section examines debates over the priorities of global feminism to explore dimensions of evidence blindness that are perhaps best understood as "sanctioned ignorance," blind spots constructed by cultural beliefs that render aspects of neocolonial power relations invisible.

Since 1975, the United Nations has created multiple sites for transnational feminist encounters through its four World Conferences on Women (Mexico 1975, Copenhagen 1980, Nairobi 1985, Beijing 1995), its Conferences on Human Rights (Vienna 1993), Population and Development (Cairo 1994), and its Conference Against Racism, Racial Discrimination, Xenophobia, and Related Intolerance (Durban 2001). The continuing activities of the UN Development Program, UNIFEM, the Commission on the Status of Women, and the Conference of NGOs in Consultative Relationship to the Economic and Social Council of the UN (CONGO) also constitute key venues for feminist mobilization and strategic negotiation. Although the platforms for action produced in these forums suggest a global feminist consensus, "the dominance of the voices of the First World women in articulating their version of the problems and priorities of Third World women frequently led to acrimonious debates in a number of international forums" (Kabeer 2003, 31; see also A. Fraser 1987). For example, the 1975 International Women's Conference generated the "World Plan of Action," which has been characterized as a "bold women's agenda to achieve equality between the sexes within the context of changed relations between North and South" (Maguire 1984, 12). While the language of the World Plan reflects multiple compromises among participants at the Conference, the privileged place accorded to "equality between the sexes" indicates the dominance of Western feminist conceptions of women's interests. "Equality," a normative ideal with strong ties to the American and French revolutions, does not have the same meaning or cultural purchase in nations whose histories have been marked by colonization and imperialism.

Contestation over the worthiness of "equality" as a transnational feminist priority has been a staple of global feminism for more than three decades. Coalitions of feminists from nations of the South took issue with the formulation of priorities during the 1975 World Conference on Women and postcolonial feminist scholars have reiterated their substantive concerns in numerous publications. As documented by the Association of African Women for Research and Development (AAWORD 1982, 101), Third World women "rejected the approach of Western women who insist on prioritizing problems of inequality between the sexes as the fundamental issue facing all women." DAWN (Development Alternatives with Women for a New Era), a network of feminist activists, researchers, and policymakers from African, Asian, Caribbean, and Latin American nations, pointed out that throughout the 1960s and 1970s, "the dissonant voices of poor women from racially or nationally oppressed groups could be heard stating their priorities—food, housing, jobs, services, and the struggle against racism. Equality with men who themselves suffer unemployment, low wages, poor work conditions and racism within the existing socioeconomic structures did not seem an adequate or worthy goal" (Sen and Grown 1987, 24–25).

Although women from the South have argued their positions vociferously in transnational feminist conferences, their arguments seem to fall on "deaf ears." Rather than hearing and engaging the substantive claims of Third World women, many Western feminists have fallen into the "ventriloquist's fantasy" (John 1996, 22) in making claims for and about "women," projecting a white, Western voice and view onto a silenced subaltern subject. As with other instances of evidence blindness, however, it is a mistake to construe the problem exclusively in terms of how information fails to be "received" or "comprehended" by certain listeners. For the competing theoretical assumptions underlying this transnational exchange involve not only "sound insulation," but a process of information substitution. The ventriloquism metaphor is designed to capture the way that some white, Western feminist activists and scholars substitute their own views for the views articulated by some women of the South.

Within the context of American feminism, Audre Lorde (1984) pointed out that such "silencing of Black women is not just an omission, it is part of the oppression." Similarly, Chandra Mohanty, Ann Russo, and Lourdes Torres (1991, 52–55) characterized these forms of "ethnocentric universalism" as a mode of structural domination that suppresses the heterogeneity of women in the global South. Convinced of the merits of their own views, some Western feminists replicate patterns of Western hegemony by exercising influence beyond their geographic and national borders, selectively permeating the boundaries of other nation-states and other women's lives (John 1996, 16). Conflating the interests of some North American and European women with the interests of all women, some transnational feminist activists and scholars from the North create and exacerbate inequalities. Applying Western concepts and frameworks to the global South, some Western feminists seem unaware of how poorly their theories "travel" and of the dangers of forcing women in the South into these ill-fitting and oppressive molds. It is important to interrogate this lack of awareness. It cannot be explained as a problem of ignorance pure and simple. For the Western feminists who have participated in multiple transnational conferences, "ignorance" should be dispelled when feminists of the South eloquently articulate their own priorities for feminist action and advance their cogent critiques of Western feminist positions. Closer examination of some competing theoretical assumptions informing these debates can illuminate factors that produce and accredit evidence blindness.

In addition to the emphasis on gender equality and the apparent indifference to the structural asymmetries within and between nations, many Western feminists have retained a "persistent faith in the reformability of a market-led development process" (Kabeer 2003, 32; V. Taylor 2000). Despite the evidence of the deteriorating conditions of the majority of women in the South after four decades of "development," many Western feminists remain convinced that women's liberation remains closely linked to "modernization," which they construe in terms of the experiences of Western nations. Drawing upon the experiences of affluent white women who sought to escape the constraints of "homemaking" careers, Western "liberal" feminists assume "that liberation hinges on work outside the home" (G. Mink 1999, 182), on "opportunities for paid work in the formal sector" (Giele 2001, 181), which will loosen patriarchal strictures and create economic independence. Accepting the economic determinism of modernization theory, they assume that capitalist economic ventures will foster political liberalization and the cultivation of civil society. Thus they advocate women's entry into "male spheres" from which they have been excluded, whether those spheres be economic, educational, ethnic, national, international, political, professional, religious, or tribal. The individualist bias and elitist implications of such advice are seldom acknowledged. And potent legacies of colonialism and neocolonialism disappear behind the rhetoric of individual upward mobility.

Feminists of the global South have insisted that modernization cannot be understood apart from centuries of colonization, economic exploitation, and environmental degradation, which produce markedly uneven "development" within the South, as well as between North and South. Meaningful liberation, on this view, must take into account the needs and interests of very different kinds of women marked by membership in particular class, caste, ethnic, national, racial, and religious groups. Once complex social hierarchies are acknowledged, then "feminism cannot be monolithic in its issues, goals and strategies since it constitutes the expression of the concerns and interests of women from different regions, classes, nationalities and ethnic backgrounds. While gender subordination has universal elements, feminism cannot be based on a rigid concept of universality that negates the wide variation of women's experiences" (Sen and Grown 1987, 18).

Western feminist prescriptions involving the liberatory force of the market, work outside the home, and employment within the formal sector produce a form of universalization marred by systemic class and regional biases. Even within nations of the North, "women of color and poor, white women have not usually found work outside the home to be a source of equality. On the contrary, such work has been the site of oppression and a mark of inequality," as the case of African American and Latina domestic workers demonstrates (G. Mink 1999, 182).

Some conceptual tools that feminists have put to good effect in analyzing relations of domination and subordination within Western liberal democratic states do not "fit" the experiences of women in other parts of the world. Within agricultural societies, for example, the demarcation of "public and private" is far less clear cut than some Western feminists have presumed. In India, for example, "it is mainly women belonging to upper class and caste who are confined to 'private' activities within the domestic sphere, while a large number of women belonging to the poorer section of society, those of lower caste, and members of peasant and tribal communities work outside the house participating extensively in agricultural, animal husbandry, and allied activities. Their work is often seen as the extension of their household activities and no clear demarcation occurs between the private and public realms in such situations" (Chauhan 2001, 74). Nor does such work provide a clear path to emancipation.

Strategies that emphasize employment in the formal sector also fail to take into account the realities of most women's lives in the South. "More women and men around the world are in informal employment arrangements than are in formal market jobs. . . . Most of the world's women who are economically active are in the informal economy, frequently as micro-entrepreneurs. More than half of the economically active women in Sub-Saharan Africa and South Asia are self-employed in the informal economy, as are about a third in Northern Africa and Asia. In Latin American countries, 30 [to] 70 percent of women workers are employed in the informal economy" (Esim 2001, 165). Working in micro-enterprises or as micro-entrepreneurs, in sweatshops or home-based units, in the most vulnerable forms of employment exempt or hidden from national employment and labor legislations, the majority of the world's women may see "modernization" in starkly different terms than do affluent Western women (V. Taylor 2000). Empowerment strategies that focus on moving women into employment in the formal sector, such as those endorsed by the World Bank, may simply impose another shift upon women who must continue their work in subsistence agriculture, informal sector activities, and their reproductive labor to keep their families alive (Bedford 2005). Rather than contributing to their empowerment, women in the global South may experience capitalist strategies of modernization as a means of heightening their oppression.

"In striking contrast to the benign view of modernity held by many Western and Northern feminists, many women from the global South believe that economic development is by and large destructive" (Giele 2001, 183). Rather than experiencing improvements in health, education, and living standards, women across the South have found their living conditions worsened as they are forced off the land, as they lose space for their subsistence crops to export agriculture, as aggregate food production falls, as malnutrition increases, as structural adjustment policies cut back educational opportunities, health care, and other minimal social services, as growing worldwide militarization diminishes physical security and unleashes powerful social forces such as national chauvinism, racism, and sexism (Sen and Grown 1987; V. Taylor 2000; Kabeer 2003).

If Western prescriptions for capitalist development conflict with the views of feminists from the South about what is needed to improve their lives, so too does the notion that the North can save the South and that technical expertise provides the means to do so. One of the most consistent themes articulated by feminists from the South over the past forty years is that solutions to develop-ment crises in the South require "people-centered approaches: overall policies (monetary, fiscal, agricultural, industrial, employment, and social services) di-rectly oriented to meeting people's basic needs," which presuppose the involve-ment of local people in project choice, planning and implementation (Sen and Grown 1987, 40). Insisting that Third World women are "agents of change, not objects or recipients of change" (Denis 2001, 155), feminists in the South have called for open, participatory processes that involve local "stakeholders" in diag-noses of problems and identification of solutions.

Across the South, grassroots feminist activists have advanced strategies for "empowerment from below" (Kabeer 2003, 224) that posit "self-definition as a key ingredient of relevant political action" (Sen and Grown 1987, 80). By in-voking long-standing arguments about the benefits of direct democracy, feminist activists suggest that local women's participation in decision-making will gener-ate benefits for the individuals involved (self-development), as well as for the community (collective solidarity and improved policies to alleviate poverty). "Where a space is created for women's own voices to be heard, either through participatory processes of needs identification or by organizational practices that encourage participation in shaping and changing the 'decisionable agenda,' a different set of needs may come into view" (Kabeer 2003, 230). In case after case across the global South, the involvement of local women in decision making has helped to "challenge conventional stereotypes about gender needs, make visible hitherto hidden categories of women's needs, and laid bare the interconnections between different aspects of women's lives" (Kabeer 2003, 231). Contrary to ste-reotypes of illiterate peasant women, feminist activists suggest that "peasant women are fully conscious of the reasons for their poverty and their subordina-tions" (Mazumdar 1989, 29). They lack information, however about their "new rights—as human beings, as workers, as citizens, their rights and responsibilities to participate in all decisions within the family, the community, and the state, to influence the process of change and claim a share of state assistance for them-selves" (Mazumdar 1989, 29).

Providing women with information about their rights under national con-stitutions and international treaties, such as CEDAW (The Convention to Elim-inate All Forms of Discrimination Against Women), has been a continuing

focus of grassroots feminist activism in the South. But in contrast to individualist deployments of rights discourses focusing on discrimination, feminist activists
in the South have linked rights rhetoric to the building of collective identities
for women. Drawing upon Paolo Freire's conception of *conscientization* and feminist notions of consciousness-raising, feminist activists in the South have devised strategies to heighten women's understanding so that they can stand
together and act together, cultivating their strength to resist and transform oppressive practices through collective organization and mobilization.

Enhancing women's capacities to organize, mobilize, build alliances, and
form coalitions to demand accountability and to create social change is a staple
of the "transversal" politics in the South (Grewal and Kaplan 1994; Yuval-Davis
1997). Deploying these skills at home and abroad, feminist activists from the
South have developed vibrant transnational networks, which they use to am-
plify their voices. At subregional, regional, and global conferences, as well as
through websites, listservs, cyberjournals, newsletters, and public reports and
books, feminists from the South have articulated strategies to break down structural inequality between the North and South, to redress the depredations of
colonial and neocolonial domination, to fight institutional, cultural, and individual racisms, to alleviate poverty through debt forgiveness, land and income
redistribution, expanded educational opportunity, and accessible and affordable
health care, to foster national self-reliance, to control multinational corporations, and to reduce military expenditures. They have worked with international
organizations, transnational NGOs, national, regional, and local governments,
and progressive solidarity networks to redefine development as "equitable and
sustainable allocation of resources in order to meet the basic needs and strategic
interests of all" (Denis 2001, 157). On this view, development is inseparable
from the empowerment of local women to determine their own priorities and
the means to address them. Aggregating the views of autonomous women's
movements across the South, Third World feminist activists identify the most
pressing priorities facing women as poverty, racism, unequal trade relations,
structural adjustment policies, coercive population control strategies, militarism,
environmental degradation (compare World Women's Congress for a Healthy
Planet, 1992; Sen and Grown 1987; V. Taylor 2000; Demos and Segal 2001;
Tauli-Corpuz 2001; Kabeer 2003).

Despite thirty years of mobilization around these issues in transnational
feminist forums, Third World women continue to experience frustration with
some feminists in the North who seem neither to hear nor heed their messages.
How do we make sense of this prolonged instance of evidence blindness?
Markedly different theories about the world inform the debates between these
feminists of the North and South. Disagreements involve individualist versus
collectivist strategies of social transformation, capitalist versus socialist modes of

development, top-down versus bottom-up development planning practices, instrumental versus feminist approaches to women's empowerment. Arguments supporting competing views on these many issues are complex and require detailed knowledge of economic, political, cultural, and environmental conditions in specific contexts. Part of the frustration of feminists from the South stems from the failure of many Northern feminists to acknowledge the need for and the validity of such local knowledge. Third World women seek to contest the arrogance of Northern feminists who assume that "modernization" is a cure without knowing the scope or dimensions of local problems and without understanding the traditions, cultures, and modes of life that are being destroyed by the imposition of market imperatives. When feminists of the South criticize "neocolonialism," they are attempting to make visible the troubling assumption that all nations must follow the path chosen by the West. From the perspective of women in the global South, cavalier assumptions that accredit the inherent superiority of Western ideas, institutions, and practices constitute a "blind spot," an angle from which one cannot see. Indeed, unexamined assumptions about the superiority of liberal democracy and the inevitability of liberal democracy support a form of sanctioned ignorance, which suggests that Westerners need not attend to the views of those in the global South. They can simply rely on their own judgments concerning what needs to be done.

If feminist researchers are to avoid replicating neocolonial power relations, then they must engage rather than ignore the contentious theoretical assumptions at the heart of these transnational feminist debates. Excavating and analyzing competing theoretical assumptions will not eliminate the structural differences between the nations of the global North and South, but it will disrupt sanctioned ignorance, end oppressive modes of feminist ventriloquism, and expand feminist awareness of additional dimensions of the politics of knowledge.

Producing Invisibility

The ventriloquism metaphor hints at active processes through which sanctioned ignorance is produced and sustained. A quotation from Nietzsche (1983) provides another clue to the forces that sustain evidence blindness: "It requires a great deal of strength to be able to live and to forget the extent to which to live and to be unjust is one and the same thing." Nietzsche suggests that evidence blindness may not be "inability to perceive" but rather an active process of forgetting, social amnesia as a protective camouflage that confers strength. Nietzsche's formulation—that it takes great strength *not* to live with the recognition of injustice, but to *forget* the injustice constitutive of life—suggests that there are additional dimensions of evidence blindness that feminists need to understand. Focusing on examples drawn from the works of nonfeminist scholars, the final section of the chapter investigates mechanisms that assist forgetting, strategies that foster "unknowing."

Feminist activists and scholars have noted that being rendered invisible is an experience familiar to many women. Having one's presence go unnoticed, having one's views ignored, having one's arguments dismissed or attributed to a male speaker are often cited as symptoms of racism and sexism. Are there comparable mechanisms that render feminist evidence invisible? Reflection on the means by which women's subordination and feminist activism to redress that subordination are kept below the threshold of visibility may afford some insight into the production of social amnesia, forms of unknowing actively produced and legitimated by dominant discourses.

Consider, for example, how difficult it has been for feminists to keep their activism and their issues in the public eye. Despite unprecedented levels of feminist activism around the globe since 1995, feminism is pronounced dead, obsolete, outmoded with remarkable frequency by pundits and the Western press (Hawkesworth 2004). Stories of successful feminist campaigns seldom make the news. As Melissa Deem (1999, 87) has pointed out, "feminists do not control the timing of their appearance or the content of their message" in print or visual media. Accounts of women's oppression surface not when feminists sound the alarm, but when they are useful to legitimate military or police operations of questionable legality as the recent invasion of Afghanistan makes painfully clear. Within this global frame, "powerless women" need to be saved by "powerful men," not to be empowered in their own right by their own activism.

The mechanisms that produce this invisibility are multiple and complex. Some tactics, however, are easier to trace than others. Consider, for example, a recent article in the *New York Times Magazine*, "Globalization: The Free Market Fix," by Tina Rosenberg (2002). While Rosenberg explicitly notes that "almost all sweatshop workers are young women [who] endure starvation wages, forced overtime, and dangerous working conditions" (32), the two global workers she describes in detail in the article are both men. Thus, any fledgling recognition of the gendered dimensions of globalization is quickly displaced by identification with and concern for the plight of male workers. Rhacel Salazar Parrenas (2001b) has pointed out a similar strategy of gender displacement in the Philippine government's discursive construction of the heroic overseas contract worker. Although government statistics indicate that Filipinas constitute 60 percent of the migrant labor force, the government intentionally promotes the image of a male migrant as the "iconic figure of the modern-day heroes. . . . The Philippine government prefers to project a representative male instead of a female image so as to downplay the reality that more women than men are leaving the Philippines. The government does so in order to downplay one of the greatest costs of exportation, which is the vulnerability of female migrant workers. Concentrated in domestic and entertainment work, Filipina migrants—77.8 percent of whom could be found in service occupations in 1996—enter more vulnerable occupations than do their male counterparts" (Parrenas 2001b, 1137). Whether an unintentional slip or as part of an intentional strategy to divert public attention, gender displacement is quite successful as a tactic to remove women from the global frame. Such gender displacement surfaces regularly in academic texts on globalization, as well as in the popular press and in government policy.

Consider, for example, the gendered rhetoric that permeates Michael Hardt and Antonio Negri's massive tome, *Empire* (2000), which was celebrated within academic circles as the vehicle though which a new, progressive global coalition could be mobilized. Although Hardt and Negri cite several feminist texts and embrace Donna Haraway's cyborg imagery, women's work in the production of subsistence, on the global assembly line, as migrant service workers, in physical and social reproduction, and as transformative agents is thoroughly occluded in this massive account of globalization. Indeed, unless "affective labor" is read as a synonym for women's work (a move that feminists find deeply problematic), women play virtually no role in the deterritorialized politics and economics of *Empire*. Allegedly gender-neutral nouns, such as "the proletariat" or "the multitude" engulf and subsume women, while reproduction, a process in which women figure prominently in past and present worlds, is miraculously taken over by men.

The production of life figures prominently in Hardt and Negri's critique of global capital and in their prophetic vision of social change. But these modes of reproduction are homosocial at best. Thus in criticizing the reduction of all relations to the cash nexus, Hardt and Negri (2000, 32) note that: "Production and reproduction are dressed in monetary clothing. . . . The great industrial and financial powers thus produce not only commodities but also subjectivities. They produce agentic subjectivities within the biopolitical context: they produce needs, social relations, bodies, and minds—which is to say, they produce producers." By conflating social reproduction with all modes of reproduction, Hardt and Negri can dispense with women and attribute pride of place in the generation of life to "the great industrial and financial powers"—a cohort in which women are markedly underrepresented. As Anne McClintock (1995, 13) has noted, women do two-thirds of the world's work and earn 10 percent of the world's income; yet they own less than 1 percent of the world's property.

Hardt and Negri are critical of on-going local struggles for social change, where feminist activism has been extensive, because these modes of activism appear "always already old, outdated, and anachronistic . . . precisely because they can not communicate, because their languages are untranslatable" (56). In lieu of these "incommunicable" local tactics, Hardt and Negri advocate new global strategies.

> We need a force capable of not only organizing the destructive capabilities of the multitude, but also constituting through the desires of the multitude an alternative. The counter-Empire must also be a new global vision, a new way of living in the world. . . . Those who are against, while escaping from the local and particular constraints of their human condition, must also continually attempt to construct a new body and a new life. This is necessarily a violent, barbaric passage. . . . Bodies themselves transform and mutate to create new posthuman bodies. . . . The new body must also be able to create a new life. . . . We have to arrive at constituting a coherent political artifice, an artificial becoming in the sense that the humanists spoke of a *homohomo* (*sic*) produced by art and knowledge, and that Spinoza spoke of a powerful body produced by that highest consciousness that is infused with love. The infinite paths of the barbarians must form a new mode of life. (214–216)

The substitution of mental production for biological reproduction as a mode of systemic privileging of men over women has been a staple of Western political thought. Perhaps Hardt and Negri are simply the latest manifestation of the Aristotelian impulse to privilege form (supposedly the unique property of men) over matter (the residual category to which women have been assigned). But as a politics for a new millennium, their effective negation of women's on-going struggles for justice in order to assert the privilege of "the virtual multitude regenerating" leaves a great deal to be desired. One virtue of their work, however, is that it provides a prime example of the production of feminist invisibility. Women are erased through the rhetorical substitution of allegedly gender-neutral terms for gender specificity. Reproductive labor that has been the near exclusive terrain of women is attributed to men under the guise of social reproduction. And feminist efforts to challenge gendered relations of domination and subordination are delegitimized by assertions that they are outmoded and divisive.

Like many Marxists before them, Hardt and Negri identify the "manipulation and management of difference" as part of the "current ideology of corporate capital" (150). Thus they suggest that feminist activists/theorists who foreground gender difference, like postcolonial and critical race theorists who foreground national, racial, or ethnic differences, are simply—albeit unwittingly—playing on a terrain that serves the interests of capital (150–155). According to Hardt and Negri, far from being liberatory, such difference-based strategies are futile and destructive, for they continue to undermine the solidarity of the "emerging multitude," which constitutes the "universal" and "revolutionary" global class (395–408). Thus not only are women displaced in Hardt and Negri's account of globalization, but feminist activism is roundly rejected as reactionary.

While Hardt and Negri afford a powerful example of the means by which women are displaced from "progressive" academic accounts of globalization, proponents of neoliberalism, a theoretical framework that celebrates individualism, the capitalist market, and the laissez-faire state, have their own repertoire for rendering women, women's issues, and feminist activism invisible. Chief among these are invocations of individual choice and privatization. Tina Rosenberg's essay again provides a helpful point of departure. After providing a gruesome account of the physically harmful and financially exploitive working conditions of a Chilean man who is employed in a chicken processing plant whose products are exported to Europe, Asia, and other countries in Latin America, Rosenberg asks, "Is this man a victim of globalization?" Rosenberg's response to the question is telling. For while she notes that at one time she might have thought him a victim, she now realizes that such a stance is mistaken. Exploitation of the sort experienced by the Chilean worker is a mistaken focus for antiglobalization protests, on her view, because the global assembly-line worker chose to take this job and is benefiting from it.

> But today if I were to picket globalization, I would protest other inequities. In a way, the chicken worker, who came to the factory when driving a taxi ceased to be profitable, is a beneficiary of globalization. So are the millions of young women who have left rural villages to be exploited gluing tennis shoes or assembling computer keyboards. The losers are those who get laid off when companies move to low-wage countries, or those forced off their land when imports undercut their crop prices, or those who can no longer afford life-saving medicine— people whose choices in life diminish because of global trade. Globalization has offered this man a hellish job, but it is a choice he did not have before, and he took it; I don't name him because he is afraid of being fired. When this chicken company is hiring, the lines go around the block. (Rosenberg 2002, 32)

A number of neoliberal stock arguments are packed into this brief paragraph. First and foremost, is the appeal to individual choice. A contract voluntarily entered into by a worker, understood as a rational economic maximizer, is deemed an inappropriate target for those interested in social justice. The agency manifested by the individual, who consents to exploitive working conditions, negates efforts to categorize the worker as oppressed. The Chilean man, a rational calculator of his economic interests by virtue of his conscious decision to opt for the global assembly line over the entrepreneurial venture of taxi driving, circulates as the sign under which the millions of young women are subsumed. Nothing need be said about the options which structured their "choices" of work. Within this theoretical framework, the familiar prejudices that pit modernization unequivocally against tradition carry additional argumentative weight.

The global factory rescues the Chilean man (and the millions of young women who trail in his wake) from "the idiocy of rural life" (Marx and Engels 1848, 14). Global capitalism is portrayed as affording opportunities for waged-labor in the formal sector, which makes individuals better off. Proof of the benefits that global capital affords: individuals compete for the opportunity to be exploited. QED: the situation is desirable.

Such an account of the generic worker masks the unique vulnerabilities that women workers face in global factories. Invasive pregnancy tests to which women employees are regularly subjected as a condition of work and the sexual harassment on the job disappear behind the mask of the self-interested maximizer. Local mobilizations by women workers against abusive working conditions are rendered invisible by depictions of jobs freely taken. Feminist mobilizations against gender-specific abuses are repudiated as a mode of hegemony that fails to comprehend the agency of women workers in export-processing zones. Third World feminist critiques of the negative consequences of marketization are trumped by the individual choices of workers who allegedly embrace their economic exploitation.

The neoliberal depiction of globalization is unquestionably the dominant view circulating in the United States. Thus it is not surprising that those who take their news exclusively from dominant media outlets may not know anything about the gendered inequities of globalization or "glocal" feminist mobilizations to address them. Such social amnesia is produced and accredited by mainstream politicians, journalists, economists, and social scientists. While such ubiquitous forms of "unknowing" may be understandable given the pervasiveness of neoliberal assumptions, feminists researchers, who are committed to improving the life-prospects of women, cannot rest content with such ubiquity. An understanding of the diverse dimensions of evidence blindness allows feminist scholars to make the production of social amnesia visible. Rather than accepting metaphors that reduce evidence blindness to unalterable physical states, feminist analysis illuminates theoretical and rhetorical processes that produce and sustain shared modes of unknowing and forgetting central to the perpetuation of injustice. By interrogating contentious theoretical assumptions and illuminating rhetorical processes of gender displacement and erasure, feminist inquiry makes manifest dimensions of the politics of knowledge that traditional scholarship renders invisible.

Fighting Evidence Blindness

Many scholarly interventions of feminist researchers can be understood as efforts to thwart evidence blindness. Dispelling the myth of the given, probing the tacit presuppositions of dominant discourses, challenging naturalization of oppressive relations, investigating processes that produce invisibility, engaging difference and plurality, denouncing reductive explanations are analytic tactics that feminists have championed. Chapters 6, 7, and 8 will examine specific analytic tools that feminists have developed and deployed in a wide range of contexts to contest dominant paradigms in academic disciplines. Gender as an analytical category, standpoint as an analytical tool, and intersectionality as a mechanism for preserving analytic complexity constitute three of the primary methodological innovations of feminist inquiry. Their deployment in concrete research contexts demonstrate how feminist political commitments can contribute to heightened objectivity by identifying new questions for investigation and illuminating dimensions of social life and institutional practices rendered invisible by traditional disciplinary approaches.

Part II

Methodological Innovations

Chapter 6	Gender as an Analytic Category

$\mathbf{W}$ HAT DOES IT MEAN to use gender as an analytic category? How is an analytic category different from a universal explanation? What kinds of innovative research questions are raised by the feminist deployment of gender as an analytic category? What exactly does gender explain? What is the relation between sex and gender, sexuality and gender, the ideology of procreation and gender? How does gender as an analytical tool produce new understandings of power? What theoretical assumptions are imported into feminist research by the adoption of gender as a central analytical category? Can the reliance upon gender as a research tool create problems for feminist analysis? If so, when and under what conditions do these problems arise? Are there strategies to circumvent troublesome theoretical underpinnings of gender while preserving the innovative areas of inquiry it enables?

This chapter investigates the development of gender as an analytical tool within feminist scholarship, tracing the transformation of the concept from a grammatical class to a descriptor of particular modes of embodiment to a research guide or "heuristic" that illuminates new questions for feminist inquiry. To probe the theoretical assumptions embedded in conceptions of gender, the chapter compares and contrasts methodological deployments of gender within phenomenology, deconstruction, dialectical materialism, and ethnomethodology. Tracing some troubling presuppositions that surface in these diverse theoretical accounts of gender, the chapter concludes with the identification of particular uses of gender that feminist researchers should avoid, if they hope to preserve the emancipatory impulse that inspired the development of gender as an analytical category.

Gender: From Grammar to Embodiment to Analytic Category

In every day usage, there are multiple meanings of the term, gender, but the most common connotation conflates gender with sex. The "natural attitude" (Garfinkel

1967) toward gender encompasses a series of "unquestionable" axioms about gender including the belief that there are two and only two genders; the belief that gender is invariant; the belief that genitals are the essential sign of gender; the belief that the male/female dichotomy is natural; the belief that being masculine or feminine is natural and not a matter of choice; and the belief that all individuals can (and must) be classified as masculine or feminine—any deviation from such a classification being either a joke or a pathology. According to Harold Garfinkel, the beliefs constituting the natural attitude are "incorrigible" in that they are held with such conviction that it is near impossible to challenge their validity (Garfinkel 1967, 122–128).

Over the past three decades, the concept of gender has undergone a metamorphosis within feminist scholarship. Although originally a linguistic category denoting a system of subdivision within a grammatical class (Corbett 1991), feminist scholars adopted the concept of gender to distinguish culturally specific characteristics associated with masculinity and femininity from biological features associated with sex (male and female chromosomes, hormones, as well as internal and external sexual and reproductive organs). In early feminist works gender was used to repudiate biological determinism by demonstrating the range of variation in cultural constructions of femininity and masculinity. In subsequent works gender has been used to analyze the social organization of relationships between men and women (Rubin 1975; Barrett 1980; MacKinnon 1987), to investigate the reification of human differences (Vetterling-Braggin 1982; Hawkesworth 1990b; Shanley and Pateman 1991), to conceptualize the semiotics of the body, sex, and sexuality (Sulieman 1985; de Lauretis 1984; Silverman 1988; Doane 1987), to explain the distribution of burdens and benefits in society (Walby 1986; Connell 1987; Boneparth and Stoper 1988), to illustrate the microtechniques of power (de Lauretis 1987; Bartky 1988; Sawicki 1991), to illuminate the structure of the psyche (Chodorow 1978), and to account for individual identity and aspiration (Butler 1990; Epperson 1988).

Interdisciplinary feminist scholars have used the concept of gender in markedly different ways. Gender has been analyzed as an attribute of individuals (Bem 1974, 1983), as an interpersonal relation (Spelman 1988), and as a mode of social organization (Firestone 1970; Eisenstein 1979). Gender has been defined in terms of status (Lopata and Thorne 1978), sex roles (Epstein 1971; Janeway 1971; Amundsen 1971), and sexual stereotypes (Friedan 1963; Anderson 1983). It has been conceived as a structure of consciousness (Rowbotham 1973), as triangulated pscyhe (Chodorow 1978), and as internalized ideology (Barrett 1980; Grant 1993). It has been discussed as a product of attribution (Kessler and McKenna 1978), socialization (Gilligan 1982; Ruddick 1980), disciplinary practices (Butler 1990; Singer 1993), and accustomed stance (Devor 1989). Gender has been depicted as an effect of language (Spender 1980; Daly

1978), a matter of behavioral conformity (Epstein 1971; Amundsen 1971), a structural feature of labor, power, and cathexis (Connell 1987), and a mode of perception (Kessler and McKenna 1978; Bem 1993). Gender has been cast in terms of a binary opposition, variable and varying continua, and in terms of a layering of personality. It has been characterized both as difference (Irigaray 1985a, 1985b) and as relations of power manifested in domination and subordination (MacKinnon 1987; Gordon 1988). It has been construed in the passive mode of seriality (Young 1994) and in the active mode, either as a process creating interdependence (Levi-Strauss 1969, 1971; Smith 1992) or as an instrument of segregation and exclusion. (Davis 1981; Hill Collins 1990). Gender has been denounced as a prisonhouse (Cornell and Thurschwell 1986) and embraced as inherently liberating (Irigaray 1985b; Smith 1992). It has been identified as a universal phenomenon (Lerner 1986) and as an historically specific consequence of modernity's increasing sexualization of women (Laqueur 1990; Riley 1988).

As the interpretations of gender have proliferated in feminist scholarship, a number of feminist scholars have raised questions about the utility of gender as an analytic category. Susan Bordo identified two currents fueling the emergence of a new "gender skepticism" (1993, 216). One current flows from the experiences of women of color and lesbian feminists who have suggested that the "multiple jeopardy" characteristic of their lives raises serious questions about the validity of gender generalizations. If gender is always mediated by race, class, ethnicity, nationality, and sexual orientation, then an analytical framework that isolates gender or construes gender in terms of an "additive model" is seriously flawed and may serve only to mask the numerous privileges of white, middle-class feminists who have the luxury of experiencing only one mode of oppression. (Spelman 1988; King 1988; Higginbotham 1992; Brewer 1993). The second current flows from postmodern criticism which depicts gender narratives as totalizing fictions that create a false unity out of heterogeneous elements. In addition to questioning the binary opposition that fixes men and women in permanent relations of domination and subordination, postmodern critics have also challenged the "ground" of the sex/gender distinction. If gender was devised to illuminate the social construction of masculinity and femininity and naively took the sexed body as given, then it has little to offer in a postmodern world that understands the body, sex, and sexuality as socially constructed.

Acknowledging the importance of the issues raised by women of color, lesbian-feminists, and postmodern-feminists, several feminist scholars have offered a defense of feminist uses of gender; they suggest that a sophisticated conception of gender can incorporate the central points made by these critics. In an important and influential essay, Joan Scott defines gender as a concept involving two interrelated but analytically distinct parts. "Gender is a constitutive element of social relationships based on perceived differences between the sexes, and gender is a primary way of signifying relationships of power" (1986, 1067). In explicating gender as a constitutive element of social relationships, Scott emphasizes that gender operates in multiple fields, including culturally available symbols that evoke multiple representations, normative concepts that set forth interpretations of the meanings of symbols, social institutions and organizations, and subjective identities (1067–1068). According to Scott, gender is a useful category of analysis because it "provides a way to decode meaning and to understand the complex connections among various forms of human interaction" (1070). Noting that gender is always contextually defined and repeatedly constructed, Scott cautions that gender analysts must not replicate the mistakes of early feminist accounts which credited gender as a universal causal force. On the contrary, gender analysts must seek a "genuine historicization and deconstruction of the terms of sexual difference" (1065). Scott demonstrates that problematic theoretical assumptions informing radical feminism, Marxist feminism, and psychoanalytic feminism gave rise to a variety of misapplications of gender as an analytic category, all of which resulted in ahistorical analyses, oversimplified and reductive explanations, universal generalizations impervious to change in history, exclusive fixation on the "subject," and to restrictive foci on the family or the household. Such flaws need not be endemic to gender analysis, however. Indeed, Scott argues that a self-critical deployment of gender analysis could provide meaningful explanations of historically and culturally specific relations obtaining between individual subjects and modes of social organization. If feminist scholars examine "how things happened in order to find out why they happened" (1067), then their analytical investigations will enable them to reverse and displace the binary and hierarchical construction of gender by refuting the naive belief that gender "is real or self-evident or in the nature of things" (1066).

Sandra Harding has also advanced a defense of gender as an analytic category. "The fact that there are class, race, and cultural differences between women and between men is not, as some have thought, a reason to find gender difference either theoretically unimportant or politically irrelevant. In virtually every culture, gender difference is a pivotal way in which humans identify themselves as persons, organize social relations, and symbolize meaningful natural and social events and processes" (1986, 18). The very pervasiveness of gender requires systematic feminist analysis. Thus Harding argues that feminists must theorize gender; they must conceive it as "an analytic category within which humans think about and organize their social activity rather than as a natural consequence of sex difference, or even merely as a social variable assigned to individual people in different ways from culture to culture" (17). Recognizing that gender appears only in culturally specific forms in no way mitigates the force of gender analysis. On the contrary, gender as an analytic category illuminates crucial cultural processes. "Gendered social life is produced through three distinct processes: it is the result of assigning dualistic gender metaphors to various perceived dichotomies that rarely have anything to do with sex differences (gender symbolism); it is the consequence of appealing to these gender dualisms to organize social activity, dividing necessary social activities between different groups of humans (gender structure); it is a form of socially contructed individual identity only imperfectly correlated with either the reality or the perception of sex differences (individual gender)" (17–18). According to Harding, feminist investigations of gender symbolism, gender structure, and individual gender challenge the basic presuppositions of the natural attitude, thereby helping to dispel essentialized identities, while creating the possibility of a politics grounded in solidarities that cross the divisions of race, class, age, ethnicity, nationality, and sexual orientation.

The defense of gender as an analytic category advanced by Scott and Harding suggests that the concerns of gender skeptics can be incorporated into a sophisticated conception of gender. Their defense also tends to mute concern about the multiplicity of meanings accorded gender in contemporary feminist scholarship. For they provide a coherent account of the intricate connections linking psyche to social organization, social roles to cultural symbols, normative beliefs to "the experience" of the body and sexuality. Indeed, they suggest that feminist research into such connections can undermine the mistaken beliefs informing the natural attitude. Thus their defense also provides a bridge linking feminist scholarship to feminist politics outside the academy. Feminist research designed to confound gender provides the analytic tools to loosen the strictures of the natural attitude and the oppressive social relations that the natural attitude legitimates.

Are Scott and Harding correct about the potential of gender as an analytic category? Can gender be deployed as an analytical tool that escapes (or dispels) the natural attitude? Can attention to the historicity of gender enable feminists to avoid universal causal claims, grand narratives, and totalizing accounts? How does the use of gender as an analytic category fit in with a thorough-going understanding of the social construction of the body?

To explore these questions, this chapter investigates four systematic efforts to deploy gender as an analytic category, Steven Smith's *Gender Thinking* (1992), Judith Butler's *Gender Trouble* (1990), R. W. Connell's *Gender and Power* (1987), and Suzanne Kessler and Wendy McKenna's *Gender: An Ethnomethodological Account* (1978). These four works are the most ambitious efforts that I have found to theorize gender in ways that connect psyche, self, and social relations. They also represent some major methodological approaches (phenomenology, postmodern deconstruction, dialectical materialism, ethnomethodology) currently vying for the allegiance of feminist scholars. Each account casts itself as a systematic, feminist analysis of gender. Each examines the multiple domains of gender, ranging across cultural symbols, normative concepts, social institutions, and subjective identities. Each conforms to Scott's directive to focus on *how* in order to explain *why* gender works. Each starts from the premise that the body is socially constituted and culturally mediated. And each advances arguments that challenge fundamental presuppositions of the natural attitude. Emerging from and drawing upon different methodological traditions, each advances a markedly different explanation of gender. Yet, despite the richness and diversity of these accounts, each also constructs a tale of gender that is markedly unsettling.

Despite important differences in their approaches to and their conceptions of gender, these works construct a narrative that implicates gender in the "ideology of procreation," a conception of sexuality that reduces the erotic to reproduction (Barrett 1980, 62–77). In so doing, these texts illuminate presuppositions that replicate rather than undermine the natural attitude. That such troubling presuppositions surface in accounts of gender that grow out of very different theoretical projects should be of concern to feminist scholars, for the presuppositions that structure this narrative of gender stand in stark contrast to the emancipatory project of feminist scholarship. Excavating the assumptions in these works, then, can help to identify the danger points in certain deployments of gender, dangers that arise in a subtle shift from using gender as analytic tool to attributing to gender explanatory force. Interrogating the conceptual tools of feminist inquiry can help feminist scholars avoid these potential pitfalls. I offer this analysis in an effort to mark the dangers that lurk in uncritical deployments of gender as a mode of universal explanation, rather than as an analytic category. The next section explores the meaning of gender as an analytic category and introduces a number of conceptual distinctions that feminists have developed to challenge assumptions of the natural attitude toward gender.

Mapping the Conceptual Terrain

What does it mean to use gender as an analytic category? Neither Scott nor Harding explicitly addresses this question, but both seem to use the term in a semitechnical sense drawn from the philosophy of science. In this sense, an analytic category can be understood as a heuristic device that performs both positive and negative functions in a research program (Lakatos 1970). As a "positive heuristic," gender illuminates an area of inquiry by framing a set of questions for investigation. It need not (although it may) involve any explicit methodological commitment, merely identifying puzzles or problems in need of exploration or clarification, but it does provide concepts, definitions, and hypotheses to guide research. By demonstrating in their own work, the intricate interrelations of symbol systems, normative precepts, social structures, and subjective identities subsumed under gender's rubric, Scott and Harding invite other scholars to probe these diverse domains to discover how culturally specific gender relations are created, sustained, and transformed. The very notion of a positive heuristic is tentative, which suggests a trial-and-error method of problem solving requiring the collective efforts of multiple scholars to advance the field. But the notion of a "negative heuristic" developed by Imre Lakatos also suggests a shared set of assumptions so central to a mode of analysis that they cannot be jettisoned (1970, 132). Given gender's original meaning in feminist discourse and the frequency with which feminist scholars reiterate this goal, the negative heuristic of gender analysis could be "to contest the naturalization of sex differences in multiple arenas of struggle" (Haraway 1991b, 131). The use of gender as an analytic category then would be intimately bound up with challenges to the natural attitude.

The terminology developed within feminist discourses on gender certainly suggests the centrality of efforts to challenge the natural attitude. Feminist scholars have introduced a number of important distinctions to illuminate the complexity of gender: sex, sexuality, sexual identity, gender identity, gender role, gender role identity. Virtually all scholars working in the field employ some of these distinctions; although all scholars do not use the terms in the same way. Sex, for example, can refer to biological features such as chromosomes, hormones, internal and external sexual and reproductive organs or to acts romantically characterized as love-making. Gender identity typically refers to the individual's own feeling of being a man or a woman, but this "feeling" may be defined in a rudimentary sense as having a conviction that one's sex assignment at birth was "anatomically and psychologically correct" (Stoller 1985, 11) or more expansively as a patterned subjectivity that bears some relation to cultural conceptions of masculinity/femininity. It should be noted that what is meant by "identity" in this formulation can also mean markedly different things. It can mean a psychological sense of "who I am," a sociological notion of a person qua agent prior to assuming specific social roles, a Foucauldian concept that captures an array of regulatory practices to produce the internal coherence of the subject, a philosophical concern with the individuation and unity of a person in the face of change, or a narrative construction the individual develops to make sense of his/her life.

Although usage varies from text to text, most feminist scholars would grant that there are important conceptual differences between sex construed in biological terms; sexuality understood to encompass sexual practices and erotic behavior; sexual identity referring to designations such as heterosexual, homosexual/gay/lesbian/queer, bisexual, or asexual; gender identity as a psychological sense of oneself as a man or a woman; gender role as a set of prescriptive, culture-specific expectations about what is appropriate for men and women; and gender role identity—a concept devised to capture the extent to which a person approves of and participates in feelings and behaviors deemed to be appropriate to his/her culturally constituted gender (Kessler and McKenna 1978, 7–11; Barrett 1980, 42–79). This terminology provides the analytic vocabulary that enables feminist scholars to challenge the natural attitude. Consider the distinction between gender identity and gender role identity, for example, which admits of the possibility that one can have a clear sense of oneself as a woman (or a man) while being thoroughly disaffected from and refusing participation in prevailing conceptions of femininity (or masculinity). This distinction breaks any connection between masculinity/femininity and sexed bodies by interpreting masculinity and femininity as culture-specific abstractions notoriously plagued by gender symbolism that mark a chasm between romanticized ideal and lived experience, attributed and actual, propaganda and practice.

Once feminists introduce conceptual distinctions that differentiate sex, sexuality, sexual identity, gender identity, gender role, and gender role identity, then critical questions emerge: What do these phenomena have to do with one another? How are they related? How do their complex interrelations pertain to gender as lived experience? The natural attitude postulates sex as the determinant of gender identity that flows naturally into a particular mode of (hetero)sexuality and that mandates certain rational gender roles embraced happily by individuals with uniformly positive gender role identities. In keeping with the negative heuristic of gender as an analytic category, feminist scholars have challenged each of these posited relations. Drawing upon linguistics, historical analysis, structuralism, deconstruction, Freudian and Lacanian psychoanalysis, phenomenology, existential and cognitive psychology, as well as dialectical materialism, feminists have advanced a variety of accounts not only of the relations that obtain among these diverse domains but also of how such complex social processes are naturalized. The following section examines four feminist accounts of the facticity of gender, which move from use of gender as an analytic category to an explanation of gender as lived experience.

Complementarity Models

GENDER WITHIN A FUNCTIONALIST FRAME

Gender initially existed as a grammatical category. Some attention to linguistics then may help illuminate the concept's appeal to feminist scholars. Etymologically, gender derives from the Latin, *genus*, via old French, *gendre*, roughly translated as "kind" or "sort." Designated "the most puzzling of grammatical categories, . . . genders are classes of nouns reflected in the behavior of associated words" (Corbett 1991, 1). Gender is puzzling for linguists precisely because it is *not* universal or invariant. In some languages gender is central and pervasive, while in others it is totally absent. Corbett's examination of more than two hundred languages revealed that "the number of genders is not limited to three; four is common, and twenty is possible" (5). As the proliferation of genders in specific languages makes clear, gender need not have anything to do with sex. "In some languages, gender marks the distinction masculine/feminine/nonsexed; but in other languages the divisions animate/inanimate, human/nonhuman, rational/ nonrational, male human/other, strong/weak, augmentative/diminutive, male/ other, female/other function exactly as does the division into male/female" (Corbett 1991, 30). As the etymology suggests, grammatical gender is based on a wide range of "kinds" including "insects, non-flesh food, liquids, canines, hunting weapons, items whose lustrous surfaces reflect light. . . . The worldview of the speakers determines the categories" (Corbett 1991, 30–32). Given the enormous range of grammatical genders, the determining criterion of gender is agreement: genders are distinguished syntactically by the agreements they take. In some languages, adjectives and verbs show agreement; in others, adverbs, numerals and even conjunctions agree; but in all cases agreement is the way in which the genders are reflected in the behavior of associated words (Corbett 1991, 5).

Gender's conceptual appeal for feminists is closely tied to its versatility in linguistics. As a linguistic construction, the cultural origins and historicity of gender are unmistakable. Gender's relation to the belief systems of determinate peoples frees it from the specter of biological determinism. Moreover, linguistic gender is not inherently enmeshed in binary opposition. Yet another facet of gender's linguistic legacy should give feminists pause. If feminists were to draw an explicit analogy from grammatical gender, then they would conceive genders as categories of persons constituted in and through the behavior of associated others by emphasizing that the relevant behavior involves concord or harmony. Although this aspect of the grammatical heritage is seldom acknowledged in feminist accounts of gender, notions of agreement, harmony, complementarity surface obliquely and problematically in numerous feminist accounts of gender. Indeed, a close reading of some of the most intricate and sophisticated recent accounts of gender reveals that notions of agreement or complementarity form the secret core of the authors' efforts to explain gender and to use gender to explain other social relations. Explanations of this sort situate gender in a functionalist frame. Within this frame, gender is depicted as a cultural construct devised to promote particular social functions that bear a marked resemblance to the presuppositions of the natural attitude.

A PHENOMENOLOGICAL ACCOUNT OF GENDER

Perhaps the most explicit version of this view can be found in Steven G. Smith's phenomenology of gender, *Gender Thinking* (1992). A philosopher steeped in the continental tradition, Smith argues that an accurate analysis of gender must begin with an explication of the "life world," the fundamental structures of consciousness: "The first false move . . . is the identification of gender with sex, or sex-as-socially constructed, or sex role, when in fact ordinary talk of 'feminine' and 'masculine' is not necessarily or even most often about any of these things but instead has to do typically with intentional qualities and indeed, ideals" (xiv). Thus Smith seeks to illuminate how gender operates in the life world.

Defining gender as a "conventional formation of a plastic humanity," Smith describes "gendering as a cultural process: a cultivation of human nature determined by the vicissitudes of early childhood and the customs of one's community" (15). Rather than invoking the metaphor of cultivation to imply growth or development, Smith uses the term to convey the imposition of certain constraints on human potential. Thus he suggests that gendering "qualifies" our humanity. Indeed, it is one of two critical social forces that shape human potential. "Humanity is a generic nature that stands in two chains of mutually qualifying categories, one physical (which includes sex) and the other intentional (which includes gender)" (23). Physical and intentional constraints admit of a range of differentiation, hence the phenomenon of individuality, but according to Smith, there are "limits to our plasticity, to the range of differentiations possible" (27). On Smith's view, "there are observable human phenomena that give definite shape to our openness" (25), and sex is perhaps the most powerful of these limits. "The sexes have the status of physical fact, almost always instantly and unproblematically ostensible" (46). Although he refers to "the sexes" as almost unproblematically ostensible, Smith acknowledges that culture shapes what is perceived as a body. Through "embodiment," "the community stipulates what counts as a male/female body, what life will be like in a male/female body in relation to other bodies, what norms (and latitudes) of character and conduct are associated with these bodies, and who is male and female" (91). When culture takes up the task of molding human nature, then, its aim is to enhance its own *construction* of what is naturally given, to mark sex differentiations through language, character, roles. For this reason, gender always entails a "dual reference to sex and character for purposes of description and evaluation" (36).

For Smith, language is paradigmatic of the cultural desire to mark sex differences. "In grammar, genders are *sex-related* systems of syntactical concord. . . . Human genders also work as systems of concord in so far as distinctive ways of speaking and acting are assigned to persons of different sexes" (43). Smith's mistaken claim that grammatical gender is exclusively sex-related enables him to suggest that the core content of the human gender system is not chosen but given. "Human gender schemes possess centers of meaning in (what are taken to be) sexed bodies" (44). Thus, cultural constructions of masculinity and femininity are not arbitrary. They are rooted in sex, which in turn has its own "center of meaning rooted in reproduction: woman as egg-producer; man as sperm producer" (46). Starting with an overly restrictive account of grammatical gender, Smith links gender to sex to reproduction and hence to heterosexuality. "Confronting sex differences makes me realize that I need a partner to reproduce. . . . A gendered being teams with other gendered beings" (71, 55).

Smith's claim that gender merely marks differences and meanings given by sexed bodies does not rest comfortably with his acknowledgment of how much work gendering involves. He notes that "we are continually subjected to gender attributions in all phases of our lives and that this gendering scheme has more orienting force for most of us, most of the time, than any other human differentiation" (36). Gender involves a "fundamental shaping of selfhood" that produces not only differences in "attunement and appreciativeness" but also "a normative solicitation of our intentions" and "an already granted permission to think, feel, act, and appear in ways that everyone does not and cannot" (53, 55, 184). Lifelong subjection to such gendering makes the experiences of the genders partly incommensurable. Smith suggests that gender both "marks the limit of comprehension" between men and women and yet gives these gendered beings a reason to live together: "Gender's normative force consists of nothing other than its ability to answer the life-interpreting question of how intenders should live together" (53, 56). Gender creates sex-specific experience and cognition, makes men and women mysteries to each other, and thereby inculcates a desire for cohabitation. For it is the culturally constructed incommensurability that enables men and women to regard each other as complementary (80). Hence genders constitute "generic realities . . . complementary kinds of a kind" (49, 52).

Why does culture engage in the double effort to differentiate bodies through embodiment and gendering? If the center of sexual meaning is unproblematically reproduction, why is this double effort necessary? Smith's response is reminiscent of Levi-Strauss. "Culture and gender are both normative organizations of intention binding the group together" (68). Gender as "a culturally-engineered central meaning with a culturally-influenced physical base" is necessary because certain "functions (e.g., childbearing and fighting) are necessary and require that our lives be substantially adapted to them" (69, 73). Underlying the cultural creation of complementarity is the species demand for survival. "Since men and women have significantly different reproductive risks and opportunities in evolutionary terms, their guiding sex-related emotions must be sex-differentiated, that is, there must be different female and male sexual natures" (124). In a somewhat bizarre inversion of sociobiological premises, Smith suggests that species reproduction requires sexual differentiation; therefore, culture creates that differentiation to insure the perpetuation of the species but masks its role by attributing the original difference to sex itself. Hence, "heterosexuality's postulated union of male and female specializations is the basic premise of the gender system" (80).

Returning to the theme of concord, Smith concludes his analysis by legitimating the cultural creation of difference with an appeal to a classical conception of the "natural." "Gender dualizing is humanly natural, if nature means that which satisfies conditions of harmonious adjustment. The adjustment in question is humans to themselves. Because humanity is a social reality, it has to be balanced within itself; the category of complementarity is bound to be invoked in the self-interpretation of beings who form their own environment. . . . Reciprocal dependency may take a number of forms, but duality is a preferred principle for elaborating such forms because of the nature of the problem of balancing" (247–248).

From a feminist perspective, the shortcomings of Smith's account of the intricate connections between sex, sexuality, gender, and gender role are numerous. He develops an enormously complex phenomenological analysis of "gender thinking" only to vindicate the natural attitude. Like Levi-Strauss (1969, 1971), Smith accepts a conception of culture as an elaborate mechanism devised to create interdependence and cooperation in the reproduction of the species. Yet culture's mission in inducing complementarity makes sense only if one presupposes an atomistic, asocial, or even antisocial conception of human nature, a conception with strong ties to capitalist ideology, but little validity as universal description. Smith tries to mask the inadequacy of his conceptions of culture and human nature by repeated references to sex construed in terms of "natural kinds," but none of the typical correlates of sex conform to the demands of that classification. Within philosophical discourses, a natural kind refers to a category that exists independent of the observer and that can be defined in terms of an essence, a set of properties common to all members of the kind. Feminist scholarship has repudiated the notion of any sexual essence precisely because "there are no behavioral or physical characteristics that always and without exception are true only of one gender" (Kessler and McKenna 1978, 1). Chromosomes, hormones, sperm production, and egg production, all fail to differentiate all men from all women or to provide a common core within each sex. "No matter how detailed an investigation science has thus far made, it is still not possible to draw a clear dividing line even between male and female" (Devor 1989, 1). If one moves from the natural sciences to the social sciences, efforts to identify behavioral differences that conform to the definition of a natural kind have again ended in failure. Attitudinal and behavioral "sex differences" attributed to men and women are mired in gender symbolism. Indicators of "biologically based femininity" typically include interest in weddings and marriage, preference for marriage over career, interest in infants and children, and enjoyment of childhood play with dolls. While indicators of "biologically based masculinity" include high activity levels, self-assurance, and a preference for career over marriage (Devor 1989, 11–15). Psychological inventories of masculinity and femininity have fallen prey to the misogynist tendency to define socially valued traits as male (logical, self-confident, ambitious, decisive, knows way around world) and less valued characteristics as female (talkative, gentle, sensitive to others' feelings, interest in appearance, strong need for security) (Devor 1989, 32). Even with all the cultural bias built into such studies, they have not been able to clearly differentiate men and women in the cultures that produced them. "'Normal femininity' of the psychological test variety may actually be a rare commodity. In one study of college-aged females, only 15 percent of the heterosexual sample tested as feminine on a widely accepted sex role inventory. The remaining 85 percent scored as either masculine or as some combination of masculine and feminine" (Devor 1989, 15). Differences cast in terms of averages, tendencies, and percentages do not meet the criteria of a natural kind. Nor do such cultural characterizations of masculinity and femininity constitute clear manifestations of "complementarity." If gender is to be judged by the standard Smith sets for it, the creation of reciprocal dependence, then much contemporary evidence (divorce rates, out-of-wedlock births, levels of domestic violence, numbers of "deadbeat dads") suggests that it fails dismally in its mission.

The main virtue of Smith's account is its graphic illustration of how gender, a category specifically devised to avoid biological determinism, covertly invokes the very biological ground it set out to repudiate. Smith's account, like many feminist analyses, like the natural attitude itself, operates within the confines of a "base/superstructure" model of the sex/gender distinction (Connell 1987, 50; Laqueur 1990, 124). Within this model, the body is assumed to provide the raw material which culture can refine in various, but limited ways. Gender is assumed to be "hard-wired," at least, in part. The presumed naturalness (understood as the absence of force or coercion) of gender turns on that presumption of hard-wiring. Thus discussions of gender seldom move far beyond presuppositions concerning inherent sex differences. R.W. Connell has attempted to explain this recurrent problem in feminist accounts of gender by suggesting that in our culture "the notion of natural sex difference forms a limit beyond which thought cannot go" (1987, 66). Similarly, Holly Devor describes biological determinism as the dominant cognitive schema in North America, that is, as the conceptual structure that organizes social experience on the basis of shared understandings (1989, 45–46). Thomas Laqueur (1990), Mary Poovey (1988), and Ludmilla Jordanova (1989) have provided fascinating accounts of the emergence of the base/superstructure model of gender since the seventeenth century. According to Laqueur, "It is a sign of modernity to ask for a single, consistent biology as the source or foundation for masculinity and femininity" (61). Whatever the "cause" of this tendency toward biological determinism, it is an impossible ground for

feminist accounts of gender. As Smith's account makes clear, appeal to a biological ground traps gender in "the ideology of procreation," which construes sexuality and erotic practices only in relation to reproduction (Barrett 1980, 62–77),
according women an essential maternal role mandated by culture and nature—a
role undifferentiated by race, ethnicity, nationality, age, class, sexual orientation, or any mode of individuality.

Is there any escape from the base/superstrucure model of the sex/gender distinction? Must feminist scholars incorporate functionalist assumptions about
culture in their conceptions of gender? Although references to "limits beyond
which thought cannot go" or to "dominant cognitive schemas" suggest quite pes-
simistic responses to these questions, attempts to locate the base/superstructure
model of gender in the politics of modernity offer more optimisitic possibilities.
If this problematic conception of gender is rooted in modernity, then a postmodern feminist strategy specifically devised to abandon all binary oppositions
should afford a conception of gender that escapes the traps of biological determinism. An examination of Judith Butler's complex and innovative analysis of
gender in *Gender Trouble* may be instructive then in revealing the prospects for
a feminist conception of gender beyond the functionalist frame.

A POSTMODERN INTERPRETATION OF GENDER

Judith Butler's *Gender Trouble* (1990) sets out to explain how the "naturalness"
of sex, sexuality, and gender are "constituted through discursively constrained
performative acts that produce the body through and within the categories of
sex" (x). She cautions at the outset that " 'being' a sex or a gender is fundamentally impossible" (18). The binary oppositions male/female and masculine/femi-
nine are incompatible with the continuous variability of human characteristics,
constructing a false opposition between "the sexes" and an artificial coherence
within each term of the binary. Stereotypical genders, then, must be understood
as "ontological locales that are fundamentally uninhabitable" (146). Rejecting
the "old dream of symmetry," Butler argues that gender must be understood, not
as a noun, nor as a set of attributes, but as a "doing," a performative that constitutes the identity that it purports to be (24).

According to Butler, gender is the process that constructs the internal coherence of sex, (hetero)sexual desire, and (hetero)sexual practice within the
modern subject. Gender is the mechanism that produces a notion of a "pre-social
body" shaped by culture. And it provides the standard of intelligibility for persons that informs both the naturalistic paradigm and the authentic-expressive
paradigm of the self. "Gender is the discursive/cultural means by which 'sexed
nature' or 'a natural sex' is produced and established as 'prediscursive,' prior to
culture, a politically neutral surface on which culture acts" (7). Gender performs
this work of naturalization through the "stylized repetition of actions through

time" (141). The natural attitude is produced through the repetition of words, acts, and gestures. The sheer weight of these repetitions leads the actor to believe in and act in the mode of belief. Gender functions, then, as a regulatory fiction, "a fabrication, a fantasy instituted and inscribed on the surface of bodies" (136). Becoming gendered is a laborious process; bringing the self into belief in the natural attitude is arduous; yet the intensity of effort and the power relations that produce this effect are hidden by the very "naturalization" at the core of the gendering process.

Butler's account reverses the direction of causality presumed by the natural attitude: "gender designates the apparatus of production whereby sexes are established" (7). But Butler insists that gender itself is the effect of specific formations of power, of institutions, practices, and discourses that establish and regulate its shape and meaning. What practices produce gender? Butler identifies phallogocentrism and compulsory heterosexuality as the discursive sites that produce gender. "The heterosexualization of desire requires and institutes the production of discrete and asymmetrical oppositions between 'feminine' and 'masculine' understood as expressive attributes of 'female' and 'male'" (17). Like Smith, Butler appeals to the cultural creation of complementarity qua heterosexuality as the ultimate explanans of gender. Her route to this conclusion, however, is markedly different, relying upon a critical rereading of Freud and Lacan.

The incest taboo plays a central role in psychoanalytic accounts of the individual's relation to culture/civilization. It has been advanced as an explanation of the cost that civilization exacts from individuals in return for life-enhancing artifacts, as an explanation of the primary repression through which the individual enters culture, and as an explanation of the formation of gender identity. Butler suggests that the incest taboo itself naturalizes heterosexuality and masculine sexual agency. Through a close reading of Freud's discussion of the "sexual dispositions" that frame the Oedipal conflict, Butler demonstrates that the incest taboo that fuels the Oedipal conflict makes no sense without a prior prohibition of homosexuality. On Butler's reading, Freud's "polymorphous perversity" itself turns on a truncated conception of bisexuality. "The conceptualization of bisexuality in terms of *dispositions*, feminine and masculine, which have heterosexual aims as their intentional correlates, suggests that for Freud *bisexuality is the coincidence of two heterosexual desires within a single psyche*. . . . Within Freud's thesis of primary bisexuality, there is no homosexuality, and only opposites attract" (60–61, italics in the original). The absence of homosexuality in Freud's account attests to the power of culture's original prohibition. Culture produces two prohibitions that regulate the shape and meaning of sexuality: the first is the taboo against homosexuality, and the second is the taboo against incest. "The prohibitive law both produces sexuality in the form of 'dispositions' and appears disingenuously at a later point in time to transform these ostensibly 'natural'

dispositions into culturally acceptable structures of exogamic kinship" (64). Butler notes that the law qua prohibition is also productive: it creates that which it
prohibits. Thus homosexuality and bisexuality cannot be understood as either
"before" or "outside" culture, for they too are constructed within the terms of the
constitutive discourse. "If the incest taboo regulates the production of discrete
gender identities, and if that production requires the prohibition and sanction of
heterosexuality, then homosexuality emerges as a desire which must be produced
in order to remain repressed. In other words, for heterosexuality to remain intact
as a distinct social form, it requires an intelligible conception of homosexuality
and also requires the prohibition of that conception in rendering it culturally
unintelligible" (77).

Butler's account of the formation of gender identity illustrates the complex
relations of prohibition, production, and naturalization. Drawing upon Freud's
notion of melancholia, a process of identification through which the ego incorporates attributes of a lost loved one to minimize the pain of the loss, Butler construes gender identity as a kind of melancholia. The incest taboo's prohibition of
the maternal body triggers an identification with the prohibited object. Abjur-
ing the language of internalization, Butler suggests the process of identification
is better understood as a mode of incorporation or "encrypting." As a technical
psychological term, incorporation refers to an "antimetaphorical activity [that]
literalizes the loss on or in the body and so appears as the facticity of the body,
the means by which the body comes to bear 'sex' at its literal truth. The local-
ization and/or prohibition of pleasures and desires in given 'erotogenic' zones is
precisely the kind of gender-differentiating melancholy that suffuses the body's
surface" (68). The incest taboo's prohibition produces gender identity as a process that minimizes loss through identification's complex disavowal of loss. The
systemacticity of this disavowal erodes the conditions of metaphorical signification resulting in encrypting, a literalizing fantasy that deadens the body, even as
it masks its genealogy, producing a body experienced as "natural fact." Becoming
a gender is becoming naturalized. The taboo against homosexuality in conjunction with the taboo against incest differentiate bodily parts and pleasures on the
basis of gendered meanings, as melancholia deadens some organs to pleasure and
brings others to life (68–70).

Butler's psychoanalytic account accords primacy to compulsory heterosexuality both as an explanation of culture's production of complementarity and as
an explanation of gender's production of a naturalized body. Where Smith endorses cultural mechanisms that "harmonize" human relations and foster social
integration, Butler denounces the modes of power that produce homosexuality
as necessary, yet prohibited; within culture, yet marginalized. Butler is careful to
note that homosexual/heterosexual is itself a problematic discursive formation, a
binary relation premised upon a false opposition and a fraudulent unity within

each term of that binary. Indeed, in criticizing Monique Wittig's radical disjunction between homosexuality and heterosexuality, Butler insists that there are "structures of psychic homosexuality within heterosexual relations, and structures of heterosexuality within gay and lesbian sexuality and relationships" (121). And in criticizing Lacan, Butler cautions against totalizing conceptions of identity that follow from too efficacious and univocal a conception of "the Law." She calls instead for a recognition that "multiple and coexisting identifications produce conflicts, convergences, and innovative dissonances within gender configurations which contest the fixity of masculine and feminine placements with respect to the paternal law" (67). The very possibility of such multiple identifications are central to Butler's strategy for confounding gender. Arguing that power can never be escaped, only redeployed, Butler endorses parody as a tactic designed to subvert "the real" or the "sexually factic." Strategies of subversive repetition can dispel belief in the illusions of the "natural" body/desire/sexuality, thereby rendering gender incredible (141, 146).

As a postmodern critic, Butler's genealogy of gender is designed to probe what is left out of discursive formations that construe sex/gender/desire as natural. She points out that homosexuality as a legitimate mode of sexuality is omitted from naturalistic accounts. Given the pervasiveness and persistence of the natural attitude, it makes sense to attribute its production to powerful cultural forces. In Butler's analysis, gender as performativity becomes the cultural force that produces belief in the naturalness of heterosexuality. Gender is no longer an analytical tool used to illuminate a variety of asymmetries in culture, but rather the process that naturalizes and justifies a particular asymmetry. The "effect of compulsory heterosexuality," gender reproduces a "natural" heterosexual world.

Why does gender act as such a helpful handmaiden of her progenitor (rather than as a rebellious adolescent)? Butler's response is telling: "gender is a project which has cultural survival as its end, the term strategy better suggests the situation of duress under which gender performance always and variously occurs. Hence, as a strategy of survival within compulsory systems, gender is a performance with clearly punitive consequences" (139). Butler's first formulation casts gender in the service of cultural survival. This does not explain why gender performs its designated cultural function, it merely redescribes the function. The second formulation, gender as a strategy of survival within a compulsory system, suggests that gender must perform its function to avoid punishment, a punishment presumably imposed by culture. But why does culture insist upon heterosexuality? In a discourse that explicitly eschews any sociobiological explanation, the options seem to be limited to either a simple notion that culture is a self-replicating system (begging the question of the origin of the cultural preference for heterosexuality) or a Freudian notion that renunciation of homosexual desire is the sublimation that civilization demands. The first option follows from Butler's characterization of gender as performativity, yet it has conservative implications Butler is unlikely to embrace. Butler defines performativity as repetition of words, acts, gestures. This definition is virtually indistinguishable from J.G.A. Pocock's conception of tradition, "an indefinite series of repetitions of an action," introduced both to vindicate the authority of tradition and to eliminate unhelpful and potentially destabilizing queries about origins (1973, 237). Such a conservative project is diametrically opposed to Butler's stated objectives as a genealogist. If Butler's account of gender is not to fall prey to a static conception of cultural self-replication, then her appeal to "cultural survival" must be interpreted in a Freudian vein. Sexuality is offered as the explanans of culture.

Butler's analysis drives a wedge between sex and sexuality, thereby avoiding biological determinism. The belief that sexuality "follows" from sex can be understood only as a relation of political entailment. But what is required to understand culture as "following" from compulsory heterosexuality? Can all of culture's complex domains plausibly be construed as emanating from or mandated by compulsory heterosexuality? Butler tends to conflate culture with phallogocentrism thereby privileging the Symbolic system over science, industry, engineering, or other more palpable cultural constructs. Phallogocentrism captures feminist concerns about male domination in history and culture, but it does so at an exacting cost. For by construing culture in terms of a Symbolic system that itself privileges the Phallus, Butler perpetuates women's invisibility, underestimating their role as cocreators of culture and miring them in victimization. Phallogocentrism fails to provide a sufficiently exhaustive account of culture. Moreover, it indulges a form of anthropomorphism that sustains discussions of what might be called "the cunning of culture" (Tucker 1974), the ingenious means by which culture insures its own survival through the production of organizational practices and structures independent of the needs or intentions of individuals. Such a reification makes culture appear at once omniscient, seamless, and unassailable, a markedly unhelpful point of departure for those aspiring to feminist transformation. There is also a certain irony in Butler's positing of compulsory heterosexuality as the explanans of culture. Foucault cautioned against the trap of conceiving sex (qua sexuality) as the secret of being, suggesting that such beliefs implicate the subject in ever deeper modes of subjugation. It is unlikely that a Foucauldian gesturing toward sexuality as the secret of culture can escape that trap.

What does Butler's discursive construction of gender leave out? By interpreting gender in terms of the cultural production of heterosexual desire and psychoanalytic production of gender identity, Butler's account makes gender too much a matter of the self—a self that appears peculiarly unmarked by race, class, ethnicity, or nationality. Her account privatizes gender, restricting the utility of the concept. Butler's conception offers little prospect for unraveling gender symbolism or for addressing gender structures beyond the psyche. The operation of gender in social, political, and economic institutions disappears as the psychodrama of the desiring self is played out. This occlusion of gender as an organizational feature of social life that is itself mediated by race and class may explain why Butler's reliance on parody as a transformative mechanism rings so hollow. While parody might help subvert the naturalization of desire, it is unlikely to make inroads against the economic and political forces that circumscribe women's lives.

Butler's postmodern account of gender succeeds in escaping biological determinism, but it still proffers a functionalist explanation of gender. Moreover in positing heterosexuality as the explanans of culture, Butler's account of gender comes far too close to Smith's account for comfort. Allusions to compulsory heterosexuality do nothing to dispel the ideology of reproduction that sustains the natural attitude. Despite the virtuousity of Butler's account of gender as performativity, it does not provide a conception of gender that breaks definitively from the problematic presuppositions of the ideology of procreation.

A STRUCTURAL ANALYSIS OF GENDER

R.W. Connell's *Gender and Power* (1987), which blends strains of Marxism, existentialism, and poststructuralism in developing its account of gender, is richly deserving of close examination. Connell advances a "systematic social theory of gender" that strives to account for the historicity of gender, the dynamic role of gender in economic, political, sexual and psychological domains, the relation between personal agency and social structure in gender formation and reproduction, as well as the turbulence and contradictions pertaining to gender as lived experience. Attuned to the problems associated with conceptions of gender that construe women as perennial victims, Connell develops a "practice-based" theory of gender, attentive to both the constraining power of gender and the myriad struggles people engage against those constraints. In addition, Connell provides a cogent critique of all modes of biological determinism. Noting that the body is never experienced without cultural mediation, he defines gender in terms of the cognitive and interpretive practices that "create, appropriate, and recreate reproductive biology" (79).

According to Connell, gender as a social practice is more than a mere marking of the human body, "it is the weaving of a structure of symbols which exaggerate and distort human potential" (79). Repudiating various versions of mind/body dualism, Connell insists that "the practical transformation of the body in the social structure of gender is not only accomplished at the level of symbolism. It has physical effects on the body, the incorporation is a material one" (87). Connell is also careful to point out that the social practices constituting gender bear no direct relation to what might be considered "functional" for human reproduction. The patterns of posture, movement, dress, adornment, body shape, body image, sexuality, intonation, speech, skilling, and de-skilling associated with cultural constructions of masculinity and femininity may not be at all conducive to reproduction. Arguing that the "logic" that drives gender is autonomous, Connell rejects all theories that attempt to derive gender from natural differences, biological reproduction, the functional needs of society, or the imperatives of social reproduction. Indeed, he insists that functionalist arguments must be viewed with extreme suspicion: they serve only to mask the power underlying these cultural symbolizations in order to justify inequitable distributions of social burdens and benefits.

In developing his account of the historicity of gender, Connell delineates a conception of human practices in relation to social structures informed by the works of Marx and Sartre. On this view, practices are the daily actions of human beings who appropriate and transform nature in order to satisfy their needs; in the process they transform themselves by producing new needs and new practices. Practices are inherently dynamic transformations of the natural world that open up new possibilities as well as new risks and pressures. Practices can also become solidified, entrenched, institutionalized, thereby creating a degree of intractability in the social world that limits the freedom of future practices. Connell defines social structure in terms of such limits. A social structure is a pattern of constraint on practice inherent in social relations. Operating through the complex interplay of power and institutions, "'structure' specifies the way practices (over time) constrain practices" (95). Although structures mark the fixity of the social world, the sedimentation of past practices that limit present action, the dimension of collective life that exists beyond individual intention, they are not impervious to change. "Practice can be turned against what constrains it. . . . Structure can deliberately be the object of practice. But practice cannot escape structure, it cannot float free of its circumstances" (95). According to Connell, gender can best be understood as an interrelated set of social structures that define men and women in terms of their reproductive role and organize social life around sex and sexuality. On this view, gender is far more than an attribute of an individual or a characteristic of a social collectivity; it is the active process that reduces people to, and conceives social life in terms of, reproductive function, thereby constraining individual potential (97, 140, 245).

Taking issue with feminist accounts that construe gender structure in terms of a monolithic male domination, Connell argues that gender must be conceived in terms of very specific structures tied to particular social practices of labor, power, and cathexis. He insists that gender is not an "ideological addendum" to social structures rooted in race or class, but rather an autonomous structure constitutive of these fields. As a constraint upon labor, gender structures the allocation of particular types of work, the organization of domestic activity, the division of paid versus unpaid labor, the segregation of labor markets, patterns of production and consumption, wage levels, opportunities for employment and promotion, and even the conditions and terms of labor exchange. Within the domain of power, gender structures authority, control, and coercion by establishing hierarchies in public and private sectors, creating a virtual male monopoly on institutional and interpersonal violence, and promoting particular modes of domestic and sexual asymmetries. Defining cathexis in terms of practices constructing emotionally charged relations with others, Connell notes that gender structures identities of desiring subjects and designation of desirable objects, patterns of desire, sexual practices, as well as terms and conditions for sexual exchange.

Connell notes that these diverse gender structures exist in complex interrelationship but insists that it is a mistake to characterize that relationship as either a logical or systemic unity. Even the notion of an "historical unity" tends to convey more coherence and internal consistency than may exist; the notion masks tensions, uneven developments, and internal contradictions among these structures that can precipitate crises crucial to their transformation. Connell prefers the term, "historical composition," to capture the human agency that creates the imperfect and incomplete orderliness linking diverse gender structures. As a historical composition, gender is "a linking concept. It is about linking other fields of social practice to modal practices of engendering" (140). Its central tools are the principles of separation, division, and unequal integration (97).

Human agency is essential to creating and transforming gender, yet the natural attitude sees gender as fixed by nature. Connell suggests that the apparent fixity of gender structures is maintained by "sexual ideology." Describing his approach to sexual ideology as "more akin to the sociology of knowledge than to contemporary theories of discourse," Connell suggests that ideology must be understood as "a practice, ontologically on a par with other practices and equally involved in the constitution of social interests" (244–245). Connell identifies two fundamental practices constitutive of sexual ideology, naturalization, and cognitive purification. Naturalization collapses social structure into nature to legitimate social practices and insulate them from change. "Naturalization is not a naive mistake about what biology can or cannot explain. At a collective level, it is a highly motivated ideological practice which constantly overrides biological facts" (246). Cognitive purification involves the production of ideological representations devoid of any of the messy complexity of lived relations. Shallow stereotypes, romantic narratives, "squeaky clean" sociobiological images of women as nurturers and men as providers—these are the stock-in-trade of cognitive purification.

Gender and Power presents a remarkably insightful and systematic analysis of gender. Like Smith and Butler, Connell moves from a description of gender as analytic category to an account of gender as an active process structuring multiple domains of social life. He offers a "modest" justification for his approach, "this framework is serviceable for understanding current history" (97). He might also have said that his theory accounts for virtually every feminist usage of "gender" over the past several decades and relates them in a multilayered whole.

At the level of conceptualization, however, there is some slippage in his theorization of gender. For Connell, gender is the process that relates all the rich and varied levels of human activity to biological reproduction. Gender is an active force that makes us think constantly in terms of sex. And it is precisely this reductionism that enables gender to constrain so many dimensions of social organization. Yet when Connell so deftly identifies the gender structures operative in the domains of labor and power, it is not at all clear that they gain their force by dragging the mind back to reproductive biology. Do women really earn less because they are capable of bearing children? Does gender make us think so? Is job segregation in clerical work, fast-food industries, primary and secondary education, or nursing really related to women's gestational ability? Are women subjected to domestic violence because of their reproductive role?

Connell notes that "the practices of sexual reproduction are often quite remote aspects of social encounters in which gender is constructed and sustained" (81). But if this is so, how does gender work? Connell introduces Sartre's distinction between a practico-inert series and an intentionally mobilized group to explain gender's operative mechanisms. According to Sartre, a series is a mode of collective unity structured by external social or material circumstances or what might be called the "logic of the situation." Because the commonality that unites the series is imposed by external objects or the actions of others, seriality is passive, implying no conscious awareness on the part of those who make up the series. Sartre used the example of people waiting for a bus to illustrate his conception of the series: they have certain things in common by virtue of their situation even though they may not be consciously aware of any common ties. In contrast, a group is a collection of persons who consciously acknowledge a bond uniting them, whether it be a collective identity, a common project, or shared values.

According to Connell, sex can be understood as a series. The biological differentiation of men and women in reproduction imposes an external logic upon individuals on the basis of a parallel situation. Thus women share a passive commonality by virtue of their reproductive capacity, as do men. In keeping with Sartre's description of seriality as practico-inert (that is, a product of human action that constrains), Connell notes that construing sex as a series does not imply any awareness of the postulated commonality, any incorporation of the seriality into one's identity, nor any identification with those others who share the situation. By describing gender in terms of a Sartrean group, Connell suggests that gender's task is to create a conscious awareness of reproductive capacity as the basis for solidarity. "To construct the social category 'man' or 'woman,' with a common identity and interest, requires a negation of the serial dispersion characteristic of the array of parallel situations constructed by biological categories. This is done in practices that create and assert the solidarity of the sex (or of a group within it)" (81, 137). For gender to accomplish its mission, then, it must negate the passive experience of the body and create a notion of commonality embraced by members of the group, thereby mobilizing women and men as distinctive groups. But how can gender simultaneously negate the biological ground of the series and mobilize reproductive biology as the basis of a shared identity? And if certain social expectations about the sexed body constitute sex as a practico-inert series, structuring the logic of situation in terms of reproduction, then how does gender differ from those initial social expectations? The sex/gender distinction seems to collapse into a vortex of reproduction.

Sartre conceives of the group as a collection of persons whose conscious awareness of shared characteristics serves as the basis for united action, for the initiation of a collective project. But Connell's conception of gender cannot begin to carry men and women that far, for he explicitly acknowledges the deficiencies of any construction of men and women as internally undifferentiated categories. And he is keenly aware of the social cleavages rooted in race, class, ethnicity, age, and homophobia that preclude any collective identification, much less collective action. Thus the group/series explanation of how gender accomplishes its work founders in both its account of sex as series and its account of gender as group. And despite Connell's numerous caveats, it appears to accord primacy to reproduction in cultural constructions of sex as well as gender.

The limitations of Connell's attempt to define gender as a process linking diverse fields of social relations to reproductive biology also surface in his discussion of sexual ideology. It is not at all clear how gender differs from sexual ideology. Both are described as cognitive and interpretive practices, as symbolizations that naturalize social constructions and impose untenable sex distinctions on men and women. Is gender after all, a matter of belief more than a structure of social forces? In what precise ways does it differ from sexual ideology? Connell uses sexual ideology to discuss literature, film, and modes of cultural production that do not fit into his categories of labor, power, and cathexis. But if we are to take seriously his discussions of the role of beliefs in constituting social practices and his rejection of simplistic base/superstructure models, what is the purpose of the distinction between gender and sexual ideology? In devising a conception of sexual ideology "akin to the sociology of knowledge," Connell is able to discuss the role (conservative versus radical) of intellectuals in ideological production and to introduce a conception of social interests (male hegemonic) served by

naturalization. Both of these moves allow Connell covertly to introduce functionalist premises that he had explicitly renounced earlier in his analysis.

Connell offers several functionalist speculations about why belief in gender
persists despite all the philosophical arguments and scientific evidence that
demonstrate the defects of the natural attitude. "There is a logic to paradoxes
such as gross exaggerations of difference by social practices of dress. . . . They are
part of a continuing effort to sustain the social definition of gender, an effort that
is necessary precisely because the biological logic, and the inert practice that re-
sponds to it, cannot sustain gender categories" (81). But if gender is doing its cultural work successfully, what explains the perceived necessity to shore up gender?
Connell's account is startling: "The solidarity of the heterosexual couple is
formed on the basis of some kind of reciprocity rather than on the basis of common situation or experience. . . . Sexual difference is in large part what gives
erotic flavor to relationships. It is emphasized as a means of heightening and intensifying pleasure, hence, the systematic exaggeration of gender differences"
(113). Despite the enormous complexity of Connell's account, despite his repeated cautions against functionalist explanation, the complementarity thesis
undergirds his analysis. It provides the fundamental explanation of why gender
persists.

Connell's book is remarkably sensitive to heterosexism, but the notion that
"sexual difference" heightens erotic pleasure depends on heterosexist presuppositions. Eve Sedgwick (1990) has pointed out that the heterosexual/homosexual
opposition allows equivocation in the meaning imputed to 'homo'/sexual. As one
moves from notions of one sex, to same sex, to self-same, to sameness, an enormous range of differences is elided. And this elision sustains Connell's assumption
that there is greater difference, hence greater potential erotic pleasure, across genders than within genders. "The new calculus of homo/hetero . . . owes its sleekly
utilitarian feel to the linguistically unappealable classification of anyone who
shares one's gender as the 'same' as oneself, and anyone who does not share one's
gender as Other" (Sedgwick 1990, 160). But Sedgwick points out that even the
most cursory examination of human beings will reveal that being of the same
gender cannot guarantee "similarity" anymore than being of "opposite" genders
can guarantee difference. Moreover, the belief that the gender of one's sexual
partner is the crucial difference determining pleasure (rather than differences pertaining to positions, acts, techniques, zones or sensations, physical types, symbolic
investments, relations of power, and so on) will not withstand serious scrutiny.
Thus, there appears to be a suppressed procreationist premise in Connell's allu-
sion to the best means to heighten erotic pleasure. Once again, the "cunning of
culture" seems to insert a procreationist agenda into an explanation of gender.

Connell's attempt to describe gender as a reductionist process linking divergent social fields to sexual reproduction does not adequately account for all the

modes of injustice women experience, although it certainly identifies a wide range of feminist concerns. Ultimately it founders on the complementarity thesis as the rationale for the cultural imposition of gender. No longer in the service of species or cultural survival, Connell's appeal to complementarity serves hedonistic ends. Gender is posited as a mechanism for heightening the intensity of pleasure. But whether the function attributed to gender is the production of heterosexuality or erotic pleasure, functionalist explanation leads feminists to a dead end. For feminists theorizing gender within a functionalist frame cannot escape the specter of biological determinism or the ideology of reproduction. Once again an insightful deployment of gender as analytic category slips into problematic claims about gender as explanans.

AN ETHNOMETHODOLOGICAL ACCOUNT OF GENDER

In a remarkable and insightful approach to the study of gender, Suzanne Kessler and Wendy McKenna attempt to bracket ontological claims about gender in order to explore gender attribution, the instantaneous process by which one person classifies another as a man or a woman. Their explicit goal in *Gender: An Ethnomethodological Approach* (1978) is to explain how gender attribution works. Their exposition of how the process operates does, however, sustain certain speculations about the larger question "why."

Kessler and McKenna begin their investigation by noting several factors concomitant to gender attribution: the urgency that governs gender attribution in daily life (we feel we need to know if we are interacting with a man/women, boy/girl), the conviction that every individual can be categorized as a man/woman, and the uneasiness that surrounds "ambiguous" cases. Linking the "need" to classify people by gender to the natural attitude, Kessler and McKenna provide a comprehensive demonstration that the assumptions informing the natural attitude are systematically flawed. Yet they note that the fact that the natural attitude rests upon a number of mistaken beliefs in no way mitigates its hold. On the contrary, each time particular beliefs informing the natural attitude are refuted, new ones seem to replace them. Thus, they note that the absence of any physical or behavioral grounds for a dichotomous classification of men and women has led to the emergence of a new "scientific" concern with gender identity, the individual's psychological sense of being a male or a female, as a firmer foundation for a "fixed dichotomy." "Transsexual is a category constructed to relieve ambiguity, to avoid the kinds of combinations (male genitals and female gender identity) that make people uncomfortable because they violate basic rules about gender. Since genitals can now be changed, gender identity is now seen as a less flexible criterion; thus marking the triumph of surgeons over psychotherapists in the rush to restore gender to unambiguous reality" (120).

What fuels this incessant replenishing of the natural attitude? Kessler and McKenna argue that sexual dimorphism is not given in nature, but imposed upon nature by the perceiver. "Gender is a social construction, a world of two sexes is the result of the socially shared, taken-for-granted methods which members use to construct a world" (vii). The perceiver's expectation that there are two genders leads to the perception of two genders by forcing all perceived phenomena into the posited dichotomous categories. Anomalies are hidden and ambiguities masked, allowing the perceived phenomenon to conform to and thereby confirm the validity of the original expectation. According to Kessler and McKenna, the selective perception that sustains gender attribution in daily life also shapes the socially accredited perceptions of scientists, whose work is then taken as incontrovertible proof of the validity of the perceptual categories.

> Scientists construct dimorphism where there is continuity. Hormones, behavior, physical characteristics, developmental processes, chromosomes, and psychological qualities have all been fitted into dichotomous categories. Scientific knowledge does not inform the answer to the question, 'What makes a person a man or a woman?' Rather it justifies (and appears to give grounds for) the already existing conviction that a person is either a man or a woman and that there is no problem differentiating between the two. Biological, psychological, and social differences do not lead to our seeing two genders. Our seeing two genders leads to the 'discovery' of biological, psychological, and social differences. (163)

Kessler and McKenna's goal is to discern how gender attributions are made. For once a person has been classified as a man/woman, his/her actions and intentions are interpreted on the basis of culturally specific gender expectations that have pervasive life consequences. In accordance with the modernist assumption that biology provides the foundation for masculinity and femininity, most people believe that the genitals provide the ultimate criterion for gender attribution. But Kessler and McKenna point out that in daily practice, attribution is almost always made in the absence of any information about genitals. Sex assignment at birth typically follows from the delivering physician's inspection of genitalia, but in social interactions, the decision to categorize another as male/female seldom turns on such direct inspection. The recent emphasis on gender identity as the ground for the dichotomous classification of men and women makes gender identity a possible basis for gender attribution. But as the psychological sense of being a man/woman, gender identity is not immediately perceptible. Kessler and McKenna note that the only way to ascertain someone's gender identity is to ask the individual a direct question, and such queries are not typically made prior to gender attribution.

How then is gender attributed? Kessler and McKenna argue that gender attribution depends upon cues given by the perceived which facilitate categorization on the basis of socially constructed, gender-specific norms. The dimensions of the presentation of self that provide cues for gender attribution include: modes and content of speech; styles of dress, adornment, posture, and movement; and the construction of a narrative history that conforms to gender stereotypes (126–128). For gender attribution that depends exclusively upon visual encounters, "tertiary sexual characteristics"—nonverbal behaviors such as facial expressions, movement, body posture—are the predominant gender markers. Kessler and McKenna introduce the term "cultural genitals" to characterize these culture-specific appearances that sustain inferences about gender. Gender attribution is dependent upon "genital attribution," but genital attribution "takes place irrespective of biological genitals on the basis of 'cultural genitals'—that are assumed to be there" (153–154). People believe that sound inferences about biology can be made on the basis of stylized gender cues, and this belief fixes gender symbolization in the body. "The relationship between cultural genitals and gender attribution is reflexive. The reality of 'gender' is proved by the genital which is attributed and at the same time the attributed genital only has meaning through the socially shared construction of gender attribution" (155).

Kessler and McKenna insist that gender categories are culturally specific. To demonstrate that dichotomous classification is not the only alternative, they discuss the "berdache"—people who receive social sanction to become a gender other than that to which they were originally assigned—as a "third gender" recognized by certain Native American peoples. How then are culture-specific gender categories constructed? Because psychology treats gender as a "way of seeing," Kessler and McKenna review psychoanalytic, social learning, and cognitive development theories for clues to the construction of gender categories. They argue persuasively that none of these approaches can explain adequately either the individual's acquisition of gender categories or the social construction of gender categories. They turn instead to the idea of a cognitive schema to explain the organizing expectations that shape perception. "A categorizing scheme is not dependent on any particular cue, nor is it a rule followed by robots. Rather it is a way of understanding . . . a method of applying information" (158, 161). In keeping with their ethnomethodological approach, they suggest that these categorizing schemas arise from the incorrigible propositions of specific cultures; they bracket questions concerning the origins of the incorrigible propositions themselves. Unfortunately, such a bracketing removes from consideration some difficult questions about the nature of, and possibilities for change in, categorizing schema, and this severely limits Kessler and McKenna's prescription for escaping the life-constraining force of dichotomous gender.

Kessler and McKenna suggest that the key to transforming gender lies in changing our incorrigible propositions. They suggest that this can be done by "confronting the reality of other possibilities (e.g., the berdache), as well as the possibility of other realities" (164). Enhancing awareness of other cultures could then serve to liberate people from the natural attitude. In addition, they suggest marshalling logical arguments and empirical evidence to demonstrate the deficiencies in incorrigible beliefs as a means of dispelling them. Kessler and McKenna recognize, for example, that the complementarity thesis undergirds sociobiological accounts of gender. A clear understanding of gender attribution should therefore help dispel the erroneous belief that gender differentiation saves the species from extinction by enabling "sperm-producers" and "egg-producers" to recognize each other. Their study demonstrates that gender attribution is based upon "cultural genitals," which can provide no certainty whatsoever about who might be a suitable reproductive partner. Thus, gender fails in its "evolutionary mission," a failure so significant that it should be sufficient to undermine sociobiological claims.

Despite the lucidity of their argument, the reliance upon rational argument to expunge such errors confronts a problem. If incorrigible beliefs are as impervious to evidence as their definition suggests, then this strategy is doomed to failure. And if categorizing schema routinely screen out anomalies to the extent that Kessler and McKenna claim, then it is unlikely that culture-bound individuals will be able to perceive the evidence that other cultures afford. The very presuppositions of ethnomethodology undermine the possibility of freeing people from gender by an appeal to evidence. For that evidence is theoretically constructed within a particular cultural frame, and, according to Kessler and McKenna, "ultimately there is no way to determine the truth of theoretical formulations. Theories may be more or less useful, aesthetically pleasing, or 'in vogue,' but their claim to truth is, in some sense, a matter of faith in basic assumptions" (100). And reason is no match against faith.

What is important about Kessler and McKenna's conception of gender is not merely their insightful account of the mechanics of gender attribution, but their subtle shift of gender's terrain. Gender moves from a stylization of the body to a category of the mind. It is, in an important sense, an immaterial substance—an intangible idea with palpable consequences, an a priori category that structures the phenomenal world. The notion of cognitive schema invoked in this work is seriously undertheorized. It is not clear whether such a mental category has more in common with Hume's notion of a "habit of the mind," with Kant's conception of a "category of the mind," or with cognitive psychology's version of "prototype theory." Each of these acknowledges the active role of the knower in constructing the object of knowledge, but they differ in their accounts of the origins of such categories, the role of tradition/reason/ language in structuring these categories, and in their assessments of how coherent, ubiquitous, and persistent such categorizations may be. Feminists who describe gender as a lens (Bem 1993), a way of seeing, or a cognitive category may not mean to invoke the full force of the Humean or Kantian conceptions, but they should proceed with extreme caution. Hume, for example, links "habits of the mind" to constant conjunction of empirically observed phenomena; this suggests that, where the eye perceives two things happening together, the mind imposes a "necessary connection." Extrapolating the Humean model to gender produces an account that locks cultural constructions of masculinity and femininity to sexed bodies with a degree of necessity that is nearly impossible to break. According to Kant, categories of the mind constitute the precondition of cognition. If gender is construed as a category of the mind, then no thinking subject can escape its grip. For those who would eradicate gender-based injustice, there are dire implications in the displacement of gender from external world to internal/mental terrain. It is not at all clear that one can change a "category of the mind." Within a social constructionist frame, cognitive schema may serve merely to mark the social constitution of consciousness. But if this is what is meant, then culture resurfaces in this discourse without any clear explication of why particular cultures cause dichotomous perceptions of gender. Biological determinism may be avoided in this account, but the natural attitude remains entrenched, as the cunning of culture structures the basic categories of the mind.

Gender as Analytic Category Versus Gender as Explanans

Gender as an analytic category illuminates a range of questions for feminist investigation and provides a framework for those investigations that challenges androcentric and heteronormative assumptions. A sophisticated understanding of gender as an analytical tool can enable feminist scholars to identify important issues pertaining to social institutions, relations, and symbols, as well as individual identities, which can be investigated within particular cultures and subcultures at particular historical moments. Developing conceptual distinctions that differentiate sex, sexuality, sexual identity, gender identity, gender role, gender-role identity can enable feminist scholars to deploy gender as an analytical device, illuminating power relations and engaging questions that confound the natural attitude, thereby contributing to progressive feminist goals.

If feminist scholars are to use gender as an analytical category that fosters emancipatory projects, however, there are crucial pitfalls to avoid. The foregoing analysis of a number of feminist efforts to theorize gender locates one danger in the construction of a narrative that links gender to the cunning of culture operating in the interests of reproduction. These efforts to explain the function of gender replicate problematic assumptions of the ideology of procreation rather than dispelling the natural attitude. Despite repeated references to cultural specificity, these accounts suggest a universal and invariant role for gender. Race, class, ethnicity, and nationality disappear from these accounts as the cunning of culture produces species survival, compulsory heterosexuality, heightened sexual pleasure, or categories of the mind.

I have tried to show that in each of these works the effort to theorize gender involves a subtle shift from an account of "how" gender operates under specific historical conditions to a universal claim about "why" gender performs a particular social function. In this shift, gender is transformed from an analytic category to a causal force. The heuristic tool is displaced as gender is accorded ontological status. It is described as the *cause* of certain beliefs about the world; the *force* that molds a plastic humanity, produces naturalized bodies or imposes sexual dimorphism; as the *determinant* of identity; the *process* that structures labor, power, and cathexis; or the *mental category* that structures a form of dichotomous perception. The distortion involved in the move from analytic category to causal force becomes apparent when the causal claims are subjected to critical scrutiny. Whether gender is advanced to explain the cultural production of heterosexual desire, the psychoanalytic production of individual identity, the power asymmetries in social life or the structure of perception, close examination of the claim reveals that the imputed causality is unfounded. Although gender as an analytic category can be invaluable to feminist scholarship in illuminating certain facets of social existence, it is a grave error to attribute explanatory force to gender.

Feminist analysis is not strengthened when gender is conflated with universal explanans. On the contrary, ersatz explanation is dangerous. It proffers false security by suggesting that issues, which need to be interrogated and analyzed, are already understood. Constructing a functionalist narrative of gender that appears to possess universal validity occludes cultural specificity and historical variability, according gender an intransigence that is markedly unhelpful to feminist projects. Rather than tracing the instability of gender as a cultural category, marking the fault lines, and searching for points at which feminist interventions might be possible, gender as universal explanans aggregates various forms of difference, disadvantage, and domains of social life under one vague, reproductive rubric, which masks the specificity of problems and impairs the identification of possible solutions. There is no question that women experience numerous disadvantages in male-dominated societies, forms of injustice that constrain their opportunities and life prospects. But gender can explain these constraints only by definitional fiat.

As a mode of explanation, functionalism has been faulted for insensitivity to history, a teleology that conflates putative function with genetic cause, a tendency to mask power, and a conservative propensity to legitimate the status quo.

None of these features of functionalism sits well with the liberatory impulse of feminist scholarship and feminist politics. Functionalist explanations of gender are particularly worrisome because they accord gender an intractability that renders transformative strategies either inconceivable, utopian, or impracticable. According gender a functional role in relation to reproduction also lends cultural constructions of gender unwarranted legitimacy. I have already noted that gender as universal explanans occludes mediations of race, class, ethnicity, and nationality and, in so doing, works against a feminist politics that tries to build solidarities across these hierarchies of difference. To the extent that gender as universal explanans shifts feminist politics toward issues of self, psyche, and sexuality, it structures a politics that is insufficiently inclusive. As Chandra Mohanty has pointed out, feminist strategies that privilege privatized gender fail to engage Third World women who locate their politics in a collective struggle against racism, sexism, colonialism, imperialism, and monopoly capital (Mohanty, Russo, and Torres 1991, 2–38).

The problematic accounts of gender discussed in this chapter suggest that gender as universal explanans poses grave threats to the potential benefits of gender as an analytic category. If feminist scholars are to confound gender and the natural attitude, rather than being confounded by gender, then it will be helpful to enrich our conceptual terminology, taking advantage of crucial distinctions such as sexed embodiedness, sexuality, sexual identity, gender identity, gendered divisions of labor, gendered social relations, gendered institutions, and gender symbolism, rather than collapsing such diverse notions into the single term, gender. Feminist scholars must also steadfastly resist the tendency to treat gender as universal explanans, to construe it as a causal force in domains as disparate as psyche, self and social relations. Universal claims about the invariability of gender and unwarranted assumptions about the cunning of culture securing gender's psychic and social functions are self-defeating, for they signify the persistence of the natural attitude in feminist discourses, a fundamental failure to escape its grip.

Chapter 7

Feminist Standpoint Theory as Analytical Tool

IF POLITICAL DIMENSIONS of knowledge are often embedded in contentious theoretical assumptions that guide research, how can these assumptions be excavated and engaged? Are there techniques that feminist scholars can use to identify and critique presuppositions that typically remain tacit and unexamined? Are there methodological innovations within feminist scholarship uniquely suited to the interrogation of the theoretical assumptions that play such a powerful role in structuring perception and accrediting particular forms of evidence?

The persistence of racist, sexist, and homophobic assertions within and outside the academy gives feminist scholars strong motivation to question such knowledge claims. But if the problematic theoretical presuppositions supporting these views operate tacitly, how can feminist researchers make them explicit, demonstrate their effects, and hold them to account? In this chapter, I argue that feminist standpoint theory, deployed as an analytical tool, affords an innovative means for the identification and interrogation of competing theoretical presuppositions.

The chapter begins with a discussion of what it means to use alternative standpoints as an analytical tool. It then provides two case studies to demonstrate the potential contributions of standpoint analysis. Focusing on two policy issues of great import for women, affirmative action and welfare "reform," I explore the kind of knowledge that can be produced by gathering, comparing, and contrasting views of conservative women, liberal feminists, socialist feminists, black feminists, and postmodern feminists. I suggest that systematic comparison of divergent "standpoints" illuminates the role of tacit assumptions in the selection of evidence, demonstrates questionable premises, and identifies grounds for assessing the credibility of particular claims. In addition, comparative analysis of a range of competing knowledge claims reveals omissions, distortions, and deficiencies in particular accounts, which provide rich resources for the development of feminist critiques.

Standpoint Analysis as a Method of Inquiry

From its origin in the work of Nancy Hartsock, feminist standpoint theory promised feminist scholarship a novel epistemology that could ground research in the truth embodied in women's experience. "Women's lives make available a particular and privileged vantage point on male supremacy, a vantage point which can ground a powerful critique of the phallocratic institutions and ideology which constitute capitalist patriarchy" (Hartsock 1983, 284). According to Hartsock, the feminist standpoint offered a definitive account of "the real relations among human beings as inhuman, point[ing] beyond the present, and carrying a historically liberatory role" (Hartsock 1983, 285). Thus standpoint theory promised to provide a bridge from knowledge to politics as cogent critiques gave rise to transformative praxis.

As we saw in chapter 2, feminist standpoint theory in its initial formulation followed classical Marxism in grounding ideology critique in a theory of truth that could generate political prescriptions tied to the "objective interests of women." As feminist standpoint theorists have grappled with the Althusserian conception of ideology, post-positivist conceptions of knowledge, and the powerful critiques advanced by black feminist theorists and postcolonial feminist theorists, these objectivist moorings have given way to an antifoundationalist reformulation of standpoint theory (Wylie 2000a). Feminist standpoint theorists have introduced conceptions of "situated knowledges" (Haraway 1991a), "subjugated knowledges" (Collins 1990), and "strong objectivity" (Harding 1991, 1992) to theorize the multiplicity of women's perspectives and the diversity of women's experiences without succumbing to relativism.

In this chapter, I consider the possible uses of standpoint theory as a methodological device, as a tool to guide feminist inquiry. As an analytical tool, feminist standpoint theory has a number of advantages. It suggests a way of gathering information for analysis that presupposes multiplicity and complexity. It recognizes that knowledge claims are produced and accredited within specific communities, and it provides a mechanism for comparatively assessing accounts that emerge within markedly different communities.

Feminist scholarship has shifted over the past two decades from a notion of "the" feminist standpoint to a recognition of multiple feminist standpoints and multiple standpoints of women and men. As an analytical tool, feminist standpoint analysis accepts plurality as an inherent characteristic of the human condition and uses the comparison of multiple and competing views as a strategy for knowledge production. Rather than presuming the truth of any particular standpoint, feminist standpoint as an analytical tool requires the collection and interrogation of competing claims about the same phenomenon. Rather than succumb to relativist notions that truth involves the sum of conflicting ac-counts, standpoint analysis critically engages contentious theoretical assump-tions to demarcate valid from flawed accounts. In marked contrast to social science methodologies that naively claim value-neutrality, feminist standpoint analysis acknowledges that claims about the world are theoretically mediated and value-laden—constructed in relation to a range of partial perspectives and determinate interests. Thus feminist standpoint as an analytical tool offers a methodology markedly suited to the post-positivist recognition of the role that theoretical presuppositions play in cognition. By expanding the sphere of re-search to encompass the theoretical frameworks that support competing empiri-cal claims, feminist standpoint analysis affords new mechanisms to help resolve seemingly intractable disputes. Attuned to the impact of particular theories on the selection of evidence, comparative standpoint analysis can provide reasons for doubting questionable assumptions, stimulate recognition of the intricacy and complexity of events, identify relevant criticisms of overly simplistic ac-counts, and produce more sophisticated analyses. Attentive to the multiple sources of error that can impede knowledge production, feminist standpoint analysis encourages researchers to interrogate that which seems least contestable. As an analytical tool, then, feminist standpoint theory provides feminist schol-ars with a methodological strategy to engage complexity, plurality, and fallibility.

To explore the potential uses of feminist standpoint analysis, the following two sections gather and analyze multiple and competing views concerning affir-mative action and welfare "reform." Each section provides an example of how to use standpoint analysis to guide research. The first step is to construct alternative "standpoints" by collecting and synthesizing as many competing views of the subject under investigation as possible. Standpoint analysis imposes a responsi-bility on the researcher to engage as comprehensive an array of claims as time and feasibility allow. Precisely because it starts from an acknowledgment of the partiality and contentiousness of competing claims and relies upon systematic comparison of alternative views as a method for identifying errors, standpoint analysis recognizes that omission of critical perspectives can seriously distort re-search findings. To avoid such distortion in discussions of affirmative action and welfare "reform," I have collected arguments advanced by scholars and activists in order to construct a "composite" conservative standpoint, liberal-feminist stand-point, socialist-feminist standpoint, black-feminist standpoint, and postmodern-feminist standpoint. By comparing the theoretical assumptions as well as the empirical claims within these conflicting accounts, I hope to illuminate the po-tential contributions that standpoint analysis offers for understanding pressing political issues. I also suggest that feminist standpoint analysis can address some problems pertaining to objectivity discussed in chapter 3, particularly those linked to intersubjective corroboration of truth claims, which traditional social science methods have been unable to address successfully. Feminist standpoints used as an analytical tool, then, may contribute to the construction of an objective account of political life, although not in the way that Nancy Hartsock originally suggested.

To reap the benefits of standpoint analysis, the researcher must examine alternative views fairly and in depth. In presenting competing policy stands on affirmative action and welfare "reform," I have tried to avoid caricature by using the words of the proponents of each view and tracing their arguments from most basic theoretical assumptions to constructions of evidence to generation of policy prescriptions. Juxtaposing the competing accounts is itself a way of gleaning knowledge, for it allows the contentious frameworks that inform these views to become visible. As the following examples show, when the values central to these policy stances are made evident, feminist scholars can evaluate problematic claims about the social world with far more sophistication. In the next two sections I explicate five competing standpoints concerning contemporary policy debates. Standpoints on affirmative action are explored first, followed by a survey of competing claims concerning welfare policy. Once the alternative standpoints for each policy area have been contrasted, the final section of the chapter considers ways to adjudicate conflicting claims and possible benefits of standpoint analysis for feminist political engagement, knowledge production, and conceptions of objectivity.

Comparing Standpoints on Affirmative Action

THE CONSERVATIVE CRITIQUE OF AFFIRMATIVE ACTION

Although the radical zeal of early, second-wave feminism sustained the illusion that certain "malestream" views were uniquely the products and perspectives of men (Daly 1978; O'Brien 1981), the increasing ranks of articulate antifeminist women destroy that naive vision. Phyllis Schlafly, Linda Chavez, Lynne Cheney, Beverly LeHaye, Anita Blair, Barbara Ledeen and Laura Ingraham constitute a vocal conservative force who advance arguments concerning the evils of affirmative action and welfare that rival the views of Charles Murray, Lawrence Mead, and Paul Weyrich. Conservative women deny that their views bear any relation to "backlash." On the contrary, their opposition to affirmative action and welfare stems from a deep conviction that life in the contemporary United States conforms to the fundamental promise of the doctrine of equal opportunity. They believe that the system operates as a meritocracy in which all have an equal opportunity to compete in a process designed to reward individual talent, initiative, and hard work.

Conservative women, like their male counterparts, deny that discrimination in hiring, wage scales, promotion, and admissions currently exists in the United States. While they acknowledge that African Americans and Latinos earn less than whites, and that women earn less than men, and that both minorities and women constitute a smaller percentage of managerial and professional workers than of the general population, they deny that the explanation of these facts lies in deliberate discrimination. They suggest that a combination of personal choices made by individuals of their own free will and objective forces over which discrete individuals have no control, provide a more adequate explanation of these phenomena.

Demonstrating a sophisticated grasp of issues in the philosophy of social science, conservative women cite a cardinal principle in statistical interpretation: correlation cannot prove causation. Thus they point out that statistical data concerning the relative distribution of minorities and women in particular jobs is not sufficient to prove that intentional discrimination has occurred. Statistics cannot "prove" discrimination because proof of discrimination requires a demonstration of intentional exclusion of particular individuals by particular individuals. As a descriptive indicator that operates at the aggregate level; statistics can provide no information at all about individual intentions. Thus, any conclusion concerning the existence of discrimination in admissions, hiring, promotions, or pay drawn from statistical data, involves an unwarranted inference.

Conservative women suggest that the problem of underrepresentation does not reflect discrimination against qualified applicants, but rather reflects the fact that women and minorities lack the requisite qualifications for certain positions; therefore, they either fail to apply or upon application are rightly rejected. The problem is primarily one of inadequate supply of qualified women and minority applicants, not one of demand hampered by willful discrimination. Lack of qualifications—not discrimination—impairs the employment potential of women and minorities. And the lack of qualifications among women and minorities relates to individual choices, for which ultimately individuals themselves are responsible. Women and minority individuals freely choose career patterns that differ from those of white males, and this crucial element of individual choice is routinely ignored in arguments that move from statistical underrepresentation to allegations of exclusion or discrimination. For this reason, conservatives suggest, affirmative action is clearly a misguided and inappropriate policy.

Affirmative action is designed as a social policy to end intentional discrimination in admission, employment, and promotion. Because any underrepresentation that currently exists is not related to any deliberate policies of discrimination, the disease and the cure are mismatched. The basic lack of correspondence between problem and solution stems from the failure to draw an important distinction between problems caused by deliberate individual actions, which are susceptible to solutions aimed at specific individuals, and problems caused by impersonal/objective social forces for which no individual can justly be held accountable.

Having diagnosed the cause of underrepresentation as an insufficient supply of qualified women and minority applicants, conservative women insist that affirmative action is synonymous with reverse discrimination: government policies necessitate the use of "quotas," the hiring of less qualified candidates, the obliteration of merit as a criterion of desert and consequently, the sacrifice of creative, hardworking individuals. Because qualified women and minority applicants are not available according to this analysis, it follows that school administrators and employers must engage in all these abuses in order to increase the number of women and blacks in their institutions as a demonstration to the government of their "good faith." Giving less qualified women and minority group members "preference" in admissions, hiring, and promotion can only result in new forms of discrimination that will entail the erosion of the principles of merit, scholarly quality, and integrity. Thus, affirmative action makes a mockery of the principle of desert, which itself provides the legitimation for denunciation of past discriminatory practices (Thernstrom and Thernstrom 1997).

Affirmative action arbitrarily imposes responsibility for a collective problem upon specific individuals. It requires preferential treatment for "unqualified" women and minority group applicants; consequently, affirmative action discriminates in reverse against the "best qualified" candidates who just happen to be nonminority men. Such reverse discrimination is all the more intolerable because it undermines competition while allowing government bureaucrats to impose their subjective vision of the good upon the society at large. Bureaucratic intervention places universities and employers in the position of having to placate federal officials under penalty of loss of federal grants and contracts vital to their very survival. Thus bureaucratic whim becomes a tyrannical task master which strips would-be federal contractors of their autonomy and their fidelity to standards of pure meritocratic excellence (Ladowsky 1995).

In the absence of deliberate discriminatory policies in the contemporary United States, the only possible moral justification for the government's policies is compensatory justice for groups. Affirmative action was initially developed as an effort to make reparation to blacks for a history of injustice. Yet, according to conservative women, this concept of compensatory justice to groups for past injustices suffered by them as groups is completely incompatible with individual rights afforded by the U.S. Constitution.

From the perspective of conservative women, affirmative action provides blanket preferential treatment for certain persons on the basis of race, even if those persons did not personally suffer past injustices. Thus, preferential treatment for

groups as a social policy is notoriously overinclusive. But it is simultaneously un-
derinclusive, for, in providing compensation only for African Americans, it ignores the claims of other individuals (for example, Irish-Americans, Jews) who
have personally suffered injustice yet who are not members of the groups targeted for compensation. Furthermore, reverse discrimination imposes the cost of
compensation upon individuals who did not perpetrate the injustice and who
cannot fairly be dubbed beneficiaries of the injustice: they neither sought the
benefit nor had the opportunity to reject it. Put simply, reverse discrimination
imposes the cost of compensation upon innocent parties. Thus reverse discrimination can be faulted as both arbitrary in the distribution of benefits to the disadvantaged and in the assignment of the costs of compensation. Such rampant
arbitrariness seriously impairs any moral justification for affirmative action.

Reverse discrimination substitutes concern with "abstract groups" and their
purported rights for concern with living individuals. Focusing solely upon individuals who "make themselves," conservative women reject any notion of a
legacy of group injury, just as they reject any notion of collective guilt on the
part of the group who historically imposed the suffering. Any policy of preferential treatment for groups subordinates individuals' rights to equal treatment to
the broader social aim of making amends for a past injustice, which contemporary individuals did not perpetrate—a clearly unconstitutional policy. According
to conservative women, justice can require nothing more than the use of neutral
principles, such as nondiscrimination, in admissions and employment. Because
deliberate discrimination is not a contemporary problem, the use of neutral principles promotes meritocratic decisions while simultaneously according justice to
individuals regardless of the group to which they happen to belong; such neutrality allows each individual to "make it" on his or her own.

LIBERAL FEMINIST VIEWS ON AFFIRMATIVE ACTION

Taking conservative arguments at face value, liberal feminists have mobilized to
present a different account of "equal opportunity" in the contemporary United
States. In the 1990s, feminist scholars launched the Committee of One Hundred
to join established groups such as the National Organization for Women (NOW),
the Feminist Majority, the Women's Equity Action League, and the American
Association of University Women (AAUW) to present a compelling case that
discrimination on the basis of race and gender persists in contemporary society
and can be demonstrated. Rather than assuming that the United States represents a just and primarily nondiscriminatory society, liberal feminists suggest
that empirical evidence documents widespread, albeit subtle, discrimination.

The Glass Ceiling Commission (1995), for example, found that although
white men constituted only 37 percent of the American population, they held
95 percent of the top managerial jobs in Fortune 1000 corporations. If one looks

beyond the realm of senior management, 8.5 percent of working women held jobs that are classified as executive/managerial, compared to 20 percent of working men, while 60 percent of women worked full time outside the home in clerical and service-sector jobs, compared to 15 percent of working men. The situation for African Americans is even more bleak. There was only one black CEO in the Fortune 1000 corporations. Although African Americans then constituted 12.9 percent of the American population, they held 0.6 percent of the senior management positions and 3 percent of executive/managerial positions in the United States. In 1990, 3.2 percent of American physicians were African American (down from 4 percent in 1970); 3 percent of all lawyers were African American (up from 1.5 percent in 1970); and 4.5 percent of university professors were African American (no change since 1970) (Hacker 1992).

Acknowledging that statistics cannot provide definitive indicators of discrimination, liberal feminists yet insist that the pervasiveness of statistical underrepresentation of women and minorities in higher education, in higher-paying employment and in positions of prestige and power is sufficient to establish a *prima facie* case of discrimination. But liberal feminists do not rest their arguments concerning the persistence of discrimination upon a demonstration of underrepresentation alone, for, as conservatives have argued, any number of variables can be introduced to explain such underrepresentation. Instead, they emphasize "underutilization" in an effort to explode the myth that the principle cause of underrepresentation is the inadequate supply of qualified women and minority applicants. Underutilization is defined as having fewer women/minorities actually employed in a job category than would reasonably be expected from their availability in the labor pool. In universities, for example, the Ph.D. is a legitimate prerequisite for employment. In 1993, 45 percent of all the doctorates awarded to U.S. citizens went to women, but women constituted only 35 percent of the new hires in universities (American Council on Education 1995). The phenomenon to be explained then, is not the dearth of minority or female professionals per se, but the dearth of such professionals given the availability of a certain percentage of qualified minority and female candidates. The pervasive underutilization of qualified women and minorities in the United States renders suspicious any explanation that emphasizes personal choice. For it seems unlikely that individuals who have invested great effort to become qualified for certain careers should suddenly choose not to pursue those professions.

Moving beyond statistics of underrepresentation and underutilization, liberal feminists have also examined the evidence from controlled experiments to document persistent discrimination. A 1991 Urban Institute study, for example, demonstrated pervasive racial discrimination in hiring by conducting job "audits" that paired black job candidates with identically qualified white candidates in a range of job competitions. Although possessing equal grade point averages and work experience, blacks were unable to advance as far in the hiring process as whites 20 percent of the time and were denied jobs offered to equally qualified whites 15 percent of the time. As the skill level of the job increased, so too did the tendency to discriminate (Turner, Fix and Struyk 1991).

Nearly thirty years of research in social psychology has documented a persistent and pervasive gender and race bias in evaluation. Psychologists have documented that given identical qualifications or performances, a general tendency gives men more favorable evaluations than women and gives whites more favorable evaluations than minorities. Moreover, ample evidence indicates that performance by women and minority group members is systematically downgraded by employers and school teachers and evaluated more positively when race or sex is unknown to the evaluator (Nieva and Gutek 1980; Rosen and Jerdee 1974; Shaw 1974; Haefner 1977; Gutek and Stevens 1979). Thus, women and minorities experience a form of discrimination that exists over and above the problems of underrepresentation and pay differentials (Hughes 1975, 26). Women and minorities are treated as beings less worthy of respect than the average white male, not because of any individual weakness or failing but simply because they are members of a particular group.

The disrespect shown to women and minorities on the basis of their sex, race, or ethnicity highlights the fact that the competition for educational and economic opportunities is neither neutral nor fair, for women and minorities are judged by standards irrelevant to the competition. A tacit pro-white, pro-male bias in admissions, hiring, and evaluation procedures constitutes a form of discrimination that continues to harm women and minorities not because of their individual characteristics but because of their membership in particular groups.

On this view, one great benefit of affirmative action's insistence on good faith efforts to recruit women and minority candidates lies precisely in its ability to help "whites recognize that their own advantages are, in significant measure, group benefits, rather than individual achievements and that their own success has been, in part, a matter of their own superior group opportunities, purchased at the expense of opportunities for non-whites" (Livingston 1979, 182). Recognition of the role played by race and gender privilege in decisions concerning admissions, hiring, and promotion procedures also demonstrates that neither the criteria employed in these decisions nor the individuals employing them are "neutral" or "impersonal." The market's "Invisible Hand" does not determine applicants' merit and prospects for success; decisions of fallible administrators serving as gate-keepers to the positions of power and privilege in contemporary society do.

Given their diagnosis of the problem as ongoing discrimination in the form of antiminority, antifemale bias, liberal feminists argue that affirmative action is a fair and appropriate remedy. As a mechanism for the cultivation of a recognition of the talent of all persons in society, affirmative action does not jeopardize principles of merit or standards of excellence. It simply prohibits situations in which the only ones allowed to demonstrate their merit are white males. Through the establishment of fair hiring practices and competition open to public inspection, affirmative action ensures that white men "compete fairly on the basis of merit, not fraternity, on demonstrated capability, not assumed superiority (Pottinger 1971). By focusing attention on admitting, hiring, and promoting members of particular target groups, affirmative action draws attention to both the consequences of historic racism and sexism and to the extent, the gravity, and the immediacy of the injuries still experienced by minorities and women in the United States.

Liberal feminists acknowledge that affirmative action causes white males to lose certain advantages, yet they deny that the loss constitutes a violation of individual rights. On the contrary, liberal feminists stress that white men currently occupying favored positions in existing organizations have themselves been the beneficiaries of some preferential treatment: "they are members of a group of persons who have been privileged in hiring and promotion in accordance with normal practices of long-standing, persons who have been offered better educational preparation than others of the same basic talents, persons whose egos have been strengthened more than members of other groups" (Held 1975, 34). Because these white males did not deserve such preferential treatment, because they had no right to the advantages afforded by a racist and sexist society, no rights are being violated by the removal of those advantages. Policies to promote justice for the victims of injustice may require that white men lose their unwarranted privilege in society but they do not strip these individuals of legitimate rights.

SOCIALIST FEMINIST AMBIVALENCE ON AFFIRMATIVE ACTION

Socialist feminists are profoundly ambivalent about affirmative action. As a policy developed within the bourgeois state to advance the interests of the privileged, affirmative action poses no threat to capitalism, to class hierarchy, or to the status quo. Indeed, affirmative action lends an air of credibility to capitalist patriarchy by erroneously suggesting that it can promote the interests and equality of women and people of color. It thereby situates discussions of racial and gender justice within the narrow and restrictive compass of "equal opportunity." By suggesting that discrimination is the primary problem that women and people of color face in contemporary society, affirmative action policies obscure and deny the structural and institutional framework of capitalist oppression. From a socialist feminist standpoint, policies that mask the complex dimensions of oppression are deeply problematic. "If one focuses on discrimination as the primary wrong groups suffer, then the more profound wrongs of exploitation, marginalization, powerlessness, cultural imperialism, and violence that we still suffer go undiscussed and unaddressed" (Young 1990, 196–197).

Long before affirmative action came under attack, socialist feminists offered a range of principled objections to this mode of liberal reformism. Affirmative action neither challenges nor transforms the hierarchical division of labor in the capitalist workplace. It merely seeks to change the racial and gender composition of the elite. In eliminating racist and sexist hiring and admissions practices, affirmative action benefits the "most privileged" of the formerly disadvantaged, that is, the well-educated, middle-class women and people of color. As prominent "tokens" like Clarence Thomas, Linda Chavez, and Lynne Cheney make clear, there is no reason to believe that even a substantial increase in the representation of racial and gender groups in positions of power and prestige would benefit women and minorities in general. Indeed, the votes of Clarence Thomas on the Supreme Court in cases such as *Adarand v. Pena* make it painfully clear that the career advances of some "tokens" can have disastrous consequences for the oppressed. Thus the critical issue is not more women and minorities in power *per se*, but using power for progressive/socialist/feminist political ends. Neither race nor gender constitutes a guarantee of progressive political inclinations (Barrett 1985, 242).

Socialist feminists have also pointed out that those who endorse affirmative action on the belief that women and people of color can work within the system to benefit the oppressed fail to recognize the power of institutional resistance to subversion from within and the likelihood of cooptation. On this view, feminist efforts to infiltrate hierarchies of power inevitably succumb to "careerism," to feminist accommodation to the status quo, or to the development of policies that heighten institutions' control over the oppressed (Barrett 1985, 244).

Any socialist feminist effort to defend affirmative action illuminates this problematic. To defend affirmative action is to endorse a policy that reinforces a range of myths about the market's "just distribution" of jobs on the basis of "merit." Advocates of affirmative action promise that the elimination of race and gender bias creates the possibility for "true merit hiring." They trust that the notion of individual "qualifications" poses no insurmountable problems. They believe that it is "possible to measure, compare, and rank individual performance of job-related tasks using criteria that are normatively and culturally neutral" (Young 1990, 193). Moreover, they accept the hierarchical organization of society, as well as the scarcity of positions of high income, power, and prestige, asking only that these positions be distributed on the basis of merit. The defense of affirmative action coopts feminists into endorsing an inegalitarian competition in which the vast majority of competitors are destined to lose.

Socialist feminists have pointed out that "even if strong affirmative action programs existed in most institutions, they would have only a minor effect in altering the basic structure of group privilege and oppression in the United States. Since these programs require that racially or sexually preferred candidates be qualified, indeed highly qualified, they do nothing directly to increase opportunities for Blacks, Latinos, or women whose social environment and lack of resources make getting qualified nearly impossible for them" (Young 1990, 199). To avoid being coopted and to make significant contributions to the struggle for equality, feminists would be better off fighting the myth of a market-based meritocracy, challenging the justice of any hierarchical division of labor, and changing "the overall patterns of racial and gender stratification in our society [which] would require major changes in the structure of the economy, the process of job allocation, the character of the social division of labor and access to schooling and training" (Young 1990, 199).

Although the logic of socialist feminist arguments concerning affirmative action is not changed by recent conservative attacks on affirmative action, the horizon of progressive political struggle has been constricted. Thus socialist feminists have joined coalitions to defend the small gains made through such reformist strategies. They bring to these coalitions important concerns about the meaning of the conservative attack on liberal policies and the ideological functions of the "war" against women and people of color. From a socialist feminist standpoint, it is a mistake to construe these issues solely in terms of partisan electoral politics. For the conservative vilification of women and the poor serves as a diversionary tactic that focuses attention on society's disadvantaged while masking structural transformations within capitalism. On this view, conservative arguments concerning the erosion of merit standards under affirmative action and conservative claims concerning the erosion of individual responsibility under welfare programs share crucial ideological affinities. Both reinforce individualist premises that structure policy debates in terms of individual success and failure, which blinds the public to the possibility that social problems and economic crises can only be systematically addressed when treated structurally and collectively.

BLACK FEMINIST EFFORTS TO DEBUNK RACIST CODES IN POLICY DISCOURSES

The experiences of African Americans in the contemporary United States provide a markedly different framework within which to analyze public policy. Both the attack on affirmative action and the war against poor women have been widely interpreted as racist codes, grounded in white supremacy, that reinforce racial stratification. Within this framework, race constitutes a "metalanguage" that reinscribes the master/slave relation in the policy discourses of the liberal welfare state (Higginbotham 1992). Policies that appear to be reversals or "backlash" from a white feminist standpoint, are perceived within a Black feminist frame as perpetuation and consolidation of white privilege, a prophylactic against any systemic gains for African Americans.

From a black feminist standpoint, racially coded policy discourse, operating at the boundaries of consciousness, mystifies the power dynamics of contemporary racial oppression and suggests levels of black affluence and success and degrees of white victimization altogether inconsistent with any examination of prevailing social relations (Carby 1987; Abel 1993). Only within the framework of racial codes can one make sense of polls such as that sponsored by the *Washington Post*, the Kaiser Family Foundation, and Harvard University which found that a majority of whites believe that blacks are as well off or better off than whites: 46 percent of whites said that blacks on average held jobs of equal quality to those of whites, 6 percent said that blacks had jobs that were "a little better" than those held by whites, and another 6 percent said blacks had jobs that were "a lot better" than those held by whites. "The overwhelming majority of whites said that blacks have an equal chance to succeed, that whites bear no responsibility for the problems blacks face today, and that its not the government's role to ensure that all races have equal jobs, pay, or housing" (Morin 1995, A6). Only within the framework of racial codes can one comprehend how, contrary to all empirical evidence, young white Americans have come to believe that they are more likely to be victims of reverse discrimination than African Americans or Latinos are to suffer from racial bias (Chideya 1995). By inverting prevailing power relations, racial codes insulate whites from the glaring evidence of racial inequality in our nation. Racial codes render Census Bureau statistics "unbelievable." Within racially coded discourse, Rush Limbaugh's wild imaginings have greater credibility than social science reports that document growing racial inequality. Consider, for example, data collected by the U.S. Census Bureau in 2002, which demonstrate that the enormous wealth gap between white families and black and Latino families continues to grow. "White households had a median net worth of greater than $88,651 in 2002, 11 times more than Latinos and more than 14 times that of Blacks" (Armas 2004, A10). While the white median net worth increased by 17.4 percent from $75,482 in 1996 to $88,651 in 2002, Latino median net worth increased by 14 percent from $6,961 to $7,932 during the same period. African American household median net worth plummeted 16.1 percent during this time frame, falling from $7,135 to $5,988. Comparable growth in racial inequality has been documented with respect to percentages of children living in poverty, adult and teenage unemployment rates, and distributions of income (Rowan 1995). Convinced by racially coded discourses that blacks are receiving "special" preferences, whites cannot comprehend that more black families were living in poverty in 1990 (37 percent) than in 1970 (34 percent) (Hacker 1992).

From a black feminist standpoint, the myth of preferential treatment for blacks makes sense only within a framework that presupposes white superiority.

Reinforced by the "scientific" racism of Charles Murray and Richard Hernstein's *The Bell Curve* and Dinesh D'Souza's *End of Racism*, many white Americans accept a vicious logic: blacks are intellectually inferior to whites, thus the only way they can attain positions of high pay, power, and prestige is through preferential treatment which necessarily entails hiring "unqualified" blacks for positions that qualified whites "deserve." The language of reverse discrimination thus consolidates the conviction of white superiority, while denigrating the talents of successful African Americans, sustaining the "stigma" associated with affirmative action that is so lamented by black conservatives. It also provides a soothing balm to the egos of thoroughly mediocre whites who can convince themselves that their failure to secure desired employment is the "fault" of blacks rather than the consequence of their own limited abilities.

POSTMODERN FEMINIST DISRUPTIONS OF THE
TERMS OF DISCOURSE

The premises of postmodern-feminism make the construction of "a postmodern-feminist standpoint" problematic. Arguing that "women's experience is thoroughly constructed, historically and culturally varied, and interpreted without end," postmodern feminists caution that feminists must be wary of those who speak for women in terms that totalize and exclude (W. Brown 1995, 41). Calling instead for a politics of voice within a space of contestation, postmodern feminists insist that we must attend to "who speaks for whom as much as to what is said" (Yeatman 1994, 15). In the words of Wendy Brown: "When the notion of a unified and coherent subject is abandoned, we . . . cease to be able to speak of woman or for women in an unproblematic way . . . dispensing with the unified subject does not mean ceasing to be able to speak about our experiences as women, only that our words cannot be legitimately deployed or construed as larger or longer than the moments of the lives they speak from"(1995, 40–41).

Recognizing such concerns for the particularity of individual perspective, this section takes up the view of just one postmodern feminist, one view that affords a vista markedly different from those considered to this point. In *States of Injury: Power and Freedom in Late Modernity*, Wendy Brown offers an interpretation of recent policy contestations in terms of the normalizing practices of the disciplinary state fueled by the psychological force of Nietzschean *ressentiment*. To capture the full meaning of Brown's argument, it is important not to conflate *ressentiment* with the English word, resentment, for Nietzschean *ressentiment* engages a markedly different psychological register. As characterized in *The Genealogy of Morals*, *ressentiment* encompasses envy, spite, vengefulness, vindictive hatefulness, and self-abasement that pervade the psyche of the "weak," all of which cause them to question that which is inherently good and noble and to celebrate values produced by their own subjugation.

Seeking to illuminate a number of paradoxes of contemporary politics, Brown emphasizes that the Right's antigovernment discourse has masked a steady expansion of state powers and retrenchment of citizen rights over the past twenty years. While antistatist rhetoric diverts attention from increasing state domination, it also incites liberal and leftist protectiveness toward the state.

> As the powers constituting late modern configurations of capitalism and the state have grown more complex, more pervasive, and simultaneously more difficult to track, both critical analyses of their power and a politics rooted in such a critique have tended to recede. Indeed Western leftists have largely forsaken analyses of the liberal state and capitalism as sites of domination and have focused instead on their implication in political and economic inequalities. At the same time, progressives have implicitly assumed the relatively unproblematic instrumental value of the state and capitalism in redressing such inequalities. (W. Brown 1995, 10)

According to Brown, this obliviousness to state domination locks progressive efforts that appeal to the state to remedy inequalities into a reactionary cycle that "reinstates rather than transforms the terms of domination that generated them" (7). In appealing to the state for rights, African Americans, Hispanics, Jews, women, gays, and lesbians seek a legal protection that "discursively entrenches the injury-identity connection it denounces . . . codify[ing] within the law the very powerlessness it seeks to redress . . . discursively collud[ing] with the conversion of attribute into identity, of historical effect of power into presumed cause of victimization" (21). Failing to recognize that politicized identity is itself a regulatory production of a disciplinary society, those who appeal to the liberal state for redress of injuries fail to comprehend that hard-won rights "imprison us within the subject positions they are secured to affirm and protect" (120).

Brown argues that rather than contributing to an emancipatory project, contestations over rights privatize and depoliticize, mystifying and reifying "social powers (property and wealth, but also race, sexuality, and gender) as the natural possessions of private persons" (123). In so doing, rights do not liberate us from relations of class, sexuality, gender, or race; on the contrary, they obfuscate power relations by creating a fictive equality of sovereign subjects before the law. According to Brown, precisely this conversion of social problems into matters of individualized, dehistoricized injury and entitlement gives rise to claims of reverse discrimination.

Within the framework of Nietzschean *ressentiment*, a peculiar affinity emerges between the reverse discrimination claims of white men and the claims of sexual and racial discrimination advanced by women and people of color. Both are incited by "the moralizing revenge of the powerless, 'the triumph of the weak as weak'" (67). According to Brown, "this incitement to *ressentiment* inheres in two related constitutive paradoxes of liberalism: that between individual liberty and social egalitarianism, a paradox which produces failure turned to recrimination by the subordinated, and guilt turned into resentment by the 'successful'; and that between the individualism that legitimates liberalism and the cultural homogeneity required by its commitment to political universality, a paradox which stimulates the articulation of politically significant differences on the one hand, and the suppression of them on the other" (67).

From this Nietzschean perspective, the political tactics of both the proponents and opponents of affirmative action are fueled by the same desire to inscribe past and present injury in the law. As such, the tactics of both sides conform to the same impetus to avenge hurt and redistribute pain. In both instances, *ressentiment* "produces an affect (rage, righteousness) that overwhelms the hurt; and it produces a site of revenge to displace the hurt (a place to inflict hurt as the sufferer has been hurt). Together these operations both ameliorate (in Nietzsche's term 'anaesthetize') and externalize what is otherwise 'unendurable'"(68).

Comparing Standpoints on Welfare "Reform"

THE CONSERVATIVE CRITIQUE OF WELFARE POLICY

Concern with the value of self-reliance and the development of social policies that hold individuals responsible for their own actions fuels conservative women's attack on welfare. Accepting that the market economy affords employment opportunities to all who seek them, conservative women understand the causes of poverty in terms of the attitudes, the psychology, and the behavior of the poor. On this view, the problem to be addressed is a direct consequence of existing welfare policies that produce a class of people who adopt welfare as a way of life, who intentionally waste their skills and talents by willfully refusing to work.

Conservative women point to stories of individual upward mobility and success (for example, Clarence Thomas, Condoleeza Rice) as proof that high rates of unemployment among disadvantaged groups cannot be explained by appeals to lack of jobs, discrimination, or other social conditions over which the disadvantaged have no control. The poor remain poor because they are unwilling to accept the jobs available to them. The underdevelopment of the work ethic is the fundamental problem of the poor, a problem attributable to welfare programs that provide benefits to recipients while expecting nothing in return. In direct contrast to the market which reinforces the work ethic in individuals by relating rewards to individuals' investments of effort and contributions to society, welfare undermines the value of such reciprocity by severing the connection between

benefits and obligations. To rectify this problem, welfare programs should include a mandatory work requirement. Work must replace welfare in order to ensure the future prosperity of the currently disadvantaged members of society.
Moreover, to facilitate recipients' integration into the mainstream of American
life, an absolute lifetime limit (two to five years) should be placed on receipt of
welfare benefits (Kondrtas 1995).

Once poverty is understood in terms of particular debilitating attitudes held
by the poor, welfare-to-work programs emerge as an appropriate social policy designed specifically to alter individual attitudes toward work. Conservative women
suggest that mandatory work requirements will generate a host of benefits for
both individual welfare recipients and society. Requiring welfare recipients to
work on a regular basis will help them to cultivate a work "habit" while simultaneously overcoming their fears of not being able to compete in a job market. On-
the-job experience in public service projects will increase welfare recipients'
feelings of self-worth and self-confidence as they realize they are contributing
something of value to their communities. The dependency bred by reliance
upon government hand-outs will be supplanted by a growing sense of self-
sufficiency as participants gain a sense of mastery in their job assignments. The
gradual accrual of job experience will enhance the marketable skills and hence
the employability of welfare recipients. Over time the regular exposure to the
world of work, coupled with the newfound confidence and the acquisition of
marketable skills, will facilitate the individual's transition from welfare to permanent paid employment in the private sector. Thus, in the long term, state and
federal expenditures for welfare will be reduced as the total number of recipients
is reduced through job placements. State and federal governments will also realize immediate reductions in their welfare expenditures as those recipients who
are unwilling to assume their work responsibilities are terminated from the welfare rolls. Work requirements also produce an additional residual benefit: reduction in the stigma associated with welfare. As the rolls are purged of welfare
"cheats," welfare workers will encounter a new respect as the American public
recognizes that the poor "have earned" the benefits that they receive.

Conservative proposals to return control of welfare to the states were designed to end any notion of "entitlement" to public assistance. These proposals
called for significant reductions in expenditures for welfare. States were allowed
to cut welfare allotments by 20 percent from the 1994 benefit levels. Federal
contributions through block grants were also reduced during a seven-year period.
Benefits to recipients necessarily fell as a consequence. Reducing benefits while
simultaneously requiring recipients to work off the benefits received was designed to deter people from seeing welfare as an alternative to work. The image
of welfare as a "prepaid lifetime vacation plan," in the words of Ronald Reagan,
would be permanently replaced by a conception of welfare as minimal subsistence

support, administered with a sufficient degree of harshness and limitation in benefits that people who could work would be happy to get off and those who did work would stay off.

Like the "carrot and stick" of the market system (high wages as positive incentive, fear of unemployment as negative incentive), conservative women envision a revised welfare system that includes positive and negative incentives. As a positive incentive, work placement for welfare recipients affords the opportunity for the poor to develop work skills and habits, self-esteem and confidence, as well as a basic "marketability." The assignment of individuals to menial jobs without pay as a condition for the receipt of minimal subsistence benefits and termination of benefits after a fixed number of years constitute the negative incentive. Each aspect of the "reform" proposals is central to their appeal; in combination they help restore the value of self-reliance, the discipline of capitalism, and the role of the market in the determination of merit.

LIBERAL FEMINIST VIEWS ON WELFARE

In their efforts to engage the "war against poor women," liberal feminists have launched a barrage of facts to counter persistent misrepresentations of the poor in conservative political rhetoric. Contrary to pernicious stereotypes, poor women do not see welfare as a desirable way of life. They do not "get pregnant" to qualify for or increase welfare benefits. Indeed, Aid to Families with Dependent Children (AFDC) recipients had a lower fertility rate than other American women of childbearing age. The typical welfare recipient seeks assistance during a crisis caused by illness, unemployment, domestic violence, or divorce, relies upon public assistance for less than two years, and returns to the labor force at the earliest opportunity (S. L. Thomas 1994).

Conservative stereotypes of the poor routinely invoke the "pathological theory of poverty," which attributes the cause of poverty to the characteristics or "defects" of the poor themselves (Handler 1972, 3). Assuming that the market economy places success within the reach of any hardworking individual, conservatives assert that individual effort is all that stands between the rich and the poor. Thus, the poor are peculiarly responsible for their own fate. Those who choose to live in ignominious conditions by willfully refusing to take advantage of the opportunities that the free market affords are morally reprehensible. On this view, "laziness" or unwillingness to work is a form of moral defect for which the poor should be held strictly accountable.

Liberal feminists have pointed out that the pathological theory of poverty does not fit the facts of American poverty. An examination of the demographic characteristics of the poor suggests that the pathological theory is fundamentally flawed. In the early 1990s when the federal government began exploring policy changes to abolish welfare entitlements, "the poor" in the United States were a large and diverse group. Many of the "officially poor," that is, those who live below the "poverty line" set by the U.S. government, work full-time outside the home (Levitan and Shapiro 1987; Spalter-Roth et al. 1995). In 1995, a full-time employee working for minimum wages earned $2,000 a year less than the poverty line for a family of three (Chideya 1995). Of the "officially poor," only 38 million Americans received government assistance. Far more received Supplemental Security Income (for the elderly, blind, and disabled) than received Aid to Families with Dependent Children (AFDC). More than two-thirds of recipients of public assistance were unable to work because of age, disability, or caretaking responsibilities for preschool age children. Of households with pre-transfer incomes below the poverty line 48 percent were headed by individuals aged sixty-five or older, another 12 percent were headed by disabled individuals, and 7 percent were headed by women with children under the age of six. Of the remaining households receiving public assistance, 7.5 percent were headed by persons who work full-time year round but whose incomes are insufficient to meet family subsistence needs, 20.4 percent were headed by persons who were employed but not on a full-time basis, and 5 percent were headed by students (Danziger and Gottschalk 1983, 1993; Edin and Lein 1997).

Studies of AFDC recipients (the subset of the poor most frequently characterized in terms of the pathological theory of poverty) indicate that the belief that AFDC household heads do not work or will not work is simply mistaken. Although 63 percent of the four million women receiving AFDC benefits in 1995 had children under the age of five (Mink 1996), 70 percent of AFDC households had at least one earner during the years on welfare. In 40 percent of these households, the head of household earned the income; in the remainder, the earnings were those of older children within the household (Rein 1982; Spalter-Roth et al. 1995). In direct contrast to popular stereotypes, black women receiving AFDC worked far more often than white women. There was also much greater movement between welfare and work than the pathological theory suggests. Only 2 percent of households receiving public benefits remained on welfare for eight years or more (S. L. Thomas 1994). The vast majority resorted to welfare to upgrade their total income because their earnings from work were inadequate or because their earning capacity had been temporarily undermined through unemployment.

A number of studies of the attitudes of the poor toward work also challenge the pathological theory's accuracy. In answer to the question "Do the poor want to work?" research on the work orientations of the poor has concluded that the poor do indeed want to work. The work ethic is upheld strongly by AFDC recipients and work plays an important role in their life goals. Indeed, results from comprehensive studies of the attitudes of the poor toward work "unambiguously indicate that AFDC recipients, regardless of sex, age or race, identify their self-esteem with work as strongly as do the non-poor. . . . Despite their adverse position in society and their past failures in the labor force, these persons clearly upheld the work ethic and voiced strong commitments toward work" (Berkeley Planning Associates 1980, 92; see also Goodwin 1972; Schiller 1973; Goodale 1973; Kaplan and Tausky 1972; Gueron and Pauly 1991; Tienda and Stier 1991; Handler 1995; Edin and Lein, 1997).

From the liberal feminist standpoint, the pathological theory of poverty that underlies conservatives' demands for "welfare reform" rests upon a number of misconceptions. Contrary to the pathological view, the able bodied poor share the American commitment to the work ethic, and they do work. Their problem is not one of attitude but one of inadequate pay or inadequate employment opportunities (Handler 1995; Edin and Lein 1997). The market economy has not afforded these individuals the mythologized avenues of upward social mobility. Moreover, some economic research suggests that even in an expanding economy, the market will not provide an escape from poverty for these individuals in the future. "The evidence from the recent past suggests that economic growth will not raise the earnings of the poor enough to enable many of them to escape poverty without government assistance. The major factor contributing to the reduction of poverty since 1966 seems to have been the growth in government transfers, which offset increases in poverty resulting from demographic changes and high unemployment rates. Economic growth *per se* seems to have had little effect" (Danziger and Gottschalk 1983, 750).

The great majority of welfare recipients who have been involved with "workfare" and those who are now involved in welfare-to-work programs have been placed in low-level maintenance and clerical positions. Jobs such as cutting grass, picking up trash, washing dishes, mopping and waxing floors, driving senior citizen vans, moving furniture, childcare, and general office work have been typical (Linden and Vincent 1982; Burtless 1995; Edin and Lein 1997). Evaluation studies note that program administrators have made no effort to offer participants jobs that utilize work skills that they already possess, nor have administrators made placements that enable participants to acquire marketable skills. Moreover, assignments tend to be in unskilled jobs, precisely the kind of jobs which are prone to elimination during periods of economic recession (Briggs, Rungeling and Smith 1980; Rosen 1980; Friedman and Hausman 1975; Danziger and Gottschalk 1993; DeParle 1997). Several evaluation studies suggest that placing welfare recipients in jobs that require few job skills actually lessens their chances of obtaining employment which affords sufficient income to escape poverty. A welfare recipient who succeeds in finding a job in the workforce equivalent to the welfare work assignment earns too little to support a household (Bernstein and Goodwin, 1978; Edin and Lein 1997; DeParle 1997).

Liberal feminists situate debates about welfare "reform" in the context of partisan politics. The increasingly vitriolic attack on poor women, which emerged in Reagan's 1970 gubernatorial campaign and has been a staple of Republican political rhetoric ever since, was reinvigorated in the 1994 congressional elections in the form of the "Contract With America." California Governor Pete Wilson launched his attack on affirmative action as a tactic to advance his presidential aspirations; Senator Robert Dole introduced legislation to abolish all federal affirmative action programs for much the same reason. Consciously devising a "southern strategy," Republican politicians relied on racism and sexism to help them secure the votes of the "social conservatives" and thereby break the Democratic party's hold on the South (Melich 1996).

To fight this political mobilization of race and gender bias, then, liberal feminists took their arsenal of facts to the public forum. They took out full page ads in and submitted letters to the editors of the major national newspapers. They formed a formidable lobby in Washington. They staged vigils at the White House. They conducted letter writing campaigns, held press conferences, developed networks, and circulated information to groups across the country. They organized sophisticated e-mail distribution mechanisms to orchestrate grassroots mobilization when critical votes were pending in Congress. Under the banner, "A War Against Poor Women is a War Against All Women," liberal feminists sought to build solidarity among women in their fight to secure the minimal provisions of the American welfare state. Toward that end they launched a massive public education and voter registration campaign—"Freedom Summer '96"—to double the voter registration among eighteen- to twenty-four-year-olds and to encourage Americans to vote in order to save women's rights and civil rights (De Witt 1996).

SOCIALIST FEMINIST CRITIQUES OF WELFARE "REFORM"

From a socialist feminist standpoint, the attack on poor women under the guise of "welfare reform" involves ideological distortions that cannot be grasped within a framework of partisan politics. Indeed, both the Democratic and the Republican parties made commitments to "end welfare as we know it." Bill Clinton advanced the slogan during his 1992 bid for the presidency, and the Republicans incorporated the idea into their "Contract with America" during the congressional elections in 1994. Both parties cooperated to pass legislation to replace AFDC entitlements with Temporary Assistance for Needy Families (TANF), which was signed into law by President Clinton in August 1996. According to socialist feminists, relentless harangues against the poor in both parties' campaign rhetoric have produced systemic misperceptions in American politics. "A poll of 1994 voters found that one of five believed that welfare was *the largest* federal government expense, larger than the military budget. The reality is that AFDC spending since 1964 has amounted to less than 1.5 percent of federal outlays" (Sklar 1995, 23).

While American voters are whipped into a frenzy of resentment against the "undeserving poor," the structural forces that threaten their fragile economic security go largely unnoticed. Changes in tax policy have produced the highest income inequality in the United States since 1929. During the past two decades, the share of the nation's income received by the top 5 percent of Americans increased nearly 25 percent, from 18.6 percent to 24.5 percent, while the share of income received by the poorest 20 percent fell by nearly 25 percent, from 5.7 percent to 4.3 percent. The richest quintile of Americans "earned" 46.9 percent of the nation's total income, while the middle 60 percent of the population earned 49.4 percent and the poorest quintile earned 3.8 percent (Center on Hunger, Poverty and Nutrition Policy 1995). As corporate profits have soared since 1979, many white-collar, high-paying positions, as well as many unionized manufacturing jobs, have been eliminated through "downsizing," while newly created jobs are concentrated in the far less lucrative service sector. "The sting is in the nature of the replacement work. Whereas 25 years ago the vast majority of the people who were laid off found jobs that paid as well as their old ones, Labor Department numbers show that now only about 35 percent of laidoff workers end up in equally remunerative or better paid jobs" (Uchitelle and Kleinfield 1996, 1, 14). As the prospect of secure employment becomes increasingly rare, so too does the hope of earning a living wage. When adjusted for inflation, workforce-wide hourly wages fell 14 percent between 1973 and 1993. For those in the lowest ranks of the income pyramid, the loss in earning power has been much greater. "An unforgiving labor market, in recession and recovery alike, has hammered young, less-educated women. . . . Between 1979 and 1989, hourly wages plummeted for these women, falling most rapidly for African American women who didn't finish high school. This group's hourly wages, adjusted for inflation, fell 20 percent in that 10 year period" (Tilly and Albelda 1994, 9). Welfare recipients have fared no better: the median AFDC payment, when adjusted for inflation, has been slashed 47 percent since 1970 (Sklar 1995, 22).

From a socialist feminist standpoint, "impoverished women don't create poverty any more than slaves created slavery. But they are primary scapegoats for illegitimate economics" (Sklar 1995, 21). They provide a handy focal point for a vicious politics of resentment, while corporate greed escapes all public scrutiny. They provide the ideological camouflage for the

> fiscal doctrine of unlimited, unending deficit reduction [which] is not
> aimed at stable prices, full employment, and greater private investment.
> Rather, the motivations are to reduce the size of government, to disas-
> semble the U.S. system of social insurance, and to maintain unyielding

downward pressure on the price level. The implied economic policy is one of stagnation: a disproportionate weight is put on low inflation to the detriment of employment, investment, and general economic growth. The policy is also counter-redistributive: it favors wealth holders at the expense of wage-earners, the elderly, and the poor. If stated out-right, these goals would be manifestly unpopular, so the sales pitch for extreme deficit reduction has to focus elsewhere—on creating and per-petuating misconceptions or downright superstitions about the federal budget and the public debt. (Sawicky, cited in Sklar 1995, 23–24)

For socialist feminists, capitalism remains the underlying problem of the lib-eral democratic state. Vitriolic policy debates manage to mask the increasing con-centration of wealth by scapegoating African Americans, women, and the poor. As such, these diversionary debates must be understood as a brilliant strategic move in the "new class war," which will be systematically addressed only when the underclasses mobilize effectively to expropriate their expropriators.

BLACK FEMINIST ANALYSES OF RACIST WELFARE DISCOURSES

Black feminists point out that racially coded policy discourse is thoroughly mys-tifying. Indeed, its commodification of otherness allows opposites to embrace (hooks 1992). The very same whites who believe that blacks are *flourishing* dur-ing the era of corporate downsizing also believe that blacks *are* the pathological poor, who must be disciplined by the strictures of the market, forced from the welfare rolls (Bond 1996). The rhetoric of "welfare reform" artfully reconfigures poverty as a "social/cultural/psychological pathology, corroborated by a public discourse of deficiency and remediation" (Polakow 1993, 3). In projecting the image of "welfare cheats" as the fundamental problem of poverty policy, racially coded policy discourse constructs a poverty population of wanton, voraciously sexual, black adults, who pose a threat to American "family values." The distor-tions in this stereotype again eclipse the facts: ten million of the fourteen million AFDC recipients at the time that welfare was abolished were children under the age of eighteen, and the majority of welfare recipients were white; these facts dis-appear in the tunnel vision of white supremacist "solipsism" (Spelman 1988, 116; Edin and Lein 1997).

Interrogating these ideological distortions, black feminists have situated the debate on "welfare reform" in the unrelenting history of racist practices of the American state. On this view, the war against poor women must be understood in relation to the long tradition of white hegemony that gave birth to slavery, the "separate but equal" doctrine, disenfranchising electoral practices, and the exclusion of domestics and agricultural laborers (black-dominant occupations) from social security provision. Within this tradition, the attack on welfare can be construed as a "women first" strategy in the Republican war against "big government" (G. Mink 1996), a war that includes incursions against the economic gains made by African Americans who have found employment with the federal government. More than one-third of all African American lawyers and 30 percent of all black scientists work for the federal government (Hacker 1992). Employment in the federal bureaucracy, often in the "redistributive agencies" of the welfare state, has been the primary route to middle-class existence for many African American women. "Great society programs in the 1960s heightened the importance of social welfare employment for all groups, particularly women. Between 1960 and 1980, human services accounted for 41 percent of the job gains for women compared with 21 percent for men. Among women, there were significant differences in the importance of human services employment for whites and blacks. For white women, the social welfare economy accounted for 39 percent of the job gain between 1960 and 1980; for black women, an even more dramatic 58 percent" (Erie, Rein and Wiget 1983, 103). "Downsizing" the government, then, places the economic security, the precondition for autonomous citizenship, at risk for millions of African Americans.

Although welfare "reformers" construct themselves as the defenders of the American family, their racially coded diatribes against pregnant teens suggest that childbearing and childrearing are not rights secured to all citizens by the U.S. Constitution (Roberts 1997). On the contrary, the recent welfare "reform" creates a class of women required by law to work outside the home, a move that denies the value of work involved in mothering, while infringing intolerably upon individual choices concerning childbearing and childrearing (Mink 1996). Once again differential rights are accorded to Americans on the basis of race and economic duress. Patricia Hill Collins (1995) has suggested that the family must be understood as a discursive site of belonging that envelopes issues of space, territory, and home. When blacks are constructed as a fundamental threat to American "family values," such racist codes can be translated in various vernaculars: there is no space for racial harmony; there is no room for racial integration; blacks have no home in white America; they are simply not welcome here.

Beverly Guy-Sheftall (1995) has noted that the idealized nuclear family, with the male breadwinner and the homemaker mother, is a bourgeois Eurocentric norm that bears little resemblance to family relations allowed slaves by their masters. When this norm is invoked by white Americans in the late twentieth century, it must be understood as a hegemonic move designed to eradicate a perceived threat. In 1995, 60 percent of black children were raised in women-headed families. The love that black mothers afford their children by providing a sense of self-esteem that withstands the trials of racism and the onset of puberty, and the shared solidarity networks that foster collective responsibility among "othermothers" within the black community do indeed challenge the white bourgeois insistence that families must be heterosexual, nuclear, and male-dominant. Within this context, the castigation of welfare mothers and black teenage pregnancy (when black teenagers constitute less than 12 percent of unmarried mothers) function as a racist code that discursively constructs black families as a symbol of what must not be (P. H. Collins 1990, 1995; Usdansky 1996). When Norplant implants for black teenagers in Baltimore high schools are added into the equation, the specter of Margaret Sanger's eugenic agenda seems far too close for comfort. Welfare "reform" becomes a guise for new social control mechanisms devised to ban poor black women from reproducing (Roberts 1997). Incorporated into the policies of a racist state, "welfare reform" has a complex agenda: coercively enforcing white norms of feminine dependency, sexuality, morality, and family; eliminating the economic security essential for equal citizenship; controlling the fertility of poor black women and thereby contributing to racial engineering; and reiterating the demand, unchanged since slavery, that black women be the "mules of the world" (Hurston 1978, 29).

From a black feminist standpoint, racially coded policy discourses concerning affirmative action and "welfare reform" are symptoms of resurgent white supremacy. Although resistance must be mounted at these sites of contemporary oppression, these local struggles must be understood in the context of a larger campaign against racist hegemony. Success in securing a decent standard of living for poor women or in repulsing the conservative attack on affirmative action must be supplemented by systematic extirpation of the racism which is their root cause.

POSTMODERN FEMINIST CAUTIONS: POVERTY, DEPENDENCY, AND *RESSENTIMENT*

In the case of antipoverty policy, as in the case of affirmative action, Wendy Brown seeks to contest shared assumptions concerning the state as a reliable ally in emancipatory projects. The discursive construction of impoverished women as "dependents," an idiom that conveniently links images of addiction with images of childhood, also resonates with the reactionary, victim-blaming politics of *ressentiment*. Moreover, state interventions to "assist" the poor have been and continue to be the disciplinary practices that produce dependent state subjects. Within this frame, policy "solutions" that appeal to the state for redress are deeply problematic. Thus Brown questions feminist tactics that would expand women's relationships to state institutions. Rather than empowering women, these "expanding relationships produce regulated, subordinated, and disciplined state subjects . . . reconfigur[ing] compulsory motherhood . . . intensifying the isolation of women in reproductive work, ghettoiz[ing] women in service work . . . exchanging dependence upon individual men for regulation by contemporary institutionalized processes of male domination" (Brown 1995, 173).

Understanding welfare rights discourses in terms of *ressentiment* and the disciplinary practices of the state makes the identification of progressive political tactics enormously complex. Brown notes that her critique of liberal rights discourses relevant to both the affirmative action debate and antipoverty policies "does not build toward policy recommendations or a specific political program" (W. Brown 1995, 173). Nevertheless, she does suggest that to reconceptualize freedom in order to contest contemporary antidemocratic configurations of power, we must move beyond the political economy of perpetrator and victim that cedes political ground to moral and juridical ground thereby reducing politics to punishment (27). To the extent that a politics fixed upon revenge is mired in the past injury that produced it, an emancipatory strategy must be oriented toward the future. Brown cautions that the centrality of "erased histories and historical invisibility" to the pain of "subjugated identities" mitigates against any embrace of "Nietzsche's counsel on the virtues of 'forgetting'" (74). Instead, she suggests we begin a new political conversation in which the demand for revenge is supplanted by the demand for recognition. Within this radically democratic discourse, the ontological defensiveness of politicized identity would be replaced by contestation among "unwieldy and shifting pluralities adjudicating for themselves and their future on the basis of nothing more than their own habits and arguments" (37). Within this mode of political speech, designed to "destabilize the formulation of identity as fixed position, entrenched history, mandated moral entailment," agonistic practices discursively forging an alternative future would banish the dispersion of blame for an unlivable present (75–76).

Assessing the Merits of Standpoint Analysis

As an analytical tool, feminist standpoint theory encourages researchers to attend to competing accounts of the same phenomenon. But once multiple views have been collected, what is the analyst to do with them? How useful is the comparison of competing standpoints? Can incompatible claims be adjudicated? Are there criteria for determining the comparative merits of alternative accounts? How does comparative analysis of alternative standpoints contribute to feminism's transformative objectives?

Judith Grant has suggested that feminist standpoint theory can be reinterpreted as a "self-consciously derived theoretical tool in service of a politics" (1993, 119). On her view, conceiving feminist standpoints as an analytical tool shifts the focus from epistemological issues to feminist politics. Within this frame, the central question concerning the utility of standpoint analysis is whether it makes policy debates more intelligible and more actionable. If comparisons of alternative accounts illuminate the forces fueling debates, such as the debates over affirmative action and welfare "reform" considered in this chapter, then they can

help feminists devise political strategies that empower women to resist oppression. Within this context, then, the utility of standpoint analysis can be gauged
by answering two basic questions. Does comparative standpoint analysis enable
us to comprehend the complexity of the debates over affirmative action and welfare "reform"? Does that heightened comprehension help us to chart emancipatory political interventions in these policy domains?

The criteria Grant identifies for assessing the merits of comparative standpoint analysis are closely tied to her concern to foster democratic politics in an
increasingly bureaucratic and technocratic age. Standpoint analysis, valuable
because it expands the terms of political discussion, airs claims too frequently
silenced in the contemporary political fray. On this view, crucial differences
among these views cannot and ought not be resolved at a theoretical level. They
must be resolved through an open political struggle in which we as a people decide what kind of a political community we wish to be.

While such an account of the utility of standpoint theory has much to
commend it, in certain respects it does not reap the full benefit of comparative
analysis of contentious theoretical presuppositions. It retreats too quickly from
theoretical analysis to majority rule and in so doing replicates the subjectivist
premises so characteristic of contemporary politics (MacIntyre, 1981). How are
political participants to choose between the political prescriptions of conservative women, liberal feminists, socialist feminists, black feminists, and postmodern feminists? Is it all to be a matter of politics, interest accommodation, or the
manipulative ploys of wiles and wills? If so, is there any hope for justice for dis-
empowered groups?

If the experiences of situated knowers are identified as the grounds for the
construction of competing standpoints, how can feminists avoid forms of subjectivism, which sustain both an unshakable conviction in the veracity of one's
own experience and relativist resignation concerning the impossibility of adjudicating incompatible, experience-based claims? As pointed out in chapter 2,
competing appeals to "experience" acknowledge no criteria for choosing between incompatible accounts. In the absence of good reasons to sustain preference for one view over another, politics cannot help but become manipulative
and rancorous (MacIntyre 1981).

I would like to suggest that there is another way to understand the utility of
standpoint analysis. Post-positivist conceptions of knowledge emphasize that
theoretical presuppositions structure perception, the definition of an appropriate
research question, the nature of acceptable evidence, data collection and analysis, and the interpretation of research findings. A methodology that requires
investigation of multiple interpretations of the same phenomenon helps to illuminate the theoretical assumptions that frame and accredit the constitution of
facticity within each explanatory account. By engaging competing theoretical

frameworks, feminist standpoint analysis can make visible social and political values in need of critical assessment. Juxtaposing incompatible accounts forces the analyst to engage questions concerning the adequacy and internal consistency of the theoretical presuppositions, the standards of evidence and the models of explanation accredited by the competing accounts (Hawkesworth 1988).

The values informing the five standpoints compared in this chapter construe the social world very differently. A notion of an unfettered individual who is free to pursue his/her interests without interference structures the conservative analysis of affirmative action and welfare reform. While liberal feminists share a commitment to individualism, their understanding of the power of racism and sexism enables them to perceive forms of discrimination at the hands of individual decision-makers that conservatives do not acknowledge. Tracing the problem of race, gender, and class bias to individuals, however, allows liberal feminists to remain optimistic about the possibility for state intervention to redress such bias. Socialist feminists call this optimism into question, pointing out structural constraints on individual choice and action that flow from the intricate interrelations of capitalism and liberal democratic states. Black feminists suggest that structural constraints emanate from systemic racism, as well as from economic relations within capitalism, and that failure to recognize and address the operation of racist codes sanctions modes of social amnesia destructive to the lives of people of color. Working within Nietzschean and Foucaultian frames, postmodern feminist Wendy Brown not only challenges notions of neutral state apparatus, which can be deployed for progressive purposes, but also calls attention to the putative role of *ressentiment* in fueling contemporary contestations over rights. Once made visible, the values that inform these competing accounts can be subjected to critical scrutiny.

Consider, for example, the contradictory claims of conservative women and liberal feminists concerning the adequacy of the pathological theory of poverty. While these claims cannot be resolved by appealing to the experiences of the women who advance them, theoretical critiques of atomistic and methodological individualism, in conjunction with aggregate economic data and survey research involving poor women, can provide ample evidence of the flaws of the pathological account of poverty (Edin and Lein 1997). Given the pervasive evidence against the pathological account, standpoint analysis not only enables feminist scholars to demonstrate the defects of conservative claims, but also to probe the appeal of the problematic conceptions of individualism. Thus standpoint analysis can raise important issues pertaining to evidence blindness, sanctioned ignorance, and social amnesia.

As pointed out in previous chapters, standpoint theory as an epistemic doctrine tends to appeal either to conceptions of ideology or to the sociology of knowledge to explain individual belief. But this also raises important theoretical issues. Many women who espouse conservative, liberal feminist, socialist feminist, black feminist, and postmodern feminist views come from remarkably similar class backgrounds and engage in similar kinds of intellectual labor. How then are we to explain their acceptance of such radically divergent views? Determinist and reductionist explanations simply cannot account for the diversity of political perspectives presented in this chapter.

All the proponents of the varying views presented here claim to be dispelling distortions and mystifications. Conservative women argue that claims concerning racial and sexual discrimination distort the functioning of impersonal market forces. Liberal feminists, socialist feminists, and black feminists argue that conservative claims concerning reverse discrimination mystify relations of power and privilege in contemporary society. And postmodern feminist Wendy Brown argues that both gender-based and race-based discrimination claims and reverse discrimination claims mystify and mask the "slave morality" from which they emerge. No enumeration of the particular characteristics of individual knowers or the class background of academic women explains these divergent beliefs. But a shift of focus from subjective knowers to analysis of the adequacy of divergent theoretical accounts of contemporary social life might help us to see how different theoretical frameworks structure perception, accredit evidence, and provide the rhetorical force for particular arguments and, in so doing, help us to assess the comparative merits of competing claims.

Consider, for example, the presumption of racial and sexual superiority that fuels conservative arguments that white men have "rights" to certain educational and employment opportunities that are "violated" when women and minorities are admitted or hired. Can this conviction persist once the premise of white-male superiority is subjected to systematic critique? Can the assumption of a "right" to certain employment opportunities coexist with conservatives' acceptance of the market's premise that no one ever has a right to a job?

Consider the comparative merits of other competing claims: socialist feminists claim that a politics of resentment against the "undeserving" poor is strategic camouflage for the oppressive practices of late capitalism, while Wendy Brown claims that a "victim-blaming politics of *ressentiment*" must be understood in relation to the moralizing revenge of the powerless, who wish to inscribe their injuries into law. Does an appeal to Nietzschean *ressentiment* place claims of reverse discrimination on the same plane as centuries of racial oppression? Does the invocation of "slave morality" as the common source of *ressentiment* create a false equivalence between the conjured injuries of privileged whites and the continuing harms experienced by people of color in this country? Does the depiction of identity politics as "recrimination produced by failure" implicitly accredit liberal meritocratic myths, which construct the marginalized as "failures," cruelly presuming that their quest for political rights derives from psychological drives induced by "failure"? Can socialist feminist critiques of capitalism adequately address the racial coding of contemporary policy debates? Can liberal feminist electoral strategies adequately engage the economic and racial dimensions of these contentious policy debates?

To answer any of these questions, it is necessary to analyze and assess the theoretical presuppositions that structure contradictory observations and make divergent interpretations meaningful. In taking up such an evaluative research agenda, feminist standpoint analysis has particular strengths. Comparative analysis of competing standpoints illuminates problems that theoretical and empirical research must engage, problems masked by myths of value-free inquiry. Juxtaposing and examining competing standpoints reveal contentious theoretical assumptions and problematic prescriptions, as well as lacunae that follow from them.

As the comparison of competing views of affirmative action and welfare "reform" makes clear, all perspectives are not equally insightful. Conservative women and liberal feminists operate within the same parameters of classical liberal theory. Within this theoretical framework, liberal feminists provide cogent arguments for rejecting the erroneous claims of conservatives. But precisely because they operate within the contours of the capitalist market, liberal feminists are markedly insensitive to the structural forces that undermine the promise of equal opportunity for a very large segment of the population. Socialist feminists raise important challenges to the moral legitimacy of a hierarchical division of labor and a mode of social organization that viciously punishes the "losers," whom it both produces and requires. But socialist feminists cannot account for the distortions that racism introduces to the operations of a capitalist market. Black feminists make visible the virulence and persistence of racism, but they fall back upon liberalism or socialism for economic analysis and tactics for political transformation. Postmodern feminist Wendy Brown reminds us that the state is not a neutral instrument and that normalizing practices threaten to ensnare emancipatory projects, but her call for a free space of contestation provides little direction for feminist praxis currently under threat from reactionary forces.

Theoretical analysis is no substitute for politics. Developing a systematic critique of competing theoretical standpoints will neither determine the outcome of the next election nor translate directly into a transformed policy agenda. Nonetheless, theoretical analysis can help feminist scholars and activists become aware of the theoretical underpinnings and implications of our political arguments. It can help move feminist political debates beyond impasses created by *ad hominem* arguments, emotivist exchanges, and the devastating damage to coalition politics that flows from appeals to the authority of individual experience. If the adoption of standpoint theory as an analytical tool contributes to this end, then it makes good on Hartsock's promise to play a liberatory role, although not precisely in the way that Hartsock envisioned.

Feminist standpoint analysis also provides resources for achieving objectivity as reconceptualized by feminist scholars. The juxtaposition of competing theoretical accounts illuminates the role of social values in cognition, an illumination that has important implications for an adequate understanding of objectivity, as noted in chapter 3. Traditional methods in the social sciences are premised upon the assumption that the chief threat to objectivity is idiosyncrasy. Notions of replicability and intersubjective verification presume that the central obstacle to objectivity lies in the emotional and perceptual quirks of the subjective self that distort, confuse, and interfere with objective apprehension of the external world. Recognition of the theoretical constitution of facticity challenges the myth of radical idiosyncrasy and the optimistic assumption that intersubjective agreement can suffice to accredit knowledge once the bias of individual observers has been purged. If social values incorporated in a theoretical framework structure perceptions of the world, then intersubjective corroboration within that framework simply insulates those values from interrogation. Rather than functioning as the equivalent of objectivity, intersubjective consensus can shield shared values from critical reflection, truncate inquiry, and entrench error within intersubjectively "verified" theories. One virtue of feminist standpoint analysis is that it requires engagement of competing claims and competing theoretical frameworks. By examining the tacit presuppositions of alternative accounts, feminist standpoint analysis helps make visible potential sources of error masked by mainstream social science methods. Attuned to the complex interaction between theoretical assumptions, social values, and discipline-specific methods in the constitution of facticity, feminist standpoint analysis affords greater awareness of potential sources of error and a commitment to heightened interrogation of precisely that which is taken as unproblematic in competing accounts. As such, feminist standpoint analysis helps us confront the contentious assumptions most deeply entrenched in our conceptual apparatus by fostering sustained critique of problematic assumptions that impair an objective grasp of the complex issues confronting contemporary political life.

Chapter 8   Intersectionality

Does FEMINIST RESEARCH generate truths about race and gender that main-stream scholarship has missed? If so, do these truths challenge dominant ac-counts of social institutions and practices? How do innovative feminist analytic tools make visible processes of racialization and gendering that have been natu-ralized by research methodologies accredited within the natural sciences and the social sciences? How can feminist methodological innovations that foreground social processes through which inequalities of race, class, ethnicity, gender, and sexuality are produced and maintained contribute to a critical reinterpretation of institutions central to liberal democratic governance?

To answer these questions, the final chapter of this book focuses on "inter-sectionality," the analytical tool developed by feminists of color in their contin-uing struggle to correct the omissions and distortions in feminist analysis caused by failure to investigate the structuring powers of race, class, ethnicity, sexuality, and nationality. The chapter begins by tracing the emergence of the concept of intersectionality from the analyses of the simultaneity of oppressions advanced by African American women in the nineteenth century and considers a range of questions for investigation opened up by this important analytical tool. The chapter then turns to an extended case study, which demonstrates how the de-ployment of intersectionality as an analytical tool contributes to an understand-ing of power relations in the United States, which are rendered invisible by mainstream research methods in the social sciences.

The case study in this chapter draws together arguments and illustrates themes developed throughout the book. In keeping with the feminist goal to "de-naturalize" relations of racial and gender power, it shows how innovative femi-nist analytical tools can challenge biological reductionism by showing in concrete instances how race and gender hierarchies are produced and maintained.

Consonant with feminist efforts to dispel myths of equal opportunity, the study illustrates how interpersonal interactions and institutional practices within a legislature, formally governed by principles of equality, can situate and constrain women of color in ways that undermine formal equality. Following feminist efforts to illuminate the politics of knowledge, it shows how questions concerning racial and gender marginalization cannot be answered within the parameters set by allegedly value-free methods of behavioral analysis. To lend support to the claim that contentious theoretical presuppositions structure perception and accredit particular forms of evidence, the case study traces how some of the most powerful policymakers in the United States have relied upon the discredited pathological theory of poverty to justify public policies that make poor women and children worse off. In tracking the conversion of questionable theoretical assumptions into public law and policy, the case study shows how evidence blindness, sanctioned ignorance, and social amnesia work to shore up structures of racial and gender privilege. Finally, the case study reinforces the point that epistemological issues have palpable consequences for the lives of women and men.

The case study grew out of reports of marginalization by African American women serving in the U.S. House of Representatives. Although dominant approaches to congressional studies afford no means to engage such reports, the concept of intersectionality combines theoretical insights from feminist and critical race theory to offer new analytic strategies with which to investigate not only the experiences of congresswomen of color but also the processes of racialization and gendering in the U.S. Congress, both of which challenge dominant interpretations of congressional operations. Intersectional analysis, then, can produce transformative knowledge of the experiences of women of color and of the operations of one of the most powerful institutions in the world.

Devising a Tool to Analyze the Complexity of Oppression

As the discussion of affirmative action and welfare reform in the previous chapter illustrates, the world looks markedly different when racism is taken seriously. From the early years of the nineteenth century, African American women have attempted to make visible the simultaneity of oppressions, which structure their lives. Beverly Guy-Sheftall's anthology, *Words of Fire* (1995), documents two centuries of writing by and about black women that analyzes and theorizes the intricate interplay of race, gender, class, and sexuality in structuring their lived experiences. These insightful analyses demonstrate that multiple vectors of power are always at work in the specific modes of oppression that circumscribe black women's lives. In their astute accounts of enslavement, economic exploitation, coerced reproduction, Black Codes, lynching, eugenics, sterilization abuse, poverty, denial and infringement of constitutional rights, political repression,

institutional, attitudinal, and cultural racism, black women mapped the contours of "intersectional" analyses.

Within feminist studies, African American scholars have been joined by
Latina scholars, Asian American scholars, and postcolonial scholars in their continuing struggle against hegemonic claims by white feminists, who fail to take seriously the multiple vectors of power that structure women's lives. Enriching
Beauvoir's (1949) insight that one is not born but becomes a woman, scholars of
color have illuminated the complex racial, ethnic, national, colonial, and neocolonial processes that interact with gendering to produce specific ways of being
a woman under particular sociohistorical conditions. Coining terms such as
"multiple jeopardy" (King 1988) and "intersectionality" (Crenshaw 1989) to
capture the intricate interplay of social forces that produce particular men and
women as members of particular races, classes, sexualities, ethnicities, and nationalities, feminist scholars of color have demonstrated the grave intellectual
and moral deficiencies that result from failure to comprehend and address the
mutual constitution of identities and the social practices that produce and sustain hierarchies of difference.

Since the late 1960s, feminists scholars of color have deployed intersectionality as an analytical tool to raise new questions for research. Working within
and across a range of disciplines, feminist scholars of color have demonstrated
that attention to intersectionality changes understandings about the social constitution of subjectivities, the materialization and stylization of bodies, the identities of desiring subjects, the designation of desirable objects, patterns of desire,
sexual practices, gendered performances, the terms and conditions of sexual exchange, the asymmetries of power in public and private spheres, the politics of
reproduction, the distributions of types of work, the organization of domestic activity, the divisions of paid and unpaid labor, the structures of the formal, informal, and subsistence economies, the segregation of labor markets, patterns of
production and consumption, terms and conditions of labor exchange, opportunities for education, employment and promotion, the politics of representation,
the structures and outcomes of public decision-making, the operating procedures
of regulatory and redistributive agencies, the dynamics of diasporas and decolo-
nization, the potent contradictions of globalization, war-making and militarization, and women's manifold resistances against the oppressive forces structuring
and constraining their life prospects.

The importance of intersectionality to feminist analysis has led one astute
feminist scholar to suggest that "intersectionality is the most important theoretical contribution of women's studies so far" (McCall 2005). Although intersectionality as an analytical tool is compatible with a wide range of research methods
in the humanities and the social sciences, this chapter develops a sustained case
study to illustrate how intersectional analysis can challenge the dominant

approaches to the study of Congress accredited by the discipline of political science. Using the words of congresswomen of color as the central research heuristic, intersectional analysis makes visible processes of marginalization that mainstream accounts omit, offers better explanations of certain policy priorities of congresswomen of color, and reveals flaws in dominant accounts of representative processes central to the legitimation of democratic practices in the United States.

Equal but Marginal: Exploring a Paradox

In their pathbreaking work, A *Portrait of Marginality*, Marianne Githens and Jewel Prestage (1977, 339) noted that from its inception American politics has been "man's business" (that is, it has been "gendered") and "white folks' business" (that is, it has been "raced"). "As a consequence, black women have been doubly excluded from the political arena." The form of exclusion that Githens and Prestage sought to illuminate was the pervasive and persistent underrepresentation of women of color in elective offices. In 1977, when *Portrait of Marginality* was published, women of color held 3 percent of the elected offices in the United States, most of which were at the level of local school boards, and five seats in the U.S. Congress (King 1977, 347). A quarter century later, women of color held 3.7 percent of the seats in the U.S. Congress, 3.6 percent of seats in state legislatures, and 3.09 percent of the mayoral and council offices at the municipal level (Center for American Women and Politics 2002; National League of Cities 2002). In addition to underrepresentation, studies of elected women of color consistently document forms of marginalization, including stereotyping complemented by a policy of invisibility, exclusion of women of color from leadership positions within legislatures, and lack of institutional responsiveness to the policies women of color champion (Bryce and Warrick 1977; Bratton and Haynie 1999; Swain 2000).

In a survey of state legislators, David Hedge, James Button, and Mary Spear (1996) found that black women are more likely to experience discrimination within state legislatures than are their male counterparts: 76 percent of the African American women legislators reported encountering discrimination, compared to 60 percent of African American male legislators. In a 2001 study of African American women state legislators, Wendy Smooth (2001a, 2001b) demonstrated that experiences of marginalization are not mitigated by seniority or leadership positions. On the contrary, the longer black women have served in office and the more powerful the positions they hold within legislative institutions, the stronger are their feelings of exclusion. "The more success black women have enjoyed in passing legislation, the less likely they are to feel they are full members of the institution" (Smooth 2001b, 12).

Little in the scholarly literature on legislatures helps explain such reports of marginalization. Indeed certain legislative rules and operating procedures are designed to secure equal inclusion of members. The "legislative egalitarianism" (Hall 1996, 55, 108) institutionalized in the one-person, one-vote rule in committees and on the floor and the considerable latitude members enjoy in hiring and organizing their staffs, fixing their schedules, and setting priorities should lay the groundwork for inclusive participation. Although numerous scholars have pointed out that legislatures are not as egalitarian as they might first appear, the explanations for inequalities in participation emphasize partisan organization within the legislature (Aldrich 1995; Cox and McCubbins 1993; Fenno 1997; Rohde 1991), divisions of labor and specialization within committees (Fenno 1973), institutional norms such as hard work and seniority (Fenno 1962, 1966), "folkways" (Matthews 1960), or rational choices by members about how to invest their time and energy (Hall 1996). Race and gender do not figure in these explanatory accounts.

With the exception of the studies that survey African American legislators noted above (Hedge, Button, and Spear 1996; Smooth 2001a, 2001b), studies of race in legislatures have typically focused on roll call analysis and have concluded that once party, region, and the percentage of African Americans in the constituency are controlled for, race carries little explanatory power (Swain 1993; Taylor 1996). Beyond roll call analysis, a number of studies have suggested that legislators of color are governed largely by the same concerns as white members (Fenno 1978; Hall 1996; Swain 1993), but these accounts do not disaggregate by gender; as such, they can provide no insights into the experience of marginalization reported by African American women legislators.

Within the women and politics literature, far more attention has been directed toward the differences between male and female legislators than to differences among women legislators. Women and politics scholars have devoted their attention to documenting "gender difference" and to investigating how that difference plays out within political institutions (Rosenthal 2002; Swers 2002). Numerous studies have demonstrated that women legislators not only give higher priority than male legislators to issues such as women's rights, education, health care, families and children, the environment, and gun control, but they are willing to devote considerable effort in committee and on the floor to securing passage of progressive legislation in these areas (for example, Dodson and Carroll 1991; Kathlene 1989; Sue Thomas 1994). Women and politics scholars have also investigated women's legislative and leadership styles, suggesting that women pursue cooperative legislative strategies, while men prefer competitive, zero-sum tactics; and women are more oriented toward consensus, preferring less hierarchical, more participatory, and more collaborative approaches than their male counterparts, but race and ethnic differences among women legislators have not figured prominently in these analyses (Sue Thomas 1994; Jewell and

Whicker 1994; Rosenthal 2000). Several scholars have investigated the tensions that arise between the preferred legislative and leadership strategies of women and the institutional norms that conflate male behavioral preferences with "professionalism" and "political savvy" (Kathlene 1994; Kenney 1996; Rosenthal 2000; Jeydel and Taylor 2003). This scholarship has made it clear that neither legislative priorities nor the standard operating procedures of legislative institutions are gender inclusive or gender neutral. But they have been less attuned to the possibility that genders are raced, that institutional norms and practices may be raced and gendered, or that political institutions may play a critical role in producing, maintaining, and reproducing raced and gendered experiences within and through their organizational routines and practices.

When women legislators of color report persistent marginalization within legislative institutions despite years of seniority and impressive legislative accomplishments, they offer a clue that there is more going on in legislative institutions than has yet been captured in the political science literature. This chapter explores the experiences of marginalization reported by congresswomen of color in the 103rd and 104th Congresses in an effort to make visible power relations that have profound effects; these relations construct raced and gendered hierarchies that structure interactions among members as well as institutional practices, while also shaping public policies.

Toward that end, I first develop a conception of racing-gendering as an active process that differs significantly from the conceptions of race and sex as individual attributes or demographic characteristics. I then suggest that investigating the processes of racing-gendering requires methodological innovation to make visible that which traditional methodologies have rendered invisible. I provide examples of racing-gendering in Congress and indicate how these marginalizing experiences of congresswomen of color challenge a number of received views in Congress studies. I explore the persistence of racing-gendering across two Congresses, the Democratic-controlled 103rd and the Republican-controlled 104th to demonstrate that congresswomen of color perceive racing-gendering to be ongoing processes, regardless of party in power. In the final sections of the chapter, I identify new explanatory possibilities created by the theory of racing-gendering in Congress and consider some implications of this account for understandings of the internal operations of political institutions, the substantive representation of the interests of historically marginalized groups, and for the quality of democracy in the United States.

From Race and Sex to Racing-Gendering

Political scientists have tended to treat race and sex as biological or physical characteristics rather than as political constructs. According to this "primordial view" (Taylor 1996), race and sex precede politics. As part of the "natural" or "given" aspects of human existence, race and sex are apolitical, unless intentionally mobilized for political purposes. The effects of race or sex upon politics, then, are matters for empirical investigation, but there is no reason to believe that politics plays any role in shaping the physical characteristics of individuals or the demographic characteristics of populations.

Within the past few decades, critical race theorists and feminist theorists have challenged the primordial view of race and sex by calling attention to processes of racialization and gendering through which relations of power and forms of inequality are constructed, shaping the identities of individuals. Through detailed studies of laws, norms, and organizational practices that enforced racial segregation and separate spheres for men and women, scholars have excavated the political processes through which hierarchies of difference have been produced and maintained. They have demonstrated that the imputed "natural" interests and abilities of women and men of various races are the result of state-prescribed limitations in education, occupation, immigration, citizenship, and office holding (for example, Connell 1987; Flammang 1997; Haney Lopez 1996; Siltanen 1994). Politics has produced race and gender not only by creating and maintaining raced and gendered divisions within the population but by defining race and gender characteristics and according differential rights on the basis of those definitions (Yanow 2003). In *White By Law*, for example, Haney Lopez has demonstrated that through the direct control of human behavior and by shaping public understanding, "law translates ideas about race into material and societal conditions that entrench those ideas" (Haney Lopez 1996, 19). Thus immigration and miscegenation laws have produced the physical appearance of the nation's population by constraining reproductive choices. Laws, court decisions, and census categories defining who is "white" and who is "non-white" have ascribed racialized meanings to physical features and ancestry (Haney Lopez 1996, 14–15; Yanow 2003). Law has also produced certain behaviors and attitudes associated with women of multiple races and men of color through exclusions from citizenship and office holding, the legalization of unequal treatment, and through differential access to social benefits (Fraser 1989; Haney Lopez 1996; G. Mink 1995).

Developing a "theory of gendered institutions," feminist scholars have begun to map the manifold ways in which gender power and disadvantage are created and maintained not only through law but also through institutional processes, practices, images, ideologies, and distributional mechanisms (Acker 1990, 1992; Kenney 1996; Steinberg 1992). They have shown how organizational practices play a central role in recreating and entrenching gender hierarchies, gender symbols, and gendered identities (Duerst-Lahti and Kelly 1995). The theory of gendered institutions has been important in drawing attention to the structuring practices, standard operating procedures, rules, and regulations that disadvantage women within contemporary organizations. But the theory of gendered institutions has not yet engaged the implications of arguments of feminists of color that gender is inseparable from race, class, ethnicity, nationality, sexual orientation, and other socially constructed hierarchies of difference.

Feminist scholars of color have coined the term, intersectionality, to capture the intricate interplay of social forces that produce particular women and men as members of particular races, classes, ethnicities, and nationalities (Crenshaw 1989, 1997). Intersectionality suggests that the processes of racialization and gendering are specific yet interrelated. Racialization may produce marked commonalities of privilege between men and women of the dominant race/ethnic groups and of disadvantage among men and women of the subordinate racial/ethnic groups. Gendering may produce particular commonalities (deportment, adornment, stylizations of the body, voice intonations and inflections, skilling or deskilling, interests, aspirations) among women across race and ethnic groups and among men across race and ethnic groups.

The term, *racing-gendering*, attempts to foreground the intricate interactions of racialization and gendering in the political production of distinctive groups of men and women. Racing-gendering involves the production of difference, political asymmetries, and social hierarchies that simultaneously create the dominant and the subordinate. To investigate racing-gendering, then, it is crucial to attend to specifics and to interrelationships. The processes that produce a white male, for example, differ from, while being fully implicated in, the processes that produce a black man, a Latino, a Native American man, a white woman, a black woman, a Latina, an Asian American woman, or a Native American woman.

Racing and gendering are active processes with palpable effects. Racing-gendering occurs through the actions of individuals, as well as through laws, policies, and organizational norms and practices. The identities of women of color are constituted through an amalgam of practices that construct them as "other" (to white men, men of color, and white women) and challenge their individuality and their status as fully human. The manifold practices through which racing-gendering are generated and sustained are complex and layered. They surface epistemically in the particular knowledges ascribed to women of color and in the forms of knowledge alleged to lie beyond their grasp. They surface contradictorily as in the opposing phenomena of invisibility (when whites consistently either fail to see or simply ignore women of color; confuse them because "they all look alike"; deny them recognition) and hypervisibility (any woman of color stands for all women of color; one or two women of color in a room is somehow too many). Silencing, excluding, marginalizing, segregating, discrediting, dismissing, discounting, insulting, stereotyping, and patronizing are used singly and in combination to fix women of color "in their place."

Tokenism has been a talisman of racing-gendering. As tokens, some women of color are admitted to membership in elite institutions, but their inclusion carries an expectation that they accept the agenda of the dominant members (Lorde 1984; Hurtado 1996). Their talents are recognized only on the condition that they are used to support the status quo. Any attempt to expand the agenda or change the operating procedures by a token produces quite different racing-gendering tactics by those dominant within the institution. Hurtado (1996, 135, 166) has suggested that women of color who act in accordance with their own agendas confront "topic extinctions" and the "*pendejo* game." Topic extinctions refer to the total silence that greets substantive suggestions and policy agendas advanced by women of color. Whether fueled by willed indifference, evidence blindness, or a refusal to hear, such silence insures that women of color fail to achieve their objectives. In the pendejo game, white men and white women in positions of power "play dumb" by pretending they do not understand the policy suggestions or substantive arguments of women of color and requesting further explication and deeper elaboration. While women of color devote time and energy trying to educate members of the dominant group about the issues, those in power pretend to listen but do not hear; hence, everything remains the same. The demand for additional information is simply a delaying tactic that insures deferment of the agenda advanced by women of color.

Racing-gendering can also involve certain "Catch 22s": women of color are simultaneously pressured to assimilate to the dominant norms of the institution and denied the possibility of assimilation. They are not allowed to assume the position of the unmarked (white/male) member because racing-gendering practices continue to set them off as different. Indeed, racing-gendering involves asymmetrical power relations that simultaneously constitute the marked and unmarked members. Whites and men constitute themselves as the unmarked norm in the very process of constructing people of color and women as marked, different.

Processes of racing-gendering can be intentional or unintentional. In her study of state legislators, for example, Sue Thomas (1994, 37) found that male legislators routinely deny both that they engage in stereotyping and sexist behavior and that women legislators are in any way limited in their legislative roles by stereotypes or sexism. Yet when asked to compare women's and men's performance in the legislature, the male legislators tended to identify certain "deficiencies" that impaired women's legislative effectiveness. The imputed deficiencies conformed to sexist stereotypes. Whether deployed intentionally or unwittingly, racing-gendering practices produce relations of power that alter the conditions of work and the conditions of life for women of color in subtle and not so subtle ways. They insure that the playing field is not equal.

In addition to various direct effects, racing-gendering practices also produce unintended consequences: anger and resistance. In the words of Aida Hurtado

(1996, 21), "to be a woman of color is to live with fury." In response to racing-gendering, women of color mobilize anger for purposes of social change. Mamie Locke (1997, 378) has argued that women of color have "struggled since our nation's founding against peripheral status and the consequences of exclusion." Within the institutions in which they work and within their communities, a "central tactic of resistance is to use anger effectively" (Hurtado 1996, 21). In the struggle against exclusion and marginalization, women of color in electoral politics have envisioned themselves as social change agents "trying to achieve the visibility and recognition that were symbolically reserved for white men" (Darling 1998, 157). In exploring the dynamics of racing-gendering in the U.S. Congress, it is important to consider that the identities of congresswomen of color may be constituted not only through the racing-gendering practices that silence, marginalize, and constrain but also through resistance and the political mobilization of anger that racing-gendering engenders. Indeed, I argue that the anger and resistance engendered by congresswomen of color's experiences of racing-gendering in the halls of Congress help explain certain of their policy preferences and the intensity with which they pursue legislation that they know to be doomed.

Changing Methods

For the past half century, congressional studies have been conducted largely within the framework of behavioral analysis. Whether informed by the assumptions of structural functionalism, which foregrounds norms and sanctions related to party organization and committee structure in Congress or by the rational actor model's alternative emphasis on the explanatory power of the rational, purposive decisions of individual members, scholars of Congress have agreed that their goal is to study the political behavior of individuals in order to formulate and test hypotheses concerning uniformities of behavior within the institutional context. While the specific methods adopted to achieve these purposes have included participant observation, historical analysis, survey research, roll call analysis, structured interviews, and systematic investigation of committee and subcommittee deliberations, none of these methods have identified "scientific laws of race or gender" operating within Congress. Indeed, several scholars have pointed out that quantitative methods are peculiarly unsuited to study historically underrepresented groups in Congress. Put simply, there have been too few women and people of color in Congress to generate statistically significant results (Hall 1996, 192; Tamerius 1995, 143–155). The problem of small numbers is further complicated by the concept of intersectionality. Standard social science methodological techniques that attempt to isolate the effects of gender by controlling for race/ethnicity or to isolate the effects of race/ethnicity by controlling for gender are at odds with any effort to trace the complex interactions of race-gender in an organization, a point made cogently by Spelman (1988, 103). Sophisticated statistical models designed to investigate interaction effects of race, gender, class, region, constituency type, and so on require large data sets that restrict legislative studies to roll call analysis, which has only limited value in explaining certain aspects of congressional operations and dynamics. Moreover, quantitative techniques devised to reveal uniformities of behavior are by design insensitive to difference, treating anything that deviates from the norm as an outlier or an anomaly.

To probe the meaning of reports of marginalization by elected women of color, an alternative approach is necessary. Hermeneutics or interpretive theory has long vied with behavioralism in the social sciences, perhaps not for supremacy, but at least for accreditation as a legitimate method for social science inquiry. Hermeneutics aspires to explain social and political experiences by situating the claims of individuals or groups within a larger interpretive framework. Treating individual statements as texts, interpretive theorists probe the meaning of those texts by analyzing them in relation to cultural and linguistic practices, historical traditions, and philosophical frameworks in order to provide an enhanced explanation consistent with the meaning of the experience to the agent.

To illuminate factors that contribute to congresswomen of color's experience of marginalization, I interpret interview data from congresswomen in the 103rd and 104th Congresses in light of recent scholarship in critical race theory, feminist theory, and African American history. I draw upon the concept of intersectionality and the theory of gendered institutions to investigate racing-gendering in the U.S. Congress and identify interpersonal interactions and institutional practices that situate and constrain congresswomen of color differently from white congressmen, white congresswomen, and congressmen of color.

While this study is informed by hermeneutics, it also employs a multimethod approach that combines textual analysis of interview data with a case study of welfare reform the 103rd and 104th Congresses. The interview data are drawn from a long-term study of women in Congress conducted by the Center for American Women and Politics. Under the auspices of grants from the Charles H. Revson Foundation and the Ford Foundation, the Center for American Women and Politics conducted a comprehensive review of written sources and documents pertaining to the 103rd and 104th Congresses, as well as multiple in-depth interviews with women members of Congress, congressional staff, and lobbyists involved with the 103rd and 104th Congresses. Between June and October 1995, CAWP staff interviewed forty-three of the fifty-four women who had served in the 103rd Congress (thirty-nine representatives, four senators; thirty-two Democrats, eleven Republicans). Between October 1997 and March 1998, CAWP staff interviewed thirty-eight of the fifty-eight women who served in the 104th Congress (thirty-six representatives, two senators; twenty-six Democrats, twelve Republicans). My textual analysis is based upon transcripts from interviews with eighty-one congresswomen, including fifteen congresswomen of color who served in the 103rd and 104th Congresses (eleven African American women, three Latinas, and one Asian American woman; see Table 1), supplemented by certain policy debates recorded in the *Congressional Record*. The interviews, which ranged from twenty to ninety minutes, were taped and "on the record"; transcripts were made from the tapes of each interview. During the interviews congresswomen were asked about their legislative priorities and accomplishments, their efforts to represent women, their relationship to the Congressional Caucus for Women's Issues, as well as their role in passing legislation in the areas of crime, health, health care reform, reproductive rights, violence against women, welfare, and international trade.

Congresswomen of Color in the 103rd and 104th Congresses

African American
Representative Corrinne Brown (D-Fla.)
Representative Eva Clayton (D-N.C.)
Representative Barbara Rose Collins (D-Mich.)
Representative Cardiss Collins (D-Il.)
Representative Sheila Jackson Lee (D-Tex.)
Representative Eddie Bernice Johnson (D-Tex.)
Representative Cynthia McKinney (D-Ga.)
Representative Carrie Meek (D-Fla.)
Representative Maxine Waters (D-Calif.)
Delegate Eleanor Holmes Norton (D-D.C.)
Senator Carol Moseley-Braun (D-Il.)

Asian American
Representative Patsy Mink (D-Hawaii)

Latina
Representative Ileana Ros-Lehtinen (R-Fla.)
Representative Lucille Roybal Allard (D-Calif.)
Representative Nydia Velasquez (D-N.Y.)

There were many similarities in the responses of white congresswomen and congresswomen of color to the interview questions. All agreed that they felt an obligation to represent women, although they differed in their understanding of what constituted a women's issue, which women they sought to represent, and how they thought it best to represent those women. They also agreed that they were willing to work across party lines to achieve legislation they thought would help women, and they agreed that the Congressional Caucus for Women's Issues played an important role in coordinating bipartisan coalitions in support of particular pieces of legislation.

The interview transcripts also revealed a range of differences in the responses of white congresswomen and congresswomen of color. In discussing their legislative priorities and in identifying their specific roles in support of or in opposition to particular bills, congresswomen of color provided narratives that differed markedly from those of their white counterparts. African American congresswomen, in particular, related tales of insult, humiliation, frustration, and anger that distinguished their responses from those of their white counterparts. These tales provide concrete examples of racing-gendering in Congress that form the core of the analysis in the next two sections. But to provide an institutional context for the interpretation of these narratives, more was needed.

Several scholars have argued that special methods are required to uncover *how* institutions are raced-gendered. Ronnie Steinberg (1992, 580) has suggested that "the feminist approach to developing organizational theory has a methodological corollary: it calls for heavy reliance on intensive case studies of well-selected organizations to uncover systemic patterns of social behavior. Qualitative studies are required to map concrete practices and processes that disadvantage women of color in organizations" (Acker 1990, 1992; Cockburn 1991; Siltanen 1994). While quantitative studies can document the persistence of white male dominance in public and private sectors, only detailed case studies can identify the mechanisms through which raced-gendered power is maintained and recreated in changing organizations.

The U.S. Congress is a particularly appropriate institution for a case study. As the premier decision-making body in the federal system, it has been thoroughly studied by political scientists and its formal and informal operating procedures are believed to be well-known. Although extensive literature documents the role of political parties, the committee system, congressional member organizations, institutional norms, constituency interests, professional lobbies, campaign contributors, and friendship in structuring the operations of Congress, as noted above, race-gender dynamics are not typically believed to play any role in the operations of this institution. Thus, tales of racing and gendering told by congresswomen of color in the 103rd and 104th Congresses raise a number of challenges to the received view of Congress. To illuminate these challenges, the following section contrasts the narratives of congresswomen of color with accepted hypotheses about how Congress works.

A case study of the 103rd and 104th Congresses makes it possible to compare insights about racing-gendering drawn from the narratives of congresswomen of color with paradigmatic accounts of Congress, thereby opening new questions for further research. But even in the absence of additional research, congresswomen's accounts of racing-gendering raise important questions about the quality of democratic practices in the United States. Congress is a unique institution. Elected directly by the people and owing their seats to electoral support in their constituencies, members of Congress possess a measure of independence that distinguishes them from their counterparts within disciplined parties in parliamentary systems. With equal salaries, autonomy to hire and fire their staffs and set their own schedules, members of Congress enter into the legislative process on the basis of considerable equality, far more equality than exists in most organizations and worksites. In the following analysis, I hope to show that despite such formal equality, racing-gendering operates in the Congress in ways that insure that congresswomen of color do equal work within the institution, but not on equal terms. If racing-gendering can be shown to create power differentials among peers within a collegial institution, then it raises questions about fundamental fairness in the operations of the nation's premier legislative institution.

Racing-Gendering Enactments in Congress

Claims about racing in Congress are not altogether new. In his account of the experiences of the first African Americans to serve in Congress during the Reconstruction era, Eric Foner (1988) noted that most bills introduced by black congressmen languished in committee and that the black legislators attributed their failure to accomplish their legislative objectives to the attitudes of their white counterparts. Similarly, Carol Swain (1993, 220) has noted not only that black legislators must fight hard for the respect of their white colleagues, but many find that such respect eludes them regardless of the intensity of their efforts. Sam Rayburn's advice to "go along to get along" may lead black legislators to mute "militant impulses or radical views," but it will not necessarily afford them power and respect within the halls of the legislature (Swain 1993, 222). Research on gendering in legislatures has also demonstrated that women confront forms of obstruction and demoralization that can hinder their legislative achievements (Kathlene 1989, 1994; Thomas 1994). What happens when racing and gendering intersect?

Evelynn Hammonds (1997, 182) has suggested that for African American women intersectionality is often manifested in invisibility, otherness, and stigma produced and reproduced on black women's bodies. Accounts provided by black congresswomen about their daily experiences in Congress corroborate Hammonds's view. Consider, for example, the report of Congresswoman Cynthia McKinney [D-Ga.] that she routinely encounters difficulty getting into the House of Representatives. Security guards, it seems, "just don't think about people of color as members of Congress" (McKinney 1997). Although routine demands for proof of her congressional membership credentials may seem a small matter, this kind of daily nuisance marks a black congresswoman as "other," a perpetual outsider.

In his poignant "phenomenology of blackness," Frantz Fanon (1952) indicated that racialization involves a particular kind of stigmatization that eclipses individuality. History freezes the black's identity on the epidermis. Thus, the black cannot assert individuality or subjectivity because he or she is thought of in the collective—as former slave. Another episode recounted by Representative Cynthia McKinney demonstrates the currency of Fanon's insight, while simultaneously challenging Herb Asher's claim that one fundamental norm of Congress is "to maintain friendly relationships" (1973, 243). According to McKinney, several of her white colleagues raise the topic of slavery when they encounter her. "When Helen Chenowith tells me that I'm lucky to have survived slavery, I think I have a problem with her. When Linda Smith thinks about slavery because I happen to be on an elevator with her, then I think I have a problem with her. . . . I don't have anything to say or do with people who still think of me as a slave" (McKinney 1997). There is no relation at greater remove from friendship and equality than that between a master and a slave. Rather than interacting on the basis of collegiality, when white members of Congress situate a black congresswoman in the context of slavery, they call into question not only her status as an equal member of the House of Representatives, but her status as a human being. Invoking constitutional doctrines concerning their subhuman status (three-fifth of a person) and Supreme Court decisions affirming their status as property, "possessing no rights a white man was bound to respect" (*Dred Scott v. Sanford* 1857), any discursive imposition of slave status upon a contemporary African American is fraught with insult and degradation. But a rhetorical frame that demands gratitude such as that implicit in a claim that contemporary blacks are "lucky to have survived slavery," adds to insult by erasing white responsibility for the institution of slavery and by assuming that whites may legitimately instruct blacks about the appropriate emotional response to the end of brutal oppression. Such racist communication between colleagues demonstrates how racing-gendering works in at least two directions simultaneously: it constitutes white women as those with authority to set the terms in which slavery is discussed, and it simultaneously constitutes a black woman as an imagined slave, lacking sufficient gratitude to whites for emancipation. Such conversational references to slavery might be isolated incidents, but as Representative McKinney's response makes clear, they have profound consequences for subsequent interactions. Such instances of racing produce Congresswoman McKinney's warranted anger and wariness while undermining the possibility that she would seek out such colleagues for collaborative efforts in Congress. Having colleagues (mis)take one for a slave may be the most blatant form of racing congresswomen of color encounter in the House, but it is certainly not the only form.

Invisibility—depending on the context and depending on whether it is de-ployed tactically by a member or imposed unwillingly upon a member—can mean markedly different things in Congress. When one is a member of the mi-nority party, working with and through members of the majority party may be the only tactic possible to accomplish a legislative end. Thus Delegate Eleanor Holmes Norton [D-D.C.] (1997) notes that even in the minority, it is possible to "have a lot of success. . . . I get things in bills all the time because I look around for somebody to work with." To illustrate the strategy, Delegate Holmes Norton recounted the legislative history of a bill that she authored to make tax exempt the benefits awarded to widows of District of Columbia police officers killed in the line of duty. Working with Republicans on the House Ways and Means Committee, she had the bill brought to the attention of committee chair, Bill Archer (R-Tex.) who added it to the budget bill. The cost of such a legislative tactic is invisibility. Officially, committee chair Archer takes credit for authoring the legislation. Consistent with the "workhorse" account of effective legislative strategies, legislators intent on attaining their policy objectives are willing to ac-cept invisibility as a trade-off for effectiveness (Clapp 1963; Matthews 1959; Payne 1980). In principle, such tactical invisibility is race and gender neutral.

But even tactical invisibility may produce outcomes that vary from those predicted by the congressional "workhorse" account when deployed by a black congresswoman. An incident reported by Representative Barbara Rose Collins [D-Mich.] (1998) suggests that tactical invisibility may generate punitive sanc-tions rather than legislative effectiveness. Alerted to the problem of environ-mental racism by a University of Michigan study, which documented that most toxic waste plants were located in African American communities, Represen-tative Collins used her position on the House Transportation and Infra-structure Committee in the 103rd Congress to draft legislation and organize hearings on an "Environmental Equity Act" (H.R. 1925, The Environmental Response, Compensation, and Liability Act). The bill stipulated that con-struction of hazardous waste plants could not be authorized without first ascer-taining the possible damage to minorities living in the vicinity. Despite her persistent efforts on its behalf, in the 103rd Congress, the bill died in commit-tee. As a member of the minority party in the 104th Congress, Representative Collins knew she would not be able to make headway on the environmental equity bill on her own. So she approached a Republican friend in the Michigan delegation, Representative Vernon Ehlers, who also served on the Transporta-tion and Infrastructure Committee and asked him to introduce the environ-mental equity bill. Ehlers agreed to introduce the bill as an amendment to the Federal Water Pollution Control Act, which was pending before the commit-tee. During a markup session, Ehrler's amendment was easily passed by the committee.

Immediately prior to the committee vote, Representative Collins was lobbied by Republican colleagues to support the proposal. In her words, "I imprudently said, well of course I'll vote for it, it's my amendment" (B. R. Collins 1998). Her inadvertent reference to her role in authoring the legislation was not allowed to go unnoticed. It was reported back to committee chair, Bud Shuster (R-Pa.). The following day, Shuster rescinded the committee vote. Representative Collins's request that the committee reconsider the legislation was denied. Although she framed the issue as a matter of water safety of concern to all residents in areas targeted for hazardous waste plants, the committee chair refused to allow the amendment to be reconsidered. Representative Bill Emerson (R-Mo.), who had gotten to know Collins as part of a congressional delegation to Somalia, offered to try to mediate the dispute. Although Emerson presented both the scientific evidence that warranted the legislation and a political rationale beneficial to Republicans for its approval, he was unable to persuade the committee chair to allow the committee to reconsider the legislation.

Within the explanatory framework provided by the "theory of purposive behavior in an institutional context" (Hall 1996), Representative Shuster's decision is puzzling in a number of respects. Within committee markups, no procedural rules prevent minority members of the committee from offering amendments. Although committee chairmen enjoy considerable latitude in conducting markups, they regularly "insert special provisions in legislation to win members' support. . . . Because the chairman is likely to be responsible for managing the bill on the floor, he or she will try throughout the markup to gather as much support within the committee as possible" (Oleszek 2001, 96). Indeed, it is standard operating procedure within House markups for the chair to "alternate between the majority and minority side in recognizing members to offer amendments or to debate pending proposals" (Oleszek 2001, 98). According to normal procedures, then, Representative Collins and/or Representative Emerson should have been allowed to reintroduce the amendment. Given that the committee majority had already voted in support of the amendment and that Representative Collins was willing to accept strategic invisibility, the theory of purposive behavior would predict that the chair would support the measure to secure committee cohesion and political leverage or as conducive to "district-endearing credit claiming" (Hall 1996, 156), especially because Republicans on the committee were lobbying the chair to support it. According to Hall's economic account of Congress, then, Representative Shuster's strategic agenda manipulation in this case counts as an anomaly. The case is also anomalous in that it departs from Representative Shuster's assessment of his own standard operating procedures. Long known for his "pork barrel" politics, Bud Shuster has described himself as politically adept at coalition-building on the Transportation and Infrastructure Committee. "He talks with pride about having the biggest committee in the

House, with 66 members. He says that will enable him to solicit many view-points when writing legislation, and give him more clout in the House. 'When we go to the floor, I've got 66 votes to start with,' he said" (Hosansky 1996). According to his own account of his legislative style, then, Representative Shuster should have allowed Representative Collins to reintroduce the proposed amendment so that he could count on her support on the House floor.

What combination of factors explains Representative Shuster's behavior? While many might wish to interpret this episode solely in terms of the heightened partisanship of the 104th Congress, in Congresswoman Barbara Collins's view, "It wasn't just partisan" (1998). She interprets this experience as a form of punitive racing-gendering. In thwarting a piece of legislation that had the Committee's bipartisan support, Shuster departed from norms of congressional courtesy and rejected the advice of senior Republicans on the committee in order to punish a black congresswoman for having manifested political skill in attempting to work the system. Regardless of his intentions, the chairman humiliated Representative Barbara Collins and undermined her effort to move legislation designed to protect the interests of African Americans. Exercising his power as committee chair, Shuster indulged the political equivalent of a "topic extinction." For the duration of the 104th Congress, Representative Collins's environmental equity legislation was effectively extinguished.

Congresswomen of color can be rendered invisible even when they are not deploying tactical invisibility to accomplish their legislative goals. In the 104th Congress, Representative Cardiss Collins [D-Il.] with more than twenty years seniority was the ranking minority member of the Government Reform and Oversight Committee, whose highly fragmented jurisdiction (Deering and Smith 1997) combines broad legislative, investigative, and oversight responsibilities. The legislative jurisdiction of the committee includes federal civil service, municipal affairs of the District of Columbia, federal paperwork reduction, government management and accounting measures, efficiency of government operations and activities, holidays and celebrations, national archives, the Census, the postal service, public information and records, intergovernmental relations, and reorganizations of the executive branch. The rules of the Committee on Government Reform require collaboration between the committee chair and the ranking minority member with respect to calling witnesses, scheduling and establishing the format of hearings, issuing investigative reports, and preparation of the committee budget. The committee rules also stipulate that when determining the order of questioning witnesses, "the chairman shall, so far as practicable, recognize alternately based on seniority those majority and minority members present at the time the hearing was called to order and others based on their arrival at the hearing" [Rules of the Committee on Government Reform 14(1)]. In contrast to the carefully delineated rules governing committee hearings, the norms governing legislative operations of the committee are far less formal. As ranking minority member, Cardiss Collins (2000) expected the collaborative relations characteristic of the investigative and oversight activities of the committee to carry over into legislative practices, but that is not what she encountered in the 104th Congress. Rather than being granted a measure of respect by the chair and allowed to amend legislation before the committee, Representative Cardiss Collins was thwarted in every effort she made to shape legislation. According to fellow committee member, Representative Carrie Meek [D-Fla.] (1997), Cardiss Collins "was not allowed to get anything passed, nothing. And many times, she and I were not even recognized to speak." Rather than being able to use her position on the committee to articulate an alternative view, Representative Collins was silenced by the chair's gavel, subjected to what she perceived as a form of humiliation as a part of the committee's routine operation throughout the 104th Congress.

The example of racing-gendering in the House Government Reform and Oversight Committee recounted by Cardiss Collins and Carrie Meek challenges respected accounts of the role of minority party members in congressional committee deliberations. In his meticulous study of participation in subcommittee and committee deliberations in Congress, Richard Hall (1996, 141–142) argues that "full-committee markups, however, provide full-committee members fully guaranteed opportunities to participate. . . . Official barriers to entry into the legislative game are proscribed at this stage. All committee members enjoy full, formal eligibility. Parliamentary rules are in force. There is no equivalent of a restrictive rule to delimit the ability of some committee members—however mischievous their intentions—to speak to the merits of the bill, speak to the merits of individual amendments, propose amendments of their own, exploit procedural options, or engage in dilatory tactics." Indeed Hall suggests that minority party participation is central to the "practice of democratic consent" (238). For expression of minority opinions within the deliberative process is precisely "what obligates minorities to outcomes they do not like" (Hall 1996, 238; Herzog 1989). In contrast to an inclusive process limited only by the strategic choices of the individual participants, Cardiss Collins and Carrie Meek, like Barbara Collins, experienced recurrent exclusion in committee markups. While some might argue that the committee chairs' strategic manipulation of the agenda in the 104th Congress should be attributed to the confrontational politics of an inexperienced Republican majority under the leadership of Newt Gingrich (Fenno 1997), neither the Transportation and Infrastructure Committee nor the Government Reform and Oversight Committee conform straightforwardly to the ideological operations of the "Contract Congress" (Deering and Smith 1997, 48). Indeed, in a study of House committee support for the "conservative coalition" in the 104th Congress, Norman Ornstein, Thomas Mann, and Michael

Malbin (1996) found these two committees among the most moderate in the House. Eschewing both the conservative and liberal ends of the voting spectrum, these committees hovered at the chamber's political center in the 104th Congress, as they had consistently since 1959. Moreover, it is important to note that the African American congresswomen immediately involved in these exchanges were unwilling to reduce their experiences to partisan politics.

Topic extinctions and silencing can undermine the legislative efforts of congresswomen of color and contribute to a form of invisibility accompanied by ineffectiveness. Congresswomen of color have also been rendered invisible, however, in instances of significant legislative achievement. The role of congresswomen of color in pressing for minimum wage legislation in the 104th Congress is well documented in the *Congressional Record*. The demand for a "livable wage" was a recurrent motif in their floor statements during the debates over welfare reform. Arguing that poverty could be eliminated for minimum wage workers only if the minimum wage were increased sufficiently to lift those who worked fulltime above the federal poverty level, congresswomen of color organized to put minimum wage legislation on the agenda. In the tradition of legislative entrepreneurs (Kingdon 1984) and coalition leaders (Arnold 1990), Democratic congresswomen of color wrote to the minority leader to press him to put a minimum wage bill at the top of his priorities. They wrote multiple "Dear Colleague" letters to all members of Congress in an effort to persuade Democrats and Republicans of the importance of an increase in the minimum wage for working women, who constitute more than 60 percent of minimum wage workers. They circulated evidence generated by economists that an increase in the minimum wage was correlated with an increase in business activity rather than a decrease as opponents of the measure suggested (Clayton 1997). When the Republican House leadership was reluctant to schedule a vote on the proposed legislation, Representative Ileana Ros Lehtinen [R-Fla.], who was a cosponsor of HR 3265, The Minimum Wage Increase Act of 1996, worked with Jack Quinn [R-N.Y.] to pressure the leadership to hold a straight up or down vote. When the vote was held, the legislation passed. Despite the activism of congresswomen of color on both sides of the aisle in support of the Minimum Wage Increase Act, when the press conference was called to announce the enactment of the legislation, all the spokespersons for the Administration and for the Congress were male.

Representative Patsy Mink [D-Hawaii] (1997) reported that the all-male delegation taking credit for the legislation was not inadvertent. On the contrary, she had lobbied the secretary of labor without success to include some women in the press conference. Thus, Republican men who had been most opposed to the legislation while it was under consideration in Congress, claimed full credit in public for its passage. In casting themselves as the real representatives of women's interests in Congress, these white men effectively rendered invisible the intensive labor of congresswomen of color to advance the interests of the nation's working poor.

Although some analysts might interpret this imposition of invisibility strictly in terms of partisan politics with the Republican majority in the House claiming credit for legislation passed on their watch; in a period of divided government, the story is more complicated. In part the decision of a Democratic secretary of labor excluded Democratic congresswomen of color from credible claims of credit (Mayhew 1974) in this instance. Moreover, partisan politics cannot explain why the Republican House leadership excluded Ileana Ros Lehtinen, a Republican cosponsor of the bill from visible credit-claiming. Nor, given the trenchant opposition to an increase in the minimum wage among significant sectors of the Republican Party's attentive public, is it altogether clear why white, male Republicans would want to claim credit for this legislation. The "blame avoidance hypothesis" advanced by Hall (1996, 63) would predict that rational optimizing Republicans would shun public credit-claiming to avoid incurring the wrath of their primary constituency. In this instance, then, the racing-gendering account of the imposition of invisibility may make sense of a puzzle that alternative accounts cannot explain adequately.

To speak of an institution as raced-gendered is to suggest that race-specific constructions of masculinity and femininity are intertwined in the daily culture of the institution (Kenney 1996). Rather than preexisting the institution and being imported into it, raced-gendered identities are negotiated within the operating practices and professional roles of the organization. To accomplish their legislative goals, congresswomen of color must attend to the cues they receive from their white colleagues and make decisions about how best to work within the institution. In contrast to decisions concerning tactical invisibility in committee negotiations, efforts to garner votes in support of their legislative priorities in committees and on the floor pose different challenges for congresswomen of color. Members of Congress routinely lobby one another for support of preferred legislation, but the permissible tactics of bargaining, negotiating, and conciliating may be race-gender specific. In describing her successful effort to include funding for lupus research in the appropriations bill passed by 103rd Congress even in the absence of authorizing legislation, Representative Carrie Meek [D-Fla.] (1995) provides insight into an interpersonal dynamic she deems it helpful to adopt to achieve her legislative ends.

> I call it groveling. . . . I have a technique of getting people to do things
> many times when they don't want to do it. I don't do it by being conten-
> tious or combative. But I do it by trying to tell the facts and then
> telling them how I know that they don't mean to overlook this, that

they were not aware of the situation or of the seriousness of the situation, of the incidence of lupus and how it causes so many deaths and so
much sterility. That's the way I do things, not by blasting out in front of
a lot of people, but behind the scenes in talking to them and appealing
to them.

Representative Meek's account of her tactics of persuasion carries a particular res-
onance in the history of U.S. race relations. By describing her mode of soliciting
her colleagues' voting support as "groveling," she links her tactics to a form of sub-
servience far too familiar to women and racial minorities. Within systems of racial
and gender power, when subordinates "tell the facts," they must do so in a way
that assuages the egos of their superiors. Within such a hierarchical frame, it just
won't do for women and people of color to inform a white male that he is mistaken; they must also acknowledge and appeal to his noble nature, in accordance
with which he would have done the right thing if only he had been in command
of full information. In contrast to communicative modes of self-assertion (to demand, insist, argue, demonstrate, convince, and so on), groveling suggests that
the speaker humble or abase himself/herself, muting an indication that he or she
has superior knowledge or equal power. Carrie Meek understands that "groveling"
can be an effective means to accomplish her legislative objectives, but that understanding does not imply that she will choose to deploy that tactic under all circumstances in the House, nor that all congresswomen of color must follow suit; it
does, however, indicate a power dynamic that congresswomen of color must take
into account in devising their legislative strategies. To the extent that such
racing-gendering dynamics are operative in interpersonal interactions in Congress, they suggest that in contrast to the affirmation of self that accompanies
men's legislative victories, women of color may experience a loss of dignity even
in victory. Rather than glorying in their legislative accomplishment, they may
have to grapple with the personal cost of such success.

One tactic underrepresented groups in Congress developed to try to minimize the personal costs of raced-gendered interactions was the creation of legislative service organizations (LSOs), such as the Congressional Black Caucus
and the Congressional Caucus for Women's Issues, which could not only serve as
support networks for members but also provide a mechanism for collective action outside of party structures. Funded by contributions from members' staff allowances, the legislative service organizations hired staff to conduct research,
draft legislation, and help the members devise successful legislative strategies to
advance shared interests.

In the opening days of the 104th Congress, House Speaker Newt Gingrich
[R-Ga.] introduced a number of structural changes to streamline House operations. The abolition of twenty-eight legislative service organizations, including the Congressional Black Caucus (CBC) and the Congressional Caucus for

Women's Issues (CCWI), is of particular interest in the context of racing-gendering practices. Gingrich's decision to eliminate the LSOs was perceived by many as an effort to mute the organized voices of both blacks and women within the halls of Congress. The withdrawal of office space, furnishings, and equipment and the edict prohibiting members from using their staff allowances to support such collective endeavors were perceived as an assault motivated by racism and sexism. Representative Barbara Collins explained.

> They abolished the caucuses because of the Black Caucus. We were a force to be reckoned with. When our members swelled, they really took steps. . . . They confiscated our money. They said it was Congressional money anyway, because we paid our CBC dues from our operating budgets. Our staff was coming to work unpaid and then they took the furniture, including our typewriters and Xerox machines, and auctioned it off to anybody who wanted it. And the staff still came, and then they changed the locks on the doors and said the staff could not meet on government property. That is what they did to us. . . . We were under siege. (1998)

Confiscation, dispossession, physical removal, lock-outs are not tactics typically deployed between equals. Nor do such draconian measures make much sense in terms of rational power maximization. Because almost all of the members of the CBC were Democrats, the tactics they had attempted to employ as a voting bloc to gain leverage within the Democratic party would not have worked with the new Republican majority. For this reason, they posed little threat to the Republican leadership of the House. Within the context of racing-gendering, however, the demarcation of government property as off-limits for the CBC staff takes on ominous meaning. For it racializes congressional space by constructing the black members of the House as somehow not fully part of the government, not entitled to use their resources to advance black interests. To physically bar black staff working without pay from House office buildings is to send a message about the majority leader's preference for the House as a white enclave. Thus the forcible eviction of the CBC staff from the Capitol was taken by congresswomen of color as a particularly egregious example of institutional racism.

Virtually all the congresswomen of color described the House Speaker's institutional reforms in terms of a frontal assault on their persons, their status in Congress, and their power that went well beyond partisan politics. "Black women were forced into a defensive posture" (Jackson Lee 1998). "We had to fight a rear-guard defensive battle" (Holmes Norton 1997). "We were disemboweled during that time" (Meek 1997). Another of the institutional changes introduced by the House Speaker as part of the rules package, House Resolution 6, adopted January 5, 1995, helps explain why congresswomen of color took these changes so personally. Among the changes in floor procedure mandated by Newt Gingrich was a restriction on voting rights for congressional delegates. The delegates for the District of Columbia, the Virgin Islands, American Samoa, and the resident commissioner of Puerto Rico—all people of color—could no longer vote in or preside over the Committee of the Whole, into which the House dissolves when debating and amending legislation on the floor.

For congresswomen of color, eliminating rights of participation, hampering efforts to devise collective strategies, and dampening the organized voice of underrepresented groups constituted unmistakably raced and gendered politics. While the institutional rules changes that sustained this politics of exclusion were neutral on their face, they were experienced by congresswomen of color as race-gender specific in their effects. As such, they engendered new strategies for collective action. Representative Corinne Brown [D-Fla.] described the process:

> "We just had to figure out a new way for us to caucus and meet. We weren't going to let men tell us we can't meet. Come on now. . . . I don't think I have to ask a white man whether I need to meet. I wanted to go into my own personal pocket and pay. We can't meet on Capitol Hill, but we're going to meet. In fact, that made me feel that we needed to be meeting every day." (1998)

Within Congress, the CBC and the CCWI reorganized as Congressional Members Organizations (CMOs), a form of organization that was not prohibited by Gingrich's institutional restructuring, and continued to meet to devise strategies to provide substantive representation for what they perceived as their national constituencies, women and people of color. CBC and CCWI staff excluded from the Capitol reorganized and continued their policy research within the private sector through the CBC Foundation and Women's Policy, Inc., respectively.

Explanatory Possibilities of a Theory of Racing-Gendering

To this point, most of the examples of racing-gendering have been drawn from the 104th Congress. Some might then claim that what appears to be racing-gendering is really a matter of partisan politics. I have noted that such a reductive move is incompatible with the views of congresswomen of color themselves. To further support the claim that racing-gendering is distinctive from partisan maneuvers, I want expand the analysis to compare instances of racing-gendering in the Democratically-controlled 103rd Congress with those in the Republican-controlled 104th Congress in one policy area—welfare reform. Welfare policy is a particularly appropriate case for the examination of racing-gendering for a number of reasons.

Since its inception, U.S. welfare policy has reinforced structural inequalities rooted in race-gender (N. Fraser 1989; G. Mink 1995). Restricted primarily to women recipients deemed morally worthy by the state bureaucrats, welfare has been "dispensed in a disparate and racially unequal manner not just in the Jim Crow era, but since the Voting Rights Act" (Darling 1998, 161). Racial bias in determinations of eligibility insured that "African American and Latinos remained underrepresented on the welfare rolls, despite high levels of need" (Mettler 2000, 12). Although racial disparities in the allocation of benefits have typified welfare policy, and the majority of welfare recipients are white, cultural stereotypes of the typical welfare recipient are highly racialized. Several studies have demonstrated that the racist attitudes fueling the misperception of welfare recipients as overwhelmingly black influence white opposition to welfare (Gilens 1995, 1996). There is also evidence that entrenched racism has shaped decades of policymakers' efforts to reform welfare (Lieberman 1995; Quadagno 1994).

Welfare reform is also an appropriate focus, for it helps to illuminate the explanatory possibilities of the theory of racing-gendering in Congress. I argue that the theory of racing-gendering provides a better explanation of the motivations and intensity of involvement of congresswomen of color in welfare reform legislation than other accounts of congressional behavior. According to studies of constituency influence in Congress, welfare recipients are not a constituency likely to receive strong representation in the halls of Congress. As Hall (1996, 201) has pointed out: "The proposition that lower-class interests will suffer from relatively weak representation in the American political system dates at least back to E. E. Schattschneider's *The Semi-Sovereign People* (1960)." While welfare recipients are concentrated in the geographic constituencies of legislators representing inner cities, they are neither an attentive public nor the "primary constituency" (that is, strongest supporters) of urban representatives (Fenno 1978). They do not donate time or money to campaigns, and often they do not vote. They do not tend to be well-informed about legislation pending in Congress. And with the exception of the activism mobilized by the National Welfare Rights Organization in the early 1970s (Sparks 1997), they tend to be unorganized. Why then did congresswomen of color devote such time and energy to the representation of an unorganized majority-white underclass?

According to the view of legislators as rational optimizers (Hall 1996, 252), it would have been rational for congresswomen of color to "abdicate"—that is, to refrain from investing substantial time, energy, and legislative capital in welfare reform legislation. For the most part they lacked positions on key subcommittees, committees, and task forces shaping the legislation. Drafting alternative legislation involved high information costs. Their intensive efforts behind the scenes and on the floor involved exceptionally high transaction costs. In the

103rd Congress, their advocacy of an alternative approach to welfare reform pit-
ted them against the president and the leadership of the Democratic majority in
the House. In the 104th Congress, with the exception of Republican Ileana Ros
Lehtinen, the congresswomen of color were members of the minority party.
Working against the Republican majority and in opposition to the wishes of the
Democratic president for a cause they knew was doomed makes little sense in
terms of rational actor accounts of Congress. For those who construe legislators
as "rational calculators of advantage" (Jacobson and Kernell 1981) or "strategic
politicians" (Gertzog 2002), congresswomen of color's opposition to the welfare
reform legislation must be characterized as either too costly (given the insufficient benefits) or irrational.

If we are to avoid characterizing fifteen talented congresswomen as "irrational," how can we explain their intensive attacks on the president's and the
Republican majority's proposals for welfare reform? Noting that the "behavioral
importance of race and ethnicity in Congress requires more systematic evidence,
Hall (1996, 192) advances a conception of "group identification" to supplement
rational optimizing accounts of legislators of color. "Underrepresented in the
House, women, blacks, and Hispanics, appear motivated to take compensatory
action, pursuing issues that are more likely to appear relevant to members of
their group. In this way, they transcend district boundaries and represent the interests of a historically underrepresented constituency" (Hall 1996, 209; Canon
1999; Cramer Walsh 2002). While the concept of group identification offers a
welcome respite from the charge of irrational legislative behavior, it leaves many
questions unasked and unanswered. When and under what circumstances does
group identification emerge? Given the membership in multiple groups high-
lighted by the concept of intersectionality, how does a legislator decide which
group with which to identify? Given the diversity of interests among blacks and
among women, which interests will a black congresswoman choose to represent?
Why did congresswomen of color maintain a united front in opposition to welfare proposals promoted by the president and by the Republican majority, while
white women and black men in both the Democratic and the Republican parties
split in their responses to each of these proposals?

The theory of racing-gendering offers some insights into such questions.
Through the following case study, I attempt to show that the intense involvement of congresswomen of color in welfare reform legislation over the course of
the 103rd and 104th Congresses can best be understood as an instance of resistance engendered in response to racing-gendering in Congress. I argue that as
white Democrats and Republicans shifted the terrain of welfare debates from
poverty alleviation to pathologizing and racializing the poor, congresswomen of
color mobilized at considerable political cost to make a public stand on the issue.
In addition to the political harms of going against their own party and their

president in the 103rd Congress and against the Republican majority in the 104th, the costs congresswomen of color paid for their resistance was subjection to intensified forms of racing-gendering in Congress. Their willingness to incur those costs can be understood as a political manifestation of willed resistance to racing-gendering. In the case of welfare reform, to live with anger is to legislate against the grain. The theory of racing-gendering in Congress thus illuminates a form of minority participation at great remove from the "expression of minority opinion central to the practice of democratic consent" (Hall 1996, 238). Far from legitimating the legislative process and the policy it produces, legislating against the grain provides a trenchant indictment of the system.

WELFARE REFORM IN THE 103RD CONGRESS
In the 103rd Congress when welfare reform was placed on the political agenda by President Clinton and the Republican minority, congresswomen of color were fully supportive of the prospect of reforming the welfare system. The re-forms they sought, however, placed them at odds with dominant forces in the Democratic and the Republican parties. The congresswomen of color sought a welfare reform that would eliminate poverty. Thus, they sought legislation that would address the structural causes of poverty, such as low wages and unemploy-ment. They also sought strategies to address the needs of welfare recipients, such as lack of training, lack of transportation, lack of childcare, which constituted major barriers to workforce participation.

In 1993 President Clinton appointed a multi-agency task force to hold hear-ings and develop a welfare reform strategy for the White House. Congresswomen of color tried to work within the task force and from outside the task force to in-fluence the proposed welfare legislation. Representative Patsy Mink [D-Hawaii] served on the Democratic task force and worked tirelessly to represent the inter-ests of "poor women who have no representation in Congress . . . and who are left out in much of this debate" (P. Mink 1997). By her own account, she was largely unsuccessful: "I was on the task force for the Democrats and tried to argue my point of view in all of the meetings. Then I introduced my own substitute so they could clearly see where I differed from the Administration and from many of the mainstream attitudes. . . . The reason why we formulated our own bill was because we were just going around and around in circles, arguing to the Admin-istration to change, clarify, amend, alter, and they wouldn't budge" (1997). Mink's experience stands in marked contrast to Hall's claim that among policy insiders, participation in shaping policy is largely a matter of self-selection. "Even with only a modest staff, the lowliest member whose interest in an issue is sufficiently intense will find none of the barriers to entry insurmountable" (Hall 1996, 108). As a member of the president's task force, Mink was an insider. And although she supplemented her staff resources with research provided by the

Institute for Women's Policy Research, the NOW Legal Defense Fund, the National Women's Law Center, MANNA (an organization working for pay equity), Wider Opportunities for Women, and the Coalition of Presidents (a coalition of presidents of one hundred women's organizations), she was not able move the draft legislation in a more progressive direction.

Congresswomen of color who tried to influence the Democratic task force from the outside reported similar frustration. Representative Barbara Rose Collins recounted her intentions:

> I felt very ineffective. I had my own ideas about welfare reform and nobody was interested in listening to what I had to say. This is one reason I cast against the Democrats. In the Democratic Party, if you're not in the inner circle with a lot of seniority, chairing a powerful committee, one of the "good old boys," you can just forget it. All you can do is throw a bomb in the workings, you can't work to fix things. I had my own ideas about welfare reform because I lived among welfare people. I sent a letter to Senator Moynihan who was doing a task force on it. I wanted to sit down and talk with him. He never responded to the letter or to telephone calls. I thought I had something I could help the President with but I didn't have the means to get to him on that. So all I could do was fight against the parts I thought were detrimental. (1998)

Central to the concerns of congresswomen of color was the circulation of racialized stereotypes about welfare recipients, particularly the construction of welfare recipients as women of color—too lazy to work—who sought to cheat the system. To counteract the "stereotypes that were alive and well" (McKinney 1997), congresswomen of color tried to inject social science research into the debate. On October 23, 1993, Representatives Patsy Mink [D-Hawaii] and Maxine Waters [D-Calif.] joined their colleagues Ed Pastor [D-Ariz.] and Lynn Woolsey [D-Calif.] in cochairing a conference on "Women and Welfare Reform: Women's Opportunities and Women's Welfare." Sponsored by the Institute for Women's Policy Research in Washington, D.C., the conference brought together academics and policymakers in an effort to "break myths and create solutions." The elements of progressive welfare reform outlined at this conference became the basis for the alternative welfare reform legislation introduced by Patsy Mink and supported by all the congresswomen of color. The alternative welfare reform included a proposal for a living wage (that is, increases in minimum wages to insure that full-time workers earned income adequate to meet their basic financial obligations), education and training opportunities to equip welfare recipients for jobs that would enable them to escape poverty, job creation to counteract unemployment, childcare to meet the needs of working parents, transportation allowances to make remote worksites accessible. The congresswomen of color supported enhanced entitlements to eradicate poverty, but their policy recommendations remained far more progressive than the proposals endorsed by the Democratic task force, which were announced by President Clinton in June 1994. Introduced immediately prior to the congressional summer recess and the fall congressional elections, the Clinton proposal to "end welfare as we know it" died with the 103rd Congress.

The experiences of the Democratic women of color in the 103rd Congress as the Democratic majority crafted welfare legislation exemplify marginalization. Many reported that they could not gain access to key white male decision makers and as such, could not influence the shape of the legislation. Despite repeated efforts to shift the terms of debate away from erroneous perceptions of welfare cheats and cycles of dependency, neither the social science knowledge they circulated nor the personal experiences they related was taken as authoritative or compelling. Even Representative Patsy Mink's substitute proposal, which garnered ninety Democratic votes in the House was dismissed rather than selectively incorporated into the president's plan.

WELFARE REFORM IN THE 104TH CONGRESS

In contrast to the concern with structural causes of poverty, which lay at the heart of the approach to welfare reform taken by Congresswomen of color, the Republican proposals for welfare reform framed poverty as a matter of personal responsibility, particularly in relation to marriage and responsible fatherhood and motherhood. Asserting that the nation confronted a "crisis of out-of-wedlock births," the Republicans proposed legislation designed to "ensure that the responsibility of having a child belongs to the mother and father, rather than to the mother and the U.S. taxpayer" (Meyers 1993). Several key provisions of the Republican welfare reform targeted teen pregnancy in particular and out-of-wedlock births more generally on the assumption that "the increase in the number of children receiving public assistance is closely related to the increase in births to unmarried women" (The Personal Responsibility and Work Opportunity Reconciliation Act of 1996, Public Law 104-193, 42 USC 601, Sec. 101 (5)C). In the words of Dick Armey [R-Tex.] (1995), "We need to understand . . . that it is illegitimacy and childbirth, fatherless children, that is so much at the heart of the distress that seems to be unending and growing worse and larger each year. So we insist that we must have a new approach that brings down illegitimacy, and quite rightly so many of us say, yes, bring down illegitimacy, but not through increased abortions."

Both H.R. 4, The Personal Responsibility Act, which was passed by the 104th Congress and vetoed by President Clinton, and H.R. 3734, which was enacted as The Personal Responsibility and Work Opportunity Reconciliation Act of 1996, denied welfare benefits to unwed teenaged mothers, allowed states to impose a benefits cap to encourage limits on recipients' family size, and required that paternity be established as a condition of welfare eligibility. The Republican-sponsored welfare reform also eliminated the federal entitlement program, Aid to Families with Dependent Children (AFDC), and replaced it with a block grant for Temporary Assistance for Needy Families, which required work as a condition for receipt of benefits and set a lifetime limit of five years for welfare eligibility. Additional provisions of the Personal Responsibility and Work Opportunity Reconciliation Act (PRWORA) reduced federal expenditures for welfare and for Supplemental Security Insurance and eliminated legal immigrants from eligibility for Supplemental Security Income, Food Stamps, and a range of social services.

Congresswomen of color perceived the attack on single mothers at the heart of welfare reform proposals as an attack on the black family, an attack that resurrected pathological theories of poverty, which had circulated in policy circles since the Moynihan Report in the 1960s. To counter Republican claims about the causes of poverty, congresswomen of color turned to social science. To engage the mistaken notion that single-parent families are the cause of increasing poverty in the United States, Representative Patsy Mink (1997) circulated to all members of the House and Senate copies of a 1995 study (J. L. Brown 1995) conducted by the Center on Hunger, Poverty and Nutritional Policy at Tufts University. Drawing upon the research of seventy-six scholars who specialize in the areas of poverty and welfare, Mink contested the conflation of single-motherhood with poverty and presented an alternative account.

> Fact No. 1: Growth in the number of single-parent families has been primarily among the non-poor. From 1970 to 1990, the number of female-headed households increased from 6 million to 11 million, mostly among the non-poor. Sixty-five percent of the increase in single-parent families were not living in poverty.
> Fact No. 2: the Census Bureau found that economic factors such as low-wage jobs accounted for approximately 85% of the child poverty rate. A 1993 Census Bureau study showed that the poverty rate was due mainly to changes in the labor market and the structure of the economy. (P. Mink 1995)

Despite Representative Mink's attempt to invoke the authority of the social science community and the U.S. Census Bureau to shift the terms of the welfare debate, the empirical evidence did nothing to dispel the correlation mistaken for causation at the heart of PRWORA.

Congresswomen of color were deeply concerned that the Republican focus on out-of-wedlock births, unwed mothers, and single-women heads-of-household was a thinly veiled attack upon poor women of color. During a number of increasingly vitriolic floor debates the legitimacy of their concern became apparent as even the pretense of using race-neutral language to characterize the poor disappeared, and Republican legislators denounced illegitimacy in the black community. For example, in his floor speech Representative Randy Cunningham [R-Calif.] (1995) linked illegitimacy in the black community with not only welfare but also crime and drug addiction. Representatives Patsy Mink [D-Hawaii] (1995), Sheila Jackson Lee [D-Tex.] (1995a, 1995b), Maxine Waters [D-Calif.] (1996), Eva Clayton [D-N.C.] (1995a, 1995b, 1995c), and Nydia Velazquez [D-N.Y.] (1995) repeatedly emphasized in floor debate that the majority of welfare recipients were white, but their factual claims failed to dispel racialized welfare myths. In the words of Representative Barbara Collins [D-Mich.] (1998): "The Congress unfortunately had the image of a welfare recipient as an urban black woman, who irresponsibly had children, was lazy, refused to work, was uneducated. Whereas the truth of the matter was that the majority of welfare recipients were white, white women and white families."

As a white woman and the only member of Congress to have once been a welfare recipient, Representative Lynn Woolsey (D-Calif.) also took to the House floor to tell her colleagues that most welfare recipients were white. "My strategy was to be out there, to take the heat and show people . . . that welfare moms were like me, that I was the typical welfare mom. They had to see that. Then I'd hear on the other side of the aisle, 'yeah, but you're different'" (1998). The racialization of the poor had conflated welfare recipient and black women so powerfully in the minds of some members of the House that they refused to accept that the typical welfare recipient is a white woman who resorts to welfare for a short time after a divorce in order to support her kids while she got back on her feet. Facts that did not conform to raced-gendered stereotypes about welfare recipients were simply dismissed.

Because argument rooted in personal experience was not carrying much weight in welfare reform debates, congresswomen of color relied heavily on social science research in their efforts to dispel other erroneous and damaging myths about welfare. In floor debates, Republicans constructed welfare recipients as "welfare addicts who will do anything to stay on the public dole" (Vucanovich 1995) and as people who need "tough love" to free "a whole class of people that have been held in bondage for generation after generation and cannot get out of bondage" (Chenowith 1995). In contrast to this image of perpetual dependency, Pasty Mink (1995) repeatedly emphasized that the majority of welfare recipients resort to welfare when beset by crises such as illness, unemployment, domestic violence, or divorce and remain on welfare for less than a year; indeed 80 percent of recipients rely on welfare for less than two years. Representative Lucille Roybal-Allard [D-Calif.] (1996) emphasized domestic violence as the reason that many women resort to welfare for short periods of time.

"A recent study by the Taylor Institute of Chicago . . . found that 50–80 percent of women on AFDC are current or past victims of domestic violence. . . . For victims of abuse, the welfare system is often the only hope they have for escape and survival." As in the case of causal claims about poverty and empirical claims about the demographic characteristics of welfare recipients, social scientific evidence about welfare use made no impact on the terms of congressional debate. Reflecting upon these frustrating floor debates, Representative Eva Clayton [D-N.C.] (1997) said, "I was trying to speak out for reason. I'm not sure I succeeded in that. . . . I would like to think that my role was to present common sense. Again I don't think I succeeded in that."

In addition to empirical arguments based upon social science research, congresswomen of color raised constitutional arguments about the permissibility of discriminating against legal immigrants, punishing children for actions of their parents, and violating the rights of poor women to privacy in reproductive decision making (Velazquez 1995; Meek 1995b). They also tried to humanize welfare recipients, to depict welfare recipients as mothers struggling against adversity to meet the needs of their children, and as children who themselves are grappling with material deprivation that marginalizes them from the mainstream. Challenging the stereotype of the welfare cheat who gets pregnant to qualify for or to increase welfare benefits, Representative Sheila Jackson Lee [D-Tex.] (1995a) asserted unequivocally on the basis of her own interactions with welfare recipients and on the basis of social science evidence that "women do not get pregnant to get welfare." Representative Patsy Mink also quoted evidence from the Census Bureau and the Department of Health and Human Services to prove that there is no causal relationship between the availability of welfare benefits and the size or structure of poor families. To illustrate the absurdity of the notion that women have babies to get welfare, she fleshed out the claim: "The suggestion that welfare mothers will be encouraged to have another child because they can increase their cash benefit is ridiculous, because the average additional cash assistance ranges from $45 to $65 across the States. I cannot imagine any person deliberately deciding they should have another baby for that amount of money. In point of fact, that does not occur" (P. Mink 1995).

Providing information about benefit levels in their states, congresswomen of color asked their colleagues to try to imagine raising a child on $184/month, the prevailing rate for a mother with one child in Texas in 1995 (Jackson Lee 1995a). They pointed out that the proposed block grants would allow states to cut funding for the program by 20 percent, slashing already inadequate benefits and further impoverishing children, the majority of welfare beneficiaries (Clayton 1995a). Indeed, Representative Eva Clayton pointed out that in contrast to "the best welfare reform [which] is a job at a livable wage. This bill as it is currently written by the majority, requires as much as 80 hours of work for as little as $69 worth of benefits, the smallest amount of benefit they will get under food stamps. One amendment would increase work requirements to 120 hours for the same $69 benefit, which is equivalent to a pay rate of about 20 cents/hour" (Clayton 1995c).

Congresswomen of color were among the most outspoken opponents of welfare reform in congressional debates. Like her Democratic counterparts in the House, Senator Carol Moseley-Braun (D-Il.), the only woman of color in the Senate, was an outspoken critic of the welfare reform bills in the Senate. She too tried to persuade her fellow senators that the legislation under consideration would not address the underlying problem of welfare—poverty: "Mr. President, policy based on rhetoric is wrong. This debate has focused on the stereotypes and it gets in the way of understanding the facts. . . . The conference report will push 1.5 million children into poverty. This country already has a higher child poverty rate than any other industrialized nation. Why would this body knowingly exacerbate that already shameful figure? It is clear to me that this plan fails those who need a national safety net the most" (Moseley-Braun 1995). Like her counterparts in the House, Senator Moseley-Braun tried to use her power on the Senate Finance Committee to alter the welfare reform bill. She drafted a substitute proposal, The Personal Self-Sufficiency Act, which she introduced as an amendment to the draft welfare bill prepared by Committee Chair Bob Packwood. Her amendment was defeated in the Finance Committee by a 12–8 vote. She also tried to amend the welfare reform bill from the Senate floor, but her amendment was again defeated by a 58–42 vote.

In the House and in the Senate, women of color worked arduously to air an alternative vision of welfare recipients and to advance an alternative version of welfare reform. According to one congressional staffer, "they spoke disproportionate to their seniority" on welfare reform (Hawkesworth et al. 2001). Yet their words seemed to have no effect. The statistical evidence they adduced was discounted. Their cogent arguments were dismissed. Authoritative knowledge was deemed to lie beyond their grasp. Gayatri Spivak (1988) has suggested that the refusal of the dominant to hear the voices of and for the oppressed is a perennial tactic in technologies of race-gender. It is a form of racing-gendering that permeated welfare reform debates in the 103rd and the 104th Congresses, ensnaring congresswomen of color in a prolonged and painful *pendejo* game.

As the majority in the 104th Congress insisted upon circulating misrepresentations of the poor in the context of welfare reform, congresswomen of color felt themselves increasingly marginalized. In the words of Representative Barbara Rose Collins (1998): "We more or less commiserated amongst ourselves. We asked, 'Don't they know more white people are on welfare than black?' Then we came to the conclusion that they didn't care, as long as they hurt black people, they didn't care if they hurt white people too. There was a lot of hostility and animosity towards blacks in that Congress."

The perception of hostility toward African Americans was heightened by several episodes involving congresswomen of color. In the midst of her floor speech addressing H.R. 4, The Personal Responsibility Act, congressional veteran Cardiss Collins was interrupted by laughter from the Republican side of the aisle. Having characterized the Act as a "callous, cold-hearted, and mean-spirited attack on this country's children" that "punishes Americans for being poor" at the same time Congress was considering tax cuts for the rich, Representative Collins was dismayed by the laughter and all that it betokened. Interrupting her prepared comments, she addressed her colleagues directly.

> I see some of the Members on the other side of the aisle laughing. I ask this question: How many of them have ever been hungry. How many of them have ever known what it was not to have a meal? How many of them have known what it was not to have decent shoes, decent clothing, a nice place to live. . . . They do not know about poverty. So I challenge them to come to the Seventh Congressional District of Illinois, my district, and walk in the path of these children that they are cutting off from welfare. Walk in the path of the truly needy people who live by welfare because they have no other means by which to live. (C. Collins 1995)

At this point, Representative Scott McInnis (R-Colo.) who was presiding over the floor debate, recognized himself on a point of personal privilege. He rebuked Representative Collins for noting the laughter. But in doing so, he made a telling error. "Mr. Speaker, as to the gentlewoman's comments from the *State of Florida* [emphasis added], I take strong exception to her comments that there is laughter on this side of the aisle. While we may disagree with her point, her comments are taken with respect. I rather suspect that her comment about laughter was probably written into her speech" (McInnis 1995). In rising to challenge Representative Collins's perceptions of floor activity, impugn her credibility, and accuse her of intentional deceit, even as he insisted she was being respectfully heard, Representative McInnis demonstrated just how little attention he had been paying to her words. For he confused, twenty-two-year congressional veteran Cardiss Collins from Illinois with Florida Congresswoman Carrie Meek, who was just beginning her second term. That the two congresswomen look nothing alike raises interesting questions about how seriously congresswomen of color are taken. That the very words she was being chastised for uttering included a reference to her home district in Illinois only intensifies the insult to Representative Collins. Feeling no obligation to know who she was or to hear what she was saying, Representative McInnis nonetheless felt at liberty to instruct her about what she may or may not say on the House floor.

Representative McInnis was not the only Republican to impugn the credibility of congresswomen of color during welfare floor debates. Representative Jack

Kingston (R-Ga.) dismissed the constitutional arguments and the empirical evidence about welfare recipients advanced by congresswomen of color as "the same rhetoric that we hear from the same group, from the same people" advanced to mask their own interest in perpetuating poverty. "They are the poverty brokers in Washington. They keep the poor dependent so bureaucrat after bureaucrat in Washington can benefit from a government poverty program. . . . To my knowledge, we have not heard from one Democrat who has ever supported a welfare reform measure" (Kingston 1996). Objecting to this distortion of the record, Representative Maxine Waters [D-CA] (1996) responded that "every Democrat has voted for a welfare bill. Remember the Deal bill? The gentleman needs to correct the record." Although Representative Waters requested an apology and a correction of the record multiple times, none was offered.

On several occasions, events outside the halls of Congress spilled over onto floor debates. Representative Cynthia McKinney (1997) reported a painful incident that she considered emblematic of the racing-gendering practices of her colleagues in the 104th Congress.

> I was trying to be bipartisan in my approach, so I was working with Nancy
> Johnson [R-Conn.] on a teenage pregnancy bill. Jim Greenwood [R-Pa.]
> had invited us to go on his cable television show, so we could talk about
> what we were doing, which was good I thought. So [during the show] he
> and Nancy have this entire conversation about teenage pregnancy and
> the legislation, and he doesn't direct a single question to me until he de-
> cides that he wants to ask 'why is it that women have babies so they can
> get extra money?' That was the question that was directed at me.

The racing-gendering in this episode manifests the same epistemic configuration witnessed in floor debates. A white congressman refuses to accredit a congresswoman of color as an authoritative source of knowledge, even about the legislation she had written. A white congresswomen is complicit in this discrediting by failing to turn some questions over to Representative McKinney as a means of inviting her into the conversation. Then having discounted her as a source of sociological and legislative knowledge, Representative Greenwood turns to a congresswoman of color for a corroboration of racist stereotypes. She is positioned as the voice of the scheming welfare recipient who is trying to cheat the system.

Incensed by the racism she perceived in the welfare debate on the part of white colleagues and white constituents, Representative McKinney drew parallels between the values informing the Republican welfare reform proposals and vicious racism circulating among some segments of the U.S. population.

> Mr. Speaker, as the Gingrich Republicans prepare for their blitzkrieg
> against the poor, and say things I hope they do not mean, I would like to
> read a letter from one of their supporters, obviously inspired by their

rhetoric. The letter reads: "After watching your Negro boss do her jungle act about bringing back the brown shirts, I think we need some color shirts to control these Negro females who pop out [expletive deleted] Negro children like monkeys into the jungle. No, I think the monkeys are more civilized. We real Americans don't intend to support [expletive deleted] Negro children who live like rats in a hole and don't have a chance to become human. The welfare system is the cause. Even whites are becoming trash just like Negroes who pop out all these [expletive deleted] Negro children. Don't you understand that we Americans are trying to civilize you? Why do you fight it so hard. The jungle is in Africa, though you have turned D.C. into an American jungle. Grow up and become an American." Mr. Speaker, the spirit of GOP welfare reform lives in these words. (McKinney 1995)

Rather than contesting racism and race hatred, Representative McKinney suggested that the Congress was reinscribing racism in the welfare reform legislation, intentionally circulating distorted stereotypes of welfare recipients, and reinforcing a long-standing tendency toward racial hatred among some American citizens. Congress was not simply reflecting prevailing views but actively shaping public perceptions of welfare policy's target population.

Representative Maxine Waters also took exception to the way that certain members of Congress were constructing welfare recipients during their television appearances, suggesting that their gross misrepresentation of welfare recipients was nothing short of irresponsible.

Mr. Speaker, this morning a Republican member of this body, the gentleman from Florida, Clay Shaw, was shown on national TV making a most irresponsible and outrageous statement disparaging welfare mothers by saying, and I quote: "You wouldn't leave your cat with them for the weekend." Clay Shaw owes the welfare mothers of this country an apology. How dare he single out welfare mothers and refer to them in such negative terms. There are responsible people in all segments of our society and there are irresponsible people. Some politicians are responsible and some are irresponsible. Mr. Clay Shaw falls into the category of the irresponsible. There are many solid responsible welfare recipients who love and care for their children, who attend Church on Sunday, who work part-time jobs, who search for jobs, who attend school in an effort to better themselves. Welfare mothers and fathers, it is time to speak up. Call Newt Gingrich at 202-225-0600 and tell him to help you with a job. (Waters 1995)

Despite Representative Waters's call for an apology, none was forthcoming. Instead, the distorted racialized stereotypes of welfare recipients continued to circulate in discussions of welfare reform on the floor and in committees of the

House and Senate until the Congress passed The Personal Responsibility and Work Opportunity Reconciliation Act in August 1996. Representative Waters, like many of the congresswomen of color, transformed her anger at the calumnies against the poor into efforts to mobilize public opposition to welfare reform.

Mobilization of anger is a tactic that several congresswomen of color reported deploying in response to the welfare reform legislation. Representative Corrine Brown [D-Fla.] (1998), for example, said that she felt it was her responsibility "to educate my constituents as to what was going on so they could be enraged and call their Senators. . . . In August I conducted 50 town meetings [to which] anybody could come and listen." In response to the proposal to drastically cut the school lunch program, Representative Eva Clayton (1997) "organized Forums called 'Feed the Folks' down in our district, and we must have received about 1300 different petitions to save the school lunch program."

In addition to their efforts to mobilize the anger of voters in their districts, I suggest that the intensive and varied participation of congresswomen of color in welfare reform efforts behind the scenes, in committees, and on the floor be understood as a mode of resistance against racing-gendering. Through a wide array of tactical maneuvers, congresswomen of color attempted to stem the stigmatization, racialization, and punitive regulation of poor women. They proposed multiple amendments to the welfare reform bills. Although none of the twenty amendments that Representative Carrie Meek introduced as a member of the budget committee passed, of the eleven amendments proposed by congresswomen of color to the House Rules Committee, two amendments did succeed and were eventually approved by the House. Representative Eva Clayton succeeded in inserting language that required that individuals employed or participating in a work or workfare program be paid at least at the minimum wage. Ileana Ros-Lehtinen secured an exemption for mentally or physically disabled immigrants from provisions excluding legal immigrants from access to state and local public benefits.

Congresswomen of color also protested parliamentary maneuvers used by the Republican leadership to minimize debate on the welfare legislation. Representative Eva Clayton objected to the restrictive rule assigned to H.R. 4 by the House Rules Committee:

> I rise in opposition to this rule. More than 150 amendments were filed
> timely on this rule, but yet there are only 26 Republicans and 5 Demo-
> crats who have amendments that were allowed. I must ask, what is the
> majority afraid of? Why must they deny thoughtful proposals that would
> improve this bill? Are they trying to muzzle discussion? . . . Perhaps they
> are afraid because they know that this bill will harm women, infants,
> and children, and they do not want the American people to know about
> that. (Clayton 1995b)

Despite such protests, the Republicans imposed even more stringent restrictions on H.R. 3734, PRWORA, introducing it as a budget resolution, thereby drastically curtailing the possibilities for amendment.

In their efforts to legislate against the grain, congresswomen of color deployed the full repertoire of strategies available to legislators. In the 103rd Congress, they used their power within the Democratic party to try to shape the content of President Clinton's welfare reform proposal. They cochaired scholarly conferences to try to shape public perceptions of the poor, as well as the content of welfare legislation. They used their power in committees to try to amend Republican sponsored legislation in the 104th Congress. They drafted one of two Democratic alternative bills to H.R. 4 considered in the House, as well as one of the Democratic alternative bills considered in the Senate during the first session of the 104th Congress. They secured a special order to allow a floor debate of the welfare legislation in the House of Representatives. They used their intellectual and rhetorical power in floor debates to try to alter congressional understandings of poverty. They scheduled press conferences featuring welfare recipients to try to get alternative images of the poor before the Congress and the public. They wrote "Dear Colleague" letters and circulated them with comprehensive social scientific studies in an effort to break the hold of pernicious stereotypes of the poor. They held town meetings across their constituencies to mobilize voters against the pending legislation. Even in the final hours they joined with a bipartisan group of twenty-six women members from both houses in sending a letter to the Conference Committee to try to shape the compromise bill that would eventually become law. But ultimately they failed to convince their colleagues to move beyond what they perceived to be racist stereotypes and policies that punished the poor. In the end, they used the power of their votes in Congress to oppose both versions of the welfare reform legislation. All fifteen congresswomen of color— fourteen Democrats and one Republican—voted against the Personal Responsibility Act and the Personal Responsibility and Work Opportunity Reconciliation Act. Their opposition was intense and consistent across two Congresses, but there is no indication that in airing their minority view, they accorded legitimacy to either the process or the bill that resulted from it. On the contrary, their stories of marginalization and thwarted effort, of the silencing of reason and evidence, and of the pervasive racing-gendering of welfare recipients and congresswomen of color, provide a resounding indictment of this form of majority rule.

Conclusion

Congresswomen of color are among the most powerful politicians in the United States. Like other politicians, they win some battles and lose others. Should the incidents described in this chapter be understood as the typical battle scars accrued by any politician deeply involved in the political fray? Should they be dismissed as isolated incidents, rather than as a pattern of racing-gendering practices within the U.S. Congress?

The data presented in this analysis suggest on-going racing-gendering in the institutional practices of Congress and in the interpersonal interactions among members of Congress. Through tactics such as silencing, stereotyping, enforced invisibility, exclusion, marginalization, challenges to epistemic authority, refusals to hear, legislative topic extinctions, and pendejo games, congresswomen of color are constituted as "other." In committee operations, floor debates, and interpersonal interactions, they are treated as less than equals in various ways that carry palpable consequences for both their identities and their policy priorities. They are forced to deal with institutional dynamics and interpersonal relations that constitute them as subordinate.

The case study of welfare reform makes these institutional dynamics visible within the Democratic-controlled 103rd Congress and the Republican-controlled 104th Congress; this chronicle suggests that racing-gendering is distinct from and ought not be reduced to partisanship. While the potent intersection of race, gender, and class in the welfare debate marks this policy terrain as distinctive, the examples of racing-gendering that congresswomen of color provide across other policy domains (environment, minimum wage, health appropriations) and committee jurisdictions (Transportation and Infrastructure, Government Reform and Operations) caution against the notion that racing-gendering surfaces solely in relation to policies that target the poor. Unique about the welfare case is the intensity of the racialization, an intensity that I have argued motivated the congresswomen of color to legislate against the grain by enacting a politics of resistance that ranged from open confrontation on the House and Senate floors to the mobilization of anger in their constituencies. Racing-gendering may not be nearly as pronounced or as visible in other policy areas, but in the words of Representative Eddie Bernice Johnson [D-Tex.] (1997), "the fundamentals of racism and sexism . . . [have] always been a constant." More research is needed to assess how pervasive racing-gendering practices are in Congress, to map more systematically the factors that contribute to or mitigate their virulence, and to investigate how the intensity of racing-gendering influences the legislative tactics and policy choices of congresswomen of color.

The examples of racing-gendering included here question fundamental stereotypes about gender in decision-making. One of the oldest gender stereotypes in the Western tradition—that men are rational and women emotional—has been recurrently incorporated in accounts of political decision making. According to this view, men are the rational policymakers, who ground their decisions in evidence and authoritative expertise, while women ground their decisions more on emotion, whether it be emotions pertaining to an ethics of care structuring policy priorities or a desire to preserve relationships informing transformational conceptions of leadership (Gilligan 1982; Rosenthal 2000). The evidence from the welfare reform debates raises important questions about not only these gendered stereotypes but also directions of causality in processes that produce raced and gendered subjects.

Throughout a four-year period that spanned two dramatically different Congresses, the congresswomen of color came to task-force and committee meetings, as well as floor debates, armed with social science studies, Census Bureau data, and Health and Human Services Department statistics to counter the emotional diatribes of some of their male Democratic and Republican counterparts. In their tactics and their demeanor, congresswomen of color embodied the norm of rational, comprehensive decision makers, while many men in Congress gloried in emotional, racially charged displays. The nature of the racing-gendering to which congresswomen of color were subjected—being ignored by their colleagues, experiencing others' willed refusal to hear their views, having their epistemic authority challenged, having their amendments blocked in committee and on the floor, having their positions misrepresented in floor debates, being chastised on the floor of the House, being invited to participate in TV debate only to be systematically ignored, being constructed as the voice of pernicious stereotypes of welfare recipients—pushed them from reason to anger. The emotion alleged to be their "natural" gendered disposition was instead the effect of racing-gendering in the institution of Congress. In this sense, racing-gendering in the Congress has palpable effects on individual congresswomen of color as well as upon public policies.

Within Democratic party hierarchies in the 103rd Congress and as members of the minority party in the 104th Congress, Democratic congresswomen of color, including several with considerable seniority, found themselves systematically shut out of key decision-making arenas. Their diverse policy concerns met with topic extinctions, their voices were silenced, their legislative achievements rendered invisible, their judgment impugned, their identities confused, their humanity called into question. In particular cases, they were cued to assume a menial stance in relation to their colleagues in the Congress and punished if they dared to engage in a politics of direct address. Some of their staff were locked out of House office space. A nineteenth-century distinction between political equality and social equality haunts these instances of racing-gendering, a distinction with a notoriously racist history having been used by the Supreme Court in *Plessy v. Ferguson* to legitimate the "separate but equal doctrine, which provided constitutional sanction to Jim Crow legislation and policies. Individually and collectively, such racing-gendering practices symbolically situate congresswomen of color as "outsiders within" the legislative body (Lorde 1984; P. H. Collins 1990). Although politically equal, they are not accorded social equality within the halls of Congress. On the contrary, racing-gendering actively subverts social equality. It also violates several putative congressional norms, such as the norm to "maintain friendly relationships" and "to avoid personal attacks during floor debates" (Asher 1973).

Although congresswomen of color are duly elected representatives of the people, racing-gendering in Congress insures that they are "with them, but not of them" (Haley 1964, 32). Congresswomen of color experience the limits of their white colleagues' acceptance as an obstacle they must overcome in the course of their work. This obstacle does not confront white male members of Congress whose identities and interests structure the operations of the institution and are affirmed by them. Congresswomen of color's accounts of racing-gendering suggest a form of "interested bias" (Hall 1996, 233) operating in the Congress that has not been previously documented and that is richly deserving of further investigation. To the extent that racing-gendering in Congress undermines social equality, it should be a matter of grave concern. For if there is any undisputable lesson from the history of race relations in the United States, it is that the absence of social equality undermines political equality. In that sense, racing-gendering in Congress compromises a basic principle of democracy.

The theory of racing-gendering also has implications concerning the possibility of substantive representation of minority interests. For it suggests that there are forces working against the legislative success of congresswomen of color not fully accounted for by either majority or minority party membership, subcommittee and committee assignments, and the choices of individual members about the intensity of their involvement on particular issues. During the past thirty years, black legislators have been advised to adopt a political strategy of "deracialization" to advance the interests of minority constituents (Hamilton 1977). They have been told to concentrate on legislation geared to help low-income people generally (for example, full employment, improved income-maintenance programs, universal health care), rather than to press for race-based policies that alienate whites (Aberbach and Walker 1973; Wilson 1980). They have been warned to avoid racial polarization at all costs (Swain 1993). The case study of welfare reform calls this political tactic into question. Although congresswomen of color worked diligently to deracialize welfare policy, many of their white counterparts worked equally or more assiduously to racialize welfare recipients and congresswomen of color. When a white majority in the legislature engages in racial polarization, a small minority of legislators of color cannot succeed in passing deracialized policies.

The theory of racing-gendering has implications for claims about the role of minority opinion in the process of democratic consent and for the legitimacy of policies produced by majority rule. Airing dissent in the context of recurrent exclusions, topic extinctions, pendejo games, and racial polarization does not

suffice to convince legislators of color that the process is fair. Nor does it legitimate the policy outcomes that proceed from that process. In contrast to the optimistic view that "consensus decisions are likely to be regarded as fair decisions"
(Fenno 1978, 245), the testimony of congresswomen of color recounted in this
analysis suggests that racing-gendering by the majority is recognized as a fundamentally unfair form of dehumanization, whether encountered in the legislative
process or in the policies generated by that process. And if the analysis in this
chapter is correct, such fundamental unfairness engenders anger and resistance,
not acceptance and legitimation.

If racing-gendering in Congress has palpable effects on individual congresswomen of color, on public policy, and on the basic principles and practices of
democracy, then there is good reason to begin to theorize raced-gendered institutions and to explore racing-gendering practices within a wider range of political and social institutions. The comprehensiveness of our analyses, the adequacy
of our explanatory accounts, and the prospects for inclusive democracy are
equally at stake. The innovative analytic tools developed by feminist scholars
provide the means to pursue these questions, while traditional research methodologies continue to leave such questions unasked and unanswerable.

Bibliography

Abel, Elizabeth. 1993. "Black Writing, White Reading: Race and the Politics of Feminist Interpretation." *Critical Inquiry* 19 (3): 470–498.

Aberbach, Joel, and Jack Walker. 1973. *Race in the City*. Boston: Little, Brown.

Abramovitz, Mimi. 1996. *Regulating the Lives of Women: Social Policy from Colonial Times to the Present*. Boston: South End Press.

Acker, Joan. 1990. "Hierarchies, Job Bodies: A Theory of Gendered Organizations." *Gender and Society* 4 (2): 139–158.

———. 1992. "Gendered Institutions: From Sex Roles to Gendered Institutions." *Contemporary Sociology* 21 (5): 565–569.

Albert, Hans. 1985. *Treatise on Critical Reason*. Trans. Mary Varney Rorty. Princeton: Princeton University Press.

Alcoff, Linda. 2000. "On Judging Epistemic Credibility: Is Social Identity Relevant." In Naomi Zack, ed., *Women of Color and Philosophy*, 235–262. Oxford: Blackwell.

Aldrich, John H. 1995. "A Model of Legislature with Two Parties and a Committee System." In Kenneth Shepsle and Barry Weingast, eds., *Positive Theories of Congressional Institutions*. Ann Arbor: University of Michigan Press.

American Council on Education (ACE). 1995. *Making the Case for Affirmative Action in Higher Education: A handbook for organizers*. Washington, D.C.: American Council on Education.

Amundsen, Kirsten. 1971. *The Silenced Majority*. Englewood Cliffs, N.J.: Prentice Hall.

Anderson, Margaret. 1983. *Thinking About Women*. New York: Macmillan.

Appiah, Kwame Anthony. 1992. *In My Father's House: Africa in the Philosophy of Culture*. New York: Oxford University Press.

Arditti, Rita, Renate Duelli Klein, and Shelly Mindon. 1994. *Test Tube Women*. London: Pandora Press.

Aristotle. 1941. *The Basic Works*. Ed. Richard McKeon. New York: Random House.

Armas, Genaro. 2004. "Study Finds Wider Gap in Wealth Among Races." *Philadelphia Inquirer*, October 18, A10.

Armey, Dick. 1995. *Congressional Record*, 104th Cong., 1st Sess., p. H3444, March 22.

Arnault, Lynne. 1989. "The Radical Future of a Classic Moral Theory." In Alison Jaggar and Susan Bordo, eds., *Gender/Body/Knowledge*. New Brunswick: Rutgers University Press.

Arnold, R. Douglas. 1990. *The Logic of Congressional Action*. New Haven, Conn.: Yale University Press.

Asher, Herbert. 1973. "The Learning of Legislative Norms." *American Political Science Review* 67 (2): 499–513.

Ayer, A. J. 1959. *Logical Positivism*. New York: Free Press.

Bacon, Francis. 1861. *Advancement of Learning*, book II, in *Works*. Eds. James Spedding and Robert Ellis. Boston.

Balbus, Isaac. 1982. *Marxism and Domination*. Princeton: Princeton University Press.

Barrett, Michele. 1980. *Women's Oppression Today*. London: Verso.

———. 1985. *Women's Oppression Today: Problems in Marxist Feminist Analysis*. 4th ed. London: Verso.

Barthes, Roland. 1967. *Elements of Semiology*. London: Jonathan Cape.

———. 1973. *Mythologies*. London: Paladin.

———. 1977. *Image—Music—Text*. London: Fontana.

Bartky, Sandra. 1988. "Foucault, Femininity, and the Modernization of Patriarchal Power." In Irene Diamond and Lee Quinby, eds., *Feminism and Foucault: Reflections on Resistance*. Boston: Northeastern University Press.

Beauvoir, Simone de. [1949] 1989. *The Second Sex*. Trans. and ed., H. M. Parshley. New York: Vintage Books.

Bedford, Katherine. 2005. *The World Bank's Employment Programs in Ecuador and Beyond: Empowering Women, Domesticating Men, and Resolving the Social Reproduction Dilemma*. Ph.D. diss., Rutgers University, New Bunswick.

Beechey, Victoria. 1977. "Some Notes on Female Wage Labour in the Capitalist Mode of Production." *Capital and Class* 3: 45–64.

———. 1978. "Women and Production." In Annette Kuhn and Ann Marie Wolpe, eds., *Feminism and Materialism*. London: Routledge and Kegan Paul.

Belenky, Mary, Blythe Clinchy, Nancy Goldberger, and Jill Tarule. 1986. *Women's Ways of Knowing*. New York: Basic Books.

Bem, Sandra. 1974. "The Measurement of Psychological Androgyny." *Journal of Clinical and Consulting Psychology* 42: 155–162.

———. 1983. "Gender Schematic Theory and Its Implications for Child Development." *Signs* 8 (3): 598–616.

———. 1993. *Lenses of Gender*. New Haven: Yale University Press.

Benhabib, Seyla. 1986. *Critique, Norm and Utopia*. New York: Columbia University Press.

Benston, Margaret. 1982. "Feminism and the Critique of Scientific Method." In G. Finn and A. Miles, eds., *Feminism in Canada*. Montreal: Black Rose Books.

Berger, John, and Jean Mohr. 1975. *A Seventh Man*. Harmondsworth: Penguin.

Berkeley Planning Associates, Inc. 1980. *Evaluation Design: Assessment of Work-Welfare Projects*. Washington, D.C.: U.S. Department of Health and Human Services.

Berman, Ruth. 1989. "From Aristotle's Dualism to Materialist Dialectics: Feminist Transformation of Science and Society." In Alison Jaggar and Susan Bordo, eds., *Gender/Body/Knowledge*. New Brunswick: Rutgers University Press.

Bernstein, Blanche, and Leonard Goodwin. 1978. "Do Work Requirements Accomplish Anything?" *Public Welfare* 32 (2): 36–45.

Bernstein, Richard. 1976. *The Restructuring of Social and Political Theory*. New York: Harcourt, Brace, Jovanovich.

———. 1983. *Beyond Objectivism and Relativism: Science, Hermeneutics and Praxis*. Philadelphia: University of Pennsylvania Press.

Blau, Francine. 1983. *The Economic Status of Women in the Labor Market*. Testimony Before the United States House of Representatives Committee on the Judiciary, Subcommittee on Civil and Constitutional Rights, September 14.

———. 1984. "Discrimination Against Women: Theory and Evidence." In W. Darity, ed., *Labor Economics*. Boston: Kluwer-Nijhoff.

Blee, Kathleen. 2000. "White on White: Interviewing Women in U.S. White Supremacist Groups." In France Winddance Twine and Jonathan Warren, eds., *Racing Research, Researching Race: Methodological Dilemmas in Critical Race Studies*, 93–110. New York: New York University Press.

Bleier, Ruth. 1979. "Social and Political Bias in Science." In E. Tobach and B. Rosoff, eds., *Genes and Gender*. New York: Gordian Press.

———. 1984. *Science and Gender: A Critique of Biology and Its Theories on Women.* New York: Pergamon.

Bond, Julian. 1996. "Civil Rights: Acting Affirmatively." Paper presented at the University of Louisville, February 9.

Boneparth, Ellen, and Emily Stoper. 1988. *Women Power and Policy: Toward the Year 2000.* New York: Pergamon.

Bordo, Susan. 1986. "The Cartesian Masculinization of Thought." *Signs* 11 (3): 99–114.

———. 1987. *The Flight to Objectivity.* Albany: State University of New York Press.

———. 1993. *Unbearable Weight: Feminism, Western Culture and the Body.* Berkeley: University of California Press.

Bourgeois, Philippe. 2000. "Violating Apartheid in the United States: On the Streets and in Academia." In France Winddance Twine and Jonathan Warren, eds., *Racing Research, Researching Race: Methodological Dilemmas in Critical Race Studies,* 187–214. New York: New York University Press.

Bratton, Kathleen, and Kerry Haynie. 1999. "Agenda Setting and Legislative Success in State Legislatures: The Effects of Race and Gender." *The Journal of Politics* 61 (August): 658–679.

Brewer, Rose. 1993. "Theorizing Race, Class, Gender: The New Scholarship of Black Feminist Intellectuals and Black Women's Labor." In Stanlie James and Abena Busia, eds., *Theorizing Black Feminisms.* New York: Routledge.

Briggs, Vernon, Brian Rungeling, and Lewis Smith. 1980. "Welfare Reform and the Plight of the Poor in the Rural South." *Monthly Labor Review* (April): 28–30.

Brown, Corrinne. 1998. Interview, Center for American Women and Politics, March 12.

Brown, H. 1977. *Perception, Theory and Commitment: The New Philosophy of Science.* Chicago: Precedent Publishing Company.

Brown, J. Larry. 1995. "Key Welfare Reform Issues: The Empirical Evidence." Center on Hunger, Poverty, and Nutritional Policy, Tufts University.

Brown, Wendy. 1995. *States of Injury: Power and Freedom in Late Modernity.* Princeton: Princeton University Press.

Bryce, Herrington, and Alan Warrick. 1977. "Black Women in Electoral Politics." In Marianne Githens and Jewell Prestage, eds., *A Portrait of Marginality,* 395–400. New York: David McKay.

Buker, Eloise. 1990. "Feminist Social Theory and Hermeneutics: An Empowering Dialectic?" *Social Epistemology* 4 (1): 23–39.

Burkhardt, Barry. 1983. "A Disturbing Look at Rape." *National on Campus Report,* September 23, p. 1.

Burtless, Gary. 1995. "Employment Prospects of Welfare Recipients." In Demetra Smith Nightingale and Robert Haverman, eds., *The Work Alternative.* Washington, D.C.: Urban Institute Press.

Butler, Judith. 1989. "Sexual Ideology and Phenomenological Description." In Jeffner Allen and Iris Young, eds., *The Thinking Muse.* Bloomington: Indiana University Press.

———. 1990. *Gender Trouble: Feminism and the Subversion of Identity.* New York: Routledge.

———. 2003. "Performative Acts and Gender Constitution: An Essay in Phenomenology and Feminist Theory." In Carole McCann and Sueng-Kyung Kim, eds., *Feminist Theory Reader: Local and Global Perspectives.* New York: Routledge.

Canon, David. 1999. *Race, Redistricting, and Representation.* Chicago: University of Chicago Press.

Carby, Hazel. 1987. *Reconstructing Womanhood.* New York: Oxford University Press.

Cavell, Stanley. 1979. *The Claim of Reason: Wittgenstein, Skepticism, Morality and Tragedy.* New York: Oxford University Press.

Center for American Women and Politics. 2002. "Fact Sheet: Women of Color in Elective Office." New Brunswick, N.J.

Center on Hunger, Poverty, and Nutrition Policy. 1995. "Statement on Key Welfare Reform Issues: The Empirical Evidence." Medford, Mass.: Tufts University.

Chapoval, Ieda. 2001. "The Devolution of Women as a Category in Development Theorizing." In Vasilikie Demos and Marcia Texler Segal, eds., *An International Feminist Challenge to Theory*. Amsterdam: Elsevier Science Ltd.

Chauhan, Abha. 2001. "The Nature/Culture Dualism in the Indian Context." In Vasilikie Demos and Marcia Texler Segal, eds. *An International Feminist Challenge to Theory*. Amsterdam: Elsevier Science Ltd.

Chenowith, Helen. 1995. *Congressional Record*, 104th Cong., 1st Sess., p. H3720, March 23.

Chideya, Farai. 1995. *Don't Believe the Hype: Fighting Cultural Misinformation about African Americans*. New York: Plume/NAL-Dutton.

Chodorow, Nancy, 1978. *The Reproduction of Mothering*. Berkeley: University of California Press.

Chow, Rey. 1991. "Violence in the Other Country." In Chandra Mohanty, Ann Russo, and Lourdes Torres, eds., *Third World Women and the Politics of Feminism*. Bloomington: Indiana University Press.

Churchland, P. M., and C. Hooker. 1985. *Images of Science*. Chicago: University of Chicago Press.

Cixous, Helene. 1975. "Le Rire de La Meduse." *L'Arc* 61: 39–54.

———. 1976. "Le Sexe ou La Tete." *Les Cahiers du GRIF* 13: 5–15.

Clapp, Charles. 1963. *The Congressman: His Work as He Sees It*. Washington, D.C.: Brookings Institution.

Clayton, Eva. 1995a. *Congressional Record*, 104th Cong., 1st Sess., p. H1684, February 13.

———. 1995b. *Congressional Record*, 104th Cong., 1st Sess., p. H3445, March 22.

———. 1995c. *Congressional Record*, 104th Cong., 1st Sess., p. H3511, March 22.

———. 1997. Interview, Center for American Women and Politics, November 4.

Cockburn, Cynthia. 1991. *In the Way of Women: Men's Resistance to Sex Equality in Institutions*. New York: ILR Press.

Code, Lorraine. 1981. "Is the Sex of the Knower Epistemologically Significant?" *Metaphilosophy* 12: 267–276.

———. 1991. *What Can She Know?* Ithaca: Cornell University Press.

Collins, Barbara Rose. 1998. Interview, Center for American Women and Politics, February 18.

Collins, Cardiss. 1995. *Congressional Record*, 104th Cong., 1st Sess., p. H3348, March 21.

———. 2000. Interview with author in conjunction with Women Transforming Congress Conference, Carl Albert Center, University of Oklahoma, April 14.

Collins, Patricia Hill. 1990. *Black Feminist Thought*. New York: Routledge.

———. 1995. "Through the Lens of Race/Class/Gender: Black Family Studies." Paper presented at the University of Louisville, November 3.

Connell, R. W. 1987. *Gender and Power*. Stanford: Stanford University Press.

Connolly, William E. 1985. "Taylor, Foucault and Otherness." *Political Theory* 13 (3): 365–376.

Cook, Elizabeth, Ted Jelen, and Clyde Wilcox. 1992. *Between Two Absolutes: Public Opinion and the Politics of Abortion*. Boulder, Colo.: Westview.

Corbett, Greville. 1991. *Gender*. Cambridge: Cambridge University Press.

Corea, Gena. 1985. *The Mother Machine*. New York: Harper and Row.

Cornell, Drucilla, and Adam Thurschwell. 1986. "Femininity, Negativity, Intersubjectivity." *Praxis International* 5 (4): 484–504.

Corradi, Laura. 2001. "Feminism of Color Challenges White Sociological Theory and Color-Blind Eco-Feminism." In Vasilikie Demos and Marcia Texler Segal, eds., *An International Feminist Challenge to Theory*. Amsterdam: Elsevier Science Ltd.

Cox, Gary, and Mathew McCubbins. 1993. *Legislative Leviathan: Party Government in the House*. Berkeley: University of California Press.

Cramer Walsh, Katherine. 2002. "Enlarging Representation: Women Bringing Marginalized Perspectives to Floor Debate in the House of Representatives." In C. S. Rosenthal, ed., *Women Transforming Congress*. Norman: University of Oklahoma Press.

Crenshaw, Kimberle. 1989. "Demarginalizing the Intersection of Race and Sex: A Black Feminist Critique of Antidiscrimination Doctrine, Feminist Theory and Antiracist Politics." *University of Chicago Legal Forum* 4: 139–167.

———. 1997. "Beyond Racism and Misogyny." In Cathy Cohen, Kathy Jones, and Joan Tronto, eds., *Women Transforming Politics*. New York: New York University Press.

Cunningham, Frank. 1973. *Objectivity in Social Science*. Toronto: University of Toronto Press.

Cunningham, Randy. 1995. *Congressional Record*, 104th Cong., 1st Sess., p. H3446, March 21.

Daly, Mary. 1973. *Beyond God the Father*. Boston: Beacon Press.

———. 1978. *GYN/Ecology*. Boston: Beacon.

Danziger, Sheldon, and Peter Gottschalk. 1983. The Measurement of Poverty: Implications for Anti-Poverty Policy." *American Behavioral Scientist* 26 (6): 739–756.

———. 1993. *Uneven Tides: Rising Inequality in America*. New York: Russell Sage Foundation.

Darling, Marsha. 1998. "African American Women in State Elective Office in the South." In Sue Thomas and Clyde Wilcox, eds., *Women and Elective Office*. New York: Oxford University Press.

Daston, Lorraine. 2004. "Are Your Having Fun Today?" *London Review of Books*, September 23, 29–31.

Davis, Angela. 1981. *Women, Race and Class*. New York: Random House.

Deem, Melissa. 1999. "Scandal, Heteronormative Culture and the Disciplining of Feminism." *Critical Studies in Mass Communication* 16 (1): 86–94.

Deering, Christopher, and Steven Smith. 1997. *Committees in Congress*. 3rd Ed. Washington, D.C.: Congressional Quarterly Press.

de Lauretis, Theresa. 1984. *Alice Doesn't: Feminism, Semiotics, Cinema*. Bloomington: Indiana University Press.

———. 1987. *Technologies of Gender*. Bloomington: Indiana University Press.

Demos, Vasilikic, and Marcia Texler Segal. 2001. *An International Feminist Challenge to Theory*. Amsterdam: Elsevier Science Ltd.

Denis, Ann. 2001. "Rethinking Development from a Feminist Perspective." In Vasilikie Demos and Marcia Texler Segal, eds., *An International Feminist Challenge to Theory*. Amsterdam: Elsevier Science Ltd.

Derrida, Jacques. 1973. *Speech and Phenomena*. Evanston, Ill.: Northwestern University Press.

———. 1976. *Of Grammatology*. Baltimore: Johns Hopkins University Press.

———. 1978. *Writing and Difference*. London: Routledge and Kegan Paul.

———. 1979. *Spurs/Eperons*. Chicago: University of Chicago Press.

———. 1980. *The Archaeology of the Frivolous*. Pittsburgh: Duquesne University Press.

———. 1981a. *Dissemination*. Chicago: University of Chicago Press.

———. 1981b. *Positions*. Chicago: University of Chicago Press.

De Parle, Jason. 1997. "Success and Frustration as Welfare Rules Change." *New York Times*, December 30, A1, A12–13.

De Witt, Karen. 1996. "New Cause Helps Feminists Appeal to Younger Women." *New York Times*, February 5, A6.

Devault, Marjorie. 1999. *Liberating Method: Feminism and Social Research*. Philadelphia: Temple University Press.

Devor, Holly. 1989. *Gender Blending: Confronting the Limits of Duality*. Bloomington: Indiana University Press.

DiPalma, Carolyn. 2001. "Truth Is A Woman: Rethinking Bodily-Based Vectors of Power." *Political Chronicle* 13 (2): 38–59.

Doane, Mary Ann. 1987. *The Desire to Desire*. Bloomington: Indiana University Press.

Dodson, Debra and Susan Carroll. 1991. *Reshaping the Agenda: Women in State Legislatures*. New Brunswick, N.J.: Center for American Women and Politics.

Dodson, Debra, et al. 1995. *Voices, Views, and Votes: The Impact of Women in the 103rd Congress*. New Brunswick, N.J.: Center for American Women and Politics.

Dred Scott v. Sanford. 1857. 19 How. 393.

DuBois, Carol, and Vicki Ruiz, eds. 1990. *Unequal Sisters*. New York: Routledge.

Duerst-Lahti, Georgia, and Rita Mae Kelly. 1995. *Gender Power, Leadership and Governance*. Ann Arbor: University of Michigan Press.

Duran, Jane. 2001. *Worlds of Knowing: Global Feminist Epistemology*. New York: Routledge.

Edin, Kathryn, and Laura Lein. 1997. *Making Ends Meet: How Single Mothers Survive Welfare and Low-Wage Work*. New York: Russell Sage Foundation.

Eichler, Margaret. 1980. *The Double Standard: A Feminist Critique of Social Science*. New York: St. Martins Press.

Eisenstein, Hester. 1991. *Gender Shock*. Boston: Beacon Press.

Eisenstein, Zillah. 1979. *Capitalist Patriarchy and the Case for Socialist Feminism*. New York: Monthly Review Press.

Epperson, Sharon. 1988. "Studies Link Subtle Sex Bias in Schools with Women's Behavior in the Workplace." *Wall Street Journal*, September 16, 19.

Epstein, Cynthia Fuchs. 1971. *Woman's Place*. Berkeley: University of California Press.

Erie, Steven, Martin Rein, and Barbara Wiget. 1983. "Women and the Reagan Revolution: Thermidor for the Social Welfare Economy." In Irene Diamond and Mary Shanley, eds. *Families, Politics and Public Policy*. New York: Longman.

Esim, Simel. 2001. "Sisters' Keepers: Economic Organizing Among Informally Employed Women in Turkey." In Vasilikie Demos and Marcia Texler Segal, eds. *An International Feminist Challenge to Theory*. Amsterdam: Elsevier Science Ltd.

Faludi, Susan. 1991. *Backlash: The Undeclared War Against American Women*. New York: Crown Publishers.

Fanon, Frantz. [1952] 1967. *Black Skin, White Masks*. New York: Grove Press.

Farganis, Sondra. 1989. "Feminism and the Reconstruction of Social Science." In Alison Jaggar and Susan Bordo, eds., *Gender/Body/Knowledge*. New Brunswick: Rutgers University Press.

Fausto-Sterling, Ann. 1986. *Myths of Gender*. New York: Basic Books.

Fee, Elizabeth. 1983. "Women's Nature and Scientific Objectivity." In M. Lowe and R. Hubbard, eds. *Women's Nature: Rationalizations of Inequality*. New York: Pergamon.

———. 1984. "Whither Feminist Epistemology of Science?" Paper presented at Beyond the Second Sex Conference, University of Pennsylvania.

Fenno, Richard F., Jr. 1962. "The House Appropriations Committee as a Political System." *American Political Science Review* 56 (2): 310–324.

———. 1966. *The Power of the Purse*. Boston: Little, Brown.

———. 1973. *Congressmen in Committees*. Boston: Little, Brown.

———. 1978. *Home Style*. Boston: Little, Brown.

———. 1997. *Learning to Govern*. Washington, D.C.: Brookings Institution.

Firestone, Shulamith. 1970. *The Dialectic of Sex*. New York: William Morrow.

Flammang, Janet. 1997. *Women's Political Voice*. Philadelphia: Temple University Press.

Flax, Jane. 1983. "Political Philosophy and the Patriarchal Unconscious: A Psychoanalytic Perspective on Epistemology and Metaphysics." In Sandra Harding and Merrill Hintikka, eds., *Discovering Reality*. Dordrecht: D. Reidel.

———. 1986. "Gender as a Social Problem: In and For Feminist Theory." *American Studies/Amerika Studien* 31 (2): 193–213.

———. 1987. "Postmodernism and Gender Relations in Feminist Theory." *Signs* 12 (4): 621–643.

Foner, Eric. 1988. *Reconstruction, 1863–1877.* New York: Harper and Row.

Fonow, Mary Margaret, and Judith Cook. 1991. *Beyond Methodology: Feminist Scholarship as Lived Research.* Bloomington: Indiana University Press.

Foucault, Michel. 1973. *The Order of Things: An Archaeology of the Human Sciences.* New York: Vintage.

———. 1977. *Discipline and Punish.* New York: Vintage Books.

———. 1980. *The History of Sexuality.* New York: Vintage Books.

Fox Keller, Evelyn. 1984. *Reflections on Gender and Science.* New Haven, Conn: Yale University Press.

Franks, Gary. 1995. *Congressional Record,* 104th Cong., 1st Sess., p. H15521, December 21.

Fraser, Arvonne. 1987. *The U.N. Decade for Women: Documents and Dialogue.* Boulder, Colo.: Westview Press.

Fraser, Nancy. 1989. "Women, Welfare, and the Politics of Need Interpretation." In *Unruly Practices.* Minneapolis: University of Minnesota Press.

French, Marilyn. 1985. *Beyond Power: On Women, Men and Morals.* New York: Summitt.

Friedan, Betty. 1963. *The Feminine Mystique.* New York: W. W. Norton.

Friedman, Barry, and Leonard Hausman. 1975. *Work and Welfare Patterns in Low Income Families.* Brandeis University: Heller Graduate School for Advanced Studies in Welfare.

Friedman, Susan Stanford. 1998. *Mappings: Feminism and the Cultural Geographies of Encounter.* Princeton: Princeton University Press.

Frye, Marilyn. 1993. "The Possibility of Feminist Theory." In Alison Jaggar and Paula Rothenberg, *Feminist Frameworks,* 3rd ed., 103–112. Boston: McGraw Hill.

Gadamer, Hans-Georg. 1979. "Historical Transformations of Reason." In Theodore Geraets, ed., *Rationality Today.* Ottawa: University of Ottawa Press.

Garfinkel, Harold. 1967. *Studies in Ethnomethodology.* Englewood Cliffs, N.J.: Prentice Hall.

Geertz, Clifford. 1994. "Thick Description: Toward an Interpretive Theory of Culture." In Michael Martin and Lee McIntyre, eds., *Readings in the Philosophy of Social Science.* Cambridge, Mass.: MIT Press.

Geiger, Susan. 1990. "What's So Feminist About Women's Oral History?" *Journal of Women's History* 2 (1): 169–182.

Gertzog, Irwin. 2002. "Women's Changing Pathways to the U.S. House of Representatives: Widows, Elites, and Strategic Politicians." In C. S. Rosenthal, ed., *Women Transforming Congress.* Norman: University of Oklahoma Press.

Giddens, Paula. 1984. *When and Where I Enter: The Impact of Black Women on Race and Sex in America.* New York: Bantam Books.

Giele, Janet Zollinger. 2001. "In Search of the Good Life: Feminist Correctives to Modernization Theory." In Vasilikie Demos and Marcia Texler Segal, eds., *An International Feminist Challenge to Theory.* Amsterdam: Elsevier Science Ltd.

Gilbert, Susan. 2004. "New Clues to Women Veiled in Black." *New York Times,* March 16, F1.

Gilens, Martin. 1995. "Racial Attitudes and the Opposition to Welfare." *Journal of Politics* 57 (4): 994–1014.

———. 1996. "Race Coding and White Opposition to Welfare." *American Political Science Review* 90 (3): 593–604.

Gilligan, Carol. 1982. *In a Different Voice.* Cambridge: Harvard University Press.

Githens, Marianne, and Jewell Prestage. 1977. "A Minority within a Minority." In Githens and Prestage, eds., *Portraits of Marginality: The Political Behavior of the American Woman,* 339–345. New York: David McKay Company.

Glass Ceiling Commission. 1995. *Good for Business: Making Full Use of the Nation's Human Capital*. Washington, D.C.: U.S. Government Printing Office (029–016–00157–3).

Glymour, C. 1980. *Theory and Evidence*. Princeton: Princeton University Press.

Goodale, James. 1973. "Effects of Personal Background and Training on Work Values of the Hard-Core Unemployed." *Journal of Applied Psychology* 57 (1): 1–9.

Goodwin, Leonard. 1972. *Do the Poor Want to Work? A Socio-Psychological Study of Work Orientations*. Washington, D.C.: Brookings Institution.

Gordon, Linda. 1988. *Heroes of their Own Lives: The Politics and History of Family Violence*. New York: Viking.

Gould, Stephen. 1981. *The Mismeasure of Man*. New York: W. W. Norton.

Grant, Judith. 1987. "I Feel Therefore I Am: A Critique of Female Experience as the Basis for a Feminist Epistemology." *Women and Politics* 7 (3): 99–114.

———. 1993. *Fundamental Feminism: Contesting the Core Concepts of Feminist Theory*. New York: Routledge.

Greenfield, Lawrence. 1997. *Sex Offenses and Offenders: An Analysis of Data on Rape and Sexual Assault*. Washington, D.C.: U.S. Department of Justice, Office of Justice Programs, Bureau of Justice Statistics. NCJ-163392.

Greer, Germaine. 1971. *The Female Eunuch*. London: St. Albans.

Grewal, Inderpal, and Caren Kaplan. 1994. *Scattered Hegemonies: Postmodernity and Transnational Feminist Practices*. Minneapolis: University of Minnesota Press.

Griffiths, Martha. 1996. In Marcy Kaptur, ed., *Women of Congress*. Washington, D.C.: Congressional Quarterly Press.

Griffin, Susan. 1980. *Woman and Nature: The Roaring Inside Her*. New York: Harper Colophon.

Grimshaw, Jean. 1986. *Philosophy and Feminist Thinking*. Minneapolis: University of Minnesota Press.

Gueron, Judith M., and Edward Pauly. 1991. *From Welfare to Work*. New York: Russell Sage Foundation.

Gunnell, John. 1986. *Between Philosophy and Politics*. Amherst: University of Massachusetts Press.

———. 1995. "Realizing Theory: The Philosophy of Science Revisited." *Journal of Politics* 57 (4): 923–940.

———. 1998. *The Orders of Discourse: Philosophy, Social Science and Politics*. Lanham, Md.: Rowman and Littlefield.

Gutek, B., and D. Stevens. 1979. "Differential Responses of Males and Females to Work Situations that Evoke Sex-Role Stereotypes." *Journal of Vocational Behavior* 14: 23–32.

Guy-Sheftall, Beverly. 1995. *Words of Fire*. New York: New Press.

Habermas, Jurgen. 1981. Dialectics of Rationalization. *Telos* 49: 5–31.

Hacker, Andrew. 1992. *Two Nations: Black and White, Separate, Hostile, and Unequal*. New York: Scribners.

Hacking, Ian. 1999. *The Social Construction of What?* Cambridge: Harvard University Press.

Haefner, J. 1977. "Race, Age, Sex, and Competence in Employee Selection of the Disadvantaged." *Journal of Applied Psychology* 62: 199–202.

Haley, Alex. 1964. *The Autobiography of Malcolm X*. New York Ballantine Books.

Hall, Richard. 1996. *Participation in Congress*. New Haven: Yale University Press.

Hamilton, Charles. 1977. "De-racialization: Examination of a Political Strategy." *First World* (March–April): 3–5.

Hammonds, Evelynn. 1997. "Toward a Genealogy of Black Female Sexuality: The Problematic of Silence." In M. Jaqui Alexander and Chandra Talpade Mohanty, eds., *Feminist Genealogies, Colonial Legacies, Democratic Futures*. New York: Routledge.

Handler, Joel. 1972. *Reforming the Poor.* New York: Basic Books.

——. 1995. *The Poverty of Welfare Reform.* New Haven: Yale University Press.

Haney Lopez, Ian. 1996. *White By Law.* New York: New York University Press.

Haraway, Donna. 1989. *Primate Visions.* New York: Routledge.

——. 1991a. *Simians, Cyborgs and Women: The Reinvention of Nature.* New York: Routledge.

——. 1991b. "Gender For a Marxist Dictionary: The Sexual Politics of a Word." In *Simians, Cyborgs and Women.* New York: Routledge.

Harding, Sandra. 1986. *The Science Question in Feminism.* Ithaca: Cornell University Press.

——. 1991. *Whose Science? Whose Knowledge? Thinking from Women's Lives.* Ithaca: Cornell University Press.

——. 1992. "After the Neutrality Ideal: Science, Politics, and Strong Objectivity." *Social Research* 59 (3): 567–587.

——. 1993. "Rethinking Standpoint Epistemology: What is Strong Objectivity." In Linda Alcoff, ed., *Feminist Epistemologies,* 49–82. New York: Routledge.

Harding, Sandra, and Merrill Hintikka. 1983. *Discovering Reality: Feminist Perspectives on Epistemology, Metaphysics, Methodology and Philosophy of Science.* Dordrecht: D. Reidel.

Hardt, Michael, and Antonio Negri. 2000. *Empire.* Cambridge: Harvard University Press.

Harre, Rom. 1986. *Varieties of Realism.* Oxford: Basil Blackwell.

Hartsock, Nancy. 1983. "The Feminist Standpoint: Developing the Ground for a Specifically Feminist Historical Materialism." In Sandra Harding and Merrill Hintikka, eds., *Discovering Reality: Feminist Perspectives on Epistemology, Metaphysics, Methodology and Philosophy of Science,* 283–310. Boston: D. Reidel.

——. 1990. "Foucault on Power: A Theory for Women?" In Linda Nicholson, ed., *Feminism/Postmodernism.* New York: Routledge.

Hawkesworth, Mary. 1988. *Theoretical Issues in Policy Analysis.* Albany: State University of New York Press.

——. 1989. "Knowers, Knowing, Known: Feminist Theory and Claims of Truth." *Signs* 14 (3): 533–557.

——. 1990a. *Beyond Oppression: Feminist Theory and Political Strategy.* New York: Continuum.

——. 1990b. "The Reification of Difference." In *Beyond Oppression.* New York: Continuum.

——. 1992. "From Objectivity to Objectification: Feminist Objections." *Annals of Scholarship* 8 (3/4): 451–477.

——. 1999. "Analyzing Backlash: Feminist Standpoint Theory as Analytical Tool." *Women's Studies International Forum.* 22 (2): 135–155.

——. 2004. "The Semiotics of Premature Burial: Feminism in a Postfeminist Age." *Signs* 29 (4): 961–986.

Hawkesworth, Mary, Debra Dodson, Katherine Kleeman, Kathleen Casey, Krista Jenkins. 2001. *Legislating By Women and For Women: A Comparison of the 103rd and 104th Congresses.* New Brunswick, N.J.: Center for American Women and Politics.

Hedge, David, James Button, and Mary Spear. 1996. "Accounting for the Quality of Black Legislative Life: The View from the States." *American Journal of Political Science* 40 (1): 82–98.

Hegel, G.W.F. 1977. *Phenomenology of Spirit.* Trans. A. V. Miller. Oxford: Oxford University Press.

Hekman, Susan. 1987. "The Feminization of Epistemology." *Women and Politics* 7 (3): 65–83.

——. 1992. *Gender and Knowledge.* Boston: Northeastern University Press.

——. 1997. "Truth and Method: Feminist Standpoint Theory Revisited." *Signs* 22 (2): 341–365.

Held, Virginia. 1975. "Reasonable Progress and Self-Respect." In Tom Beauchamp, ed., *Ethics and Public Policy*. Englewood Cliffs, N.J.: Prentice Hall.

Herzog, Donald. 1989. *Happy Slaves: A Critique of Consent Theory*. Chicago: University of Chicago Press.

Hesse, Mary. 1980. *Revolutions and Reconstructions in the Philosophy of Science*. Brighton: Harvester Press.

Hesse-Biber, Sharlene, Christina Gilmartin, and Robin Lydenberg. 1999. *Feminist Approaches to Theory and Methodology: An Interdisciplinary Reader*. New York: Oxford University Press.

Hesse-Biber, Sharlene, and Patricia Leavy. 2004. *Approaches to Qualitative Research*. New York: Oxford University Press.

Higginbotham, Evelyn Brooks. 1992. "African-American Women's History and the Metalanguage of Race." *Signs* 17 (2): 251–274.

Hirschmann, Nancy. 1993. *Rethinking Obligation: A Feminist Method for Political Theory*. Ithaca: Cornell University Press.

Hobbes, Thomas. [1651] 1968. *Leviathan*. C. B. Macpherson, ed. London: Penguin Books.

Hoff Summers, Christine. 1994. *Who Stole Feminism: How Women Have Betrayed Women*. New York: Touchstone/Simon and Shuster.

Holmes, Helen, Betty Hoskins, and Michael Goss. 1981. *The Custom-Made Child*. Clifton, N.J.: Humanities Press.

Holmes Norton, Eleanor. 1997. Interview, Center for American Women and Politics, November 4.

hooks, bell. 1981. *Ain't I a Woman: Black Women and Feminism*. Boston: South End Press.

———. 1984. *Feminist Theory: From Margin to Center*. Boston: South End Press.

———. 1989. *Talking Back: Thinking Feminist, Thinking Black*. Boston: South End Press.

———. 1990. *Yearning: Race, Gender, and Cultural Politics*. Boston: South End Press.

———. 1992. *Black Looks: Race and Representation*. Boston: South End Press.

Horkheimer, Max, and Theodor Adorno. 1972. *The Dialectic of Enlightenment*. New York: Herder and Herder.

Hosansky, David. 1996. "Shuster: A Veteran Road Warrior." *Congressional Quarterly Weekly Report*, December 14, 3395.

Hubbard, Ruth, M. S. Hennifin, and Barbara Fried. 1982. *Biological Woman: The Convenient Myth*. Cambridge, Mass.: Schenkman.

Hughes, Graham. 1975. "Reparations for Blacks." In Tom Beauchamp, ed., *Ethics and Public Policy*. Englewood Cliffs, N.J.: Prentice Hall.

Hull, Gloria, Patricia Bell Scott, and Barbara Smith. 1982. *All the Women Are White, All the Blacks Are Men, But Some of Us Are Brave*. Old Westbury: The Feminist Press.

Hume, David. [1748] 1927. *An Enquiry Concerning Human Understanding*. L. A. Selby-Bigge, ed. Oxford: Clarendon Press.

Humphreys, W. 1969. *Perception and Discovery*. San Francisco: Freeman, Cooper.

Hurston, Zora Neale. 1978. *Their Eyes Were Watching God*. Urbana: University of Illinois Press.

Hurtado, Aida. 1996. *The Color of Privilege: Three Blasphemies on Race and Feminism*. Ann Arbor: University of Michigan Press.

Irigaray, Lucy. 1985a. *Speculum of the Other Woman*. Trans. Gillian Gill. Ithaca: Cornell University Press.

———. 1985b. *This Sex Which Is Not One*. Trans. Catherine Porter. Ithaca: Cornell University Press.

Islam, Naheed. 2000. "Research as an Act of Betrayal: Researching Race in an Asian Community in Los Angeles." In France Winddance Twine and Jonathan Warren, eds., *Racing Research, Researching Race: Methodological Dilemmas in Critical Race Studies*, 35–66. New York: New York University Press.

Jackson Lee, Sheila. 1995a. *Congressional Record*, 104th Cong., 1st Sess., p. H3554, March 22.

————. 1995b. *Congressional Record*, 104th Cong., 1st Sess., p. H 3872, March 28.

————. 1998. Interview, Center for American Women and Politics, July 19.

Jacobson, Gary C., and Samuel Kernell. 1981. *Strategy and Choice in Congressional Elections*. New Haven: Yale University Press.

Jaggar, Alison. 1983. *Feminist Politics and Human Nature*. Totowa, N.J.: Rowman and Allenheld.

————. 1989. "Love and Knowledge: Emotion in Feminist Epistemology." In Alison Jaggar and Susan Bordo, eds., *Gender/Body/Knowledge*. New Brunswick: Rutgers University Press.

Janeway, Elizabeth. 1971. *Man's World, Women's Place*. New York: Delta Books.

Jardine, Alice. 1982. "Gynesis." *Diacritics* 12: 54–65.

————. 1985. *Gynesis: Configurations of Woman and Modernity*. Ithaca: Cornell University Press.

Jelen, Ted, and Clyde Wilcox. 2003. "Causes and Consequences of Public Attitudes Toward Abortion." Paper presented at the Annual Meeting of the Western Political Science Association, Long Beach, Calif., March 22–24.

Jewell, Malcolm E., and Marcia Lynn Whicker. 1994. *Legislative Leadership in the American States*. Ann Arbor: University of Michigan Press.

Jeydel, Alana, and Andrew Taylor. 2003. "Are Women Legislators Less Effective? Evidence from the U.S. House in the 103rd–105th Congress." *Political Research Quarterly* 56 (1): 19–27.

Joergenson, J. 1951. "The Development of Logical Empiricism." *International Encyclopedia of Unified Science*, Vol. 2, no. 9. Chicago: University of Chicago Press.

John, Mary. 1996. *Discrepant Dislocations: Feminism, Theory, and Postcolonial Histories*. Berkeley: University of California Press.

Johnson, Eddie Bernice. 1997. Interview, Center for American Women and Politics, October 31.

Jordanova, Ludmilla. 1989. *Sexual Visions: Images of Gender in Science and Medicine Between the 18th and 20th Centuries*. Madison: University of Wisconsin Press.

Joseph, Gloria, and Jill Lewis. 1981. *Common Differences: Conflicts in Black and White Feminist Perspectives*. New York: Anchor Press/Doubleday.

Kabeer, Nayla. 2003. *Reversed Realities: Gender Hierarchies in Development Thought*. London: Verso.

Kaplan, Roy, and Curt Tausky. 1972. "Work and the Welfare Cadillac: The Function of the Commitment to Work among the Hard Core Unemployed." *Social Problems* 19: 469–483.

Kathlene, Lyn. 1989. "Uncovering the Political Impacts of Gender: An Exploratory Study." *Western Political Quarterly* 42 (4): 397–421.

————. 1994. "Power and Influence in State Legislative Policymaking: The Interaction of Gender and Position in Committee Hearing Debates." *American Political Science Review* 88 (3): 560–576.

Kelly, Rita, Bernard Ronan, and Margaret Cawley. 1987. "Liberal Positivistic Epistemology and Research on Women and Politics." *Women and Politics* 7 (3): 11–27.

Kenney, Sally. 1996. "New Research on Gendered Political Institutions." *Political Research Quarterly* 49 (2): 445–466.

Kenny, Lorraine. 2000. "Doing My Homework: The Autoethnography of A White Teenage Girl." In France Winddance Twine and Jonathan Warren, eds. *Racing Research, Researching Race*, 111–134. New York: New York University Press.

Kessler, Suzanne, and Wendy McKenna. 1978. *Gender: An Ethnomethodological Approach*. New York: John Wiley.

Ketchum, Sara Ann, and Christine Pierce. 1979. "Separatism and Sexual Relationships." In Sharon Bishop and Marjorie Weinzweig, eds., *Philosophy and Women*. Belmont, Calif.: Wadsworth.

King, Deborah. 1988. "Multiple Jeopardy, Multiple Consciousness: The Context of Black Feminist Ideology. *Signs* 14 (1): 42–72.

King, Mae. 1977. "The Politics of Sexual Stereotypes. In Marianne Githens and Jewell Prestage, eds., *A Portrait of Marginality*, 346–365. New York: David McKay and Company.

Kingdon, John. 1984. *Agendas, Alternatives, and Public Policies*. Boston: Little, Brown.

Kingston, Jack. 1996. *Congressional Record*, 104th Cong., 2d Sess., p. H7749, July 17.

Kondrtas, Anna. 1995. *News and Views*. Independent Women's Forum, (May/June).

Koss, Mary. 1992a. "The Measurement of Rape Victimization in Crime Surveys." *Criminal Justice and Behavior* 23 (1): 55–69.

———. 1992b. "The Underdetection of Rape: Methodological Choices Influence Incidence Estimates." *Journal of Social Issues* 48 (1): 61–65.

———. 1993. "Detecting the Scope of Rape: A Review of Prevalence Research Methods." *Journal of Interpersonal Violence* 8 (2): 198–222.

———. 1996. "The Measurement of Rape Victimization in Crime Surveys." *Criminal Justice & Behavior* 23 (1): 55–69.

Kraft, V. 1952. *The Vienna Circle*. New York: Philosophical Library.

Kristeva, Julia. 1982. *Powers of Horror: An Essay on Abjection*. Trans. Leon S. Roudiez. New York: Columbia University Press.

Kruks, Sonia. 2001. *Retrieving Experience: Subjectivity and Recognition in Feminist Politics*. Ithaca, N.Y.: Cornell University Press.

Ladowsky, Ellen. 1995. "That's No White Male, That's My Husband." *The Women's Quarterly*. Washington, D.C.: The Independent Women's Forum.

Lakatos, Imre. 1970. "Falsification and the Methodology of Scientific Research Programmes." In Imre Lakatos and Alan Musgrave, eds., *Criticism and the Growth of Knowledge*. Cambridge: Cambridge University Press.

Laqueur, Thomas. 1990. *Making Sex: Body and Gender From the Greeks to Freud*. Cambridge: Harvard University Press.

Lather, Patti. 1991. *Getting Smart: Feminist Research and Pedagogy With/In the Postmodern*. New York: Routledge.

Laudan, L. 1990. *Science and Relativism*. Chicago: University of Chicago Press.

Le Doeuff, Michele. 1991. *Hipparchia's Choice: An Essay Concerning Women, Philosophy, etc*. Trans. Trista Selous. Oxford: Blackwell.

Lerner, Gerda. 1986. *The Creation of Patriarchy*. New York: Oxford University Press.

Letherby, Gayle. 2003. *Feminist Research in Theory and Practice*. Buckingham and Philadelphia: Open University Press.

Levi-Strauss, Claude. 1969. *The Elementary Structures of Kinship*. Boston: Beacon Press.

———. 1971. "The Family." In H. Shapiro, ed., *Man, Culture and Society*. London: Oxford University Press.

Levitan, Sar A., and Isaac Shapiro. 1987. *Working But Poor: America's Contradiction*. Baltimore: Johns Hopkins University Press.

Lieberman, Robert C. 1995. "Race and the Organization of Welfare Policy." In Paul E. Peterson, ed., *Classifying by Race*, 157–187. Princeton: Princeton University Press.

Linden, Barbara, and Deborah Vincent. 1982. *Workfare in Theory and Practice*. Washington, D.C.: National Social Science and Law Center.

Livingston, John. 1979. *Fair Game: Inequality and Affirmative Action*. San Francisco: W. H. Freeman and Company.

Lloyd, Genevieve. 1982. *The Man of Reason: Male and Female in Western Philosophy*. London: Methuen.

Locke, Mamie. 1997. "From 3/5ths to Zero: Implications of the Constitution for African American Women, 1787–1870." In Cathy Cohen, Kathy Jones, and Joan Tronto, eds., *Women Transforming Politics*. New York: New York University Press.

Longino, Helen. 1990. *Science as Social Knowledge*. Princeton: Princeton University Press.

———. 1993. "Feminist Standpoint Theory and the Problems of Knowledge." *Signs* 19 (1): 201–212.

Lopata, Helene, and BarrieThorne. 1978. "On the Term, 'Sex Roles'" *Signs* 3 (3): 718–721.

Lorde, Audre. 1984. *Sister Outsider*. New York: Crossing Press.

Lowe, Marian, and Ruth Hubbard. 1983. *Woman's Nature: Rationalizations of Inequality*. New York: Pergamon.

Lublin, David. 1997. *The Paradox of Representation*. Princeton: Princeton University Press.

MacIntrye, Alasdair. 1981. *After Virtue*. Notre Dame, Ind.: University of Notre Dame Press.

MacKinnon, Catharine. 1987. *Feminism Unmodified*. Cambridge: Harvard University Press.

Maguire, Kathleen, and Ann Pastore. 1996. *Sourcebook of Criminal and Justice Statistics*. Washington, D.C.: U.S. Department of Justice, Bureau of Justice Statistics.

Maguire, P. 1984. *Women in Development: An Alternative Analysis*. Amherst, Mass.: Center for International Education.

Mannheim, Karl. 1936. *Ideology and Utopia*. Trans. Louis Wirth and Edward Shils. New York: Harcourt, Brace, and World.

Maracle, Lee. 1996. *I Am A Woman: A Native Perspective on Sociology and Feminism*. Vancouver, B.C.: Press Gang Publishers.

March, James G., and John P. Olsen. 1989. *Rediscovering Institutions*. New York: Free Press.

Martin, Emily. 1990. "The Egg and Sperm: How Science Has Constructed a Romance Based on Stereotypical Male and Female Roles." *Signs* 16 (3): 485–501.

Marx, Karl, and Friedrich Engels. [1848] 1955. *The Communist Manifesto*. New York: Meredith Corporation.

Matthews, Donald. 1959. "The Folkways of the United States Senate: Conformity to Group Norms and Legislative Effectiveness." *American Political Science Review* 53 (4): 1064–1089.

———. 1960. *U.S. Senators and Their World*. Chapel Hill: University of North Carolina Press.

Mayhew, David. 1974. Congress: *The Electoral Connection*. New Haven: Yale University Press.

Mazumdar, V. 1989. "Peasant Women Organize for Empowerment: The Bankura Experiment." Occasional Paper 13. New Delhi: Centre for Women's Development Studies.

McCall, Leslie. 2001. *Complex Inequality: Gender, Race, and Class in the New Economy*. New York: Routledge.

———. 2005. "The Complexity of Intersectionality." *Signs: Journal of Women in Culture and Society* 30 (3): 1771–1800.

McClintock, Anne. 1995. *Imperial Leather: Race, Gender, and Sexuality in Colonial Context*. New York: Routledge.

McInnis, Scott. 1995. *Congressional Record*, 104th Cong., 1st Sess., p. H3349, March 21.

McKinney, Cynthia. 1995. *Congressional Record*, 104th Cong., 1st Sess., p. H3741, March 24.

———. 1997. Interview, Center for American Women and Politics, October 29.

McMillan, Ann. 1983. "The Angel in the Text: Christine de Pisan and Virginia Woolf." Paper presented at the Modern Languages Association Annual Convention.

Meek, Carrie. 1995a. Interview, Center for American Women and Politics, June 27.

———. 1995b. *Congressional Record*, 104th Cong., 1st Sess., p. H15524, December 21.

———. 1997. Interview, Center for American Women and Politics, October 31.

Megill, Allan. 1985. *Prophets of Extremity: Nietzsche, Heidegger, Foucault, Derrida*. Berkeley: University of California Press.

Melich, Tanya. 1996. *The Republican War Against Women*. New York: Bantam Books.

Merton, Robert. 1945. "The Sociology of Knowledge." In George Gurwitch and Wilbert Moore, eds., *Twentieth Century Sociology*. New York: Philosophical Library.

Mettler, Suzanne. 2000. "States Rights, Women's Obligations: Contemporary Welfare Reform in Historical Perspective." *Women and Politics* 21 (1): 1–34.

Meyers, Jan. 1993. *Congressional Record*. 103rd Congress, 1st Session, p. H1084, March 10.

Mies, Maria. 1984. "Toward a Methodology for Feminist Research." In Edith Altbach, Jeanette Clausen, Dagmar Schultz, and Naomi Stephan, eds., *German Feminism*. Albany: State University of New York Press.

Mill, John Stuart. [1869] 1970. *The Subjection of Women*. Cambridge: MIT Press.

Miller, R. 1987. *Fact and Method*. Princeton: Princeton University Press.

Mink, Gwendolyn. 1995. *The Wages of Motherhood: Inequality in the Welfare State*. Ithaca, N.Y.: Cornell University Press.

———. 1996. "Welfare 'Reform': The Attack on Poor Women." Paper presented at the Annual Meeting of the Western Political Science Association, San Francisco, March 15.

———. 1998. *Welfare's End*. Ithaca, N.Y.: Cornell University Press.

———. 1999. "Aren't Poor Single Mothers Women? Feminists, Welfare Reform, and Welfare Justice." In Gwendolyn Mink, ed., *Whose Welfare?* Ithaca, N.Y.: Cornell University Press.

Mink, Patsy. 1995. *Congressional Record*. 104th Cong., 1st Sess., pp. H1685–1686, February 13.

———. 1997. Interview, Center for American Women and Politics, November 4.

Mohanty, Chandra Talpade. 1991. "Under Western Eyes: Feminist Scholarship and Colonial Discourses." In Chandra Mohanty, Ann Russo, and Lourdes Torres, eds., *Third World Women and the Politics of Feminism*. Bloomington: Indiana University Press.

Mohanty, Chandra, Ann Russo, and Lourdes Torres. 1991. *Third World Women and the Politics of Feminism*. Bloomington: Indiana University Press.

Moi, Toril. 1985. *Sexual/Textual Politics*. New York: Methuen.

Moon, Donald. 1975. "The Logic of Political Inquiry: A Synthesis of Opposed Perspectives." In Fred Greenstein and Nelson Polsby, eds., *Handbook of Political Science*, vol. 1. Reading, Mass.: Addison-Wesley.

Morin, Richard. 1995. "A Nation Divided." *Louisville Courier Journal*, October 8.

Morgan, Jennifer. 2004. *Laboring Women: Reproduction and Gender in New World Slavery*. Philadelphia: University of Pennsylvania Press.

Mosely-Braun, Carol. 1995. *Congressional Record*, 104th Cong., 1st Sess., p. S19095, December 21.

Murray, T. 1983. "Partial Knowledge." In Daniel Callahan and Bruce Jennings, eds., *Ethics, The Social Sciences and Policy Analysis*. New York: Plenum Press.

Nagel, Thomas. 1986. *The View from Nowhere*. New York: Oxford University Press.

Naples, Nancy. 2003. *Feminism and Method: Ethnography, Discourse Analysis and Activist Research*. New York: Routledge.

Narayan, Uma. 1997. *Dislocating Cultures*. New York: Routledge.

Narayan, Uma, and Sandra Harding. 2000. *Decentering the Center*. Bloomington: Indiana University Press.

National League of Cities. 2002. "Women of Color in Local Elective Offices." [Includes all cities with populations greater than 10,000].

National Victim Center and Crime Victim Research and Treatment Center. 1992. *Rape In America: A Report to the Nation*. Washington, D.C.: National Victim Center.

Nelson, Candace, and Marta Tienda. 1997. "The Structuring of Hispanic Ethnicity: Historical and Contemporary Perspectives." In Mary Romero, Pierrette Hondagneu-Sotelo, and Vilma Ortiz, eds., *Challenging Fronteras*, 7–29. New York: Routledge.

Nelson, Lyn. 1990. *Who Knows? From Quine to a Feminist Empiricism*. Philadelphia: Temple University Press.

Newton-Smith, W. 1981. *The Rationality of Science*. London: Routledge.

Nicholson, Linda. 1990. *Feminism/Postmodernism*. New York: Routledge.

Nielsen, Arrah. 2004. "Feminist Statistics Skew Issues." *University Daily Kansan*, September 24.

Nietzsche, Friedrich. 1969. *On the Genealogy of Morals*. Trans. Walter Kaufman. New York: Vintage Books.

———. 1983. "The Uses and Disadvantages of History." Trans. R. J. Hollingdale. In Daniel Breazeale, ed., *Untimely Meditations II*. Cambridge: Cambridge University Press.

Nieva, Veronica, and Barbara Gutek. 1980. "Sex Effects on Evaluation." *Academy of Management Review* 5: 267–276.

Nochlin, Linda. 1971. "Why Have There Been No Great Women Artists?" *Art News* 69 (9). Reprinted in Linda Nochlin, *Women, Art and Power and Other Essays*. New York: Harper & Row, Publishers, 1988.

O'Brien, Mary. 1981. *The Politics of Reproduction*. London: Routledge and Kegan Paul.

Oakley, Ann. 2000. *Experiments in Knowing: Gender and Method in the Social Sciences*. New York: New Press.

Oleszek, Walter. 2001. *Congressional Procedures and the Policy Process*. 5th ed. Washington, D.C.: CQ Press.

Ornstein, Norman, Thomas E. Mann, and Michael Malbin. 1996. *Vital Statistics on Congress, 1995–1996*, 218. Washington, D.C.: CQ Press.

Painter, Nell Irwin. 1996. *Sojourner Truth: A Life; A Symbol*. New York: W.W. Norton.

Parrenas, Rhacel Salazar. 2000. "Migrant Filipina Domestic Workers and the International Division of Reproductive Labor." *Gender and Society* 14 (4): 560–581.

———. 2001a. *Servants of Globalization: Women Migration and Domestic Work*. Stanford: Stanford University Press.

———. 2001b. "Transgressing the Nation-State: The Partial Citizenship and 'Imagined Community' of Migrant Filipina Domestic Workers." *Signs* 26 (4): 1129–1154.

Parrot, Andrea, and Laurie Bechhofer. 1991. *Acquaintance Rape: The Hidden Crime*. New York: Wiley.

Pateman, Carole, and Elizabeth Grosz. 1986. *Feminist Challenges: Social and Political Theory*. Boston: Northeastern University Press.

Payne, James. 1980. "Show Horses and Work Horses in the U.S. House of Representatives." *Polity* 12: 428–456.

Pearce, Diana. 1993. "Feminization of Poverty: Update." In Alison Jaggar and Paula Rothenberg, eds., *Feminist Frameworks*. Boston: McGraw Hill.

Peirce, Charles Sanders. [1883] 1982. "The Logic of Relatives." In *Studies in Logic by Members of the Johns Hopkins University*. Reprinted in Max Fisch, ed., *Writings of Charles S. Peirce: A Chronological Edition*. Bloomington: Indiana University Press.

Pirog-Good, Maureen, and Jan Stets. 1989. *Violence in Dating Relationships*. New York: Praeger.

Pisan, Christine de. [1405] 1982. *The Book of the City of the Ladies*. Trans. Earl Jeffrey Richards. New York: Persea.

Plato. 1961. *The Collected Dialogues*. Eds. Edith Hamilton and Huntington Cairns. Princeton: Princeton University Press.

Plessy v. Ferguson. 1896. 163 U.S. 537.

Pocock, J.G.A. 1973. *Politics, Language, and Time*. New York: Atheneum.

Polakow, V. 1993. *Lives on the Edge: Single Mothers and Their Children in the Other America*. Chicago: University of Chicago Press.

Polanyi, M. 1958. *Personal Knowledge*. Chicago: University of Chicago Press.

Poovey, Mary. 1988. *Uneven Developments*. Chicago: University of Chicago Press.

Popper, Karl. 1959. *The Logic of Scientific Discovery.* New York: Basic Books.
————. 1962. *Conjectures and Refutations.* New York: Basic Books.
————. 1972a. *Conjectures and Refutations: The Growth of Scientific Knowledge,* 4th rev. ed. London: Routledge and Kegan Paul.
————. 1972b. *Objective Knowledge: An Evolutionary Approach.* Oxford: Clarendon Press.
Pottinger, J. Stanley. 1971. "Affirmative Action." *New York Times,* December 18.
Putnam, H. 1981. *Reason, Truth and History.* Cambridge: Cambridge University Press.
————. 1983. *Realism and Reason.* Cambridge: Cambridge University Press.
————. 1988. *Representation and Reality.* Cambridge: MIT Press.
————. 1990. *Realism with a Human Face.* Cambridge: Harvard University Press.
Quadagno, Jill. 1994. *The Color of Welfare: How Racism Undermined the War on Poverty.* New York: Oxford University Press.
RAINN (Rape, Abuse, and Incest National Network). 2004. "Department of Justice Study Shows Rape Down." http://www.rainn.org/stat.html.
Ramazanoglu, Caroline, with Janet Holland. 2002. *Feminist Methodology: Challenges and Choices.* London and Thousand Oaks: Sage Publications.
Rand Corporation. 2004. "Do Public Attitudes Toward Abortion Influence Attitudes Toward Family Planning?" *Population Policy Briefs. http://www.rand.org/publications/RB/RB5042/.*
Rein, Mildred. 1982. *Dilemmas of Welfare Policy.* New York: Praeger.
Reinharz, Shulamit. 1992. *Feminist Methods in Social Research.* New York: Oxford University Press.
Ricci, David. 1984. *The Tragedy of Political Science: Politics, Scholarship, Democracy.* New Haven, Conn.: Yale University Press.
Rich, Adrienne. 2003. "Notes Toward a Politics of Location." In Carol McCann and Seung-Kyung Kim, eds., *Feminist Theory Reader: Local and Global Perspectives,* 447–459. New York: Routledge.
Richards, Janet. 1982. *The Skeptical Feminist.* London: Penguin.
Riley, Denise. 1988. *Am I that Name? Feminism and the Category of 'Women' in History.* Minneapolis: University of Minnesota Press.
Rixecker, Stefanie. 1994. "Expanding the Discursive Context of Policy Design: A Matter of Feminist Standpoint Epistemology." *Policy Sciences* 27 (2–3): 119–142.
Roberts, Dorothy. 1997. *Killing the Black Body: Race, Reproduction, and the Meaning of Liberty.* New York: Vintage.
Rohde, David. 1991. *Parties and Leaders in the Postreform House.* Chicago: University of Chicago Press.
Roiphe. Katie. 1994. *The Morning After: Sex, Fear, and Feminism on Campus.* Boston: Little Brown.
Rorty, Richard. 1979. *Philosophy and the Mirror of Nature.* Princeton: Princeton University Press.
Rose, Hilary. 1983. "Hand, Brain and Heart: A Feminist Epistemology for the Natural Sciences." *Signs* 9 (1): 73–90.
Rosen, B., and T. Jerdee. 1974. "Influence of Sex-Role Stereotypes on Personnel Decisions." *Journal of Applied Psychology* 59: 9–14.
Rosen, Richard. 1980. "Identifying States and Areas Prone to High and Low Unemployment." *Monthly Labor Review* (March): 22–24.
Rosenberg, Tina. 2002. "Globalization: The Free Market Fix." *New York Times Magazine,* August 18, 28–33, 50, 74–75.
Rosenthal, Cindy Simon. 2000. "Gender Styles in State Legislative Committees: Raising their Voices and Resolving Conflict." *Women and Politics* 21 (2): 21–45.
————. 2002. *Women Transforming Congress.* Norman: University of Oklahoma Press.
Rowan, Carl. 1995. "The 'Reverse Discrimination' Myth." *Louisville Courier Journal,* November 13.

Rowbotham, Sheila. 1973. *Women's Consciousness, Man's World*. London: Penquin.

Roybal-Allard, Louise. 1996. *Congressional Record*, 104th Cong., 2d Sess., p. H7508, July 12.

Rubin, Gayle. 1975. "The Traffic in Women: Notes on the Political Economy of Sex." In Rayner Reiter, ed., *Toward an Anthropology of Women*. New York: Monthly Review Press.

Ruddick, Sara. 1980. "Maternal Thinking," *Feminist Studies* 6 (2): 342–367.

———. 1983. "Pacifying the Forces: Drafting Women in the Interests of Peace." *Signs* 8 (3): 471–489.

Russell, Diana, and Nancy Howell. 1983. "The Prevalence of Rape in the United States Revisited." *Signs* 8 (4): 688.

Ruth, Sheila. 1981. "Methodocracy, Mysogyny and Bad Faith: The Response of Philosophy." In Dale Spender, ed., *Men's Studies Modified*. Oxford: Pergamon.

Sandoval, Chela. 2000. *Methodology of the Oppressed*. Minneapolis: University of Minnesota Press.

Saussure, Ferdinand de. [1916] 1974. *Course in General Linguistics*. London: Fontana.

Sawicki, Jana. 1991. "Foucault and Feminism: Toward a Politics of Difference." In Mary Shanley and Carole Pateman, eds., *Feminist Interpretations and Political Theory*. University Park: University of Pennsylvania Press.

Schattschneider, E. E. 1960. *The Semi-Sovereign People*. New York: Holt, Reinhart and Winston.

Schiller, Bradley. 1973. "Empirical Studies of Welfare Dependency: A Survey." *Journal of Human Resources* 8 (Supplement).

Schott, Robin. 1988. *Cognition and Eros: A Critique of the Kantian Paradigm*. Boston: Beacon Press.

Scott, Joan. 1986. "Gender: A Useful Category for Historical Analysis." *American Historical Review* 91: 1053–1075.

———. 1988. "Deconstructing the Equality vs. Difference Debate: Or the Uses of Poststructuralist Theory for Feminism." *Feminist Studies* 14 (1): 575–599.

———. 1992. "Experience." In Judith Butler and Joan Scott, eds., *Feminists Theorize the Political*, 22–40. New York: Routledge.

Seccombe, Wally. 1974. "The Housewife and her Labour Under Capitalism." *New Left Review* 83: 3–24.

Sedgwick Eve. 1990. *Epistemology of the Closet*. Berkeley: University of California Press.

Sellars, Wilfred. 1963. *Science, Perception and Reality*. New York: Humanities Press.

Sen, Amartya. 1988. "Africa and India: What Do We Have To Learn From Each Other?" In Kenneth Arrow, ed. *The Balance between Industry and Agriculture in Economic Development*. London: Macmillan.

———. 1990. "More Than a Hundred Million Women Are Missing." *New York Review of Books*, December 20.

———. 1992. "Missing Women." *British Medical Journal* 304 (March 1992).

Sen, Gita, and Caren Grown. 1987. *Development, Crises, and Alternate Visions: Third World Women's Perspectives*. New York: Monthly Review Press.

Shanley, Mary, and Carole Pateman. 1991. *Feminist Interpretations and Political Theory*. University Park: Pennsylvania State University Press.

Shaw, T. 1974. "Differential Impact of Negative Stereotypes on Employee Selection." *Personnel Psychology* 25: 333–338.

Sherman, Beth. 1985. "The New Realities of Date Rape." *New York Times*, October 23, 17, 19.

Showalter, Elaine. 1987. "Women's Time, Women's Space: Writing the History of Feminist Criticism." In Shari Benstock, ed., *Feminist Issues in Literary Scholarship*. Bloomington: Indiana University Press.

Siltanen, Janet. 1994. *Locating Gender: Occupational Segregation, Wages and Domestic Responsibilities*. London: UCL Press.

Silverman, Kaja. 1988. *The Acoustic Mirror*. Bloomington: Indiana University Press.

Singer, Linda. 1993. *Erotic Welfare: Sexual Theory and Politics in the Age of Epidemic*. New York: Routledge.

Sklar, Holly. 1995. "Back to the Raw Deal." *Z Magazine* (November): 19–24.

Smith, Dorothy. 1979. "A Sociology for Women." In Julia Sherman and Evelyn Beck, eds., *The Prism of Sex: Essays in the Sociology of Knowledge*, 137–187. Madison: University of Wisconsin Press.

Smith, Steven G. 1992. *Gender Thinking*. Philadelphia: Temple University Press.

Smooth, Wendy. 2001a. "African American Women State Legislators: The Impact of Gender and Race on Legislative Influence." Ph.D. diss., University of Maryland.

———. 2001b. "African American Women State Legislators and the Politics of Legislative Incorporation." Prepared for the Center for American Women and Politics Forum for Women State Legislators, November 15–18.

Soble, Alan. 1983. "Feminist Epistemology and Women Scientists." *Metaphilosophy* 14: 291–307.

Spalter-Roth, Roberta, Beverly Burr, Heidi Hartmann, and Louise Shaw. 1995. "Welfare that Works: The Working Lives of AFDC Recipients." Report to the Ford Foundation. Washington, D.C.: Institute for Women's Policy Research.

Sparks, Holloway. 1997. "Dissident Citizenship: Democratic Theory, Political Courage, and Activist Women." *Hypatia: A Journal of Feminist Philosophy* 12 (December): 74–109.

Speier, Hans. 1938. "The Social Determination of Ideas." *Social Research* 5: 182–205.

Spelman, Elizabeth. 1988. *Inessential Woman: Problems of Exclusion in Feminist Thought*. Boston: Beacon Press.

Spender, Dale. 1980. *Man Made Language*. London: Routledge and Kegan Paul.

———. 1981. *Men's Studies Modified: The Impact of Feminism on the Academic Disciplines*. Oxford: Pergamon.

———. 1983. *Women of Ideas and What Men Have Done to Them*. London: Ark Paperbacks.

Spivak, Gayatri. 1988. "Can the Subaltern Speak?" In Cary Nelson and Lawrence Grossberg, eds., *Marxism and the Interpretation of Culture*. Champagne-Urbana: University of Illinois Press.

Stanley, Liz, and Susan Wise. 1983. *Breaking Out: Feminist Consciousness and Feminist Research*. London: Routledge and Kegan Paul.

Steinberg, Ronnie. 1992. "Gender on the Agenda: Male Advantage in Organizations." *Contemporary Sociology* 21 (5): 576–581.

Stimpson, Catherine. 1991. "On Cultural Democracy and the Republic of Letters." Phi Beta Kappa Lecture, University of Louisville, January 31.

Stockman, N. 1983. *Anti-Positivist Theories of Science: Critical Rationalism, Critical Theory and Scientific Realism*. Dordrecht: D. Reidel.

Stoller, Robert. 1985. *Presentations of Gender*. New Haven: Yale University Press.

Strum, Shirley, and Linda Fedigan. 2000. *Primate Encounters: Models of Science, Gender, and Society*. Chicago: University of Chicago Press.

Suleiman, Susan Rubin. 1985. *The Female Body and Western Culture*. Cambridge: Harvard University Press.

Suppe, F. 1977. *The Structure of Scientific Theories*, 2d ed. Urbana: University of Illinois Press.

Swain, Carol. 1993. *Black Faces, Black Interests*. Cambridge: Harvard University Press.

———. 2000. "Minorities in the House: What Can We Expect in the Next Century?" In Joseph Zimmerman and Wilma Rule, eds., *The U.S. House of Representatives: Reform or Rebuild*, 36–50. Westport, Conn.: Praeger.

Swers, Michele. 2002. *The Difference Women Make: The Policy Impact of Women in Congress*. Chicago: University of Chicago Press.

Tamerius, Karin. 1995. "Sex, Gender, and Leadership in the Representation of Women." In Georgia Duerst-Lahti and Rita Mae Kelly, eds., *Gender Power, Leadership and Governance*. Ann Arbor: University of Michigan Press.

Tanesini, Allesandra. 1999. *An Introduction to Feminist Epistemologies*. Oxford: Blackwell.

Tauli-Corpuz, Victoria. 2001. "Diversity, Universality, and Democracy: A Perspective of an Indigenous Woman." *The South Touching Base: Women in Action*. ww.isiswomen.org/pub/wia/wia301/index.html.

Tavris, Carol. 1992. *The Mismeasure of Woman*. New York: Simon and Schuster.

Taylor, Charles. 1984. "Foucault on Freedom and Truth." *Political Theory* 12 (2): 152–183.

Taylor, Rupert. 1996. "Political Science Encounters 'Race' and 'Ethnicity.'" *Racial and Ethnic Studies* 19 (October): 884–895.

Taylor, Viviene. 2000. *Marketisation of Governance: Critical Feminist Perspectives from the South*. Cape Town, South Africa: DAWN/SADEP.

Thernstrom, Abigail, and Stephan Thernstrom. 1997. *America in Black and White: One Nation Indivisible*. New York: Simon and Schuster.

Thomas, Sue. 1994. *How Women Legislate*. New York: Oxford University Press.

Thomas, Susan L. 1994. "From the Culture of Poverty to the Culture of Single Motherhood." *Women and Politics* 14 (2): 65–97.

Tienda, Marta, and Haya Stier. 1991. "Joblessness and Shiftlessness: Labor Force Activity in Chicago's Inner City." In Christopher Jencks and Paul Peterson, eds., *The Urban Underclass*. Washington, D.C.: Brookings Institution.

Tilly, Chris, and Randy Albelda. 1994. "It's Not Working: Why Many Single Mothers Can't Work their Way Out of Poverty." *Dollars and Sense* (November/December): 8–10.

Trask, H. K. 1986. *Eros and Power: The Promise of Feminist Theory*. Philadelphia: University of Pennsylvania Press.

Tuana, Nancy. 1989. *Feminism and Science*. Bloomington: Indiana University Press.

Tucker, R. W. 1974. "The Cunning of Reason in Hegel and Marx." *Review of Politics* 18 (3): 269–295.

Turner, Margery Austin, Michael Fix, and Raymond Struyk. 1991. *Opportunities Denied, Opportunities Diminished: Discrimination in Hiring*. Washington, D.C.: The Urban Institute.

U.S. Census Bureau. 2002. *Poverty in the United States: 2001*. Washington, D.C.: U.S. Department of Commerce, Economics and Statistics Administration.

Uchitelle, Louis, and N. R. Kleinfield. 1996. "On the Battlefields of Business: Millions of Casualties." *New York Times*, March 3.

Usdansky, Margaret. 1996. "While Out-of-Wedlock Births Soar, Unwed Moms Don't Fit Stereotypes." *Louisville Courier Journal*, February 25: H3.

van Fraassen, Bas. 1980. *The Scientific Image*. Oxford: Oxford University Press.

Velazquez, Nydia. 1995. *Congressional Record*, 104th Cong., 1st Sess., p. H15520, December 21.

Vetterling-Braggin, Mary. 1982. *"Femininity," "Masculinity," and "Androgyny."* Totowa, N.J.: Littlefield Adams.

Vickers, Jill M. 1982. "Memoirs of an Ontological Exile: The Methodological Rebellions of Feminist Research." In Geraldine Finn and Angela Miles, eds., *Feminism in Canada*. Montreal: Black Rose Books.

Vivas, Eliseo. 1960. "Science and the Studies of Man." In Helmut Schoek and James Wiggins, eds., *Scientism and Values*. Princeton: Princeton University Press.

Vucanovich, Barbara. 1995. *Congressional Record*, 104th Cong., 1st Sess., p. H2587, March 3.

Walby, Sylvia. 1986. *Patriarchy at Work*. Minneapolis: University of Minnesota Press.

———. 2001. "Against Epistemological Caverns: The Science Question in Feminism Revisited." *Signs:* 26 (2): 486–509.

Warshaw, Robin. 1988. *I Never Called It Rape*. New York: Harper and Row.

Waters, Maxine. 1995. *Congressional Record*, 104th Cong., 1st Sess., p. H3578, March 23.

———. 1996. *Congressional Record*, 104th Cong., 2d Sess., p. H7749, July 17.

Watkins, J.W.N. 1957. "Epistemology and Politics." *Proceedings of the Aristotelian Society* 58: 79–102.

Weber, Max. 1958. *The Protestant Ethic and the Spirit of Capitalism*. Trans. Talcott Parsons. New York: Charles Scribner's Sons.

West, Candace, and Sarah Fenstermaker. 1995. "Doing Difference." *Gender and Society* 9 (1): 8–37.

Westkott, Marcia. 1979. "Feminist Criticism of the Social Sciences." *Harvard Educational Review* 49: 422–430.

White, Hayden. 1978. *Tropics of Discourse*. Baltimore: Johns Hopkins University Press.

Wilcox, Clyde, and Barbara Norrander. 2001. "Of Mood and Morals: The Dynamics of Opinion on Abortion and Gay Rights." In Clyde Wilcox and Barbara Norrander, eds., *Understanding Public Opinion*. Washington, D.C.: CQ Press.

Williams, Bernard. 1985. *Ethics and the Limits of Philosophy*. Cambridge: Harvard University Press.

Wilson, William J. 1980. *The Declining Significance of Race*. Chicago: University of Chicago Press.

Winddance Twine, France, and Jonathan Warren. 2000. *Racing Research, Researching Race*. New York: New York University Press.

Wing, Susanna. 2002. "Women Activists in Mali: The Global Discourse on Human Rights." In Nancy Naples and Manisha Desai, eds., *Women's Activism and Globalization*. New York: Routledge.

Wingrove, Elizabeth. 1999. "Interpellating Sex." *Signs* 24 (4): 869–893.

Wittig, Monique. 1979. "One is Not Born A Woman." *Proceedings of the Second Sex Conference*. New York: Institute for the Humanities.

Wolf, Diane. 1996. *Feminist Dilemmas in Fieldwork*. Boulder, Colo.: Westview Press.

Wolin, Sheldon. 1981. "Max Weber: Legitimation, Method, and the Politics of Theory." *Political Theory* 9 (3): 401–424.

Wollstonecraft, Mary. [1792] 1975. *A Vindication of the Rights of Woman*. New York: W. W. Norton.

Woolsey, Lynn. 1998. Interview, Center for American Women and Politics, February 12.

World Women's Congress for a Healthy Planet. 1992. *Action Agenda 21*. http://www.iisd.org/women/action21.htm.

Wright Mills, C. 1939. "Language, Logic, and Culture." *American Sociological Review* 4: 670–680.

Wylie, Alison. 2000a. "Why Standpoint Matters." Paper presented at the Annual Meeting of the American Philosophical Association, Eastern Division, December 30.

———. 2000b. "Feminism in Philosophy of Science: Making Sense of Contingency and Constraint." In Miranda Fricker and Jennifer Hornsby, eds., *The Cambridge Companion to Feminism in Philosophy*. Cambridge: Cambridge University Press.

Yanow, Dvora. 2003. *Constructing "Race" and "Ethnicity" in America: Category-Making in Public Policy and Administration*. Armonk, N.Y.: M. E. Sharpe.

Yeatman, Anna. 1994. *Postmodern Revisionings of the Political*. New York: Routledge.

Young, Iris. 1986. "Impartiality and the Civic Public: Some Implications of Feminist Critiques of Moral and Political Theory." *Praxis International* 5 (4): 381–401.

———. 1987. "The Ideal of Community and the Politics of Difference." *Social Theory and Practice* 12: 1–26.

———. 1989. "Throwing Like a Girl: A Phenomenology of Feminine Comportment, Motility, and Spatiality." In Jeffner Allen and Iris Young, eds., *The Thinking Muse*. Bloomington: Indiana University Press.

———. 1990. *Justice and the Politics of Difference*. Princeton: Princeton University Press.

———. 1994. "Gender as Seriality: Thinking About Women as a Social Collective." *Signs* 19 (3): 713–738.

Yuval-Davis, Nira. 1997. *Gender and Nation*. Thousand Oaks, Calif.: Sage Publications.

Zuckerman, Diana. 2000. "Welfare Reform in America." *Journal of Social Issues* Winter: 587–599.

Index

100; meaning of, 98; in phenomenological analysis, 107–108; in presupposition theories of science, 46; resistance to, 118; statistical, 108–109, 111; of survey research, 112–113; in systemic analysis, 108–109; in textual analysis, 101–107; and theoretical frameworks, 10; truth and, 99

evidence blindness, 10, 111, 117; competing explanations of, 119–123; criminalization of, 120; example of, 126–127; feminist analysis of, 140; as feminist problem, 118; fighting, 140–142; and historical figures, 128; medicalization of, 120; F. Nietzsche's formulation of, 135; and public policy, 208; sanctioned ignorance, 129; and standpoint analysis, 203; understanding of, 118

exclusion, of elected women of color, 210

experimental methods, in F. Bacon's science, 29. *See also* methodology

explanation: formal, 24; and social values, 96

explanans, gender as, 173–175

facticity: constitution of, 123; theoretical constitution of, 28, 117, 206

facts: defined, 66; identification of, 45; post-positivist conception of, 45–46; "self-evidence" of, 117

fallibility, and feminist standpoint theory, 178

falsifiability, criterion, 41–42

falsification: in critical rationalism, 43; problem of, 47; for testing theories, 46–47

family, and beliefs, 27

family value, nuclear family as, 199

Fanon, Frantz, 221

fantasy, gender as, 159

federal budget, AFDC spending in, 197

Federal Water Pollution Control Act, 222

Fee, Elizabeth, 83

'Feed the Folks' forums, 243

female, definition of, 85

femininity: biologically based, 156; cultural characteristics of, 146, 157; cultural constructions of, 164; and heterosexualization of desire, 159; social construction of, 147

feminism: and complex social hierarchies, 131; diverse histories of, 63; emancipatory objectives of, 7; global, 129;

Marxist, 148; postmodern, 69–72; second-wave, 125, 179; transnational, 129

feminist analysis: conception of objectivity in, 82; gender in, 148; intersectionality in, 209; privileged perspective in, 56; and standards of evidence, 98

feminist inquiry: breadth of, 5; characteristics of, 4; and evidence blindness, 10–11; scope of, 3–14

Feminist Majority, 182

feminists: activism of, 136; and anti-rape activism, 113; of global South, 131, 134; invisibility of, 138; North and South, 134–135; Third World, 134. *See also* black; liberal; postmodern; socialist; Western feminists

feminist scholars, of color, 209

feminist scholarship, relevance of, 1–2

feminists of global South, people-centered approaches of, 133. *See also* women of global South

feminist standpoint analysis: as analytical tool, 177; objectivity of, 206; strengths of, 205

feminist standpoint theory, 8, 55, 56, 62, 176; and antifoundationalism, 73–74; goal of, 201; notion of common experience in, 63; and postmodern construction, 189–191

feminist studies, ix

feminization of poverty, 110

fiction, gender as, 159

field work, 77

figure-ground relations, 21. *See also* perception

Foner, Eric, 220

Food Stamps, 236

Ford Foundation, 217

formal explanation, 24

formalists, and textual analysis, 102–103

forms, Plato's theory of, 22

Foucault, Michel, 70, 94, 151, 162, 203

foundationalism: critiques of, 64; doctrine of, 30

Freire, Paolo, 134

Freud, Sigmund, 103, 159, 160, 161, 162

Frye, Marilyn, 3

functionalism: criticism of, 175–176; limitations of, 60; modes of, 59–60

fundamentalism, contemporary, 28

fundamentalist religious leaders, 17

sanctioned ignorance, 11, 129
Sanger, Margaret, 200
Sartre, Jean Paul, 164, 166
Schattschneider, E. E., 231
Schlafly, Phyllis, 179
scholarship, feminist: analytical categories in, 57; hallmarks of, 11; and sexist beliefs, 60. *See also* feminist analysis
scholasticism, 25, 28, 29
Schott, Robin, 89
science: goal of, 41; Popperian account of, 47; positivist conception of, 37–39; post-positivist conceptions of, 52; presupposition theories of, 45; as public enterprise, 27; social and cultural construction of, 95; unity of, 38
science, philosophy of: critical rationalism, 41–44; positivism, 37–41; post-positivist presupposition theories, 44–53; 20th-century debates in, 36–37
scientific inquiry, 25. *See also* feminist inquiry
scientific laws, 78
scientific method: belief in, 79; objectivity in, 77–83 (*see also* objectivity); positivist conception of, 38, 40; and presupposition theory, 51
scientific study, parts of human existence deemed amenable to, 92
scientific theories: adequacy of, 42; alternative, 49; positivist conception of, 42; presupposition conceptions of, 45
scientism, authoritarian tendencies sustained by, 69
Scott, Joan, 12, 147–151
Sedgwick, Eve, 168
selfhood, and gender, 155
semantics, defined, 103
semiotics: defined, 103; and evidence blindness, 127
Sen, Amartya, 109
Senate, U.S., welfare reform bills in, 239
seriality, J. P. Sartre's conception of, 166
series, sex as, 166
service economy, 109
service work, gendered differences in, 109
sex: and gender, 154–155; and gender identity, 151, 152; primordial view of, 213; and racing-gendering, 212–216
sex differences, biologically based, 156
sexism, 9; and dislocation of truth, 94; invisibility produced by, 136; liberal feminist views of, 203; in scientific

research, 79–80; and "southern strategy," 196; and systematic observation, 56; Western culture, 86; and worldwide militarization, 136. *See also* gendering
sexist beliefs, and early feminist scholarship, 60
sex-selection, 85
sexual difference, 148
sexual differentiation, for species reproduction, 155
sexual dimorphism, imposition of, 170
sexual identity, and gender identity, 151
sexual intercourse, without consent, 116–117. *See also* rape
sexuality: and African American women, 208; and culture, 159; and gender identity, 151; and social processes, 207
Shaw, Rep. Clay, 242
Showalter, Elaine, 105, 106
Shuster, Rep. Bud, 223–224
silence: probing, 3; and women of color, 215. *See also* invisibility
similarity, and gender, 168
situatedness: and objective inquiry, 96; postmodern feminists' view of, 56, 69
skepticism: in Ancient World, 19–25; F. Bacon on, 29; defined, 18; of feminist postmodernists, 57; in modern world, 25–36; from trust to, 18–19
slave morality, 204
slavery, situation of black congresswomen in context of, 221
Smith, Linda, 221
Smith, Steven G., 149, 153–158, 154, 155, 160, 163
Smooth, Wendy, 210
Soble, Alan, 83
"social amnesia," 11
social change, and feminist activism, 137
social contract, T. Hobbes' view of, 32
social control: in early feminist scholarship, 60; and scientific inquiry, 81
social Darwinists, 17
social determination, 121
socialist feminists, 202, 204, 205; and affirmative action, 185–187; critiques of capitalism of, 205; on reverse discrimination, 204; standpoint analysis of, 203; and welfare "reform," 196–198
socialization: and acquisition of knowledge, 65; and phenomenological analysis, 108
social science studies, 246. *See also* research

tradition: D. Hume's conception of, 36;
  and knowledge, 27. *See also* culture;
  values
transparency: goal of, 66; notion of, 66
Transportation and Infrastructure Committee, House, 222–224, 225–226
transsexual category, 169
Tribe, Idols of, 27
truth: evidence and, 99; and feminist
  politics, 54; in feminist scholarship,
  69; in feminist standpoint theory, 74;
  and objectification of women, 88; ontological discussions of, 31; pragmatic
  theory of, 29; and presupposition theories, 47–48; quest for, 3; and scientific
  method, 79
Truth, Sojourner, 126, 127
Tufts University, Center on Hunger,
  Poverty and Nutritional Policy at, 236

underrepresentation: in Congress, U.S.,
  216; of congresswomen of color, 232;
  conservative view of, 180–181; of
  elected women of color, 210; statistics
  for, 183
underutilization: and discrimination, 183;
  statistics for, 183
Uniform Crime Reporting Program, 114
United Nations, world conferences
  of, 129
unity of science, principle of, 38
universalism, ethnocentric, 130
universal validity, notion of, 39
unknowing, forms of, 140
Urban Institute, 183

value choices, in critical rationalism, 43
value-neutrality: and feminist standpoint
  theory, 178; and objectivity, 80–81
values: and conceptions of objectivity,
  94; in cultural narratives, 106; and
  research, 7; and scientific inquiry, 96
Van Wagenen, Isabella, 126
Velaquez, Rep. Nydia, 237
ventriloquism: feminist, 135; forms
  of, 128
verification criterion, and theoretical
  presuppositions, 40–41
verstehen, 107–108
Vickers, Jill McCalla, 83
victims of abuse, and welfare system, 238
vocabulary, and positivism, 38. *See also*
  grammar; language

Washington Post, 188
Waters, Rep. Maxine, 234, 237, 241,
  242–243
Watkins, J. W. N., 122
welfare "cheats," 192
welfare policy, U.S.: black feminists'
  views of, 198–200; conservative critique of, 191–193; liberal feminist
  views on, 193–196; racial bias in, 231;
  and racing-gendering, 230–231
welfare recipients, 111; alternative vision
  of, 239; attempts to humiliate, 238; as
  constituency, 231; misrepresentation
  of, 242; racialized myths about, 237;
  statistics for, 237–238; stereotypes of,
  234, 242; typical, 193
welfare "reform," 12–13, 176; agenda of,
  200; comparing standpoints on,
  191–201; and congresswomen of color,
  232; conservative analysis of, 203; and
  evidence blindness, 119; in 103rd Congress, 233; in 104th Congress,
  235–244; and racing-gendering, 231;
  rhetoric of, 198; socialist feminist critiques of, 196–198; and social science
  research, 237, 238; and standpoint
  analysis, 178
welfare rights discourses, and *ressentiment*,
  201
welfare-to-work programs, 192, 195
Western feminists, evidence blindness of,
  130–131
Western intellectual tradition, 58
Western press, on feminism, 136
Western tradition, epistemology in,
  18–19
Weyrich, Paul, 179
white males, in U.S. Congress, 228. *See
  also* men
white-male superiority, criticism of, 204
Wider Opportunities for Women, 234
Wilcox, Clyde, 112
will to power: and evidence blindness,
  122; in knowledge production, 71
Wilson, Gov. Pete, 196
Winnicott, Donald, 103
"wishful thinking," 27
Wittig, Monique, 161
Wolf, Diane
women: African American, 207, 220,
  298; conservative view of, 180; erroneous claims about, 78; First World,
  129; impoverished, 197; "missing," 109;

About the Author

Mary Hawkesworth is a professor of women's and gender studies at Rutgers University. Her teaching and research interests include feminist theory, women and politics, contemporary political philosophy, philosophy of science, and social policy. An award-winning teacher and scholar, Hawkesworth has published in the leading journals of feminist scholarship. She is currently serving as editor of *Signs, Journal of Women in Culture and Society*.